Everyman, I will go with thee,
and be thy guide

THE EVERYMAN
LIBRARY

*The Everyman Library was founded by J. M. Dent
in 1906. He chose the name Everyman because he wanted
to make available the best books ever written in every
field to the greatest number of people at the cheapest possible
price. He began with Boswell's 'Life of Johnson';
his one-thousandth title was Aristotle's 'Metaphysics',
by which time sales exceeded forty million.*

*Today Everyman paperbacks remain true to
J. M. Dent's aims and high standards, with a wide range
of titles at affordable prices in editions which address
the needs of today's readers. Each new text is reset to give
a clear, elegant page and to incorporate the latest thinking
and scholarship. Each book carries the pilgrim logo,
the character in 'Everyman', a medieval morality play,
a proud link between Everyman
past and present.*

Henry James

THE AMERICAN

Introduction by
MALCOLM BRADBURY

Other critical material by
STEPHEN PAIN
University of East Anglia

Consultant Editor for this volume
CHRISTOPHER BIGSBY
University of East Anglia

EVERYMAN
J. M. DENT · LONDON
CHARLES E. TUTTLE
VERMONT

The American first published
by Everyman Paperbacks in 1997
Introduction and other critical material
© J. M. Dent 1997

All rights reserved

J. M. Dent
Orion Publishing Group
Orion House
5 Upper St Martin's Lane
London WC2H 9EA
and
Charles E. Tuttle Co. Inc.
28 South Main Street
Rutland, Vermont 05701, USA

Typeset in Sabon by CentraCet, Saffron Walden
Printed in Great Britain by
The Guernsey Press Co. Ltd, Guernsey, C. I.

This book if bound as a paperback is subject to the
condition that it may not be issued on loan or otherwise
except in its original binding.

British Library Cataloguing-in-Publication Data
is available upon request.

ISBN 0 460 87657 0

CONTENTS

NOTE ON THE AUTHOR AND EDITORS

HENRY JAMES was born in New York City on 15 April 1843 of Scottish and Irish descent. His father James Sr was a well-known theologian and philosopher. His elder brother William was also a famous philosopher. He had a sophisticated education with private tutors and at schools in New York, London, Paris and Geneva, entering the law school at Harvard in 1862. In 1864 he began to contribute reviews and short stories to American journals. He visited Europe in 1869–70 and 1872–4, the first of many such trips. In 1875 he settled for a year in Paris, where he met Flaubert, Turgenev and other literary and art-world figures. The same year his first novel, *Roderick Hudson* (1875) was published. A year later he moved to London, and became immensely popular as a Society dinner guest. In 1898 he left London and went to live at Lamb House, Rye, Sussex. Henry James became a British citizen in 1915 following the outbreak of the Great War, was awarded the Order of Merit, and died in 1916.

In addition to many short stories, plays, books of travel, autobiography, and criticism he wrote some twenty novels including *The Europeans* (1878), *Washington Square* (1880), *The Portrait of a Lady* (1881), *The Bostonians* (1886), *The Princess Casamassima* (1886), *The Tragic Muse* (1890), *The Spoils of Poynton* (1897), *What Maisie Knew* (1897), *The Awkward Age* (1899), *The Wings of the Dove* (1902), *The Ambassadors* (1903) and *The Golden Bowl* (1904).

MALCOLM BRADBURY is a novelist, critic, television dramatist and, until 1995, was Professor of American Studies at the University of East Anglia, in Norwich, England. His novels include *Eating People is Wrong* (1959), *The History Man* (1975), *Rates of Exchange* (1983) and *Doctor Criminale* (1992). Amongst his critical works are *The Modern American Novel* (rev. ed., 1992), *No, Not Bloomsbury* (1987, essays), *The*

Modern World: Ten Great Writers (1989), and, with Richard Ruland, *From Puritanism to Postmodernism: A History of American Literature* (1991). He has edited *Modernism* (1976) and *An Introduction to American Studies* (1981), and he holds the CBE.

STEPHEN PAIN is a writer and lecturer. He has taught and lectured both in Britain and Japan. He has degrees in literature and law. He has edited several works in the Everyman Paperbacks series. His creative writings include poems, plays and short stories. A number of his poems have appeared in Britain and abroad in the following publications: *Asahi Shinbun, Dada, New Poetry, Pen & Sword, Snakeskin, TELS* and *Zanzibar*. He is married with three children.

CHRONOLOGY OF JAMES'S LIFE

Year	Age	Life
1843		Born on 15 April in New York City
1843–5	0–2	James family travels abroad
1845–7	2–4	Family returns to New York and moves to Albany
1847–55	4–12	Family moves to New York City
1855–8	12–15	Family travels abroad; James educated in Europe (Geneva, Paris, Boulogne)

CHRONOLOGY OF HIS TIMES

Year	Literary Context	Historical Events
1843	Dickens, *A Christmas Carol*, *Martin Chuzzlewit*	
1844–5	Browning, *Dramatic Romances and Lyrics*	
1846	Balzac, *La Cousine Bette*	
1847	Thackeray, *Vanity Fair* Charlotte Brontë, *Jane Eyre* Emily Brontë, *Wuthering Heights* Balzac, *Le Cousin Pons*	
1848	Dickens, *Dombey and Son*	European Revolutions; California Gold Rush
1850	Dickens, *David Copperfield* Hawthorne, *The Scarlet Letter* Turgenev, *A Month in the Country* Death of Balzac	
1851	Melville, *Moby-Dick*	Great Exhibition
1852		Louis Napoleon proclaimed Emperor of France
1853	Dickens, *Bleak House*	
1854–6	Dickens, *Hard Times*	Crimean War
1855	Trollope, *The Warden*	

Year	Age	Life
1858–9	15–16	Family returns to United States and moves to Newport
1859–60	16–17	Family travels to Europe; James studies in Geneva and Bonn
1860–2	17–19	Family returns to Newport
1862–3	19–20	James enters Harvard Law School; withdraws from law school to commence writing
1864	21	'A Tragedy of Error' published (unsigned) in *Continental Monthly*. Begins writing reviews for *North American Review*
1865	22	Publishes first signed story, 'The Story of a Year' in *Atlantic Monthly*. Writes reviews for *The Nation*

Year	Literary Context	Historical Events
1856	Flaubert, *Madame Bovary* Turgenev, *Rudin*	
1857	Dickens, *Little Dorrit* Elizabeth Barrett Browning, *Aurora Leigh* Trollope, *Barchester Towers*	Indian Mutiny
1858	George Eliot, *Scenes of* *Clerical Life* Trollope, *Doctor Thorne* Dickens, *A Tale of Two* *Cities*	
1859	George Eliot, *Adam Bede* Trollope, *The Bertrams*	Darwin, *The Origin of* *Species*
1860	George Eliot, *The Mill on the* *Floss* Turgenev, *On the Eve* Hawthorne, *The Marble* *Faun*	
1861	Dickens, *Great Expectations* George Eliot, *Silas Marner* Turgenev, *Fathers and Sons*	American Civil War begins
1861–5		Presidency of Lincoln
1862	Flaubert, *Salammbô*	
1863	George Eliot, *Romola*	
1864	Trollope, *Can You Forgive* *Her?*	
1865	Dickens, *Our Mutual Friend*	End of American Civil War; assassination of Lincoln
1866	Dostoevsky, *Crime and* *Punishment* George Eliot, *Felix Holt*	
1867	Zola, *Thérèse Raquin* Trollope, *Phineas Finn*	Marx, *Das Kapital* I

Year	Age	Life
1869–70	26–7	European tour
1870	27	Beloved cousin, Minnie Temple, dies. Returns to Cambridge, Massachusetts
1871	28	Publishes first novel, *Watch and Ward*, in *Atlantic Monthly*
1872–4	29–31	Visits Europe with sister Alice. Writes travel sketches for *The Nation*
1875	32	*Roderick Hudson* serialised in *Atlantic Monthly*. Publishes *A Passionate Pilgrim and Other Tales*. Tries living in New York, but decides to return to Europe; arranges to write Paris letters for *New York Tribune*
1875–6	32–3	Arrives in Paris and meets Turgenev, Flaubert, Zola, Daudet, Maupassant; moves to London in December
1877	34	Publishes *The American*. Meets Robert Browning and George du Maurier
1878	35	Publishes *Daisy Miller* to international acclaim; also publishes 'An International Episode', and *The Europeans*
1879	36	Publishes *Hawthorne*; *Confidence* serialised in *Scribner's*
1880	37	Meets Constance Fenimore Woolson. Publishes *Washington Square*; *The Portrait of a Lady* begins to appear in *Macmillan's Magazine* and *Atlantic Monthly*

Year	Literary Context	Historical Events
1868	Dostoevsky, *The Idiot* Trollope, *He Knew He Was Right*	Gladstone prime minister
1869	Flaubert, *L'Education sentimentale* Tolstoy, *War and Peace*	Suez Canal opened
1870	Death of Dickens	Franco-Prussian War; fall of Napoleon III; Education Act
1871	George Eliot, *Middlemarch*	Darwin, *The Descent of Man*
1873	Tolstoy, *Anna Karenina*	
1874	Hardy, *Far from the Madding Crowd*	Disraeli prime minister; first Impressionist exhibition in Paris Factory Act
1875	George Eliot, *Daniel Deronda*	Invention of telephone
1876	Twain, *Tom Sawyer*	
1878	Hardy, *The Return of the Native*	
1880	Dostoevsky, *The Brothers Karamazov* Deaths of George Eliot and Flaubert	Gladstone prime minister

Year	Age	Life
1881	38	*The Portrait of a Lady* published in novel form
1882	39	Visits United States; death of parents
1883	40	Death of brother Wilky
1886	43	Publishes *The Bostonians, The Princess Casamassima*
1888	45	Publishes *The Aspern Papers, The Reverberator*
1890	47	Publishes *The Tragic Muse*; turns to play-writing
1892	49	Death of sister, Alice
1894	51	Constance Fenimore Woolson commits suicide in Italy
1895	52	Booed off stage on opening night of *Guy Domville*. Returns to fiction-writing
1896–7	53–4	Takes lease of Lamb House in Rye, Sussex

Year	Literary Context	Historical Events
1881		Married Woman's Property Act; Irish Land Act
1883	Maupassant, Une Vie	Fabian Society founded; death of Marx
1884	Twain, The Adventures of Huckleberry Finn	
1885	Howells, The Rise of Silas Lapham Maupassant, Bel Ami Zola, Germinal	Salisbury prime minister
1886	Stevenson, The Strange Case of Dr Jekyll and Mr Hyde	Year of the 'Great Upheaval' (United States): 700,000 on strike; demand for eight-hour working day
1887		Queen Victoria's Golden Jubilee
1889	Death of Browning	
1890	Wilde, The Picture of Dorian Gray	William James, Principles of Psychology
1891	Hardy, Tess of the d'Urbervilles Gissing, New Grub Street Howells, A Modern Instance	
1892		Gladstone prime minister
1894		Death of Alexander III; accession of Nicholas II
1895	Hardy, Jude the Obscure Conrad, Almayer's Folly Wells, The Time Machine Wilde, The Importance of Being Earnest	Trial of Oscar Wilde; Salisbury prime minister; Marconi's 'wireless' telegraphy
1896	Chekhov, The Seagull	Klondike Gold Rush

Year	Age	Life
1897	54	Publishes *The Spoils of Poynton, What Maisie Knew*. Begins friendship with Joseph Conrad
1898	55	Publishes *The Turn of the Screw, In the Cage*
1899	56	Publishes *The Awkward Age*
1901	58	Publishes *The Sacred Fount*
1902	59	Publishes *The Wings of the Dove*
1903	60	Publishes *The Ambassadors*. Meets Edith Wharton
1904	61	Publishes *The Golden Bowl*
1905	62	Visits United States; delivers lectures
1907	64	Publishes *The American Scene*. Travels in France with Edith Wharton; visits Henrik Andersen in Italy
1907–9	64–6	Publishes the New York Edition of his fiction

Year	Literary Context	Historical Events
1897	Conrad, *The Nigger of the 'Narcissus'*	Queen Victoria's Diamond Jubilee
1899	Chopin, *The Awakening* Norris, *McTeague*	
1899–1902		Boer War
1900	Dreiser, *Sister Carrie* Conrad, *Lord Jim* Wells, *Love and Mr Lewisham* Chekhov, *Uncle Vanya* Death of Wilde	Freud, *Interpretation of Dreams*
1901	Kipling, *Kim*	Death of Queen Victoria; accession of Edward VII
1901–9		Presidency of Theodore Roosevelt
1902	William James, *Varieties of Religious Experience* Conrad, *Heart of Darkness*	Balfour prime minister
1904	Conrad, *Nostromo*	Russo-Japanese War begins
1905	Wells, *Kipps* Edith Wharton, *The House of Mirth* Forster, *Where Angels Fear to Tread*	First Russian Revolution
1906	Sinclair, *The Jungle*	
1907	Adams, *The Education of Henry Adams* Conrad, *The Secret Agent* William James, *Pragmatism*	
1908	Forster, *A Room with a View*	Asquith prime minister
1909	Wells, *Ann Veronica* and *Tono-Bungay*	First Ford Model-T car

Year	Age	Life
1910	67	Death of brothers, William and Robertson
1911	68	Receives honorary degree from Harvard
1912	69	Receives honorary degree from Oxford
1913	70	Publishes first autobiographical memoir, *A Small Boy and Others*
1914	71	Publishes second autobiographical memoir, *Notes of a Son and Brother*
1915	72	Becomes British subject. Helps with war relief. Dines with the prime minister and Cabinet. Receives certificate of naturalisation. Satirised by H. G. Wells in *Boon*. Suffers a stroke followed by respiratory complications and is cared for by Mrs William James
1916	73	Awarded Order of Merit; dies on 28 February

Year	Literary Context	Historical Events
1910	Wells, *The History of Mr Polly* Forster, *Howards End* Death of Tolstoy	Death of Edward VII; accession of George V
1911	Conrad, *Under Western Eyes* Mann, *Death in Venice* Edith Wharton, *Ethan Frome*	
1912		The *Titanic* disaster
1913	Lawrence, *Sons and Lovers* Edith Wharton, *The Custom of the Country* Proust, *Swann's Way*	Panama Canal opened
1914	Joyce, *Dubliners*	Outbreak of First World War
1915	Lawrence, *The Rainbow* Ford Madox Ford, *The Good Soldier*	
1916	Joyce, *A Portrait of the Artist as a Young Man*	Lloyd George prime minister
1917		Russian Revolution

INTRODUCTION

In mid-November of 1875, when he was thirty-two years old, Henry James decided, for excellent literary reasons (he was still trying to find the shape of his career as a novelist) to settle a while in Paris. It was by no means his first visit there; it would certainly not be his last. His father, Henry James Senior – citizen of Albany, a New York millionaire, a Swedenborgian thinker – was a passionate republican who always liked to claim he preferred to spend his time with the Indians. Even so, he could not stay away from Europe and its intellectual, cultural and social rewards, and regularly crossed the Atlantic with his growing family. First taken to Paris in 1843–4, when he was only six months old, Henry Junior was thus always to claim that the first memory of his life was of the Napoleonic column in the Place Vendôme. So 'the poison had entered my veins', he recalled in his late-life memoirs; the poison in question, Europe, was to run through his bloodstream ever after. The vivid childhood glimpse was but the first of a very considerable number of visits. 'Looking on our four stout boys,' Henry Senior addressed his Transcendentalist philosopher friend Ralph Waldo Emerson in 1849, when Henry Junior was six, 'who have no playroom within doors, and import shocking bad manners from the street, with much pity, we gravely ponder whether it would be better to go abroad for a few years with them, allowing them to absorb French and German and get a better sensuous education than they are likely to get here. To be sure, this is but a glimpse of our ground of proceeding – but perhaps you know of some decisive word which shall dispense us from any further consideration of the subject.' But Emerson evidently didn't find the decisive comment ('Stay at home' might have done it), and not too surprisingly, since he had really discovered his own seemingly home-grown Romantic Transcendentalism in Europe. Henry's sensuous education and his linguistic experience continued to develop across the Atlantic, and so did his love of art.

Between 1855 and 1858 the whole James family were back in Europe, touring extensively. This trip, to Geneva, London and pre-Haussmann Paris, kept the James family in Paris from June 1856 to the summer of 1857. It left the twelve-year-old Henry with an episode of typhus, a passion for the novel and drama, a 'general sense of glory', a vivid sense of a 'whole perfect Parisianism I seemed to myself always to have possessed mentally', and an indelible recollection of the artistic splendours of 'the bridge to Style' in the Galerie d'Apollon of the Louvre. These youthful visits to the Louvre were, he said, 'so many explorations of the house of life, so many circlings and hoverings around the image of the world'. Appropriately enough, it's in this great museum (evidently as much a social meeting place as a gallery), that *The American*, his most Parisian novel, begins. A couple of years later, in 1859, the Jameses were back in Europe once more. The teenage Henry went to school and university in Geneva and Bonn, and began to think of becoming a painter. Returned home to Newport, Rhode Island, in the palmier days of the place, before the great Euro-mansions of the American robber barons were built there (he would use those later), he took artistic training, and sustained some 'obscure injury', apparently while extinguishing a stable fire. This began a period of illness which would duly keep him out of the American Civil War, which started a year before he went, in 1862, to Harvard College in Cambridge, Massachusetts, to study law. The nation was now going through its greatest crisis since the foundation of the Republic. Boston and Cambridge were in their intellectual heyday, packed with writers – the Boston Brahmins, the Transcendentalists, the writers of what's been called 'the American Renaissance'. Round them were the teachers, the editors, the publishing houses and the magazines of a Boston that was still very much the cultural 'hub' of the United States. In 1864 the James family itself moved to Boston, and Henry began a number of important friendships with several of the leading figures.

Now beginning to see where destiny beckoned, he began reviewing for the *North American Review* and *The Nation*, and published a story in *The Atlantic Monthly*. He also thought more and more of Europe, itself a very Bostonian thing to do. Then, with the war over, the world widened again. Americans were, Henry told a friend, the 'heirs to all the ages', and could claim and assimilate their property wherever they found it. In

1869–70, at twenty-six, he was off to Europe once more, on his first adult visit. His plan was to make his own grand tour and write travel pieces, which – as other American writers, like Hawthorne, Mark Twain and William Dean Howells had already shown – were just about as popular in America as travel itself. For, with peace come at last, there was a massive rise in industrial wealth, and a growing ease and speed of travel. Americans were taking up their Baedekers, packing aboard the fast new steamships, becoming the new imperial innocents abroad. Henry, already less innocent than most, went to England ('a good-natured matron'), to Switzerland ('a magnificent man'), to Italy ('a beautiful dishevelled nymph'). Rome excited him to such delirium he wandered over its sites for five hours without breakfast. 'At last – for the first time – I live!' he wrote home to his father – who summoned him to come home immediately. James did return, and duly produced a modest and still little-read first novel, *Watch and Ward* (1871), with an American setting. But he was quickly back in Europe again, for a twenty-eight-month visit over 1872–4. He travelled across much of the continent, and lived for a while in Paris, Rome and Florence. In Florence he wrote his first serious novel, *Roderick Hudson* (1875), a book which shows the strong influence of Nathaniel Hawthorne on his work. Hawthorne had written his version of Americans abroad in his last novel, *The Marble Faun* (1860), a romance about Rome, and art, and puritanism, published not long before his death in 1864. This was his one European novel, and James travelled with it in his pocket. In his tale, Hawthorne had finally opted to take himself and his characters home, away from the Gothic mysteries of history and art, and back to the plain world of American puritanism. But James, who was ever more tempted by what he nicely called 'the apple of Europe', evidently saw matters far more ambiguously, recognising in his own new version of the story that Europe was 'knowledge, pleasure, experience', a rounded apple indeed. However, once more he returned to America, determined to 'try New York', and 'thinking it my duty to attempt to live at home before I should grow older'.

Yet the very titles of his collection of European stories, *A Passionate Pilgrim and Other Tales* and his essay-collection, *Transatlantic Sketches* (both 1875), made it evident where his interests lay. In November 1875 he was off to Europe again, and this time it seemed decisive. 'Harry James has gone abroad again, not to return, I fancy, even for visits,' reported his friend William Dean Howells, who had also once bitten of the apple. But where to settle? He considered Italy, the beautiful dishevelled nymph; she seemed too tempting to allow his writing to flourish. He considered London, the good-natured matron, 'but London appeared to me then impossible', he said. That left Paris, now in its Third Republic, where in November he rented 'a snug little *troisième*' at 29 Rue de Luxembourg, later the Rue Cambon, near to the Place Vendôme, with the great Napoleonic column that had become his first memory. He wrote travel letters for the New York *Tribune*, studied French theatre. And now, since there was no time to waste, he also started within a month of arrival a new novel, *The American*. He also went often to the Comédie-Française, visited the Salon of 1876, inspected the work of the new French Impressionist painters and did not much admire them (his views would change later). He wrote about the new French novelists, most of whom belonged to the new movements of Realism and Naturalism. He did not, it seemed, greatly admire these tendencies either – though, again, his views would change later. He met a fair number of the leading writers and joined the edges of their selective circle. There was Gustave Flaubert, whom he found 'wonderfully simple, honest, kindly, and touchingly articulate'. He added rather grandly: 'I think I easily – more than easily – see round him intellectually.' Around him were other notable figures: Guy de Maupassant, the two brothers Goncourt, Alphonse Daudet, all of them realists, and Émile Zola, just becoming the prophet of the novel of scientific naturalism. He was proud to be taken into their company, but found their preoccupations, aesthetic and naturalistic, and their endless concern with this school or that, this movement or that (the kind of thinking without which Paris would not think), decidedly narrow. It all seemed to him, he said, like 'an excellent engine for the production of limited perfection'. They lacked the capaciousness he associated with English writers like George Eliot, they lacked the grand sweep of their predecessor Balzac. 'I don't like their wares, and they don't like any others,' he complained at last to his friend William Dean Howells, who was now editing *The Atlantic Monthly* back at home, 'and besides, they are not *accueillants*'.

But this was a little over-stated. It is true that, despite his excellent contacts and fluency in the language, James was not really at home in Paris. But he would always relish his experience in these arcane and important literary circles, and would write, often and brilliantly, about the modern French writers – challenging their excessive preoccupation with form and indifference to the claims of the moral power of art, but no less using them as a yardstick with which to beat the limited aesthetic aims of British and American authors. His disappointment perhaps reflects the fact that he was still a more or less unknown American novelist and storywriter; and that, what is more, the kind of work he was doing himself at the time – not least the demanding pages of *The American*, unfolding back there in the Rue de Luxembourg – didn't really consort with the current French theories of perfection of form and realism of subject. He wrote home to Howells: 'As editor of the austere *Atlantic* it would startle you to hear of some of their projected subjects. The other day Edmond de Goncourt (the best of them) said he had been working very well on his novel – he had got into an episode that greatly interested him, and into which he was going very far. *Flaubert*: "What is it?" *E de G*: "A whorehouse *de province*."' Still, James's horizons plainly widened in Paris. As he told Howells, a little nudgingly: 'The great merit of the place is that one can arrange one's life here exactly as one pleases – that there are facilities for every kind of habit and taste, and that everything is accepted and understood.' He made good friends, one of the closest being the Russian writer-in-exile Ivan Turgenev, who admired his work, even though James did admit that 'I do not think my stories quite struck him as meat for men.' However the American colony in Paris seemed to him generally oppressive. He was also struck, as many intellectual and literary visitors to Paris have been, by the phenomenon of French national conceit, though he found it understandable in the aftermath of the Franco-Prussian War. But the literary community, however brilliant, seemed to him strangely closed and mandarin, uninterested in anything that chose not to be French. James was probably also beginning to confess to himself that he did possess the moralistic imagination of Protestantism – and that, what's more, he was really no natural bohemian. The lesson at the time was plain: 'I saw, moreover, that I should be an eternal outsider.'

Finally, with a year gone, the episode was decisively concluded.

'I have done with 'em forever, and I am turning English all over,' he wrote to his brother William, 'I desire only to feed on English life and the contact of English minds – I wish greatly I knew some.' Happily, and perhaps even unusually, he found some; and in December 1876 he moved to London, taking a lodging at 3 Bolton Street, Piccadilly, at the heart of 'the place in the world where there was most to observe'. He remained in Britain for the rest of his life, though always travelling constantly in Europe. As for the Parisians, he had not done with 'em forever. Indeed he was back again in 1877, and he – and his fictional characters – would thereafter revisit the city often. The great fact was that the year in Paris carried with it many long-lasting literary rewards. One was that from it flowed many aspects of his own great adventure in the making of modern fiction. When the mature James became, as he soon did, a far more aesthetic and experimental novelist – exploring the measure of Realism, the reaches of Naturalism, the implications of Impressionism, and in time the excitements of Modernism – the sense he had of the novel as a discovering, self-creating form of art and knowledge owed a very great deal to his French experience. Much more immediate, and no less important, was the very fact of the novel that he had begun there, *The American*. In his later years, it was not to remain a book he was completely proud of. With its rather dramatic plot and its rather grand note of renunciation, it came to seem to him far too much a youthful and intuitive 'arch-romance' – the kind of book where 'the way things don't happen may be artfully made to pass for the way things do'. In any case he wondered if he hadn't betrayed the ending, suspecting that the 'outrage' perpetrated in Europe against his hero was 'far more showy than sound'.

But when we judge things from the standpoint of the young James, matters were entirely the opposite. Writers must start somewhere, find their way, their vision, their great themes and myths. In *The American* James had, quite decisively, written his first mature novel, a wonderfully intelligent and cunning comic romance, even if it had a somewhat exotic shape to its plot. It was the first great flight, the brilliant opening out to mythic proportions of his central 'international theme', the transatlantic encounter between his contemporary America – the America of the new 'Gilded Age' after the Civil War – and Europe. It was the book where one of the most essential dramas that would sustain his fiction – the transaction between the bold, wandering American 'innocent' and the complex, mannered, labyrinthine social world of Europe – first took on substantial and powerful shape, a mythic shape which later books would refine, complicate, deconstruct, but never lose touch with altogether. For the reader who wants to understand the larger, more detailed maps of James's later fiction, this is quite the best book to start with. But it was something else; *The American* was also the book where, for James, the full joy of being a writer started to flow. Surveying it magisterially from the end of his great writing life, he had to confess that he found himself, 'at this late hour', feeling 'a certain sad envy of so much unchallenged instinct', gladly recalling that the book came from 'the happiest season of surrender to the invoked muse and the projected fable'. For writers, the time must one day come, he says, 'when questions rule the roost'. Yet, he acknowledges, the moments of instinct and gamble, of the wonderful thrill of immersion in the observed scene, are no less important to writing, no less urgent to the chase. *The American* was James's first truly great gamble in the adventure of the novel. It was the Jamesian tale in its purest early form, and he was right to take delight in it, as so many readers have done since.

*

The American was begun in Paris in December 1875, serialised from June 1876 in twelve instalments in *The Atlantic Monthly* from June 1876, and appeared in book form in 1877. The whole enterprise was in fact a decidedly dangerous adventure into the practices of Victorian serial publication, since the first chapters began appearing while most of the book was still unwritten. For a young writer, this Dickensian method of publication was a considerable act of courage; the older James noted 'I can but speculate all vainly today on the oddity of my composure.' The initial idea, the first glimpse, had come not in Paris at all, but, James tells us, on an American street-car:

> I recall sharply the felicity of the first glimpse, though I forget the accident of thought that produced it. I recall that I was seated in an American 'horse-car' when I found myself, of a sudden, considering with enthusiasm, as the theme of a 'story', the situation, in another country and an aristocratic society, of some

robust, but insidiously beguiled and betrayed, some cruelly wronged, compatriot: the point being in especial that he should suffer at the hands of persons pretending to represent the highest possible civilisation and to be of an order in every way superior to his own. What would he 'do' in that predicament, how would he right himself, or how, failing a remedy, would he conduct himself under his wrong?

However, this idea had faded back into the well of 'unconscious cerebration', until his arrival in Paris and his commission from the *Atlantic* brought it back into the light. For, after all, it was crucial that such a tale should take place on a 'high and lighted stage', which would make the story 'go of itself'. It needed its perfect local colour, and Paris did its gilded service, 'the life of the splendid city playing up in it like a flashing fountain in a marble basin'. What's more, as James always emphasised, the interest of fiction lay not simply in the story-idea – the *'donnée'*, as he liked to call it – but in the 'treatment'. In fact such was the 'treatment' he was able to mete it in Paris that, to some degree at least, the initial story faded into the background. The real excitement of the novel lies in the hero's first dramatic encounter with that 'high and lighted stage', and the encounters and initiations that would occur on it as James himself, writing in the city, himself begins to penetrate its veils, comprehend its customs, capture the social energy and the hidden segments of its cityscape and its life.

Moreover, the essential point of his 'treatment' is indeed that the story does acquire grand mythic proportions, taking on the character of a transatlantic drama in which the energetic and dramatic forces on both sides are arrayed. The signs are all clearly there in the primary invention – that of Christopher Newman, the figure who 'rose before me, on a perfect day of the divine Paris spring', and on whom the whole plot depended. In creating Newman, James was creating what the sociologists call 'an ideal type', a prime representative of culture, nationality and region. 'An observer with anything of an eye for national types would have had no difficulty in determining the local origin of this undeveloped connoisseur, and indeed such an observer might have felt a certain humorous relish of the almost ideal completeness with which he filled out the national mould,' James tells us. Newman is quickly endowed with many associations appropriate to his scale and national origins, not least in the choice of his name. Newman is the American, that new man ('What then is this American, this new man?' Hector St John de Crévecoeur famously asked in his *Letters from an American Farmer* (1782), and answered: 'He is an American who, leaving behind him all his ancient prejudices and manners, receives new ones from the new mode of life he has embraced, the new government he obeys, and the new rank he holds'). His first name associates him with the most famed of the American discoverers. 'Your English names are so droll,' says pert Mlle. Noéme Nioche, the imperfect copyist who has so artfully arranged herself before the art of the Louvre at the start, mistaking his nationality. 'Did you ever hear of Christopher Columbus?' asks Newman. '*Bien sûr!* He invented America; a very great man. And is he your patron?' 'Oh, exactly; my parents named me for him,' Newman says. 'Monsieur is American?' cries Mlle. Nioche. Newman is an American discoverer, this time exploring in reverse, and inventing Europe.

James constantly insists on his distinctive traits. He is 'the great Western Barbarian, stepping forth in his innocence and his might, gazing a while at this poor effete Old World and then swooping down on it', observes his new-found friend Mrs Tristram – who, though American, has been educated in a French convent and is therefore a specialist in the French 'labyrinth of appearances'. He is the 'superlative American', the narrator tells us, who stands in 'a posture of general hospitality to the chances of life'. He's a rags-to-riches hero from his own place and time, having served a little obscurely in the American Civil War, then 'made money largely' in common commodities like leather and wash-tubs ('Successful in copper, only so-so in railroads, and a hopeless fizzle in oil,' is how he puts it). His is 'an intensely Western story', of which James gives us just enough glimpses to make his point. He has 'a relish of bold processes', and his capital lies not just in dollars but in 'his dogged resolution and his lively perception of ends and means'. He is lounging and ranging, bulky and healthy: 'a more completely healthy mortal had never trod the elastic soil of the West'. His manners are loose; he's always extending his legs, and, like his friend Tristram, engages a good deal in 'loafing' (an early use of the word). Until his thirty-fifth year, making money has been his sole aim. Now he has 'a sort of mighty hankering, a desire to stretch out and haul in'. A representative of American nature, he seeks to range just as freely and largely in European culture. He has won at last, and carried off his winnings: the big question for him – as for his nation – is what he shall do with them: 'the question was sure to present itself, and the answer to it belongs to our story'. Indeed in the first instance the story isn't about a plot contrived against him, but about his own problem in deciding what to do with his life. 'I seemed to feel a new man inside my old skin, and I longed for a new world,' he says. It so happens that his New World is the Old one, which has a great sufficiency of its own history, culture and social practice. Newman is a new kind of innocent, with experience. Like Columbus, he sails off to his new continent mythically endowed, with great and fanciful expectations – only to find it has reality and meanings rather more complex and ambiguous than he is capable of predicting.

So, like a good many transatlantic stories, this one is about the adventurous, risky exploration of a badly signposted other continent whose meanings constantly slip or rebound. Newman has come with his own easy and genial ways, his materialist and realist code, above all his distinctive kind of American capitalist and commercial mathematics. When we first encounter him, in a gilded salon of the Louvre, he's already suffering from an 'aesthetic headache' from looking at too many pictures, a kind of indoor exercise to which he isn't used. Like Mark Twain's innocents abroad – Twain had published his comic account of one of the first American package tours to Europe, *Innocents Abroad*, not much earlier, in 1869, a year after James's own story is set – he's an uneasy but unintimidated visitor to the museums and art-storehouses of the past. He's as likely to prefer a copy to an original, a big painting to a small one. The practices and codes of culture are new to him, a different calculus: 'Raphael and Titian and Rubens were a new kind of arithmetic, and they inspired our friend, for the first time in his life, with a vague self-mistrust.' Newman is a capable consumer of facts, a willing seizer of pleasures, an indefatigable tourist ('He lounged through Belgium and Holland and the Rhineland, through Switzerland and Northern Italy, planning about nothing, but seeing everything'). Unlike the wonderfully solemn Rev Babcock, with whom he takes part of his Grand Tour, he is neither 'extremely devoted to "culture"' nor obsessed with moral encounter and the risk of a dangerous vision of evil. He simply believes that Europe is made for him, and not he for Europe. Though Babcock gives him the proper and solemn warning ('*do* remember that Life and Art *are* extremely serious'), Newman has merely 'given his mind a chance to "improve", if it would.' Plainly it does; the European Tour plays a key role in distancing Newman from his commercial world – the world at home in which he had never done anything very ugly, but likewise anything particularly beautiful: 'It had come back to him simply that what he had been looking at all the summer was a very rich and beautiful world, and that it had not all been made by sharp railroad men and stock-brokers.' The episode is a good deal more than an engaging and witty travelogue. It is this that confirms him in the attraction of Mme. Claire de Cintré, and sets him on his obscure romantic quest.

Hence what tempts, beguiles, eventually deceives Newman isn't, at the start, a cunning conspiracy, but his own desires, expectations, illusions. And what he is first deceived by is not deliberate exploitation but the very practices of culture itself: that deeper 'labyrinth of appearances' to which Mrs Tristram chooses to introduce him, again not to deceive him, but to see what will happen when the two different worlds she knows confront each other. Newman's conception of the world at large is of a place of surfaces without tricky depths, a realm that is openly on offer to the independent and benign consumer: 'The world, to his sense, was a great bazaar, where one might stroll about and purchase handsome things; but he was no more conscious, individually, of social pressure than he admitted the existence of such a thing as an obligatory purchase.' He's not a stern moralist, but he does have a conscience; and James reminds us that in his earlier business life he should really have begun to moralise a little more delicately. And throughout the story, though his moral education enlarges, he retains his benign, his material, his common-sense relation to everything. His first desires are direct: 'I've come to see Europe, to get the best out of it I can. I want to see all the great things and do what the best people do.' He possesses a mixture of innocence and experience, but to complex situations he always has frank empirical answers, though they often do not satisfy the situation. A girl who is poor needs enough of a dowry to marry an ordinary fellow, and that's it; it is not the course that Mlle. Nioche, one of the book's most interesting characters, chooses to follow. An amiable and aristocratic French friend who is impoverished and makes nothing of his life needs a job in American business; Valentin de Bellegarde, the friend in question, makes an irrationally opposite choice. A widow of rank but no means must be in want of a husband, who will give her the wealth and respect so rightfully hers; he is hence the natural suitor of Madame de Cintré. And here is the heart of it. Newman means to decorate his leisure, utilise his wealth, and develop his sentiments by acquiring a wife in Europe: 'the best article in the market': 'I want a great woman. I stick to that. That's one thing I *can* treat myself to, and if it is to be had I mean to have it. What else have I toiled and struggled for all these years? I have succeeded, and now what am I to do with my success? To make it perfect, as I see it, there must be a beautiful woman perched on the pile, like a statue on a monument. She must be as good as she is beautiful, and as clever as she is good.'

The prime fact about *The American* is that it starts out not as it ends, as an 'arch-romance', but something like its opposite. It's a transatlantic social comedy of cultural differences and incomprehensions, distinctive for its high touches of irony, its good dramatic scenes, its sure bi-partisan control of tone. The irony plays, benignly but always pointedly, over Newman, and his directness, his materialism, his wonderful innocence (plays over him to a far greater degree than many critics seem to observe). Where it takes on force is when his qualities are brought into contact and conflict with the opposed French sense, of veiled complexity, hierarchy and indirection. Newman knows what he thinks, says what he means; the story has him encounter people who have learned to decorate what they think and not say what they mean. Instead they signify indirectly, through the codes, practices, detachments and condescensions of an inherited and hierarchical culture. Newman speaks as he finds; the French have perfected a quite different form of speech called 'conversation'. 'Our French conversation is famous, you know,' explains M. Nioche, when his daughter Noémie offers Newman his services as a language tutor, 'It's a great talent.' Language is not simply an instrument; it is above all a social form. Newman's 'loafing' American friend Tristram confirms the point: 'It's a splendid language. You can say all sorts of bright things in it' – even if you happen not to be bright. Mademoiselle Nioche (who is bright, and says all sorts of bright things in it) repeatedly indicates to Newman that things do not signify their meanings directly. She herself makes copies of originals, but as anyone of taste would know they are not good copies; the point is that they are designed for a different artistic use – to attract attention to her other splendid attributes.

In the finely done early scenes, James again and again creates vivid and dramatically subtle encounters between directness and indirectness – two quite contrasting social currencies that are in constant ironic juxtaposition once the Western barbarian swoops down on Old World society. As Newman's French friend Valentin shrewdly tells him, in Paris there is nothing that's too scanty not to be transformed into the aesthetic: 'Why, my dear fellow, we here in Paris want to make as much as possible out of everything. That's how we differ, I conceive, from the people of your country: the objects of your exploitation appear to be fewer, and above all of fewer kinds.' To this Newman is benignly open. He's prepared to buy fakes if they delight him, or is interested in their maker. The fine scene in Chapter 4, where Mlle. Nioche, skilfully removing veil after veil, confesses her deception of him – her bad painting, her overcharging, her exploitation of her father, her use of him – in order to tempt further, and no doubt sexual, contact, is exemplary in its mounting revelations and duplicities. Newman recognises her 'world of ambiguous intentions', realises that her 'sudden frankness was not essentially more honest than her leaving him in error would have been', and makes his moral judgements accordingly; meantime James constructs for us a convincing portrait of the psychology and formation of a French courtesan. The key to Newman's character is his 'tranquil unsuspectingness of the relativity of his own place on the social scale'. But he enters a world where exactly the opposite is true, where identities and lives are differently constructed, and he is unfathomable. These different attitudes to self and selflessness, worth and worthlessness are essential to the story. To Newman, the aristocratic spectacle he observes in Paris is one of 'uninvested capital': rank and possession are resources not put to their 'highest use' – 'The highest uses known to Newman's experience were certain transcendent sagacities in the handling of railway stock.' Making a good friend of Valentin, and taking a benevolent concern in his seemingly useless life, he offers him the American promise: a life in business. Yet from this Valentin is, to Newman's eyes, incomprehensibly diverted, preferring to undertake what will prove a fatal duel over the worthless honour of Noémie Nioche. Meantime, by contrast, Newman is to the French people he meets a 'commercial person': 'It's very disagreeable to know how Americans have made their money,' says Mrs Tristram, who may be conceived to be chiefly on his own side, and who tells a truth Newman in fact finally has to reckon with. To those who belong to what James calls the 'forlorn aristocracies' Newman, who lacks both rank and the sense of it (he thinks of it as something in the army), has humour but not wit, and does not know most of what is considered knowable, is simply someone who might be useful or essential in a moment of financial necessity – but ideally, as a placeless 'commercial person', is someone with whose services one would ultimately wish to dispense.

*

Of course the primary tale of *The American* is its odd love story, as we follow Newman's easy-going pursuit of Madame de Cintré, the 'rare and precious' poor widow who is in disappointed despair after her first arranged marriage, through the French labyrinth of appearances. Crucially, as we shall see, James tells this whole matter primarily from Newman's point of view. 'I have written my story from Newman's side of the wall,' he wrote to Howells, and the image of the wall is appropriate – in fact it is essential to the story. James's presentation of the story through the standpoint of Newman doesn't have the grand sophistication this matter would acquire later on in his career – when he would concern himself so seriously with questions of angle of vision, centres of consciousness, *points d'appuye*, and the discriminated scene. That refined Jamesian method would reach its peak of perfection in works like *What Maisie Knew* (1897), where James implies everything that is corrupt and adulterous in his adult story without transgressing the perimeters of what the child Maisie herself might know. Here the method is a good deal more instinctive and innocent, consorting with James's own present sense of being something of an outsider in French society, and reinforced by his role 'above' the story, as a near-omniscient Victorian narrator prepared to leave the 'discriminated occasion' and explicate motives or backstories from above. Even so, as he points out in his late-life preface, Newman is the essence, 'the lighted figure', and 'the interest of everything is all that is *his* vision, *his* conception, *his* interpretation; at the window of his wide, quite sufficiently wide, consciousness we are seated, from that admirable position we "assist".' We assist from a position of compassionate irony, watching, stage by stage and scene by scene, as Newman follows out his half-baffled, half-wise, ever benign quest through the labyrinth of appearances – even though it is up to us to deduce far more than he does of what is happening.

One part of James's brilliance in the book thus lies in his creation of Newman – the richest character he has so far constructed, innocent but essentially good-natured, a rangy Noble Savage in the salons of the great, a centre not just of consciousness but of sympathy, a figure of certain distinct vulgarities who is none the less capable of intense moral experience. The other lies in his constructing the opposite world of the Bellegardes and all who surround them: the formidable Comtesse, with her English background and her implacable dignity, the urbane Urbain de Bellegarde ('Newman had never been confronted with such an incarnation of the art of taking one's self seriously; he felt a sort of impulse to step backward, as you do to get a view of a great façade'), the impish Mme. de Bellegarde, the sympathetic Valentin, the 'comical Duchess', with her remarkable command of social practice, the 'greatest lady in France', a 'reverend effigy' who reminds the irreverent Newman of the Fat Lady at a fair. The Bellegardes are all that Newman is not; they are from the 'forlorn aristocracies', conservative, pre-Napoleonic, pro-Bourbon, and, interestingly, Anglo-French in background. They think ill of public affairs, and consider the age rotten to its core. They are, as Valentin says, 'strange': 'Old trees have crooked branches, old houses have queer cracks, old races have odd secrets. Remember that we are eight hundred years old!' Without being commercial, they are materialist, avaricious and impoverished. And the essential item of their trade, financial and social, is not railway stock but their daughter – who for them too is 'the best article on the market'.

In creating Claire de Cintré, James creates a different kind of character: the *princesse lointaine*, the mystery at the heart of the labyrinth. Her nature, sentiments, passions and familial

obligations are obscure from the start. So is her very appearance:
Tristram and Mrs Tristram, who are there to offer two different
accounts of everything, give two quite different versions of
whether she is beautiful or not. For Newman, Claire is the
obscure object of desire, who remains almost always on the
other side of the wall. In nearly every scene with her he observes
her over long distances, either in the social company of others,
or standing far away from him in large aristocratic rooms. His
performance with her is always ambiguous ('He had little of the
small change of conversation, and his stock of ready-made
formulaes and phrases was of the scantiest'), as indeed are his
fundamental emotions towards her ('He flattered himself that he
was not in love; but his biographer may be supposed to know
better'). From the first formal visit he makes to her in the family
hôtel in the Faubourg St Germain – where the houses 'present
to the outer world a face as impassive and as suggestive of the
concentration of privacy within as the blank walls of Eastern
seraglios ... The place was all in the shade; it answered to
Newman's conception of a convent' – she is immured, almost as
much so at the beginning as she will be at the end. Entering the
house, Newman enters a world of obstructions, indirections,
closures, spaces with barriers, surfaces with depths: 'For a
moment he felt as if he had plunged into some medium as deep
as the ocean, and as if he must exert himself to keep from
sinking.' Even once Claire de Cintré has been acknowledged,
through his elaborate negotiations with the whole familial
labyrinth, as his wife-to-be, and seems to be deeply affectionate
towards him ('I was glad you were different'), she retains her
passive obscurity, and poses the same problems of aesthetic
understanding as the paintings and their copies. So Newman
wonders where, 'in so exquisite a compound, nature and art
showed their dividing line ... Where did fine urbanity end and
fine sincerity begin?'

This question, as James acknowledges in some wonderfully
frank passages in his preface, is never properly answered. A key
scene is the occasion of the Comtesse's ball (Chapter 16), where
all the obscurities of the social and emotional relationship are
cunningly developed ('I feel as if I were looking at you through
a telescope. It is very strange,' says Newman to his betrothed;
'But I am not a heavenly body,' she replies). To Newman the
glittering occasion appears a great success ('I am satisfied with

everything'), but we see that once again he has failed to observe hidden signs – not least the presence of the aply named Lord Deepmere, whose arrival has deepened the waters of the plot. Newman passes over the moment of the private encounter between him and Mme. de Cintré; we sense it has a profounder significance, as it does (Deepmere is there as the family's now preferred candidate for her hand, but has done the honourable thing and revealed the household plan to her). James's preface very rightly observes a basic literary difficulty in the scene that then follows in Chapter 17. Once the engagement has been officially celebrated and displayed to Paris society, it would only be logical for Newman to take his fiancée with him on his visit to the opera, where further key events unravel. However, says James, to preserve her good faith in her later decision to reject Newman, it's necessary for their relationship not to deepen at this point, since 'every touch in the picture of her apparent loyalty would add to her eventual shame'. In other words, she must remain the obscure object of desire, since the family intrigue must develop at a distance, the complicated, manipulated motives for her rejection both of Newman and her family need room to unfold. Hence we never quite do know those motives, nor the kinds of pressure that have been exercised upon her from within the labyrinth of appearances on the other side of the wall. From this point on, the novel changes, to become the 'arch-romance' James called it. A great Gothic apparatus – of deathbed revelation, a hidden wicked secret, a dark stain on the family badge of honour, a compliant servant, a revealed letter from the past, a chance of revenge – takes over the development. Finally discovering he has been plotted against, Newman – and the art of the novel – require that he should be able to plot in return. He inherits the fictional task of detection, then the moral dilemma of how to prevent the outcome, right the wrong and punish the wrongdoers.

To the end, Claire de Cintré remains the ambiguous figure – not herself a deceiver, but a standing sign of the deceptiveness Newman encounters when he chooses to swoop down on the Old World. She opts, it seems, for resignation, and a solace set beyond human satisfaction, gratifying neither her family nor Newman's dreams of possessing a 'great woman'. She looks for her salvation in her Catholic religion, and disappears into what Newman, with his 'contemporaneous optimism', regards as the 'tragic travesty' of the convent in the Rue d'Enfer. To him it is a place beyond all sentiment, set in a trans-human world that 'revealed no symptoms of human life: the place looked dumb, deaf, inanimate'. Yet this is also the goal of Newman's journey, a grim satisfaction – 'and yet it was a satisfaction; the barren stillness of the place seemed to be his own release from ineffectual longing. It told him that the woman within was lost beyond recall, and that the days and years of the future would pile themselves above her like the huge immovable slab of the tomb.' Many critics, including Howells, challenged the ending; after all, it seemed that James had provided himself with the means for a happier one, if only Newman had chosen to press on with his revenge. Instead he too chooses resignation, ceases to be 'a man with a plot in his head'. He burns the incriminating letter, 'burns them', lets all the Bellegardes go. They, in defying him, have calculated neither on their innocence nor their power to contradict his charges, but on his benign good nature; that good nature is all he carries away with him at the end. For a romance, it is not a romantic ending, but it does have moral and literary truth. James opts not for a romantic conclusion but a moral reconciliation, not a happy ending but an intelligent one, based on a choice, a forfeiture. Like his inventor James, Newman can only enter so far into the French labyrinth of appearances. The difficulties are insuperable; what is obscure and distanced remains forever unread on the other side of the wall. 'I saw, moreover, that I should be an eternal outsider,' James reflected on leaving Paris; that is how Newman leaves too.

*

In 1907, just thirty years after he had published *The American*, the elderly James undertook the great New York edition of his collected fiction. *The American* – Volume 2 in the great plum-coloured edition – evidently struck him as a special problem. Ever since the serial publication, he had been worried by his brother William James's criticisms of Newman's vulgarities (one particular objection was to a phrase of Newman's calling Mme. de Cintré a 'high class of goods') and had made corrections for its book publication. Now he made extensive revision to the text, correcting other inelegancies he saw, and refining the imagery. For this edition he also wrote the brilliant prefaces, his 'story of the story', as they've been called. They were, he said, a plea for criticism along other than infantile lines, and no less an attempt at self-criticism (for 'to criticise is to appropriate, to appropriate, to take intellectual possession, to establish in fine a relation with the criticised thing and make it one's own'). The prefaces – which were independently collected in 1934 in *The Art of the Novel* – were, he said himself, an attempt to 'remount the stream of composition', and they are some of the most brilliant creative criticism of fiction we possess, especially for those of us who aspire to write ourselves.

None is more remarkable than the preface to *The American*. It reveals his anxious fascination with a book which, he thinks, he might have taken better care of, but which contains all the wonder, eagerness and intuition of early composition. He tells us about the way he had made the 'limping' thing go, explaining how he initiated and undertook it, how it all depended on a miracle. As we've seen, the primary idea arose from a vision of a wrong done in Europe to a compatriot, and how the protagonist would deal with it. He wouldn't forgive: 'he would simply turn, at the supreme moment, away, the bitterness of his personal loss yielding to the very force of his aversion. All he would have at the end would be therefore just the moral convenience, indeed the moral necessity, of his practical, but quite unappreciated, magnanimity . . . James then takes us through the creative stages: telling us how, in Paris, he found 'the whole formidable list, the who? the what? the where? the when? the why? the how?', and the way he worked out by what means the affront to him was to occur. It would be 'done [to] him by a lover; and yet not that done by his mistress herself, since injuries of this order are the stalest stuff of romance'. The lover would need to be an equal victim, and his hero would have to be confronted by others, 'great people', against whom he must in turn be given some power of revenge. But here was the problem. 'I had been plotting arch-romance without knowing it,' he says, and so the result was unintentionally romantic – romance 'undesigned and unabashed', romance that comes simply from following the silver thread of the story in all its buoyant joy.

What then follows are some quite remarkable reflections on the nature of romance, and its dialectical relation to fiction's sense and power of reality. Both elements are part of fiction; both are hard to designate. James attempts a distinction: 'The real represents to my perception the things we cannot possibly *not* know, soon or later, in one way or another . . . The romantic stands, on the other hand, for the things that, with all the facilities in the world, all the wealth and all the courage and all the wit and all the adventure, we never *can* directly know; the things that can reach us only through the beautiful circuit and subterfuge of our thought and our desire.' Then comes a passage, striking for its central analogy as well as its thought, that has often been quoted, but merits quoting again:

> The balloon of experience is in fact of course tied to the earth, and under that necessity we swing, thanks to a rope of remarkable length, in the more or less commodious car of the imagination; but it is by the rope we know where we are, and from the moment that cable is cut we are at large and unrelated: we only swing apart from the globe – though remaining as exhilarated, naturally, as we like, especially when all goes well. The art of the romancer is, 'for the fun of it', insidiously to cut the cable, to cut it without our detecting him. What I have recognised then in 'The American', much to my surprise and after long years, is that the experience here represented is the disconnected and uncontrolled experience – uncontrolled by our general sense of 'the way things happen' – which romance alone more or less successfully palms off on us.

The key to the hocus-pocus is that the outrage that must be performed on Newman is, he says, 'more showy than sound'. From elderly retrospect he considers he hasn't imparted an air of truth to the deeds of the Bellegardes: 'They would positively have jumped then, the Bellegardes, at my rich and easy American, and not have "minded" in the least any drawback . . .' He then goes on to reconceive the plan of the whole book. It would have been better, more ironical, if they had taken with alacrity 'everything he could give them, only asking for more and more, and then adjusting their pretensions and their pride to it with all the comfort in life. Such accommodation of the theory of a noble indifference to the practice of a deep avidity is the real note of policy in forlorn aristocracies'. Clearly, had Newman been allowed to enter inside the citadel, been permitted to marry Claire de Cintré, a very different battle and a very different book would have ensued. But it would not have been the adventure Newman had always been intended to have. So the reason why things had to develop as they do, says James, 'now glimmers interestingly out'. The main point was always to keep Newman consistent: 'he was to be the lighted figure, the others – even doubtless to an excessive degree the woman who is made the agent of his discomfiture – were to be obscured'. In consequence, he says, with Mme. de Cintré 'a light plank, too light a plank, is laid for the reader over a dark "psychological" abyss'. Many readers, no doubt stirred by what James called 'the fabulous felicity of my candour', have had the same feeling – that the price of telling the story of Newman's moral evolution beyond business and to his final 'unappreciated magnanimity' is the ritual sacrifice of Mme. de Cintré, who remains simply the centre of tragic romance, lacking the fictional weight given to those around her, not least her courtesan surrogate Noémie Nioche.

But we can draw other lessons from the preface. 'I sat for a long time with the closed volume [of the New York edition of *The American*] in my hand going over the preface in my mind and thinking – that is how it began, that's how it was done,' wrote Joseph Conrad, expressing his gratitude and that of many a novelist since. James shows us with utter clarity the novelist at his choices, and the way choices plainly have their consequences: by plotting a wrong, by putting the centre of consciousness in Newman, then following out 'the intensity of the creative effort to get into the skin of the creature', while at the same time trying for the effect of a 'centre', James came to the shape, the problems, the 'beautiful difficulties' of his novel. In the novel as we have it, he constructs a fable of his own youthful American sense of exclusion from the Parisian soul and sensibility. Newman is left uncertain not just about Claire de Cintré but his own role in the great drama – the encounter between his American commercial clarity and the secreted, finally religiously-veiled world hidden in the pavilion and the dark castle of the Bellegardes, then behind the closed, windowless walls of a Carmelite convent in the emblematically named Rue d'Enfer. But, as James says, the moral weight of the story is compensated for in following Newman's own moral progression: 'So much remains true then on behalf of my instinct of multiplying the fine touches by which Newman should live and communicate life.' He is left wondering whether he has been 'more commercial than was pleasant', and whether his decision to come to Europe in search both of 'aesthetic entertainment' and a wife has been a matter of wisdom: 'it may therefore be understood that he was able to conceive that a man may be too commercial'. The lesson is drawn by Mrs Tristram, who has set the whole dangerous enterprise in motion. While her husband wonders what made the Bellegardes drop their desire for what they wanted, Newman's wealth, she notes that their confidence was in 'your remarkable good nature! You see they were right.'

The American is one of those novels which, coming early in the career of a very great writer, show us what he then could and couldn't manage, what places he could and couldn't reach, which parts of the story have the feel of being an inherited and mechanical Victorian apparatus, which have a sense of deeply observed truth. But it is the mature James himself who best deconstructs The American, doing so as no one else could, dismantling it, reconceiving it in front of our eyes. Likewise later in his work he would vary, change, dissolve, deconstruct this whole fictive America, this fictive Paris, this 'great and gilded' Europe. He would consider, over and over again, the weight and worth of the American 'black ebony god of business' and its role in American life; he would look again at the 'forlorn aristocracies' of Europe; he would explore the ever-shifting transatlantic relation between the two, as both became exemplary cases of the social, moral, technological and psychological changes happening on each side of the Atlantic as the modern world steered its course. He would no longer be 'an eternal outsider' but the transatlantic insider, privy to much in the labyrinth of appearances. Hence many more alternative stories start in The American than the one he sketches: they are nothing less than the stories that would make up the great sum of James's work.

MALCOLM BRADBURY

NOTE ON THE TEXT

This Everyman edition uses the same text as the Penguin edition (1981), which was edited by William Spengemann. Spengemann 'elected to present the novel in its earlier, "unmodernised" form'. In other words he chose the Macmillan edition (1879) as emended for the uniform edition (1883) and not the later, heavily revised, New York edition (1907). As an example of James's revision one might cite his controversial decision to delete the final sentence of the English editions: 'Newman instinctively turned to see [. . .] it.' This edition includes however typographical corrections made by James for the New York edition. There are also some changes made by Spengemann. One of these, a change (suggested by Hershel Park – see Suggestions for Further Reading, p. 390) to a paragraph (1879 edition) in Chapter 11 (p. 151) beginning 'Well,' said Newman [. . .] found in Paris.' This has been altered so that there are now three short paragraphs. This alteration makes it clear who is speaking. Other changes are: in Chapter 3 (p. 55) the sentence reading: 'What do yo mean?' has had the 'u' inserted; in Chapter 5 (p. 72): 'wofully' now reads as woefully; in Chapter 10 (p. 140): Nevertheless he continued (the 1877 punctuation) replaces 'Nevertheless,' he continued . . . (the 1879 punctuation) as it makes more sense; in Chapter 11 (p. 148) quotemarks have been removed from the end of the sentence reading: And she began to put up her utensils.

1876–7: *The American* serialised in *The Atlantic Monthly*.

Editions of The American

1877: James R. Osgood and Co., Late Ticknor & Fields, and Fields, Osgood & Co. (Boston). Three printings: 30 April 1877; 18 May 1877; 29 August 1877.

1877: Ward, Lock (London), 18 December 1877.

1878: Bernhard Tauchnitz (Leipzig), authorised edn in 2 vols in *Collection of British Authors Series.*

1879: Macmillan (London), 8 March 1879.

1883: Macmillan (London), vols in *Novels and Tales of Henry James.*

1894: Ward, Lock & Bowden (London), 5 May 1894.

1907: Scribners (New York), preface pp. v–xxiii, 1907.

1921: Macmillan (London), Percy Lubbock (ed.), *The Novels and Stories of Henry James*, 1921–3.

LIST OF CHARACTERS

Rev Mr Benjamin Babcock: a Unitarian minister from Dorchester, Mass.

Blanche de Bellegarde: daughter of Urbain de Bellegarde and his wife.

Marquis Henri-Urbain de Bellegarde: the murdered husband of Mme. de Bellegarde.

Mme. Henri-Urbain (Emmeline) de Bellegarde: the widow of above. Formerly Lady Emmeline Atheling.

Bellegarde Urbain (Henri-Urbain): son of the Marquis and Mme. Henri-Urbain. The head of the household.

Mme. Urbain de Bellegarde: married to Urbain.

Valentin de Bellegarde: a younger brother of Urbain.

Princess Borealska: a Polish Princess who invites Christopher Newman, but he declines.

Mrs Catherine Bread: English servant and governess to Bellegarde family.

Claire de Bellegarde de Cintré: a widow and the heroine in the novel.

Blanche de Cintré: daughter of the young Henri-Urbain.

Dandelard: the wife batterer.

Mme. Dandelard: an Italian married to above.

Lord Deepmere: young Irish nobleman.

Dora Finch: an American visitor whom Newman met while dining at the Tristrams'.

M. de Grosjoyaux: a second with Ledoux at Valentin de Bellegarde's duel with Stanislas Kapp.

C. P. Hatch: an American friend of Newman's.

Stanislas Kapp: a duellist from Strasbourg who kills Valentin over Noémie Nioche.

Noémie Nioche: a French copyist whom Newman meets at the Louvre.

M. Nioche: father of above. He gives Newman French lessons.

Duchess d'Outreville: duchess whom Newman meets at a Bellegarde party.

General Packard: another American friend of Newman's.

Mme. Robineau: a French hostess.

Count de la Rochefidèle: a nobleman met at the Bellegarde party.

Countess de la Rochefidèle: his wife.

Lord St Dunstan's: the deceased father of Mme. Emmeline de Bellegarde.

Tom Tristram: Newman's friend in Paris.

Mrs Tom (Lizzie) Tristram: the American wife of above.

Kitty Upjohn: another American friend of Newman's.

THE AMERICAN

AUTHOR'S PREFACE TO
THE AMERICAN

'The American', which I had begun in Paris early in the winter
of 1875–76, made its first appearance in 'The Atlantic Monthly'
in June of the latter year and continued there, from month to
month, till May of the next. It started on its course while much
was still unwritten, and there again come back to me, with this
remembrance, the frequent hauntings and alarms of that com-
paratively early time; the habit of wondering what would
happen if anything *should* 'happen', if one should break one's
arm by an accident or make a long illness or suffer, in body,
mind, fortune, any other visitation involving a loss of time. The
habit of apprehension became of course in some degree the habit
of confidence that one would pull through, that, with opportunity enough, grave interruption never yet *had* descended, and
that a special Providence, in short, despite the sad warning of
Thackeray's 'Denis Duval' and of Mrs Gaskell's 'Wives and
Daughters' (that of Stevenson's 'Weir of Hermiston' was yet to
come) watches over anxious novelists condemned to the economy of serialisation. I make myself out in memory as having at
least for many months and in many places given my Providence
much to do: so great a variety of scenes of labour, implying all
so much renewal of application, glimmer out of the book as I
now read it over. And yet as the faded interest of the whole
episode becomes again mildly vivid what I seem most to recover
is, in its pale spectrality, a degree of joy, an eagerness on behalf
of my recital, that must recklessly enough have overridden
anxieties of every sort, including any view of inherent
difficulties.

I seem to recall no other like connexion in which the case was
met, to my measure, by so fond a complacency, in which my
subject can have appeared so apt to take care of itself. I see now
that I might all the while have taken much better care of it; yet,
as I had at the time no sense of neglecting it, neither acute nor
rueful solicitude, I can but speculate all vainly today on the

oddity of my composure. I ask myself indeed if, possibly, recognising after I was launched the danger of an inordinate leak – since the ship has truly a hole in its side more than sufficient to have sunk it – I may not have managed, as a counsel of mere despair, to stop my ears against the noise of waters and *pretend* to myself I was afloat; being indubitably, in any case, at sea, with no harbour of refuge till the end of my serial voyage. If I succeeded at all in that emulation (in another sphere) of the pursued ostrich I must have succeeded altogether; must have buried my head in the sand and there found beatitude. The explanation of my enjoyment of it, no doubt, is that I was more than commonly enamoured of my idea, and that I believed it, so trusted, so imaginatively fostered, not less capable of limping to its goal on three feet than on one. The lameness might be what it would: I clearly, for myself, felt the thing go – which is the most a dramatist can ever ask of his drama; and I shall here accordingly indulge myself in speaking first of how, superficially, it did so proceed; explaining then what I mean by its practical dependence on a miracle.

It had come to me, this happy, halting view of an interesting case, abruptly enough, some years before: I recall sharply the felicity of the first glimpse, though I forget the accident of thought that produced it. I recall that I was seated in an American 'horse-car' when I found myself, of a sudden, considering with enthusiasm, as the theme of a 'story', the situation, in another country and an aristocratic society, of some robust but insidiously beguiled and betrayed, some cruelly wronged, compatriot: the point being in especial that he should suffer at the hands of persons pretending to represent the highest possible civilisation and to be of an order in every way superior to his own. What would he 'do' in that predicament, how would he right himself, or how, failing a remedy, would he conduct himself under his wrong? This would be the question involved, and I remember well how, having entered the horse-car without a dream of it, I was presently to leave that vehicle in full possession of my answer. He would behave in the most interesting manner – it would all depend on that: stricken, smarting, sore, he would arrive at his just vindication and then would fail of all triumphantly and all vulgarly enjoying it. He would hold his revenge and cherish it and feel its sweetness, and then in the very act of forcing it home would sacrifice it in disgust. He would let them go, in short, his haughty contemners, even while feeling them, with joy, in his power, and he would obey, in so doing, one of the large and easy impulses *generally* characteristic of his type. He wouldn't 'forgive' – that would have, in the case, no application; he would simply turn, at the supreme moment, away, the bitterness of his personal loss yielding to the very force of his aversion. All he would have at the end would be therefore just the moral convenience, indeed the moral necessity, of his practical, but quite unappreciated, magnanimity; and one's last view of him would be that of a strong man indifferent to his strength and too wrapped in fine, too wrapped above all in *other* and intenser, reflexions for the assertion of his 'rights'. This last point was of the essence and constituted in fact the subject: there would be no subject at all, obviously, – or simply the commonest of the common, – if my gentleman should enjoy his advantage. I was charmed with my idea, which would take, however, much working out; and precisely because it had so much to give, I think, must I have dropped it for the time into the deep well of unconscious cerebration: not without the hope, doubtless, that it might eventually emerge from that reservoir, as one had already known the buried treasure to come to light, with a firm iridescent surface and a notable increase of weight.

This resurrection then took place in Paris, where I was at the moment living, and in December, 1875; my good fortune being apparently that Paris had ever so promptly offered me, and with an immediate directness at which I now marvel (since I had come back there, after earlier visitations, but a few weeks before), everything that was needed to make my conception concrete. I seem again at this distant day to see it become so quickly and easily, quite as if filling itself with life in that air. The objectivity it had wanted it promptly put on, and if the questions had been, with the usual intensity, for my hero and his crisis – the whole formidable list, the who? the what? the where? the when? the why? the how? – they gathered their answers in the cold shadow of the Arc de Triomphe, for fine reasons, very much as if they had been plucking spring flowers for the weaving of a frolic garland. I saw from one day to another my particular cluster of circumstances, with the life of the splendid city playing up in it like a flashing fountain in a marble basin. The very splendour seemed somehow to witness and intervene; it was important for the effect of my friend's discomfiture that it should take place on a high and lighted stage, and that his original ambition, the project exposing him, should have sprung from beautiful and noble suggestions – those that, at certain hours and under certain impressions, we feel the many-tinted medium by the Seine irresistibly to communicate. It was all charmingly simple, this conception, and the current must have gushed, full and clear, to my imagination, from the moment Christopher Newman rose before me, on a perfect day of the divine Paris spring, in the great gilded Salon Carré of the Louvre. Under this strong contagion of the place he would, by the happiest of hazards, meet his old comrade, now initiated and domiciled; after which the rest would go of itself. If he was to be wronged he would be wronged with just that conspicuity, with his felicity at just that pitch and with the highest aggrava- tion of the general effect of misery mocked at. Great and gilded the whole trap set, in fine, for his wary freshness and into which it would blunder upon its fate. I have, I confess, no memory of a disturbing doubt; once the man himself was imaged to me (and *that* germination is a process almost always untraceable) he must have walked into the situation as by taking a pass-key from his pocket.

But what then meanwhile would be the affront one would see him as most feeling? The affront of course done him as a lover; and yet not that done by his mistress herself, since injuries of this order are the stalest stuff of romance. I was not to have him jilted, any more than I was to have him successfully vindictive: both his wrong and his right would have been in these cases of too vulgar a type. I doubtless even then felt that the conception of Paris as the consecrated scene of rash infatuations and bold bad treacheries belongs, in the Anglo-Saxon imagination, to the infancy of art. The right renovation of any such theme as *that* would place it in Boston or at Cleveland, at Hartford or at Utica – give it some local connexion in which we had not already had so much of it. No, I should make my heroine herself, if heroine there was to be, an equal victim – just as Romeo was not less the sport of fate for not having been interestedly sacrificed by Juliet; and to this end I had but to imagine 'great people' again, imagine my hero confronted and involved with them, and impute to them, with a fine free hand, the arrogance and cruelty, the tortuous behaviour, in given conditions, of which great people have been historically so often capable. But as this was the light in which they were to show, so the essence of the matter would be that he should at the right moment find them in his power, and so the situation would reach its highest interest with the question of his utilisation of that knowledge. It would be here, in the possession and application of his power, that he would come out strong and would so deeply appeal to our sympathy. Here above all it really was, however, that my conception unfurled, with the best conscience in the world, the emblazoned flag of romance; which venerable ensign it had, though quite unwittingly, from the first and at every point sported in perfect good faith. I had been plotting arch-romance without knowing it, just as I began to write it that December day without recognising it and just as I all serenely and blissfully pursued the process from month to month and from place to place; just as I now, in short, reading the book over, find it yields me no interest and no reward comparable to the fond perception of this truth.

The thing is consistently, consummately – and I would fain really make bold to say charmingly – romantic; and all without intention, presumption, hesitation, contrition. The effect is equally undesigned and unabashed, and I lose myself, at this late hour, I am bound to add, in a certain sad envy of the free play of so much unchallenged instinct. One would like to woo back such hours of fine precipitation. They represent to the critical sense which the exercise of one's *whole* faculty has, with time, so inevitably and so thoroughly waked up, the happiest season of surrender to the invoked muse and the projected fable: the season of images so free and confident and ready that they brush questions aside and disport themselves, like the artless school-boys of Gray's beautiful Ode, in all the ecstasy of the ignorance attending them. The time doubtless comes soon enough when questions, as I call them, rule the roost and when the little victim, to adjust Gray's term again to the creature of frolic fancy, doesn't dare propose a gambol till they have all (like a board of trustees discussing a new outlay) sat on the possibly scandalous case. I somehow feel, accordingly, that it was lucky to have sacrificed on this particular altar while one still could; though it is perhaps droll – in a yet higher degree – to have done so not simply because one was guileless, but even quite under the conviction, in a general way, that, since no 'rendering' of any object and no painting of any picture can take effect without some form of reference and control, so these guarantees could but reside in a high probity of observation. I must decidedly have supposed, all the while, that I was acutely observing – and with a blest absence of wonder at its being so easy. Let me certainly at present rejoice in that absence; for I ask myself how without it I could have written 'The American'.

Was it indeed meanwhile my excellent conscience that kept the charm as unbroken as it appears to me, in rich retrospect, to have remained? – or is it that I suffer the mere influence of remembered, of associated places and hours, all acute impressions, to palm itself off as the sign of a finer confidence than I could justly claim? It is a pleasure to perceive how again and again the shrunken depths of old work yet permit themselves to be sounded or – even if rather terrible the image – 'dragged': the long pole of memory stirs and rummages the bottom, and we fish up such fragments and relics of the submerged life and the extinct consciousness as tempt us to piece them together. My windows looked into the Rue de Luxembourg – since then meagrely re-named Rue Cambon – and the particular light Parisian click of the small cab-horse on the clear asphalt, with its sharpness of detonation between the high houses, makes for the faded page today a sort of interlineation of sound. This sound rises to a martial clatter at the moment a troop of cuirassiers charges down the narrow street, each morning, to file, directly opposite my house, through the plain portal of the barracks occupying part of the vast domain attached in a rearward manner to one of the Ministères that front on the Place Vendôme; an expanse marked, along a considerable stretch of the street, by one of those high painted and administratively-placarded garden walls that form deep, vague, recurrent notes in the organic vastness of the city. I have but to re-read ten lines to recall my daily effort not to waste time in hanging over the window-bar for a sight of the cavalry the hard music of whose hoofs so directly and thrillingly appealed; an effort that inveterately failed – and a trivial circumstance now dignified, to my imagination, I may add, by the fact that the fruits of this weakness, the various items of the vivid picture, so constantly recaptured, must have been in themselves suggestive and inspiring, must have been rich strains, in their way, of the great Paris harmony. I have ever, in general, found it difficult to write of places under too immediate an impression – the impression that prevents standing off and allows neither space nor time for perspective. The image has had for the most part to be dim if the reflexion was to be, as is proper for a reflexion, both sharp and quiet: one has a horror, I think, artistically, of agitated reflexions.

Perhaps that is why the novel, after all, was to achieve, as it went on, no great – certainly no very direct – transfusion of the immense overhanging presence. It had to save as it could its own life, to keep tight hold of the tenuous silver thread, the one hope for which was that it shouldn't be tangled or clipped. This earnest grasp of the silver thread was doubtless an easier business in other places – though as I remount the stream of composition I see it faintly coloured again: with the bright protection of the Normandy coast (I worked away a few weeks at Étretat); with the stronger glow of southernmost France, breaking in during a stay at Bayonne; then with the fine historic and other 'psychic' substance of Saint-Germain-en-Laye, a purple patch of terraced October before returning to Paris. There comes after that the memory of a last brief intense invocation of the enclosing scene, of the pious effort to unwind my tangle, with a firm hand, in the very light (that light of high, narrowish French windows in old rooms, the light somehow, as one always feels, of 'style' itself) that had quickened my original vision. I was to pass over to London that autumn; which was a reason the more for considering the matter – the matter of Newman's final predicament – with due intensity: to let a loose end dangle over into alien air would so fix upon the whole, I strenuously felt, the dishonour of piecemeal composition. Therefore I strove to finish – first in a small dusky hotel of the Rive Gauche, where, though the windows again were high, the days were dim and the crepuscular court, domestic, intimate, 'quaint', testified to ancient manners almost as if it had been that of Balzac's Maison Vauquer in 'Le Père Goriot': and then once more in the Rue de Luxembourg, where a black-framed Empire portrait-medallion, suspended in the centre of each white panel of my almost noble old salon, made the coolest, discreetest, most measured decoration, and where, through casements open to the last mildness of the year, a belated Saint Martin's summer, the tale was taken up afresh by the charming light click and clatter, that sound as of the thin, quick, quite feminine surface-breathing of Paris, the shortest of rhythms for so huge an organism.

I shall not tell whether I did there bring my book to a close – and indeed I shrink, for myself, from putting the question to the test of memory. I follow it so far, the old urgent ingenious business, and then I lose sight of it: from which I infer – all exact recovery of the matter failing – that I did not in the event drag over the Channel a lengthening chain; which would have been detestable. I reduce to the absurd perhaps, however, by that small subjective issue, any undue measure of the interest of this insistent recovery of what I have called attendant facts. There always has been, for the valid work of art, a history – though mainly inviting, doubtless, but to the curious critic, for whom such things grow up and are formed very much in the manner of attaching young lives and characters, those conspicuous cases of happy development as to which evidence and anecdote are always in order. The development indeed must be certain to have been happy, the life sincere, the character fine: the work of art, to create or repay critical curiosity, must in short have been very 'valid' indeed. Yet there is on the other hand no mathematical measure of that importance – it may be a matter of widely-varying appreciation; and I am willing to grant, assuredly, that this interest, in a given relation, will nowhere so effectually kindle as on the artist's own part. And I am afraid that after all even his best excuse for it must remain the highly personal plea – the joy of living over, as a chapter of experience, the particular intellectual adventure. Here lurks an immense homage to the general privilege of the artist, to that constructive, that creative passion – portentous words, but they are convenient – the exercise of which finds so many an occasion for appearing to him the highest of human fortunes, the rarest boon of the gods. He values it, all sublimely and perhaps a little fatuously, for itself – as the great extension, great beyond all others, of experience and of consciousness; with the toil and trouble a mere sun-cast shadow that falls, shifts and vanishes, the result of his living in so large a light. On the constant nameless felicity of this Robert Louis Stevenson has, in an admirable passage and as in so many other connexions, said the right word: that the partaker of the 'life of art' who repines at the absence of the rewards, as they are called, of the pursuit might surely be better occupied. Much rather should he endlessly wonder at his not having to pay half his substance for his luxurious immersion. He enjoys it, so to speak, without a tax; the effort of labour involved, the torment of expression, of which we have heard in our time so much, being after all but the last refinement of his privilege. It may leave him weary and worn; but how, after his fashion, he will have lived! As if one were to expect at once freedom and ease! That silly safety is but the sign of bondage and forfeiture. Who can imagine free selection – which is the beautiful, terrible *whole* of art – without free difficulty? This is the very franchise of the city and high ambition of the citizen. The vision of the difficulty, as one looks back, bathes one's course in a golden glow by which the very objects along the road are transfigured and glorified; so that one exhibits them to other eyes with an elation possibly presumptuous.

Since I accuse myself at all events of these complacencies I take advantage of them to repeat that I value, in my retrospect, nothing so much as the lively light on the romantic property of my subject that I had not expected to encounter. If in 'The American' I invoked the romantic association without malice prepense, yet with a production of the romantic effect that is for myself unmistakable, the occasion is of the best perhaps for penetrating a little the obscurity of that principle. By what art or mystery, what craft of selection, omission or commission, does a given picture of life appear to us to surround its theme, its figures and images, with the air of romance while another picture close beside it may affect us as steeping the whole matter in the element of reality? It is a question, no doubt, on the painter's part, very much more of perceived effect, effect *after* the fact, than of conscious design – though indeed I have ever failed to see how a coherent picture of anything is producible save by a complex of fine measurements. The cause of the deflexion, in one pronounced sense or the other, must lie deep, however; so that for the most part we recognise the character of our interest only after the particular magic, as I say, has thoroughly operated – and then in truth but if we be a bit critically minded, if we find our pleasure, that is, in these intimate appreciations (for which, as I am well aware, ninety-nine readers in a hundred have no use whatever). The determining condition would at any rate seem so latent that one may well doubt if the full artistic consciousness ever reaches it; leaving the matter thus a case, ever, not of an author's plotting and planning and calculating, but just of his feeling and seeing, of his conceiving, in a word, and of his thereby inevitably expressing himself, under the influence of one value or the other. These values represent different sorts and degrees of the communicable thrill, and I doubt if any novelist, for instance, ever proposed to commit himself to one kind or the other with as little mitigation as we are sometimes able to find for him. The interest is greatest – the interest of his genius, I mean, and of his general wealth – when he commits himself in both directions; not quite at the same time or to the same effect, of course, but by some need of performing his whole possible revolution, by the law of some rich passion in him for extremes.

Of the men of largest responding imagination before the human scene, of Scott, of Balzac, even of the coarse, comprehensive, prodigious Zola, we feel, I think, that the deflexion toward either quarter has never taken place; that neither the nature of the man's faculty nor the nature of his experience has ever quite determined it. His current remains therefore extraordinarily rich and mixed, washing us successively with the warm wave of the near and familiar and the tonic shock, as may be, of the far and strange. (In making which opposition I suggest not that the strange and the far are at all necessarily romantic: they happen to be simply the unknown, which is quite a different matter. The real represents to my perception the things we cannot possibly *not* know, sooner or later, in one way or another; it being but one of the accidents of our hampered state, and one of the incidents of their quantity and number, that particular instances have not yet come our way. The romantic stands, on the other hand, for the things that, with all the facilities in the world, all the wealth and all the courage and all the wit and all the adventure, we never *can* directly know; the things that can reach us only through the beautiful circuit and subterfuge of our thought and our desire.) There have been, I gather, many definitions of romance, as a matter indispensably of boats, or of caravans, or of tigers, or of 'historical characters', or of ghosts, or of forgers, or of detectives, or of beautiful wicked women, or of pistols and knives, but they appear for the most part reducible to the idea of the facing of danger, the acceptance of great risks for the fascination, the very love, of their uncertainty, the joy of success if possible and of battle in any case. This would be a fine formula if it bore examination; but it strikes me as weak and inadequate, as by no means covering the true ground and yet as landing us in strange confusions.

The panting pursuit of danger is the pursuit of life itself, in which danger awaits us possibly at every step and faces us at every turn; so that the dream of an intenser experience easily becomes rather some vision of a sublime security like that enjoyed on the flowery plains of heaven, where we may conceive ourselves proceeding in ecstasy from one prodigious phase and form of it to another. And if it be insisted that the measure of the type is then in the *appreciation* of danger – the sign of our projection of the real being the smallness of its dangers, and that of our projection of the romantic the hugeness, the mark of the distinction being in short, as they say of collars and gloves and shoes, the size and 'number' of the danger – this discrimination again surely fails, since it makes our difference not a difference of kind, which is what we want, but a difference only of degree, and subject by that condition to the indignity of a sliding scale and a shifting measure. There are immense and flagrant dangers that are but sordid and squalid ones, as we feel, tainting with their quality the very defiances they provoke; while there are common and covert ones, that 'look like nothing' and that can be but inwardly and occultly dealt with, which involve the sharpest hazards to life and honour and the highest instant decisions and intrepidities of action. It is an arbitrary stamp that keeps these latter prosaic and makes the former heroic; and yet I should still less subscribe to a mere 'subjective' division – I mean one that would place the difference wholly in the temper of the imperilled agent. It would be impossible to have a more romantic temper than Flaubert's Madame Bovary, and yet nothing less resembles a romance than the record of her adventures. To classify it by that aspect – the definition of the spirit that happens to animate her – is like settling the question (as I have seen it witlessly settled) by the presence or absence of 'costume'. Where again then does costume begin or end? – save with the 'run' of one or another sort of play? We must reserve vague labels for artless mixtures.

The only *general* attribute of projected romance that I can see, the only one that fits all its cases, is the fact of the kind of experience with which it deals – experience liberated, so to speak; experience disengaged, disembroiled, disencumbered, exempt from the conditions that we usually know to attach to it and, if we wish so to put the matter, drag upon it, and operating in a medium which relieves it, in a particular interest, of the inconvenience of a *related*, a measurable state, a state subject to all our vulgar communities. The greatest intensity may so be arrived at evidently – when the sacrifice of community, of the 'related' sides of situations, has not been too rash. It must to this end not flagrantly betray itself; we must even be kept if possible, for our illusion, from suspecting any sacrifice at all. The balloon of experience is in fact of course tied to the earth, and under that necessity we swing, thanks to a rope of remarkable length, in the more or less commodious car of the imagination; but it is by the rope we know where we are, and from the moment that cable is cut we are at large and unrelated: we only swing apart from the globe – though remaining as exhilarated, naturally, as we like, especially when all goes well. The art of the romancer is, 'for the fun of it', insidiously to cut the cable, to cut it without our detecting him. What I have recognised then in 'The American', much to my surprise and after long years, is that the experience here represented is the disconnected and uncontrolled experience – uncontrolled by our general sense of 'the way things happen' – which romance alone more or less successfully palms off on us. It is a case of Newman's own intimate experience all, that being my subject, the thread of which, from beginning to end, is not once exchanged, however momentarily, for any other thread; and the experience of others concerning us, and concerning him, only so far as it touches him and as he recognises, feels or divines it. There is our general sense of the way things happen – it abides with us indefeasibly, as readers of fiction, from the moment we demand that our fiction shall be intelligible; and there is our particular sense of the way they don't happen, which is liable to wake up unless reflexion and criticism, in us, have been skilfully and successfully drugged. There are drugs enough, clearly – it is all a question of applying them with tact; in which case the way things don't happen may be artfully made to pass for the way things do.

Amusing and even touching to me, I profess, at this time of day, the ingenuity (worthy, with whatever lapses, of a better cause) with which, on behalf of Newman's adventure, this hocus-pocus is attempted: the value of the instance not being diminished either, surely, by its having been attempted in such evident good faith. Yes, all is romantic to my actual vision here, and not least so, I hasten to add, the fabulous felicity of my candour. The way things happen is frankly not the way in which they are represented as having happened, in Paris, to my hero: the situation I had conceived only saddled me with that for want of my invention of something better. The great house of Bellegarde, in a word, would, I now feel, given the circumstances, given the *whole* of the ground, have comported itself in a manner as different as possible from the manner to which my narrative commits it; of which truth, moreover, I am by no means sure that, in spite of what I have called my serenity, I had not all the while an uneasy suspicion. I had dug in my path, alas, a hole into which I was destined to fall. I was so possessed of my idea that Newman should be ill-used – which was the essence of my subject – that I attached too scant an importance to its fashion of coming about. Almost any fashion would serve, I appear to have assumed, that would give me my main chance for him; a matter depending not so much on the particular trick played him as on the interesting face presented by him to *any* damnable trick. So where I part company with *terra-firma* is in making that projected, that performed outrage so much more showy, dramatically speaking, than sound. Had I patched it up to a greater apparent soundness my own trick, artistically speaking, would have been played; I should have cut the cable without my reader's suspecting it. I doubtless at the time, I repeat, believed I had taken my precautions; but truly they should have been greater, to impart the air of truth to the attitude – that is first to the pomp and circumstance, and second to the queer falsity – of the Bellegardes.

They would positively have jumped then, the Bellegardes, at my rich and easy American, and not have 'minded' in the least any drawback – especially as, after all, given the pleasant palette from which I have painted him, there were few drawbacks to mind. My subject imposed on me a group of closely-allied persons animated by immense pretensions – which was all very well, which might be full of the promise of interest: only of interest felt most of all in the light of comedy and of irony. This, better understood, would have dwelt in the idea not in the least of their not finding Newman good enough for their alliance and thence being ready to sacrifice him, but in that of their taking with alacrity everything he could give them, only asking for more and more, and then adjusting their pretensions and their pride to it with all the comfort in life. Such accommodation of the theory of a noble indifference to the practice of a deep avidity is the real note of policy in forlorn aristocracies – and I meant of course that the Bellegardes should be virtually forlorn. The perversion of truth is by no means, I think, in the displayed acuteness of their remembrance of 'who' and 'what' they are, or at any rate take themselves for; since it is the misfortune of all insistence on 'worldly' advantages – and the situation of such people bristles at the best (by which I mean under whatever invocation of a superficial simplicity) with emphasis, accent, assumption – to produce at times an effect of grossness. The picture of their tergiversation, at all events, however it may originally have seemed to me to hang together, has taken on this rococo appearance precisely because their preferred course, a thousand times preferred, would have been to haul him and his fortune into their boat under cover of night perhaps, in any case as quietly and with as little bumping and splashing as possible, and there accommodate him with the very safest and most convenient seat. Given Newman, given the fact that the thing constitutes itself organically as *his* adventure, that too might very well be a situation and a subject: only it wouldn't have been the theme of 'The American' as the book stands, the theme to which I was from so early pledged. Since I had wanted a 'wrong' this other turn might even have been arranged to give me *that*, might even have been arranged to meet my requirement that somebody or something should be 'in his power' so delightfully; and with the signal effect, after all, of 'defining' everything. (It is as difficult, I said above, to trace the dividing-line between the real and the romantic as to plant a milestone between north and south; but I am not sure an infallible sign of the latter is not this rank vegetation of the 'power' of bad people that good get into, or *vice versa*. It is so rarely, alas, into *our* power that any one gets!)

It is difficult for me today to believe that I had not, as my work went on, *some* shade of the rueful sense of my affront to verisimilitude; yet I catch the memory at least of no great sharpness, no true critical anguish, of remorse: an anomaly the reason of which in fact now glimmers interestingly out. My concern, as I saw it, was to make and to keep Newman consistent; the picture of his consistency was all my undertaking, and the memory of *that* infatuation perfectly abides with me.

He was to be the lighted figure, the others – even doubtless to an excessive degree the woman who is made the agent of his discomfiture – were to be the obscured; by which I should largely get the very effect most to be invoked, that of a generous nature engaged with forces, with difficulties and dangers, that it but half understands. If Newman was attaching enough, I must have argued, his tangle would be sensible enough; for the interest of everything is all that it is *his* vision, *his* conception, *his* interpretation: at the window of his wide, quite sufficiently wide, consciousness we are seated, from that admirable position we 'assist'. He therefore supremely matters; all the rest matters only as he feels it, treats it, meets it. A beautiful infatuation this, always, I think, the intensity of the creative effort to get into the skin of the creature; the act of personal possession of one being by another at its completest – and with the high enhancement, ever, that it is, by the same stroke, the effort of the artist to preserve for his subject that unity, and for his use of it (in other words for the interest he desires to excite) that effect of a *centre*, which most economise its value. Its value is most discussable when that economy has most operated; the content and the 'importance' of a work of art are in fine wholly dependent on its *being* one: outside of which all prate of its representative character, its meaning and its bearing, its morality and humanity, are an impudent thing. Strong in that character, which is the condition of its really bearing witness at all, it is strong every way. So much remains true then on behalf of my instinct of multiplying the fine touches by which Newman should live and communicate life; and yet I still ask myself, I confess, what I can have made of 'life', in my picture, at such a juncture as the interval offered as elapsing between my hero's first accepted state and the nuptial rites that are to crown it. Nothing here is in truth 'offered' – everything is evaded, and the effect of this, I recognise, is of the oddest. His relation to Madame de Cintré takes a great stride, but the author appears to view that but as a signal for letting it severely alone.

I have been stupefied, in so thoroughly revising the book, to find, on turning a page, that the light in which he is presented immediately after Madame de Bellegarde has conspicuously introduced him to all her circle as her daughter's husband-to-be is that of an evening at the opera quite alone; as if he wouldn't surely spend his leisure, and especially those hours of it, with his intended. Instinctively, from that moment, one would have seen them intimately and, for one's interest, beautifully together; with some illustration of the beauty incumbent on the author. The truth was that at this point the author, all gracelessly, could but hold his breath and pass; lingering was too difficult – he had made for himself a crushing complication. Since Madame de Cintré was after all to 'back out' every touch in the picture of her apparent loyalty would add to her eventual shame. She had acted in clear good faith, but how could I give the *detail* of an attitude, on her part, of which the foundation was yet so weak? I preferred, as the minor evil, to shirk the attempt – at the cost evidently of a signal loss of 'charm'; and with this lady, altogether, I recognise, a light plank, too light a plank, is laid for the reader over a dark 'psychological' abyss. The delicate clue to her conduct is never definitely placed in his hand: I must have liked verily to think it *was* delicate and to flatter myself it was to be felt with finger-tips rather than heavily tugged at. Here then, at any rate, is the romantic *tout craché* – the fine flower of Newman's experience blooming in a medium 'cut off' and shut up to itself. I don't for a moment pronounce any spell proceeding from it necessarily the less workable, to a rejoicing ingenuity, for that; beguile the reader's suspicion of *his* being shut up, transform it for *him* into a positive illusion of the largest liberty, and the success will ever be proportionate to the chance. Only all this gave me, I make out, a great deal to look to, and I was perhaps wrong in thinking that Newman by himself, and for any occasional extra inch or so I might smuggle into his measurements, would see me through my wood. Anything more liberated and disconnected, to repeat my terms, than his prompt general profession, before the Tristrams, of aspiring to a 'great' marriage, for example, could surely not well be imagined. I had to take that over with the rest of him and fit it in – I had indeed to exclude the outer air. Still, I find on re-perusal that I have been able to breathe at least in my aching void; so that, clinging to my hero as to a tall, protective, good-natured elder brother in a rough place, I leave the record to stand or fall by his more or less convincing image.

CHAPTER I

On a brilliant day in May, in the year 1868, a gentleman was reclining at his ease on the great circular divan which at that period occupied the centre of the Salon Carré, in the Museum of the Louvre.* This commodious ottoman has since been removed, to the extreme regret of all weak-kneed lovers of the fine arts; but the gentleman in question had taken serene possession of its softest spot, and, with his head thrown back and his legs outstretched, was staring at Murillo's beautiful moon-borne Madonna* in profound enjoyment of his posture. He had removed his hat, and flung down beside him a little red guide-book and an opera-glass. The day was warm; he was heated with walking, and he repeatedly passed his handkerchief over his forehead, with a somewhat wearied gesture. And yet he was evidently not a man to whom fatigue was familiar; long, lean, and muscular, he suggested the sort of vigour that is commonly known as 'toughness'. But his exertions on this particular day had been of an unwonted sort, and he had often performed great physical feats which left him less jaded than his tranquil stroll through the Louvre. He had looked out all the pictures to which an asterisk was affixed in those formidable pages of fine print in his Bädeker;* his attention had been strained and his eyes dazzled, and he had sat down with an aesthetic headache. He had looked, moreover, not only at all the pictures, but at all the copies that were going forward around them, in the hands of those innumerable young women in irreproachable toilets who devote themselves, in France, to the propagation of masterpieces; and if the truth must be told, he had often admired the copy much more than the original. His physiognomy would have sufficiently indicated that he was a shrewd and capable fellow, and in truth he had often sat up all night over a bristling bundle of accounts, and heard the cock crow without a yawn. But Raphael and Titian and Rubens were a new kind of arithmetic, and they inspired our friend, for the first time in his life, with a vague self-mistrust.

An observer, with anything of an eye for national types, would have had no difficulty in determining the local origin of this undeveloped connoisseur, and indeed such an observer might have felt a certain humorous relish of the almost ideal completeness with which he filled out the national mould. The gentleman on the divan was a powerful specimen of an American. But he was not only a fine American; he was in the first place, physically, a fine man. He appeared to possess that kind of health and strength which, when found in perfection, are the most impressive – the physical capital* which the owner does nothing to 'keep up'. If he was a muscular Christian,* it was quite without knowing it. If it was necessary to walk to a remote spot, he walked, but he had never known himself to 'exercise'. He had no theory with regard to cold bathing or the use of Indian clubs; he was neither an oarsman, a rifleman, nor a fencer – he had never had time for these amusements – and he was quite unaware that the saddle is recommended for certain forms of indigestion. He was by inclination a temperate man; but he had supped the night before his visit to the Louvre at the Café Anglais* – someone had told him it was an experience not to be omitted – and he had slept none the less the sleep of the just. His usual attitude and carriage were of a rather relaxed and lounging kind, but when, under a special inspiration, he straightened himself, he looked like a grenadier on parade. He never smoked. He had been assured – such things are said – that cigars were excellent for the health, and he was quite capable of believing it; but he knew as little about tobacco as about homoeopathy.* He had a very well-formed head, with a shapely, symmetrical balance of the frontal and the occipital development, and a good deal of straight, rather dry brown hair. His complexion was brown, and his nose had a bold, well-marked arch. His eye was of a clear, cold grey, and, save for a rather abundant moustache, he was clean-shaved. He had the flat jaw and sinewy neck which are frequent in the American type; but the traces of national origin are a matter of expression even more than of feature, and it was in this respect that our friend's countenance was supremely eloquent. The discriminating observer we have been supposing might, however, perfectly have measured its expressiveness, and yet have been at a loss to describe it. It had that typical vagueness which is not vacuity, that blankness which is not simplicity, that look of being committed to nothing in particular, of standing in an attitude of general hospitality to the chances of life, of being very much at one's own disposal, so characteristic of many American faces. It was our friend's eye that chiefly told his story; an eye in which innocence and experience were singularly blended. It was full of contradictory suggestions; and though it was by no means the glowing orb of a hero of romance, you could find in it almost anything you looked for. Frigid and yet friendly, frank yet cautious, shrewd yet credulous, positive yet sceptical, confident yet shy, extremely intelligent and extremely good-humoured, there was something vaguely defiant in its concessions, and something profoundly reassuring in its reserve. The cut of this gentleman's moustache, with the two premature wrinkles in the cheek above it, and the fashion of his garments, in which an exposed shirt-front and a cerulean cravat played perhaps an obtrusive part, completed the conditions of his identity. We have approached him, perhaps, at a not especially favourable moment; he is by no means sitting for his portrait. But listless as he lounges there, rather baffled on the aesthetic question, and guilty of the damning fault (as we have lately discovered it to be) of confounding the merit of the artist with that of his work (for he admires the squinting Madonna of the young lady with the boyish coiffure, because he thinks the young lady herself uncommonly taking), he is a sufficiently promising acquaintance. Decision, salubrity, jocosity, prosperity, seem to hover within his call; he is evidently a practical man, but the idea, in his case, has undefined and mysterious boundaries, which invite the imagination to bestir itself on his behalf.

As the little copyist proceeded with her work, she sent every now and then a responsive glance toward her admirer. The cultivation of the fine arts appeared to necessitate, to her mind, a great deal of by-play, a great standing off with folded arms and head drooping from side to side, stroking of a dimpled chin with a dimpled hand, sighing and frowning and patting of the foot, fumbling in disordered tresses for wandering hair-pins. These performances were accompanied by a restless glance, which lingered longer than elsewhere upon the gentleman we have described. At last he rose abruptly, put on his hat, and approached the young lady. He placed himself before her picture and looked at it for some moments, during which she pretended to be quite unconscious of his inspection. Then, addressing her with the single word which constituted the strength of his French vocabulary, and holding up one finger in a manner which appeared to him to illuminate his meaning, 'Combien?' he abruptly demanded.

The artist stared a moment, gave a little pout, shrugged her shoulders, put down her palette and brushes, and stood rubbing her hands.

'How much?' said our friend, in English. 'Combien?'

'Monsieur wishes to buy it?' asked the young lady, in French.

'Very pretty, splendide.* Combien?' repeated the American.

'It pleases monsieur, my little picture? It's a very beautiful subject,' said the young lady.

'The Madonna, yes; I am not a Catholic, but I want to buy it. Combien? Write it here.' And he took a pencil from his pocket, and showed her the fly-leaf of his guide-book. She stood looking at him and scratching her chin with the pencil. 'Is it not for sale?' he asked. And as she still stood reflecting, and looking at him with an eye which, in spite of her desire to treat this avidity of patronage as a very old story, betrayed an almost touching incredulity, he was afraid he had offended her. She was simply trying to look indifferent, and wondering how far she might go. 'I haven't made a mistake – pas insulté,* no?' her interlocutor continued. 'Don't you understand a little English?'

The young lady's aptitude for playing a part at short notice was remarkable. She fixed him with her conscious, perceptive eye, and asked him if he spoke no French. Then, 'Donnez!'* she said briefly, and took the open guide-book. In the upper corner of the fly-leaf she traced a number, in a minute and extremely neat hand. Then she handed back the book, and took up her palette again.

Our friend read the number: '2,000 francs'. He said nothing for a time, but stood looking at the picture, while the copyist began actively to dabble with her paint. 'For a copy, isn't that a good deal?' he asked at last. 'Pas beaucoup?'*

The young lady raised her eyes from her palette, scanned him from head to foot, and alighted with admirable sagacity upon exactly the right answer. 'Yes, it's a good deal. But my copy has remarkable qualities; it is worth nothing less.'

The gentleman in whom we are interested understood no French, but I have said he was intelligent, and here is a good chance to prove it. He apprehended, by a natural instinct, the meaning of the young woman's phrase, and it gratified him to think that she was so honest. Beauty, talent, virtue; she combined everything! 'But you must finish it,' he said. '*Finish*, you know,' and he pointed to the unpainted hand of the figure.

'Oh, it shall be finished in perfection – in the perfection of perfections!' cried mademoiselle; and to confirm her promise, she deposited a rosy blotch in the middle of the Madonna's cheek.

But the American frowned. 'Ah, too red, too red!' he rejoined. 'Her complexion,' pointing to the Murillo, 'is more delicate.'

'Delicate? Oh, it shall be delicate, monsieur; delicate as Sèvres *biscuit*.* I am going to tone that down; I know all the secrets of my art. And where will you allow us to send it to you? Your address?'

'My address? Oh yes!' And the gentleman drew a card from his pocket-book and wrote something upon it. Then hesitating a moment he said: 'If I don't like it when it is finished, you know, I shall not be obliged to take it.'

The young lady seemed as good a guesser as himself. 'Oh, I am very sure that monsieur is not capricious,' she said with a roguish smile.

'Capricious?' And at this monsieur began to laugh. 'Oh no, I'm not capricious. I am very faithful. I am very constant. *Comprenez?*'

'Monsieur is constant; I understand perfectly. It's a rare virtue. To recompense you, you shall have your picture on the first possible day; next week – as soon as it is dry. I will take the card of monsieur.' And she took it and read his name: 'Christopher Newman'. Then she tried to repeat it aloud, and laughed at her bad accent. 'Your English names are so droll!'

'Droll?' said Mr Newman, laughing too. 'Did you ever hear of Christopher Columbus?'

'*Bien sûr!** He invented* America; a very great man. And is he your patron?'

'My patron?'

'Your patron-saint, in the calendar.'

'Oh, exactly; my parents named me for him.'

'Monsieur is American?'

'Don't you see it?' monsieur inquired.

'And you mean to carry my little picture away over there?' and she explained her phrase with a gesture.

'Oh, I mean to buy a great many pictures – *beaucoup*, *beaucoup*,' said Christopher Newman.

'The honour is not less for me,' the young lady answered, 'for I am sure monsieur has a great deal of taste.'

'But you must give me your card,' Newman said; 'your card, you know.'

The young lady looked severe for an instant, and then said: 'My father will wait upon you.'

But this time Mr Newman's powers of divination were at fault. 'Your card, your address,' he simply repeated.

'My address?' said mademoiselle. Then, with a little shrug: 'Happily for you, you are an American! It is the first time I ever gave my card to a gentleman.' And, taking from her pocket a rather greasy portemonnaie,* she extracted from it a small glazed visiting card, and presented the latter to her patron. It was neatly inscribed in pencil, with a great many flourishes: 'Mdlle. Noémie Nioche'.* But Mr Newman, unlike his companion, read the name with perfect gravity; all French names to him were equally droll.

'And precisely, here is my father, who has come to escort me home,' said Mademoiselle Noémie. 'He speaks English. He will arrange with you.' And she turned to welcome a little old gentleman who came shuffling up, peering over his spectacles at Newman.

M. Nioche wore a glossy wig, of an unnatural colour, which overhung his little meek, white, vacant face, and left it hardly more expressive than the unfeatured block upon which these articles are displayed in the barber's window. He was an exquisite image of shabby gentility. His little ill-made coat, desperately brushed, his darned gloves, his highly-polished boots, his rusty, shapely hat, told the story of a person who had 'had losses', and who clung to the spirit of nice habits, though the letter had been hopelessly effaced. Among other things M. Nioche had lost courage. Adversity had not only ruined him, it had frightened him, and he was evidently going through his remnant of life on tiptoe, for fear of waking up the hostile fates. If this strange gentleman was saying anything improper to his daughter, M. Nioche would entreat him huskily, as a particular favour, to forbear; but he would admit at the same time that he was very presumptuous to ask for particular favours.

'Monsieur has bought my picture,' said Mademoiselle Noémie. 'When it is finished you will carry it to him in a cab.'

'In a cab!' cried M. Nioche; and he stared, in a bewildered way, as if he had seen the sun rising at midnight.

'Are you the young lady's father?' said Newman. 'I think she said you speak English.'

'Speak English – yes,' said the old man, slowly rubbing his hands. 'I will bring it in a cab.'

'Say something, then,' cried his daughter. 'Thank him a little – not too much.'

'A little, my daughter, a little,' said M. Nioche, perplexed. 'How much?'

'Two thousand!' said Mademoiselle Noémie. 'Don't make a fuss, or he will take back his word.'

'Two thousand!' cried the old man; and he began to fumble for his snuff-box. He looked at Newman, from head to foot, at his daughter, and then at the picture. 'Take care you don't spoil it!' he cried, almost sublimely.

'We must go home,' said Mademoiselle Noémie. 'This is a good day's work. Take care how you carry it!' And she began to put up her utensils.

'How can I thank you?' said M. Nioche. 'My English does not suffice.'

'I wish I spoke French as well,' said Newman, good-naturedly. 'Your daughter is very clever.'

'Oh sir!' and M. Nioche looked over his spectacles with tearful eyes and nodded several times with a world of sadness. 'She has had an education – *très-supérieure!** Nothing was spared. Lessons in pastel at ten francs the lesson, lessons in oil at twelve francs. I didn't look at the francs then. She's an *artiste*, eh?'

'Do I understand you to say that you have had reverses?' asked Newman.

'Reverses? Oh sir, misfortunes – terrible!'

'Unsuccessful in business, eh?'

'Very unsuccessful, sir.'

'Oh, never fear, you'll get on your legs again,' said Newman cheerily.

The old man drooped his head on one side and looked at him with an expression of pain, as if this were an unfeeling jest.

'What does he say?' demanded Mademoiselle Noémie.

M. Nioche took a pinch of snuff. 'He says I will make my fortune again.'

'Perhaps he will help you. And what else?'

'He says thou art very clever.'*

'It is very possible. You believe it yourself, my father?'

'Believe it, my daughter? With this evidence!' and the old man turned afresh, with a staring, wondering homage, to the audacious daub on the easel.

'Ask him, then, if he would not like to learn French.'

'To learn French?'

'To take lessons.'

'To take lessons, my daughter? From thee?'

'From you!'

'From me, my child? How should I give lessons?'

'*Pas de raisons!** Ask him immediately!' said Mademoiselle Noémie, with soft brevity.

M. Nioche stood aghast, but under his daughter's eye he collected his wits, and, doing his best to assume an agreeable smile, he executed her commands. 'Would it please you to receive instruction in our beautiful language?' he inquired, with an appealing quaver.

'To study French?' asked Newman, staring.

M. Nioche pressed his finger-tips together and slowly raised his shoulders. 'A little conversation!'

'Conversation – that's it!' murmured Mademoiselle Noémie, who had caught the word. 'The conversation of the best society.'

'Our French conversation is famous, you know,' M. Nioche ventured to continue. 'It's a great talent.'

'But isn't it awfully difficult?' asked Newman, very simply.

'Not to a man of *esprit*,* like monsieur, an admirer of beauty in every form!' and M. Nioche cast a significant glance at his daughter's Madonna.

'I can't fancy myself chattering French!' said Newman with a laugh. 'And yet, I suppose that the more a man knows the better.'

'Monsieur expresses that very happily. *Hélas, oui!**

'I suppose it would help me a great deal, knocking about Paris, to know the language.'

'Ah, there are so many things monsieur must want to say: difficult things!'

'Everything I want to say is difficult. But you give lessons?'

Poor M. Nioche was embarrassed; he smiled more appealingly. 'I am not a regular professor,' he admitted. 'I can't nevertheless tell him that I'm a professor,' he said to his daughter.

'Tell him it's a very exceptional chance,' answered Mademoiselle Noémie; 'an *homme du monde** – one gentleman conversing with another! Remember what you are – what you have been!'

'A teacher of languages in neither case! Much more formerly and much less today! And if he asks the price of the lessons?'

'He won't ask it,' said Mademoiselle Noémie.

'What he pleases, I may say?'

'Never! That's bad style.'

'If he asks, then?'

Mademoiselle Noémie had put on her bonnet and was tying the ribbons. She smoothed them out, with her soft little chin thrust forward. 'Ten francs,' she said quickly.

'Oh, my daughter! I shall never dare.'

'Don't dare, then! He won't ask till the end of the lessons, and then I will make out the bill.'

M. Nioche turned to the confiding foreigner again, and stood rubbing his hands, with an air of seeming to plead guilty which was not intenser only because it was habitually so striking. It never occurred to Newman to ask him for a guarantee of his skill in imparting instruction; he supposed of course M. Nioche knew his own language, and his appealing forlornness was quite the perfection of what the American, for vague reasons, had always associated with all elderly foreigners of the lesson-giving class. Newman had never reflected upon philological processes. His chief impression with regard to ascertaining those mysterious correlatives of his familiar English vocables which were current in this extraordinary city of Paris was, that it was simply a matter of a good deal of unwonted and rather ridiculous muscular effort on his own part. 'How did you learn English?' he asked of the old man.

'When I was young, before my miseries. Oh, I was wide awake, then. My father was a great *commerçant*; he placed me for a year in a counting-house in England. Some of it stuck to me; but I have forgotten!'

'How much French can I learn in a month?'

'What does he say?' asked Mademoiselle Noémie.

M. Nioche explained.

'He will speak like an angel!' said his daughter.

But the native integrity which had been vainly exerted to secure M. Nioche's commercial prosperity flickered up again. '*Dame*,* monsieur!' he answered. 'All I can teach you!' And then, recovering himself at a sign from his daughter, 'I will wait upon you at your hotel.'

'Oh yes, I should like to learn French,' Newman went on, with democratic confidingness. 'Hang me if I should ever have thought of it! I took for granted it was impossible. But if you learned my language, why shouldn't I learn yours?' and his frank, friendly laugh drew the sting from the jest. 'Only, if we are going to converse, you know, you must think of something cheerful to converse about.'

'You are very good, sir; I am overcome!' said M. Nioche, throwing out his hands. 'But you have cheerfulness and happiness for two!'

'Oh no,' said Newman more seriously. 'You must be bright and lively; that's part of the bargain.'

M. Nioche bowed, with his hand on his heart. 'Very well, sir; you have already made me lively.'

'Come and bring me my picture then; I will pay you for it, and we will talk about that. That will be a cheerful subject!'

Mademoiselle Noémie had collected her accessories, and she gave the precious Madonna in charge to her father, who retreated backwards out of sight, holding it at arm's-length and reiterating his obeisances. The young lady gathered her shawl about her like a perfect Parisienne, and it was with the smile of a Parisienne that she took leave of her patron.

CHAPTER 2

He wandered back to the divan and seated himself on the other side, in view of the great canvas on which Paul Veronese* has depicted the marriage feast of Cana. Wearied as he was he found the picture entertaining; it had an illusion for him; it satisfied his conception, which was ambitious, of what a splendid banquet should be. In the left-hand corner of the picture is a young woman with yellow tresses confined in a golden head-dress; she is bending forward and listening, with the smile of a charming woman at a dinner-party, to her neighbour. Newman detected her in the crowd, admired her, and perceived that she too had her votive copyist – a young man with his hair standing on end. Suddenly he became conscious of the germ of the mania of the 'collector'; he had taken the first step; why should he not go on? It was only twenty minutes before that he had bought the first picture of his life, and now he was already thinking of art-patronage as a fascinating pursuit. His reflections quickened his good-humour, and he was on the point of approaching the young man with another '*Combien?*' Two or three facts in this relation are noticeable, although the logical chain which connects them may seem imperfect. He knew Mademoiselle Nioche had asked too much; he bore her no grudge for doing so, and he was determined to pay the young man exactly the proper sum. At this moment, however, his attention was attracted by a gentleman who had come from another part of the room, and whose manner was that of a stranger to the gallery, although he was equipped with neither guide-book nor opera-glass. He carried a white sun-umbrella, lined with blue silk, and he strolled in front of the Paul Veronese, vaguely looking at it, but much too near to see anything but the grain of the canvas. Opposite to Christopher Newman he paused and turned, and then our friend, who had been observing him, had a chance to verify a suspicion aroused by an imperfect view of his face. The result of this larger scrutiny was that he presently sprang to his feet, strode across the room, and, with an outstretched hand, arrested the gentleman with the blue-lined umbrella. The latter stared, but put out his hand at a venture. He was corpulent and rosy; and though his countenance, which was ornamented with a beautiful flaxen beard, carefully divided in the middle and brushed outward at the sides, was not remarkable for intensity of expression, he looked like a person who would willingly shake hands with anyone. I know not what Newman thought of his face, but he found a want of response in his grasp.

'Oh, come, come,' he said, laughing; 'don't say, now, you don't know me – if I have *not* got a white parasol!'

The sound of his voice quickened the other's memory, his face expanded to its fullest capacity, and he also broke into a laugh.

'Why, Newman – I'll be blowed! Where in the world – I

declare – who would have thought? You know you have changed.'

'You haven't,' said Newman.

'Not for the better, no doubt. When did you get here?'

'Three days ago.'

'Why didn't you let me know?'

'I had no idea *you* were here.'

'I have been here these six years.'

'It must be eight or nine since we met.'

'Something of that sort. We were very young.'

'It was in St Louis, during the war. You were in the army.'

'Oh no, not I. But you were.'

'I believe I was.'

'You came out all right?'

'I came out with my legs and arms – and with satisfaction. All that seems very far away.'

'And how long have you been in Europe?'

'Seventeen days.'

'First time?'

'Yes, very much so.'

'Made your everlasting fortune?'

Christopher Newman was silent a moment, and then, with a tranquil smile, he answered: 'Yes.'

'And come to Paris to spend it, eh?'

'Well, we shall see. So they carry those parasols here – the men-folk?'

'Of course they do. They're great things. They understand comfort out here.'

'Where do you buy them?'

'Anywhere, everywhere.'

'Well, Tristram, I'm glad to get hold of you. You can show me the ropes. I suppose you know Paris inside out.'

Mr Tristram gave a mellow smile of self-gratulation. 'Well, I guess there are not many men that can show me much. I'll take care of you.'

'It's a pity you were not here a few minutes ago. I have just bought a picture. You might have put the thing through for me.'

'Bought a picture?' said Mr Tristram, looking vaguely round at the walls. 'Why, do they sell them?'

'I mean a copy.'

'Oh, I see. These,' said Mr Tristram, nodding at the Titians and Vandykes, 'these, I suppose, are originals?'

'I hope so,' cried Newman. 'I don't want a copy of a copy.'

'Ah,' said Mr Tristram, mysteriously, 'you can never tell. They imitate, you know, so deucedly well. It's like the jewellers, with their false stones. Go into the Palais Royal,* there; you see "Imitation" on half the windows. The law obliges them to stick it on, you know; but you can't tell the things apart. To tell the truth,' Mr Tristram continued, with a wry face, 'I don't do much in pictures. I leave that to my wife.'

'Ah, you have got a wife?'

'Didn't I mention it? She's a very nice woman; you must know her. She's up there in the Avenue d'Iéna.'*

'So you are regularly fixed – house and children and all?'

'Yes; a tip-top house, and a couple of youngsters.'

'Well,' said Christopher Newman, stretching his arms a little, with a sigh, 'I envy you.'

'Oh no, you don't,' answered Mr Tristram, giving him a little poke with his parasol.

'I beg your pardon; I do.'

'Well, you won't, then, when – when – '

'You don't certainly mean when I have seen your establishment?'

'When you have seen Paris, my boy. You want to be your own master here.'

'Oh, I have been my own master all my life, and I'm tired of it.'

'Well, try Paris. How old are you?'

'Thirty-six.'

'C'est le bel âge,* as they say here.'

'What does that mean?'

'It means that a man shouldn't send away his plate till he has eaten his fill.'

'All that? I have just made arrangements to take French lessons.'

'Oh, you don't want any lessons. You'll pick it up. I never took any.'

'I suppose you speak French as well as English?'

'Better!' said Mr Tristram, roundly. 'It's a splendid language. You can say all sorts of bright things in it.'

'But I suppose,' said Christopher Newman, with an earnest desire for information, 'that you must be bright to begin with.'

'Not a bit; that's just the beauty of it.'

The two friends, as they exchanged these remarks, had remained standing where they met, and leaning against the rail which protected the pictures. Mr Tristram at last declared that he was overcome with fatigue, and should be happy to sit down. Newman recommended in the highest terms the great divan on which he had been lounging, and they prepared to seat themselves. 'This is a great place; isn't it?' said Newman, with ardour.

'Great place, great place. Finest thing in the world.' And then, suddenly, Mr Tristram hesitated and looked about him. 'I suppose they won't let you smoke here?'

Newman stared. 'Smoke? I'm sure I don't know. You know the regulations better than I.'

'I? I never was here before!'

'Never! in six years?'

'I believe my wife dragged me here once when we first came to Paris, but I never found my way back.'

'But you say you know Paris so well!'

'I don't call this Paris!' cried Mr Tristram, with assurance. 'Come; let's go over to the Palais Royal and have a smoke.'

'I don't smoke,' said Newman.

'A drink, then.'

And Mr Tristram led his companion away. They passed through the glorious halls of the Louvre, down the staircases, along the cool, dim galleries of sculpture, and out into the enormous court. Newman looked about him as he went, but he made no comments; and it was only when they at last emerged into the open air that he said to his friend: 'It seems to me that in your place I should have come here once a week.'

'Oh no, you wouldn't!' said Mr Tristram. 'You think so, but you wouldn't. You wouldn't have had time. You would always mean to go, but you never would go. There's better fun than that, here in Paris. Italy's the place to see pictures; wait till you get there. There you have to go; you can't do anything else. It's an awful country; you can't get a decent cigar. I don't know why I went in there today. I was strolling along, rather hard up for amusement. I sort of noticed the Louvre as I passed, and I thought I would go in and see what was going on. But if I hadn't found you there I should have felt rather sold. Hang it, I don't care for pictures; I prefer the reality!' And Mr Tristram tossed off this happy formula with an assurance which the numerous class of persons suffering from an overdose of 'culture' might have envied him.

The two gentlemen proceeded along the Rue de Rivoli and into the Palais Royal, where they seated themselves at one of the little tables stationed at the door of the café which projects into the great open quadrangle. The place was filled with people, the fountains were spouting, a band was playing, clusters of chairs were gathered beneath all the lime-trees, and buxom, white-capped nurses, seated along the benches, were offering to their infant charges the amplest facilities for nutrition. There was an easy, homely gaiety in the whole scene, and Christopher Newman felt that it was most characteristically Parisian.

'And now,' began Mr Tristram, when they had tasted the decoction which he had caused to be served to them, 'now just give an account of yourself. What are your ideas, what are your plans, where have you come from and where are you going? In the first place, where are you staying?'

'At the Grand Hotel,'* said Newman.

Mr Tristram puckered his plump visage. 'That won't do! You must change.'

'Change?' demanded Newman. 'Why, it's the finest hotel I ever was in.'

'You don't want a "fine" hotel; you want something small and quiet and elegant, where your bell is answered and your – your person is recognised.'

'They keep running to see if I have rung before I have touched the bell,' said Newman, 'and as for my person, they are always bowing and scraping to it.'

'I suppose you are always tipping them. That's very bad style.'

'Always? By no means. A man brought me something yesterday, and then stood loafing about in a beggarly manner. I offered him a chair and asked him if he wouldn't sit down. Was that bad style?'

'Very!'

'But he bolted, instantly. At any rate, the place amuses me. Hang your elegance, if it bores me. I sat in the court of the Grand Hotel last night until two o'clock in the morning, watching the coming and going, and the people knocking about.'

'You're easily pleased. But you can do as you choose – a man in your shoes. You have made a pile of money, eh?'

'I have made enough.'

'Happy the man who can say that! Enough for what?'

'Enough to rest awhile, to forget the confounded thing, to look about me, to see the world, to have a good time, to improve my mind, and, if the fancy takes me, to marry a wife.' Newman spoke slowly, with a certain dryness of accent and with frequent pauses. This was his habitual mode of utterance, but it was especially marked in the words I have just quoted.

'Jupiter! There's a programme!' cried Mr Tristram. 'Certainly, all that takes money, especially the wife; unless indeed she gives it, as mine did. And what's the story? How have you done it?'

Newman had pushed his hat back from his forehead, folded his arms, and stretched his legs. He listened to the music, he looked about him at the bustling crowd, at the plashing fountains, at the nurses and the babies. 'I have worked!' he answered at last.

Tristram looked at him for some moments, and allowed his placid eyes to measure his friend's generous longitude and rest upon his comfortably contemplative face. 'What have you worked at?' he asked.

'Oh, at several things.'

'I suppose you're a smart fellow, eh?'

Newman continued to look at the nurses and babies; they imparted to the scene a kind of primordial, pastoral simplicity. 'Yes,' he said at last, 'I suppose I am.' And then, in answer to his companion's inquiries, he related briefly his history since their last meeting. It was an intensely Western story, and it dealt with enterprises which it will be needless to introduce to the reader in detail. Newman had come out of the war with a brevet* of brigadier-general, an honour which in this case – without invidious comparisons – had lighted upon shoulders amply competent to bear it. But though he could manage a fight, when need was, Newman heartily disliked the business; his four years in the army had left him with an angry, bitter sense of the waste of precious things – life and time and money and 'smartness' and the early freshness of purpose; and he had addressed himself to the pursuits of peace with passionate zest and energy. He was of course as penniless when he plucked off his shoulder-straps as when he put them on, and the only capital

at his disposal was his dogged resolution and his lively perception of ends and means. Exertion and action were as natural to
him as respiration; a more completely healthy mortal had never
trod the elastic soil of the West. His experience, moreover, was
as wide as his capacity; when he was fourteen years old,
necessity had taken him by his slim young shoulders and pushed
him into the street, to earn that night's supper. He had not
earned it; but he had earned the next night's, and afterwards,
whenever he had had none, it was because he had gone without
it to use the money for something else, a keener pleasure or a
finer profit. He had turned his hand, with his brain in it, to
many things; he had been enterprising, in an eminent sense of
the term; he had been adventurous and even reckless, and he
had known bitter failure as well as brilliant success; but he was
a born experimentalist, and he had always found something to
enjoy in the pressure of necessity, even when it was as irritating
as the haircloth shirt* of the mediaeval monk. At one time
failure seemed inexorably his portion; ill-luck became his bed-
fellow, and whatever he touched he turned, not to gold, but to
ashes. His most vivid conception of a supernatural element in
the world's affairs had come to him once when this pertinacity
of misfortune was at its climax; there seemed to him something
stronger in life than his own will. But the mysterious something
could only be the devil, and he was accordingly seized with an
intense personal enmity to this impertinent force. He had known
what it was to have utterly exhausted his credit, to be unable to
raise a dollar, and to find himself at nightfall in a strange city,
without a penny to mitigate its strangeness. It was under these
circumstances that he made his entrance into San Francisco, the
scene, subsequently, of his happiest strokes of fortune. If he did
not, like Dr Franklin in Philadelphia, march along the street
munching a penny loaf, it was only because he had not the
penny loaf necessary to the performance. In his darkest days he
had had but one simple, practical impulse – the desire, as he
would have phrased it, to see the thing through. He did so at
last, buffeted his way into smooth waters, and made money
largely. It must be admitted, rather nakedly, that Christopher
Newman's sole aim in life had been to make money; what he
had been placed in the world for was, to his own perception,
simply to wrest a fortune, the bigger the better, from defiant
opportunity. This idea completely filled his horizon and satisfied

his imagination. Upon the uses of money, upon what one might do with a life into which one had succeeded in injecting the golden stream,* he had up to his thirty-fifth year very scantily reflected. Life had been for him an open game, and he had played for high stakes. He had won at last and carried off his winnings; and now what was he to do with them? He was a man to whom, sooner or later, the question was sure to present itself, and the answer to it belongs to our story. A vague sense that more answers were possible than his philosophy had hitherto dreamt of* had already taken possession of him, and it seemed softly and agreeably to deepen as he lounged in this brilliant corner of Paris with his friend.

'I must confess,' he presently went on, 'that here I don't feel at all smart. My remarkable talents seem of no use. I feel as simple as a little child, and a little child might take me by the hand and lead me about.'

'Oh, I'll be your little child,' said Tristram, jovially; 'I'll take you by the hand. Trust yourself to me.'

'I am a good worker,' Newman continued, 'but I rather think I am a poor loafer. I have come abroad to amuse myself, but I doubt whether I know how.'

'Oh, that's easily learned.'

'Well, I may perhaps learn it, but I am afraid I shall never do it by rote. I have the best will in the world about it, but my genius doesn't lie in that direction. As a loafer I shall never be original,* as I take it that you are.'

'Yes,' said Tristram, 'I suppose I am original; like all those immoral pictures in the Louvre.'

'Besides,' Newman continued, 'I don't want to work at pleasure, any more than I played at work. I want to take it easily. I feel deliciously lazy, and I should like to spend six months as I am now, sitting under a tree and listening to a band. There's only one thing; I want to hear some good music.'

'Music and pictures! Lord, what refined tastes! You are what my wife calls intellectual. I ain't, a bit. But we can find something better for you to do than to sit under a tree. To begin with, you must come to the club.'

'What club?'

'The Occidental.* You will see all the Americans there; all the best of them, at least. Of course you play poker?'

'Oh, I say,' cried Newman, with energy, 'you are not going to lock me up in a club and stick me down at a card-table! I haven't come all this way for that.'

'What the deuce *have* you come for! You were glad enough to play poker in St Louis, I recollect, when you cleaned me out.'

'I have come to see Europe, to get the best out of it I can. I want to see all the great things, and do what the clever people do.'

'The clever people? Much obliged. You set me down as a blockhead, then?'

Newman was sitting sidewise in his chair, with his elbow on the back and his head leaning on his hand. Without moving he looked awhile at his companion, with his dry, guarded, half-inscrutable, and yet altogether good-natured smile. 'Introduce me to your wife!' he said at last.

Tristram bounced about in his chair. 'Upon my word, I won't. She doesn't want any help to turn up her nose at me, nor do you, either!'

'I don't turn up my nose at you, my dear fellow; nor at anyone, or anything. I'm not proud, I assure you I'm not proud. That's why I am willing to take example by the clever people.'

'Well, if I'm not the rose,* as they say here, I have lived near it. I can show you some clever people, too. Do you know General Packard? Do you know C. P. Hatch? Do you know Miss Kitty Upjohn?'

'I shall be happy to make their acquaintance; I want to cultivate society.'

Tristram seemed restless and suspicious; he eyed his friend askance, and then: 'What are you up to, anyway?' he demanded. 'Are you going to write a book?'

Christopher Newman twisted one end of his moustache awhile, in silence, and at last he made answer. 'One day, a couple of months ago, something very curious happened to me. I had come on to New York on some important business; it was rather a long story – a question of getting ahead of another party, in a certain particular way, in the stockmarket. This other party had once played me a very mean trick. I owed him a grudge, I felt awfully savage at the time, and I vowed that, when I got a chance, I would, figuratively speaking, put his nose out of joint. There was a matter of some sixty thousand dollars at stake. If I put it out of his way, it was a blow the fellow would feel, and he really deserved no quarter. I jumped into a hack and went about my business, and it was in this hack – this immortal, historical hack – that the curious thing I speak of occurred. It was a hack like any other, only a trifle dirtier, with a greasy line along the top of the drab cushions, as if it had been used for a great many Irish funerals.* It is possible I took a nap; I had been travelling all night, and though I was excited with my errand, I felt the want of sleep. At all events I woke up suddenly, from a sleep or from a kind of a reverie, with the most extraordinary feeling in the world – a mortal disgust for the thing I was going to do. It came upon me like *that*!' – and he snapped his fingers – 'as abruptly as an old wound that begins to ache. I couldn't tell the meaning of it; I only felt that I loathed the whole business and wanted to wash my hands of it. The idea of losing that sixty thousand dollars, of letting it utterly slide and scuttle and never hearing of it again, seemed the sweetest thing in the world. And all this took place quite independently of my will, and I sat watching it as if it were a play at the theatre. I could feel it going on inside of me. You may depend upon it that there are things going on inside of us that we understand mighty little about.'

'Jupiter! you make my flesh creep!' cried Tristram. 'And while you sat in your hack, watching the play, as you call it, the other man marched in and bagged your sixty thousand dollars?'

'I have not the least idea. I hope so, poor devil! but I never found out. We pulled up in front of the place I was going to in Wall Street, but I sat still in the carriage, and at last the driver scrambled down off his seat to see whether his carriage had not turned into a hearse. I couldn't have got out, any more than if I had been a corpse. What was the matter with me? Momentary idiocy, you'll say. What I wanted to get out of was Wall Street. I told the man to drive down to the Brooklyn ferry and to cross over. When we were over, I told him to drive me out into the country. As I had told him originally to drive for dear life down town, I suppose he thought me insane. Perhaps I was, but in that case I am insane still. I spent the morning looking at the first green leaves on Long Island. I was sick of business; I wanted to throw it all up and break off short; I had money enough, or if I hadn't I ought to have. I seemed to feel a new man inside my old skin, and I longed for a new world. When you want a thing so very badly you had better treat yourself to it. I didn't understand the matter, not in the least; but I gave the old horse the bridle and let him find his way. As soon as I could get out of the game I sailed for Europe. That is how I come to be sitting here.'

'You ought to have bought up that hack,' said Tristram; 'it isn't a safe vehicle to have about. And you have really sold out, then; you have retired from business?'

'I have made over my hand to a friend; when I feel disposed, I can take up the cards again. I daresay that a twelvemonth hence the operation will be reversed. The pendulum will swing back again. I shall be sitting in the gondola or on a dromedary, and all of a sudden I shall want to clear out. But for the present I am perfectly free. I have even bargained that I am to receive no business letters.'

'Oh, it's a real *caprice de prince*,'* said Tristram. 'I back out; a poor devil like me can't help you to spend such very magnificent leisure as that. You should get introduced to the crowned heads.'

Newman looked at him a moment, and then, with his easy smile: 'How does one do it?' he asked.

'Come, I like that!' cried Tristram. 'It shows you are in earnest.'

'Of course I am in earnest. Didn't I say I wanted the best? I know the best can't be had for mere money, but I rather think money will do a good deal. In addition, I am willing to take a good deal of trouble.'

'You are not bashful, eh?'

'I haven't the least idea. I want the biggest kind of entertainment a man can get. People, places, art, nature, everything! I want to see the tallest mountains, and the bluest lakes, and the finest pictures, and the handsomest churches, and the most celebrated men, and the most beautiful women.'

'Settle down in Paris, then. There are no mountains that I know of, and the only lake is in the Bois de Boulogne,* and not particularly blue. But there is everything else: plenty of pictures and churches, no end of celebrated men, and several beautiful women.'

'But I can't settle down in Paris at this season, just as summer is coming on.'

'Oh, for the summer go up to Trouville.'*

'What is Trouville?'

'The French Newport.* Half the Americans go.'

'Is it anywhere near the Alps?'

'About as near as Newport is to the Rocky Mountains.'

'Oh, I want to see Mont Blanc,' said Newman, 'and Amsterdam, and the Rhine, and a lot of places. Venice in particular. I have great ideas about Venice.'

'Ah,' said Mr Tristram, rising, 'I see I shall have to introduce you to my wife!'

CHAPTER 3

He performed this ceremony on the following day, when, by appointment, Christopher Newman went to dine with him. Mr and Mrs Tristram lived behind one of those chalk-coloured façades which decorate with their pompous sameness the broad avenues manufactured by Baron Haussmann* in the neighbourhood of the Arc de Triomphe. Their apartment was rich in the modern conveniences, and Tristram lost no time in calling his visitor's attention to their principal household treasures, the gas-lamps and the furnace-holes. 'Whenever you feel homesick,' he said, 'you must come up here. We'll stick you down before a register, under a good big burner, and – '

'And you will soon get over your homesickness,' said Mrs Tristram.

Her husband stared; his wife often had a tone which he found inscrutable; he could not tell for his life whether she was in jest or in earnest. The truth is that circumstances had done much to cultivate in Mrs Tristram a marked tendency to irony. Her taste on many points differed from that of her husband; and though she made frequent concessions, it must be confessed that her concessions were not always graceful. They were founded upon a vague project she had of some day doing something very positive, something a trifle passionate. What she meant to do she could by no means have told you; but meanwhile, nevertheless, she was buying a good conscience, by instalments.

It should be added, without delay, to anticipate misconception, that her little scheme of independence did not definitely involve the assistance of another person, of the opposite sex; she was not saving up virtue to cover the expenses of a flirtation.

For this there were various reasons. To begin with, she had a very plain face, and she was entirely without illusions as to her appearance. She had taken its measure to a hair's breadth, she knew the worst and the best, she had accepted herself. It had not been, indeed, without a struggle. As a young girl, she had spent hours with her back to her mirror, crying her eyes out; and later she had, from desperation and bravado, adopted the habit of proclaiming herself the most ill-favoured of women, in order that she might – as in common politeness was inevitable – be contradicted and reassured. It was since she had come to live in Europe that she had begun to take the matter philosophically. Her observation, acutely exercised here, had suggested to her that a woman's first duty is not to be beautiful, but to be pleasing; and she encountered so many women who pleased without beauty, that she began to feel that she had discovered her mission. She had once heard an enthusiastic musician, out of patience with a gifted bungler, declare that a fine voice is really an obstacle to singing properly; and it occurred to her that it might perhaps be equally true that a beautiful face is an obstacle to the acquisition of charming manners. Mrs Tristram, then, undertook to be exquisitely agreeable, and she brought to the task a really touching devotion. How well she would have succeeded I am unable to say; unfortunately she broke off in the middle. Her own excuse was the want of encouragement in her immediate circle. But I am inclined to think that she had not a real genius for the matter, or she would have pursued the charming art for itself. The poor lady was very incomplete. She fell back upon the harmonies of the toilet, which she thoroughly understood, and contented herself with dressing in perfection. She lived in Paris, which she pretended to detest, because it was only in Paris that one could find things to exactly suit one's complexion. Besides, out of Paris it was always more or less of a trouble to get ten-button gloves.* When she railed at this serviceable city, and you asked her where she would prefer to reside, she returned some very unexpected answer. She would say in Copenhagen, or in Barcelona; having, while making the tour of Europe, spent a couple of days at each of these places. On the whole, with her poetic furbelows, and her misshapen, intelligent little face, she was, when you knew her, a decidedly interesting woman. She was naturally shy, and if she had been born a beauty, she would (having no vanity) probably have remained shy. Now, she was both diffident and importunate; extremely reserved sometimes with her friends, and strangely expansive with strangers. She despised her husband; despised him too much, for she had been perfectly at liberty not to marry him. She had been in love with a clever man, who had slighted her, and she had married a fool, in the hope that this thankless wit, reflecting on it, would conclude that she had no appreciation of merit, and that he had flattered himself in supposing that she cared for his own. Restless, discontented, visionary, without personal ambitions, but with a certain avidity of imagination, she was, as I have said before, eminently incomplete. She was full – both for good and for ill – of beginnings that came to nothing; but she had nevertheless, morally, a spark of the sacred fire.

Newman was fond, under all circumstances, of the society of women; and now that he was out of his native element, and deprived of his habitual interests, he turned to it for compensation. He took a great fancy to Mrs Tristram; she frankly repaid it, and after their first meeting he passed a great many hours in her drawing-room. After two or three talks, they were fast friends. Newman's manner with women was peculiar, and it required some ingenuity on a lady's part to discover that he admired her. He had no gallantry, in the usual sense of the term; no compliments, no graces, no speeches. Very fond of what is called chaffing, in his dealings with men, he never found himself on a sofa beside a member of the softer sex without feeling extremely serious. He was not shy, and, so far as awkwardness proceeds from a struggle with shyness, he was not awkward; grave, attentive, submissive, often silent, he was simply swimming in a sort of rapture of respect. This emotion was not at all theoretic, it was not even in a high degree sentimental; he had thought very little about the 'position' of women, and he was not familiar, either sympathetically or otherwise, with the image of a President in petticoats. His attitude was simply the flower of his general good-nature, and a part of his instinctive and genuinely democratic assumption of everyone's right to lead an easy life. If a shaggy pauper had a right to bed and board and wages and a vote, women, of course, who were weaker than paupers, and whose physical tissue was in itself an appeal, should be maintained, sentimentally, at the public expense. Newman was willing to be taxed for this purpose, largely, in proportion to his means. Moreover, many of the common traditions with regard to women were with him fresh personal impressions; he had never read a novel! He had been struck with their acuteness, their subtlety, their tact, their felicity of judgment. They seemed to him exquisitely organised. If it is true that one must always have in one's work here below a religion, or at least an ideal, of some sort, Newman found his metaphysical inspiration in a vague acceptance of final responsibility to some illumined feminine brow.

He spent a great deal of time in listening to advice from Mrs Tristram; advice, it must be added, for which he had never asked. He would have been incapable of asking for it, for he had no perception of difficulties, and consequently no curiosity about remedies. The complex Parisian world about him seemed a very simple affair; it was an immense, amazing spectacle, but it neither inflamed his imagination nor irritated his curiosity. He kept his hands in his pockets, looked on good-humouredly, desired to miss nothing important, observed a great many things narrowly, and never reverted to himself. Mrs Tristram's 'advice' was a part of the show, and a more entertaining element, in her abundant gossip, than the others. He enjoyed her talking about himself; it seemed a part of her beautiful ingenuity; but he never made an application of anything she said, or remembered it when he was away from her. For herself, she appropriated him; he was the most interesting thing she had had to think about in many a month. She wished to do something with him – she hardly knew what. There was so much of him; he was so rich and robust, so easy, friendly, well-disposed, that he kept her fancy constantly on the alert. For the present, the only thing she could do was to like him. She told him that he was 'horribly Western', but in this compliment the adverb was tinged with insincerity. She led him about with her, introduced him to fifty people, and took extreme satisfaction in her conquest. Newman accepted every proposal, shook hands universally and promiscuously, and seemed equally unfamiliar with trepidation or with elation. Tom Tristram complained of his wife's avidity, and declared that he could never have a clear five minutes with his friend. If he had known how things were going to turn out, he never would have brought him to the Avenue d'Iéna. The two men, formerly, had not been intimate, but Newman remembered his earlier impression of his host, and did Mrs Tristram, who had by no means taken him into her confidence, but whose secret he presently discovered, the justice to admit that her husband was a rather degenerate mortal. At twenty-five he had been a good fellow, and in this respect he was unchanged; but of a man of his age one expected something more. People said he was sociable, but this was as much a matter of course as for a dipped sponge to expand; and it was not a high order of sociability. He was a great gossip and tattler, and to produce a laugh would hardly have spared the reputation of his aged mother. Newman had a kindness for old memories, but he found it impossible not to perceive that Tristram was nowadays a very light weight. His only aspirations were to hold out at poker, at his club, to know the names of all the *cocottes*,* to shake hands all round, to ply his rosy gullet with truffles and champagne, and to create uncomfortable eddies and obstructions among the constituent atoms of the American colony. He was shamefully idle, spiritless, sensual, snobbish. He irritated our friend by the tone of his allusions to their native country, and Newman was at a loss to understand why the United States were not good enough for Mr Tristram. He had never been a very conscious patriot, but it vexed him to see them treated as little better than a vulgar smell in his friend's nostrils, and he finally broke out and swore that they were the greatest country in the world, that they could put all Europe into their breeches' pockets, and that an American who spoke ill of them ought to be carried home in irons and compelled to live in Boston. (This, for Newman, was putting it very vindictively.) Tristram was a comfortable man to snub; he bore no malice, and he continued to insist on Newman's finishing his evenings at the Occidental Club.

Christopher Newman dined several times in the Avenue d'Iéna, and his host always proposed an early adjournment to this institution. Mrs Tristram protested, and declared that her husband exhausted his ingenuity in trying to displease her.

'Oh no, I never try, my love,' he answered. 'I know you loathe me quite enough when I take my chance.'

Newman hated to see a husband and wife on these terms, and he was sure one or other of them must be very unhappy. He knew it was not Tristram. Mrs Tristram had a balcony before her windows, upon which, during the June evenings, she was fond of sitting, and Newman used frankly to say that he preferred the balcony to the club. It had a fringe of perfumed plants in tubs, and enabled you to look up the broad street and see the Arch of Triumph vaguely massing its heroic sculptures in the summer starlight. Sometimes Newman kept his promise of following Mr Tristram, in half an hour, to the Occidental, and sometimes he forgot it. His hostess asked him a great many questions about himself, but on this subject he was an indifferent talker. He was not what is called subjective, though when he felt that her interest was sincere, he made an almost heroic attempt to be. He told her a great many things he had done, and regaled her with anecdotes of Western life; she was from Philadelphia, and with her eight years in Paris, talked of herself as a languid Oriental. But some other person was always the hero of the tale, by no means always to his advantage; and Newman's own emotions were but scantily chronicled. She had an especial wish to know whether he had ever been in love – seriously, passionately – and, failing to gather any satisfaction from his allusions, she at last directly inquired. He hesitated awhile, and at last he said: 'No!' She declared that she was delighted to hear it, as it confirmed her private conviction that he was a man of no feeling.

'Really?' he asked, very gravely. 'Do you think so? How do you recognise a man of feeling?'

'I can't make out,' said Mrs Tristram, 'whether you are very simple or very deep.'

'I'm very deep. That's a fact.'

'I believe that if I were to tell you with a certain air that you have no feeling, you would implicitly believe me.'

'A certain air?' said Newman. 'Try it and see.'

'You would believe me, but you would not care,' said Mrs Tristram.

'You have got it all wrong. I should care immensely, but I shouldn't believe you. The fact is I have never had time to feel things. I have had to *do* them, to make myself felt.'

'I can imagine that you may have done that tremendously, sometimes.'

'Yes, there's no mistake about that.'

'When you are in a fury it can't be pleasant.'

'I am never in a fury.'

'Angry, then, or displeased.'

'I am never angry, and it is so long since I have been displeased that I have quite forgotten it.'

'I don't believe,' said Mrs Tristram, 'that you are never angry. A man ought to be angry sometimes, and you are neither good enough nor bad enough always to keep your temper.'

'I lose it perhaps once in five years.'

'The time is coming round, then,' said his hostess. 'Before I have known you six months I shall see you in a fine fury.'

'Do you mean to put me into one?'

'I should not be sorry. You take things too coolly. It exasperates me. And then you are too happy. You have what must be the most agreeable thing in the world – the consciousness of having bought your pleasure beforehand, and paid for it. You have not a day of reckoning staring you in the face. Your reckonings are over.'

'Well, I suppose I am happy,' said Newman, meditatively.

'You have been odiously successful.'

'Successful in copper,' said Newman, 'only so-so in railroads, and a hopeless fizzle in oil.'

'It is very disagreeable to know how Americans have made their money. Now you have the world before you. You have only to enjoy.'

'Oh, I suppose I am very well off,' said Newman. 'Only I am tired of having it thrown up at me. Besides, there are several drawbacks. I am not intellectual.'

'One doesn't expect it of you,' Mrs Tristram answered. Then in a moment: 'Besides, you are!'

'Well, I mean to have a good time, whether or no,' said Newman. 'I am not cultivated, I am not even educated; I know nothing about history, or art, or foreign tongues, or any other learned matters. But I am not a fool, either, and I shall undertake to know something about Europe by the time I have done with it. I feel something under my ribs here,' he added in a moment, 'that I can't explain – a sort of a mighty hankering, a desire to stretch out and haul in.'

'Bravo!' said Mrs Tristram, 'that is very fine. You are the great Western Barbarian, stepping forth in his innocence and might, gazing awhile at this poor effete Old World, and then swooping down on it.'

'Oh, come,' said Newman. 'I am not a barbarian, by a good

deal. I am very much the reverse. I have seen barbarians; I know what they are.'

'I don't mean that you are a Comanche chief, or that you wear a blanket and feathers. There are different shades.'

'I am a highly-civilised man,' said Newman. 'I stick to that. If you don't believe it, I should like to prove it to you.'

Mrs Tristram was silent awhile. 'I should like to make you prove it,' she said, at last. 'I should like to put you in a difficult place.'

'Pray do,' said Newman.

'That has a little conceited sound!' his companion rejoined.

'Oh,' said Newman, 'I have a very good opinion of myself.'

'I wish I could put it to the test. Give me time, and I will.' And Mrs Tristram remained silent for some time afterwards, as if she was trying to keep her pledge. It did not appear that evening that she succeeded; but as he was rising to take his leave, she passed suddenly, as she was very apt to do, from the tone of unsparing persiflage to that of almost tremulous sympathy. 'Speaking seriously,' she said, 'I believe in you, Mr Newman. You flatter my patriotism.'

'Your patriotism?' Christopher demanded.

'Even so. It would take too long to explain, and you probably would not understand. Besides, you might take it – really, you might take it for a declaration. But it has nothing to do with you personally; it's what you represent. Fortunately you don't know all that, or your conceit would increase insufferably.'

Newman stood staring and wondering what under the sun he 'represented'.

'Forgive all my meddlesome chatter, and forget my advice. It is very silly in me to undertake to tell you what to do. When you are embarrassed, do as you think best, and you will do very well. When you are in a difficulty, judge for yourself.'

'I shall remember everything you have told me,' said Newman. 'There are so many forms and ceremonies over here – '

'Forms and ceremonies are what I mean, of course.'

'Ah, but I want to observe them,' said Newman. 'Haven't I as good a right as another? They don't scare me, and you needn't give me leave to violate them. I won't take it.'

'That is not what I mean. I mean, observe them in your own way. Settle nice questions for yourself. Cut the knot or untie it,* as you choose.'

'Oh, I am sure I shall never fumble over it,' said Newman.

The next time that he dined in the Avenue d'Iéna was a Sunday, a day on which Mr Tristram left the cards unshuffled, so that there was a trio in the evening on the balcony. The talk was of many things, and at last Mrs Tristram suddenly observed to Christopher Newman that it was high time he should take a wife.

'Listen to her; she has the audacity!' said Tristram, who on Sunday evenings was always rather acrimonious.

'I don't suppose you have made up your mind not to marry?' Mrs Tristram continued.

'Heaven forbid!' cried Newman. 'I am sternly resolved on it.'

'It's very easy,' said Tristram; 'fatally easy!'

'Well, then, I suppose you do not mean to wait till you are fifty.'

'On the contrary, I am in a great hurry.'

'One would never suppose it. Do you expect a lady to come and propose to you?'

'No; I am willing to propose. I think a great deal about it.'

'Tell me some of your thoughts.'

'Well,' said Newman, slowly, 'I want to marry very well.'

'Marry a woman of sixty, then,' said Tristram.

' "Well" in what sense?'

'In every sense. I shall be hard to please.'

'You must remember that, as the French proverb says, the most beautiful girl in the world can give but what she has.'

'Since you ask me,' said Newman, 'I will say frankly that I want extremely to marry. It is time, to begin with; before I know it I shall be forty. And then I'm lonely and helpless and dull. But if I marry now, so long as I didn't do it in hot haste when I was twenty, I must do it with my eyes open. I want to do the thing in handsome style. I not only want to make no mistakes, but I want to make a great hit. I want to take my pick. My wife must be a magnificent woman.'

'*Voilà ce qui s'appelle parler!*'* cried Mrs Tristram.

'Oh, I have thought an immense deal about it.'

'Perhaps you think too much. The best thing is simply to fall in love.'

'When I find the woman who pleases me, I shall love her enough. My wife shall be very comfortable.'

'You are superb! There's a chance for the magnificent women.'

'You are not fair,' Newman rejoined. 'You draw a fellow out and put him off his guard, and then you laugh at him.'

'I assure you,' said Mrs Tristram, 'that I am very serious. To prove it, I will make you a proposal. Should you like me, as they say here, to marry you?'

'To hunt up a wife for me?'

'She is already found. I will bring you together.'

'Oh, come,' said Tristram, 'we don't keep a matrimonial bureau. He will think you want your commission.'

'Present me to a woman who comes up to my notions,' said Newman, 'and I will marry her tomorrow.'

'You have a strange tone about it, and I don't quite understand you. I didn't suppose you would be so cold-blooded and calculating.'

Newman was silent awhile. 'Well,' he said, at last, 'I want a great woman. I stick to that. That's one thing I *can* treat myself to, and if it is to be had I mean to have it. What else have I toiled and struggled for all these years? I have succeeded, and now what am I to do with my success? To make it perfect, as I see it, there must be a beautiful woman perched on the pile, like a statue on a monument. She must be as good as she is beautiful, and as clever as she is good. I can give my wife a good deal, so I am not afraid to ask a good deal myself. She shall have everything a woman can desire; I shall not even object to her being too good for me; she may be cleverer and wiser than I can understand, and I shall only be the better pleased. I want to possess, in a word, the best article in the market.'

'Why didn't you tell a fellow all this at the outset?' Tristram demanded. 'I have been trying so to make you fond of *me*!'

'This is very interesting,' said Mrs Tristram. 'I like to see a man know his own mind.'

'I have known mine for a long time,' Newman went on. 'I made up my mind tolerably early in life that a beautiful wife was the thing best worth having, here below. It is the greatest victory over circumstances. When I say beautiful, I mean beautiful in mind and in manners, as well as in person. It is a thing every man has an equal right to; he may get it if he can. He doesn't have to be born with certain faculties on purpose; he needs only to be a man. Then he needs only to use his will, and such wits as he has, and to try.'

'It strikes me that your marriage is to be rather a matter of vanity.'

'Well, it is certain,' said Newman, 'that if people notice my wife and admire her, I shall be mightily tickled.'

'After this,' cried Mrs Tristram, 'call any man modest!'

'But none of them will admire her so much as I.'

'I see you have a taste for splendour.'

Newman hesitated a little; and then: 'I honestly believe I have!' he said.

'And I suppose you have already looked about you a good deal.'

'A good deal, according to opportunity.'

'And you have seen nothing that satisfied you?'

'No,' said Newman, half reluctantly, 'I am bound to say in honesty that I have seen nothing that really satisfied me.'

'You remind me of the heroes of the French romantic poets, Rolla and Fortunio* and all those other insatiable gentlemen for whom nothing in this world was handsome enough. But I see you are in earnest, and I should like to help you.'

'Who the deuce is it, darling, that you are going to put upon him?' Tristram cried. 'We know a good many pretty girls, thank Heaven, but magnificent women are not so common.'

'Have you any objections to a foreigner?' his wife continued, addressing Newman, who had tilted back his chair, and, with his feet on a bar of the balcony railing and his hands in his pockets, was looking at the stars.

'No Irish need apply,' said Tristram.

Newman meditated awhile. 'As a foreigner, no,' he said at last; 'I have no prejudices.'

'My dear fellow, you have no suspicions!' cried Tristram. 'You don't know what terrible customers these foreign women are; especially the "magnificent" ones. How should you like a fair Circassian, with a dagger in her belt?'*

Newman administered a vigorous slap to his knee. 'I would marry a Japanese, if she pleased me,' he affirmed.

'We had better confine ourselves to Europe,' said Mrs Tristram. 'The only thing is, then, that the person be in herself to your taste?'

'She is going to offer you an unappreciated governess!'
Tristram groaned.

'Assuredly. I won't deny that, other things being equal, I
should prefer one of my own countrywomen. We should speak
the same language, and that would be a comfort. But I am not
afraid of a foreigner. Besides, I rather like the idea of taking in
Europe, too. It enlarges the field of selection. When you choose
from a greater number, you can bring your choice to a finer
point.'

'You talk like Sardanapalus!'* exclaimed Tristram.

'You say all this to the right person,' said Newman's hostess.
'I happen to number among my friends the loveliest woman in
the world. Neither more nor less. I don't say a very charming
person or a very estimable woman or a very great beauty; I say
simply the loveliest woman in the world.'

'The deuce!' cried Tristram, 'you have kept very quiet about
her. Were you afraid of me?'

'You have seen her,' said his wife, 'but you have no perception
of such merit as Claire's.'

'Ah, her name is Claire? I give it up.'

'Does your friend wish to marry?' asked Newman.

'Not in the least. It is for you to make her change her mind. It
will not be easy; she has had one husband, and he gave her a
low opinion of the species.'

'Oh, she is a widow, then?' said Newman.

'Are you already afraid? She was married at eighteen, by her
parents, in the French fashion, to a disagreeable old man. But
he had the good taste to die a couple of years afterward, and
she is now twenty-five.'

'So she is French?'

'French by her father, English by her mother. She is really
more English than French, and she speaks English as well as you
or I – or rather much better. She belongs to the very top of the
basket, as they say here. Her family, on each side, is of fabulous
antiquity; her mother is the daughter of an English Catholic
earl. Her father is dead, and since her widowhood she has lived
with her mother and a married brother. There is another
brother, younger, who I believe is wild. They have an old hotel
in the Rue de l'Université,* but their fortune is small, and they
make a common household, for economy's sake. When I was a
girl I was put into a convent here for my education, while my

father made the tour of Europe. It was a silly thing to do with me, but it had the advantage that it made me acquainted with Claire de Bellegarde. She was younger than I, but we became fast friends. I took a tremendous fancy to her, and she returned my passion as far as she could. They kept such a tight rein on her that she could do very little, and when I left the convent she had to give me up. I was not of her *monde*;* I am not now, either, but we sometimes meet. They are terrible people – her *monde*; all mounted upon stilts a mile high, and with pedigrees long in proportion. It is the skim of the milk of the old *noblesse*.* Do you know what a Legitimist is, or an Ultramontane?* Go into Madame de Cintré's drawing-room some afternoon, at five o'clock, and you will see the best-preserved specimens. I say go, but no one is admitted who can't show his fifty quarterings.'*

'And this is the lady you propose to me to marry?' asked Newman. 'A lady I can't even approach?'

'But you said just now that you recognised no obstacles.'

Newman looked at Mrs Tristram awhile, stroking his moustache. 'Is she a beauty?' he demanded.

'No.'

'Oh, then it's no use – '

'She is not a beauty, but she is beautiful, two very different things. A beauty has no faults in her face; the face of a beautiful woman may have faults that only deepen its charm.'

'I remember Madame de Cintré, now,' said Tristram. 'She is as plain as a pikestaff. A man wouldn't look at her twice.'

'In saying that *he* would not look at her twice, my husband sufficiently describes her,' Mrs Tristram rejoined.

'Is she good; is she clever?' Newman asked.

'She is perfect! I won't say more than that. When you are praising a person to another who is to know her, it is bad policy to go into details. I won't exaggerate. I simply recommend her. Among all women I have known she stands alone; she is of a different clay.'

'I should like to see her,' said Newman, simply.

'I will try to manage it. The only way will be to invite her to dinner. I have never invited her before, and I don't know that she will come. Her old feudal countess of a mother rules the family with an iron hand, and allows her to have no friends but of her own choosing, and to visit only in a certain sacred circle. But I can at least ask her.'

At this moment Mrs Tristram was interrupted; a servant stepped out upon the balcony and announced that there were visitors in the drawing-room. When Newman's hostess had gone in to receive her friends, Tom Tristram approached his guest.

'Don't put your foot into *this*, my boy,' he said, puffing the last whiffs of his cigar. 'There's nothing in it!'

Newman looked askance at him, inquisitive. 'You tell another story, eh?'

'I say simply that Madame de Cintré is a great white doll of a woman, who cultivates quiet haughtiness.'

'Ah, she's haughty, eh?'

'She looks at you as if you were so much thin air, and cares for you about as much.'

'She is very proud, eh!'

'Proud? As proud as I'm humble.'

'And not good-looking?'

Tristram shrugged his shoulders: 'It's a kind of beauty you must be intellectual to understand. But I must go in and amuse the company.'

Some time elapsed before Newman followed his friends into the drawing-room. When he at last made his appearance there he remained but a short time, and during this period sat perfectly silent, listening to a lady to whom Mrs Tristram had straightway introduced him and who chattered, without a pause, with the full force of an extraordinarily high-pitched voice. Newman gazed and attended. Presently he came to bid good-night to Mrs Tristram.

'Who is that lady?' he asked.

'Miss Dora Finch. How do you like her?'

'She's too noisy.'

'She is thought so bright! Certainly, you are fastidious,' said Mrs Tristram.

Newman stood a moment, hesitating. Then at last, 'Don't forget about your friend,' he said; 'Madame What's-her-name? the proud beauty. Ask her to dinner, and give me good notice.' And with this he departed.

Some days later he came back; it was in the afternoon. He found Mrs Tristram in her drawing-room; with her was a visitor, a woman young and pretty, dressed in white. The two ladies had risen and the visitor was apparently taking her leave. As Newman approached, he received from Mrs Tristram a

glance of the most vivid significance, which he was not immediately able to interpret.

'This is a good friend of ours,' she said, turning to her
companion, 'Mr Christopher Newman. I have spoken of you to
him and he has an extreme desire to make your acquaintance. If
you had consented to come and dine, I should have offered him
an opportunity.'

The stranger turned her face toward Newman, with a smile.
He was not embarrassed, for his unconscious *sang-froid** was
boundless; but as he became aware that this was the proud and
beautiful Madame de Cintré, the loveliest woman in the world,
the promised perfection, the proposed ideal, he made an instinctive movement to gather his wits together. Through the slight
preoccupation that it produced he had a sense of a long, fair
face, and of two eyes that were both brilliant and mild.

'I should have been most happy,' said Madame de Cintré.
'Unfortunately, as I have been telling Mrs Tristram, I go on
Monday to the country.'

Newman had made a solemn bow. 'I am very sorry,' he said.

'Paris is getting too warm,' Madame de Cintré added, taking
her friend's hand again in farewell.

Mrs Tristram seemed to have formed a sudden and somewhat
venturesome resolution, and she smiled more intensely, as
women do when they take such resolutions. 'I want Mr Newman
to know you,' she said, dropping her head on one side and
looking at Madame de Cintré's bonnet ribbons.

Christopher Newman stood gravely silent, while his native
penetration admonished him. Mrs Tristram was determined to
force her friend to address him a word of encouragement which
should be more than one of the common formulas of politeness;
and if she was prompted by charity, it was by the charity that
begins at home. Madame de Cintré was her dearest Claire, and
her especial admiration; but Madame de Cintré had found it
impossible to dine with her, and Madame de Cintré should for
once be forced gently to render tribute to Mrs Tristram.

'It would give me great pleasure,' she said, looking at Mrs
Tristram.

'That's a great deal,' cried the latter, 'for Madame de Cintré
to say!'

'I am very much obliged to you,' said Newman. 'Mrs Tristram
can speak better for me than I can speak for myself.'

Madame de Cintré looked at him again, with the same soft brightness. 'Are you to be long in Paris?' she asked.

'We shall keep him,' said Mrs Tristram.

'But you are keeping *me*!' and Madame de Cintré shook her friend's hand.

'A moment longer,' said Mrs Tristram.

Madame de Cintré looked at Newman again; this time without her smile. Her eyes lingered a moment. 'Will you come and see me?' she asked.

Mrs Tristram kissed her. Newman expressed his thanks, and she took her leave. Her hostess went with her to the door, and left Newman alone a moment. Presently she returned, rubbing her hands. 'It was a fortunate chance,' she said. 'She had come to decline my invitation. You triumphed on the spot, making her ask you, at the end of three minutes, to her house.'

'It was you who triumphed,' said Newman. 'You must not be too hard upon her.'

Mrs Tristram stared. 'What do you mean?'

'She did not strike me as so proud. I should say she was shy.'

'You are very discriminating. And what do you think of her face?'

'It's handsome!' said Newman.

'I should think it was! Of course you will go and see her.'

'Tomorrow!' cried Newman.

'No, not tomorrow; the next day. That will be Sunday; she leaves Paris on Monday. If you don't see her, it will at least be a beginning.' And she gave him Madame de Cintré's address.

He walked across the Seine, late in the summer afternoon, and made his way through those grey and silent streets of the Faubourg St Germain,* whose houses present to the outer world a face as impassive and as suggestive of the concentration of privacy within as the blank walls of Eastern seraglios.* Newman thought it a queer way for rich people to live; his ideal of grandeur was a splendid façade, diffusing its brilliancy outward too, irradiating hospitality. The house to which he had been directed had a dark, dusty, painted portal, which swung open in answer to his ring. It admitted him into a wide, gravelled court, surrounded on three sides with closed windows, and with a doorway facing the street, approached by three steps and surmounted by a tin canopy. The place was all in the shade; it answered to Newman's conception of a convent. The portress could not tell him whether Madame de Cintré was visible; he would please to apply at the farther door. He crossed the court; a gentleman was sitting, bareheaded, on the steps of the portico, playing with a beautiful pointer. He rose as Newman approached, and, as he laid his hand upon the bell, said with a smile, in English, that he was afraid Newman would be kept waiting; the servants were scattered; he himself had been ringing; he didn't know what the deuce was in them. He was a young man; his English was excellent, and his smile very frank. Newman pronounced the name of Madame de Cintré.

'I think,' said the young man, 'that my sister is visible. Come in, and if you will give me your card I will carry it to her myself.'

Newman had been accompanied on his present errand by a slight sentiment, I will not say of defiance – a readiness for aggression or defence, as they might prove needful – but of reflective good-humoured suspicion. He took from his pocket, while he stood on the portico, a card upon which, under his name, he had written the words 'San Francisco', and while he presented it he looked warily at his interlocutor. His glance was singularly reassuring; he liked the young man's face; it strongly resembled that of Madame de Cintré. He was evidently her brother. The young man, on his side, had made a rapid inspection of Newman's person. He had taken the card and was about to enter the house with it when another figure appeared on the threshold – an older man, of a fine presence, wearing evening dress. He looked hard at Newman, and Newman looked at him. 'Madame de Cintré,' the younger man repeated, as an introduction of the visitor. The other took the card from his hand, read it in a rapid glance, looked again at Newman from head to foot, hesitated a moment, and then said, gravely, but urbanely, 'Madame de Cintré is not at home.'

The younger man made a gesture, and then turning to Newman: 'I am very sorry, sir,' he said.

Newman gave him a friendly nod, to show that he bore him no malice, and retraced his steps. At the porter's lodge he stopped; the two men were still standing on the portico.

'Who is the gentleman with the dog?' he asked of the old woman who reappeared. He had begun to learn French.

'That is Monsieur le Comte.'

'And the other?'

'That is Monsieur le Marquis.'

'A marquis?' said Christopher in English, which the old woman fortunately did not understand. 'Oh, then he's not the butler!'

CHAPTER 4

Early one morning, before Christopher Newman was dressed, a little old man was ushered into his apartment, followed by a youth in a blouse,* bearing a picture in a brilliant frame. Newman, among the distractions of Paris, had forgotten M. Nioche and his accomplished daughter; but this was an effective reminder.

'I am afraid you had given me up, sir,' said the old man, after many apologies and salutations. 'We have made you wait so many days. You accused us, perhaps, of inconstancy, of bad faith. But behold me at last! And behold also the pretty "Madonna". Place it on a chair, my friend, in a good light, so that monsieur may admire it.' And M. Nioche, addressing his companion, helped him to dispose the work of art.

It had been endued with a layer of varnish an inch thick, and its frame, of an elaborate pattern, was at least a foot wide. It glittered and twinkled in the morning light, and looked, to Newman's eyes, wonderfully splendid and precious. It seemed to him a very happy purchase, and he felt rich in the possession of it. He stood looking at it complacently, while he proceeded with his toilet, and M. Nioche, who had dismissed his own attendant, hovered near, smiling and rubbing his hands.

'It has wonderful *finesse*,' he murmured, caressingly. 'And here and there are marvellous touches; you probably perceive them, sir. It attracted great attention on the Boulevard,* as we came along. And then a gradation of tones! That's what it is to know how to paint. I don't say it because I am her father, sir; but as one man of taste addressing another I cannot help observing that you have there an exquisite work. It is hard to produce such things and to have to part with them. If our means only allowed us the luxury of keeping it! I really may say, sir' – and M. Nioche gave a little feebly insinuating laugh – 'I really may say that I envy you! You see,' he added in a moment, 'we have taken the liberty of offering you a frame. It increases by a trifle the value of the work, and it will save you the annoyance – so great for a person of your delicacy – of going about to bargain at the shops.'

The language spoken by M. Nioche was a singular compound, which I shrink from the attempt to reproduce in its integrity. He had apparently once possessed a certain knowledge of English, and his accent was oddly tinged with the cockneyism of the British metropolis. But his learning had grown rusty with disuse, and his vocabulary was defective and capricious. He had repaired it with large patches of French, with words anglicised by a process of his own, and with native idioms literally translated. The result, in the form in which he in all humility presented it, would be scarcely comprehensible to the reader, so that I have ventured to trim and sift it. Newman only half understood it, but it amused him, and the old man's decent forlornness appealed to his democratic instincts. The assumption of a fatality in misery always irritated his strong good-nature – it was almost the only thing that did so; and he felt the impulse to wipe it out, as it were, with the sponge of his own prosperity. The papa of Mademoiselle Noémie, however, had apparently on this occasion been vigorously indoctrinated, and he showed a certain tremulous eagerness to cultivate unexpected opportunities.

'How much do I owe you, then, with the frame?' asked Newman.

'It will make in all three thousand francs,' said the old man, smiling agreeably, but folding his hands in instinctive suppliance.

'Can you give me a receipt?'

'I have brought one,' said M. Nioche. 'I took the liberty of drawing it up in case monsieur should happen to desire to discharge his debt.' And he drew a paper from his pocket-book and presented it to his patron. The document was written in a minute, fantastic hand, and couched in the choicest language.

Newman laid down the money, and M. Nioche dropped the napoleons* one by one, solemnly and lovingly, into an old leathern purse.

'And how is your young lady?' asked Newman. 'She made a great impression on me.'

'An impression? Monsieur is very good. Monsieur admires her appearance?'

'She is very pretty, certainly.'

'Alas, yes, she is very pretty!'

'And what is the harm in her being pretty?'

M. Nioche fixed his eyes upon a spot on the carpet and shook his head. Then looking up at Newman with a gaze that seemed to brighten and expand, 'Monsieur knows what Paris is. She is dangerous to beauty, when beauty hasn't the sou.'*

'Ah, but that is not the case with your daughter. She is rich, now.'

'Very true; we are rich for six months. But if my daughter were a plain girl I should sleep better, all the same.'

'You are afraid of the young men?'

'The young and the old!'

'She ought to get a husband.'

'Ah, monsieur, one doesn't get a husband for nothing. Her husband must take her as she is; I can't give her a sou. But the young men don't see with that eye.'

'Oh,' said Newman, 'her talent is in itself a dowry.'

'Ah, sir, it needs first to be converted into specie!'* and M. Nioche slapped his purse tenderly before he stowed it away. 'The operation doesn't take place every day.'

'Well, your young men are very shabby,' said Newman; 'that's all I can say. They ought to pay for your daughter, and not ask money themselves.'

'Those are very noble ideas, monsieur; but what will you have? They are not the ideas of this country. We want to know what we are about when we marry.'

'How big a portion does your daughter want?'

M. Nioche stared, as if he wondered what was coming next; but he promptly recovered himself, at a venture, and replied that he knew a very nice young man, employed by an insurance company, who would content himself with fifteen thousand francs.

'Let your daughter paint half-a-dozen pictures for me, and she shall have her dowry.'

'Half-a-dozen pictures – her dowry! Monsieur is not speaking inconsiderately?'

'If she will make me six or eight copies in the Louvre as pretty

as that "Madonna", I will pay her the same price,' said
Newman.

Poor M. Nioche was speechless a moment, with amazement
and gratitude, and then he seized Newman's hand, pressed it
between his own ten fingers, and gazed at him with watery eyes.
'As pretty as that? They shall be a thousand times prettier – they
shall be magnificent, sublime. Ah, if I only knew how to paint
myself, sir, so that I might lend a hand! What can I do to thank
you? *Voyons!*'* and he pressed his forehead while he tried to
think of something.

'Oh, you have thanked me enough,' said Newman.

'Ah, here it is, sir!' cried M. Nioche. 'To express my gratitude,
I will charge you nothing for the lessons in French conversation.'

'The lessons? I had quite forgotten them. Listening to your
English,' added Newman, laughing, 'is almost a lesson in
French.'

'Ah, I don't profess to teach English, certainly,' said M.
Nioche. 'But for my own admirable tongue I am still at your
service.'

'Since you are here, then,' said Newman, 'we will begin. This
is a very good hour. I am going to have my coffee; come every
morning at half-past nine and have yours with me.'

'Monsieur offers me my coffee, also?' cried M. Nioche. 'Truly,
my *beaux jours** are coming back.'

'Come,' said Newman, 'let us begin. The coffee is almighty
hot. How do you say that in French?'

Every day, then, for the following three weeks, the minutely
respectable figure of M. Nioche made its appearance, with a
series of little inquiring and apologetic obeisances, among the
aromatic fumes of Newman's morning beverage. I don't know
how much French our friend learned; but, as he himself said, if
the attempt did him no good, it could at any rate do him no
harm. And it amused him; it gratified that irregularly sociable
side of his nature which had always expressed itself in a relish
for ungrammatical conversation, and which often, even in his
busy and preoccupied days, had made him sit on rail fences in
young Western towns, in the twilight, in gossip hardly less than
fraternal with humorous loafers and obscure fortune-seekers.
He had notions, where-ever he went, about talking with the
natives; he had been assured, and his judgment approved the
advice, that in travelling abroad it was an excellent thing to look

into the life of the country. M. Nioche was very much of a
native, and, though his life might not be particularly worth
looking into, he was a palpable and smoothly-rounded unit in
that picturesque Parisian civilisation which offered our hero so
much easy entertainment and propounded so many curious
problems to his inquiring and practical mind. Newman was
fond of statistics; he liked to know how things were done; it
gratified him to learn what taxes were paid, what profits were
gathered, what commercial habits prevailed, how the battle
of life was fought. M. Nioche, as a reduced capitalist, was
familiar with these considerations, and he formulated his information, which he was proud to be able to impart, in the neatest
possible terms and with a pinch of snuff between finger and
thumb. As a Frenchman – quite apart from Newman's napoleons – M. Nioche loved conversation, and even in his decay
his urbanity had not grown rusty. As a Frenchman, too, he
could give a clear account of things, and – still as a Frenchman
– when his knowledge was at fault he could supply its lapses
with the most convenient and ingenious hypotheses. The little
shrunken financier was intensely delighted to have questions
asked him, and he scraped together information, by frugal
processes, and took notes, in his little greasy pocket-book, of
incidents which might interest his munificent friend. He read old
almanacs at the book-stalls on the quays, and he began to frequent another *café*, where more newspapers were taken and his
post-prandial *demitasse** cost him a penny extra, and where he
used to con* the tattered sheets for curious anecdotes, freaks of
nature, and strange coincidences. He would relate with solemnity the next morning that a child of five years of age had lately
died at Bordeaux, whose brain had been found to weigh sixty
ounces – the brain of a Napoleon or a Washington! or that
Madame P——, *charcutière** in the Rue de Clichy,* had found
in the wadding of an old petticoat the sum of three hundred and
sixty francs, which she had lost five years before. He pronounced
his words with great distinctness and sonority, and Newman
assured him that his way of dealing with the French tongue was
very superior to the bewildering chatter that he heard in other
mouths. Upon this M. Nioche's accent became more finely
trenchant than ever; he offered to read extracts from Lamartine,*
and he protested that, although he did endeavour according to

his feeble lights to cultivate refinement of diction, monsieur, if he wanted the real thing, should go to the Théâtre Français.*

Newman took an interest in French thriftiness and conceived a lively admiration for Parisian economies. His own economic genius was so entirely for operations on a larger scale, and, to move at his ease, he needed so imperatively the sense of great risks and great prizes, that he found an ungrudging entertainment in the spectacle of fortunes made by the aggregation of copper coins, and in the minute subdivision of labour and profit. He questioned M. Nioche about his own manner of life, and felt a friendly mixture of compassion and respect over the recital of his delicate frugalities. The worthy man told him how, at one period, he and his daughter had supported existence, comfortably, upon the sum of fifteen sous *per diem*; recently, having succeeded in hauling ashore the last floating fragments of the wreck of his fortune, his budget had been a trifle more ample. But they still had to count their sous very narrowly, and M. Nioche intimated with a sigh that Mademoiselle Noémie did not bring to this task that zealous co-operation which might have been desired.

'But what will you have?' he asked, philosophically. 'One is young, one is pretty, one needs new dresses and fresh gloves; one can't wear shabby gowns among the splendours of the Louvre.'

'But your daughter earns enough to pay for her own clothes,' said Newman.

M. Nioche looked at him with weak, uncertain eyes. He would have liked to be able to say that his daughter's talents were appreciated, and that her crooked little daubs commanded a market; but it seemed a scandal to abuse the credulity of this free-handed stranger, who, without a suspicion or a question, had admitted him to equal social rights. He compromised, and declared that while it was obvious that Mademoiselle Noémie's reproductions of the old masters had only to be seen to be coveted, the prices which, in consideration of their altogether peculiar degree of finish she felt obliged to ask for them, had kept purchasers at a respectful distance. 'Poor little one!' said M. Nioche, with a sigh; 'it is almost a pity that her work is so perfect! It would be in her interest to paint less well.'

'But if Mademoiselle Noémie has this devotion to her art,'

Newman once observed, 'why should you have those fears for her that you spoke of the other day?'

M. Nioche meditated; there was an inconsistency in his position; it made him chronically uncomfortable. Though he had no desire to destroy the goose with the golden eggs – Newman's benevolent confidence – he felt a tremulous impulse to speak out all his trouble. 'Ah, she is an artist, my dear sir, most assuredly,' he declared. 'But to tell you the truth, she is also a *franche coquette.** I am sorry to say,' he added in a moment, shaking his head with a world of harmless bitterness, 'that she comes honestly by it. Her mother was one before her!'

'You were not happy with your wife?' Newman asked.

M. Nioche gave half-a-dozen little backward jerks of his head. 'She was my purgatory, monsieur!'

'She deceived you?'

'Under my nose, year after year. I was too stupid, and the temptation was too great. But I found her out at last. I have only been once in my life a man to be afraid of; I know it very well: it was in that hour! Nevertheless I don't like to think of it. I loved her – I can't tell you how much. She was a bad woman.'

'She is not living?'

'She has gone to her account.'

'Her influence on your daughter, then,' said Newman encouragingly, 'is not to be feared.'

'She cared no more for her daughter than for the sole of her shoe! But Noémie has no need of influence. She is sufficient to herself. She is stronger than I.'

'She doesn't obey you, eh?'

'She can't obey, monsieur, since I don't command. What would be the use? It would only irritate her and drive her to some *coup de tête.** She is very clever, like her mother; she would waste no time about it. As a child – when I was happy, or supposed I was – she studied drawing and painting with first-class professors, and they assured me she had a talent. I was delighted to believe it, and when I went into society I used to carry her pictures with me in a portfolio and hand them round to the company. I remember, once, a lady thought I was offering them for sale, and I took it very ill. We don't know what we may come to! Then came my dark days, and my explosion with Madame Nioche. Noémie had no more twenty-franc lessons; but in the course of time, when she grew older, and it became highly expedient that she should do something that would help to keep us alive, she bethought herself of her palette and brushes. Some of our friends in the *quartier** pronounced the idea fantastic: they recommended her to try bonnet-making, to get a situation in a shop, or – if she was more ambitious – to advertise for a place of *dame de compagnie.** She did advertise, and an old lady wrote her a letter and bade her come and see her. The old lady liked her, and offered her her living and six hundred francs a year; but Noémie discovered that she passed her life in her arm-chair and had only two visitors, her confessor and her nephew: the confessor very strict, and the nephew a man of fifty, with a broken nose and a government clerkship of two thousand francs. She threw her old lady over, bought a paint-box, a canvas, and a new dress, and went and set up her easel in the Louvre. There, in one place and another, she has passed the last two years; I can't say it has made us millionaires. But Noémie tells me that Rome was not built in a day, that she is making great progress, that I must leave her to her own devices. The fact is, without prejudice to her genius, that she has no idea of burying herself alive. She likes to see the world, and to be seen. She says, herself, that she can't work in the dark. With her appearance it is very natural. Only, I can't help worrying and trembling and wondering what may happen to her there all alone, day after day, amid all that coming and going of strangers. I can't be always at her side. I go with her in the morning, and I come to fetch her away, but she won't have me near her in the interval; she says I make her nervous. As if it didn't make me nervous to wander about all day without her! Ah, if anything were to happen to her!' cried M. Nioche, clenching his two fists and jerking back his head again, portentously.

'Oh, I guess nothing will happen,' said Newman.

'I believe I should shoot her!' said the old man solemnly.

'Oh, we'll marry her,' said Newman, 'since that's how you manage it; and I will go and see her tomorrow at the Louvre and pick out the pictures she is to copy for me.'

M. Nioche had brought Newman a message from his daughter, in acceptance of his magnificent commission, the young lady declaring herself his most devoted servant, promising her most zealous endeavour, and regretting that the proprieties forbade her coming to thank him in person. The morning after the conversation just narrated, Newman reverted to his intention of meeting Mademoiselle Noémie at the Louvre. M. Nioche appeared preoccupied, and left his budget of anecdotes unopened; he took a great deal of snuff, and sent certain oblique, appealing glances toward his stalwart pupil. At last, when he was taking his leave, he stood a moment, after he had polished his hat with his calico pocket-handkerchief, with his small, pale eyes fixed strangely upon Newman.

'What's the matter?' our hero demanded.

'Excuse the solicitude of a father's heart!' said M. Nioche. 'You inspire me with boundless confidence, but I can't help giving you a warning. After all, you are a man, you are young and at liberty. Let me beseech you, then, to respect the innocence of Mademoiselle Nioche!'

Newman had wondered what was coming, and at this he broke into a laugh. He was on the point of declaring that his own innocence struck him as the more exposed, but he contented himself with promising to treat the young girl with nothing less than veneration. He found her waiting for him, seated upon the great divan in the Salon Carré. She was not in her working-day costume, but wore her bonnet and gloves and carried her parasol, in honour of the occasion. These articles had been selected with unerring taste, and a fresher, prettier image of youthful alertness and blooming discretion was not to be conceived. She made Newman a most respectful curtsy and expressed her gratitude for his liberality in a wonderfully graceful little speech. It annoyed him to have a charming young girl stand there thanking him, and it made him feel uncomfortable to think that this perfect young lady, with her excellent manners and her finished intonation, was literally in his pay. He assured her, in such French as he could muster, that the thing was not worth mentioning, and that he considered her services a great favour.

'Whenever you please, then,' said Mademoiselle Noémie, 'we will pass the review.'

They walked slowly round the room, then passed into the others and strolled about for half an hour. Mademoiselle Noémie evidently relished her situation, and had no desire to bring her public interview with her striking-looking patron to a close. Newman perceived that prosperity agreed with her. The little thin-lipped, peremptory air with which she had addressed her father on the occasion of their former meeting had given place to the most lingering and caressing tones.

'What sort of pictures do you desire?' she asked. 'Sacred, or profane?'

'Oh, a few of each,' said Newman. 'But I want something bright and gay.'

'Something gay? There is nothing very gay in this solemn old Louvre. But we will see what we can find. You speak French today like a charm. My father has done wonders.'

'Oh, I am a bad subject,' said Newman. 'I am too old to learn a language.'

'Too old? *Quelle folie!*'* cried Mademoiselle Noémie, with a clear, shrill laugh. 'You are a very young man. And how do you like my father?'

'He is a very nice old gentleman. He never laughs at my blunders.'

'He is very *comme il faut*,* my papa,' said Mademoiselle Noémie, 'and as honest as the day. Oh, an exceptional probity! You could trust him with millions.'

'Do you always obey him?' asked Newman.

'Obey him?'

'Do you do what he bids you?'

The young girl stopped and looked at him; she had a spot of colour in either cheek, and in her expressive French eye, which projected too much for perfect beauty, there was a slight gleam of audacity. 'Why do you ask me that?' she demanded.

'Because I want to know.'

'You think me a bad girl?' And she gave a strange smile.

Newman looked at her a moment; he saw that she was pretty, but he was not in the least dazzled. He remembered poor M. Nioche's solicitude for her 'innocence', and he laughed out again as his eyes met hers. Her face was the oddest mixture of youth and maturity, and beneath her candid brow her searching little smile seemed to contain a world of ambiguous intentions. She was pretty enough, certainly, to make her father nervous; but, as regards her innocence, Newman felt ready on the spot to affirm that she had never parted with it. She had simply never had any; she had been looking at the world since she was ten years old, and he would have been a wise man who could tell her any secrets. In her long mornings at the Louvre she had not only studied Madonnas and St Johns; she had kept an eye upon all the variously embodied human nature around her, and she had formed her conclusions. In a certain sense, it seemed to Newman, M. Nioche might be at rest; his daughter might do something very audacious, but she would never do anything foolish. Newman, with his long-drawn, leisurely smile, and his even, unhurried utterance, was always, mentally, taking his time; and he asked himself, now, what she was looking at him in that way for. He had an idea that she would like him to confess that he did think her a bad girl.

'Oh no,' he said at last; 'it would be very bad manners in me to judge you that way. I don't know you.'

'But my father has complained to you,' said Mademoiselle Noémie.

'He says you are a coquette.'

'He shouldn't go about saying such things to gentlemen! But you don't believe it?'

'No,' said Newman gravely, 'I don't believe it.'

She looked at him again, gave a shrug and a smile, and then pointed to a small Italian picture, a Marriage of St Catherine.* 'How should you like that?' she asked.

'It doesn't please me,' said Newman. 'The young lady in the yellow dress is not pretty.'

'Ah, you are a great connoisseur,' murmured Mademoiselle Noémie.

'In pictures? Oh no; I know very little about them.'

'In pretty women, then?'

'In that I am hardly better.'

'What do you say to that, then?' the young girl asked, indicating a superb Italian portrait of a lady.* 'I will do it for you on a smaller scale.'

'On a smaller scale? Why not as large as the original?'*

Mademoiselle Noémie glanced at the glowing splendour of the Venetian masterpiece and gave a little toss of her head. 'I don't like that woman. She looks stupid.'

'I do like her,' said Newman. 'Decidedly, I must have her, as large as life. And just as stupid as she is there.'

The young girl fixed her eyes on him again, and with her mocking smile, 'It certainly ought to be easy for me to make her look stupid!' she said.

'What do you mean?' asked Newman, puzzled.

She gave another little shrug. 'Seriously, then, you want that portrait – the golden hair, the purple satin, the pearl necklace, the two magnificent arms?'

'Everything – just as it is.'

'Would nothing else do, instead?'

'Oh, I want some other things, but I want that too.'

Mademoiselle Noémie turned away a moment, walked to the other side of the hall, and stood there, looking vaguely about her. At last she came back. 'It must be charming to be able to order pictures at such a rate. Venetian portraits, as large as life! You go at it *en prince*.* And you are going to travel about Europe that way?'

'Yes, I intend to travel,' said Newman.

'Ordering, buying, spending money?'

'Of course I shall spend some money.'

'You are very happy to have it. And you are perfectly free?'

'How do you mean, free?'

'You have nothing to bother you – no family, no wife, no *fiancée*?'

'Yes, I am tolerably free.'

'You are very happy,' said Mademoiselle Noémie gravely.

'*Je le veux bien!*'* said Newman, proving that he had learned more French than he admitted.

'And how long shall you stay in Paris?' the young girl went on.

'Only a few days more.'

'Why do you go away?'

'It is getting hot, and I must go to Switzerland.'

'To Switzerland? That's a fine country. I would give my new parasol to see it! Lakes and mountains, romantic valleys and icy peaks! Oh, I congratulate you. Meanwhile, I shall sit here through all the hot summer, daubing at your pictures.'

'Oh, take your time about it,' said Newman. 'Do them at your convenience.'

They walked farther and looked at a dozen other things. Newman pointed out what pleased him, and Mademoiselle Noémie generally criticised it, and proposed something else. Then suddenly she diverged and began to talk about some personal matter.

'What made you speak to me the other day in the Salon Carré?' she abruptly asked.

'I admired your picture.'

'But you hesitated a long time.'

'Oh, I do nothing rashly,' said Newman.

'Yes, I saw you watching me. But I never supposed you were going to speak to me. I never dreamed I should be walking about here with you today. It's very curious.'

'It is very natural,' observed Newman.

'Oh, I beg your pardon; not to me. Coquette as you think me, I have never walked about in public with a gentleman before. What was my father thinking of when he consented to our interview?'

'He was repenting of his unjust accusations,' replied Newman.

Mademoiselle Noémie remained silent; at last she dropped into a seat. 'Well, then, for those five it is fixed,' she said. 'Five copies as brilliant and beautiful as I can make them. We have one more to choose. Shouldn't you like one of those great Rubenses – the marriage of Marie de Médicis?* Just look at it and see how handsome it is.'

'Oh yes; I should like that,' said Newman. 'Finish off with that.'

'Finish off with that – good!' And she laughed. She sat a moment, looking at him, and then she suddenly rose and stood before him, with her hands hanging and clasped in front of her. 'I don't understand you,' she said with a smile. 'I don't understand how a man can be so ignorant.'

'Oh, I am ignorant, certainly,' said Newman, putting his hands into his pockets.

'It's ridiculous! I don't know how to paint.'

'You don't know how?'

'I paint like a cat; I can't draw a straight line. I never sold a picture until you bought that thing the other day.' And as she offered this surprising information she continued to smile.

Newman burst into a laugh. 'Why do you tell me this?' he asked.

'Because it irritates me to see a clever man blunder so. My pictures are grotesque.'

'And the one I possess – '

'That one is rather worse than usual.'

'Well,' said Newman, 'I like it all the same!'

She looked at him askance. 'That is a very pretty thing to say,' she answered; 'but it is my duty to warn you before you go farther. This order of yours is impossible, you know. What do you take me for? It is work for ten men. You pick out the six most difficult pictures in the Louvre, and you expect me to go to work as if I were sitting down to hem a dozen pocket-handkerchiefs. I wanted to see how far you would go.'

Newman looked at the young girl in some perplexity. In spite of the ridiculous blunder of which he stood convicted, he was very far from being a simpleton, and he had a lively suspicion that Mademoiselle Noémie's sudden frankness was not essentially more honest than her leaving him in error would have been. She was playing a game; she was not simply taking pity on his aesthetic verdancy. What was it she expected to win? The stakes were high and the risk was great; the prize therefore must have been commensurate. But even granting that the prize might be great, Newman could not resist a movement of admiration for his companion's intrepidity. She was throwing away with one hand, whatever she might intend to do with the other, a very handsome sum of money.

'Are you joking,' he said, 'or are you serious?'

'Oh, serious!' cried Mademoiselle Noémie, but with her extraordinary smile.

'I know very little about pictures, or how they are painted. If you can't do all that, of course you can't. Do what you can, then.'

'It will be very bad,' said Mademoiselle Noémie.

'Oh,' said Newman, laughing, 'if you are determined it shall be bad, of course it will. But why do you go on painting badly?'

'I can do nothing else; I have no real talent.'

'You are deceiving your father, then.'

The young girl hesitated a moment. 'He knows very well!'

'No,' Newman declared; 'I am sure he believes in you.'

'He is afraid of me. I go on painting badly, as you say, because I want to learn. I like it, at any rate. And I like being here; it is a place to come to every day; it is better than sitting in a little dark damp room, on a court, or selling buttons and whalebones over a counter.'

'Of course it is much more amusing,' said Newman. 'But for a poor girl isn't it rather an expensive amusement?'

'Oh, I am very wrong, there is no doubt about that,' said Mademoiselle Noémie. 'But rather than earn my living as some girls do – toiling with a needle, in little black holes, out of the world – I would throw myself into the Seine.'

'There is no need of that,' Newman answered; 'your father told you my offer?'

'Your offer?'

'He wants you to marry, and I told him I would give you a chance to earn your *dot*.'*

'He told me all about it, and you see the account I make of it! Why should you take such an interest in my marriage?'

'My interest was in your father. I hold to my offer; do what you can, and I will buy what you paint.'

She stood for some time, meditating, with her eyes on the ground. At last, looking up: 'What sort of a husband can you get for twelve thousand francs?' she asked.

'Your father tells me he knows some very good young men.'

'Grocers and butchers and little *maîtres de cafés*!* I will not marry at all if I can't marry well.'

'I would advise you not to be too fastidious,' said Newman. 'That's all the advice I can give you.'

'I am very much vexed at what I have said!' cried the young girl. 'It has done me no good. But I couldn't help it.'

'What good did you expect it to do you?'

'I couldn't help it, simply.'

Newman looked at her a moment. 'Well, your pictures may be bad,' he said, 'but you are too clever for me, nevertheless. I don't understand you. Good-bye!' And he put out his hand.

She made no response, and offered him no farewell. She turned away and seated herself sidewise on a bench, leaning her head on the back of her hand, which clasped the rail in front of the pictures. Newman stood a moment and then turned on his heel and retreated. He had understood her better than he confessed; this singular scene was a practical commentary upon her father's statement that she was a frank coquette.

CHAPTER 5

When Newman related to Mrs Tristram his fruitless visit to
Madame de Cintré, she urged him not to be discouraged, but to
carry out his plan of 'seeing Europe' during the summer, and
return to Paris in the autumn and settle down comfortably for
the winter. 'Madame de Cintré will keep,' she said; 'she is not a
woman who will marry from one day to another.' Newman
made no distinct affirmation that he would come back to Paris;
he even talked about Rome and the Nile, and abstained from
professing any especial interest in Madame de Cintré's continued widowhood. This circumstance was at variance with his
habitual frankness, and may perhaps be regarded as characteristic of the incipient stage of that passion which is more
particularly known as the mysterious one. The truth is that
the expression of a pair of eyes, that were at once brilliant
and mild, had become very familiar to his memory, and he
would not easily have resigned himself to the prospect of never
looking into them again. He communicated to Mrs Tristram a
number of other facts, of greater or less importance, as you
choose; but on this particular point he kept his own counsel. He
took a kindly leave of M. Nioche, having assured him that, so
far as he was concerned, the blue-cloaked Madonna* herself
might have been present at his interview with Mademoiselle
Noémie; and left the old man nursing his breast-pocket, in an
ecstasy which the acutest misfortune might have been defied to
dissipate. Newman then started on his travels with all his usual
appearance of slow-strolling leisure, and all his essential directness and intensity of aim. No man seemed less in a hurry, and
yet no man achieved more in brief periods. He had certain
practical instincts which served him excellently in his trade of
tourist. He found his way in foreign cities by divination, his
memory was excellent when once his attention had been at all
cordially given, and he emerged from dialogues in foreign
tongues, of which he had, formally, not understood a word,
in full possession of the particular fact he had desired to
ascertain. His appetite for facts was capacious, and although
many of those which he noted would have seemed woefully dry
and colourless to the ordinary sentimental traveller, a careful
inspection of the list would have shown that he had a soft spot

in his imagination. In the charming city of Brussels – his first stopping-place after leaving Paris – he asked a great many questions about the street-cars, and took extreme satisfaction in the reappearance of this familiar symbol of American civilisation; but he was also greatly struck with the beautiful Gothic tower of the Hôtel de Ville,* and wondered whether it would not be possible to 'get up' something like it in San Francisco. He stood for half an hour in the crowded square before this edifice, in imminent danger from carriage-wheels, listening to a toothless old cicerone* mumble in broken English the touching history of Counts Egmont and Horn;* and he wrote the names of these gentlemen – for reasons best known to himself – on the back of an old letter.

At the outset, on his leaving Paris, his curiosity had not been intense; passive entertainment, in the Champs Élysées* and at the theatres, seemed about as much as he need expect of himself, and although, as he had said to Tristram, he wanted to see the mysterious, satisfying *best*, he had not the Grand Tour* in the least on his conscience, and was not given to cross-questioning the amusement of the hour. He believed that Europe was made for him, and not he for Europe. He had said that he wanted to improve his mind, but he would have felt a certain embarrassment, a certain shame, even – a false shame, possibly – if he had caught himself looking intellectually into the mirror. Neither in this nor in any other respect had Newman a high sense of responsibility; it was his prime conviction that a man's life should be easy, and that he should be able to resolve privilege into a matter of course. The world, to his sense, was a great bazaar, where one might stroll about and purchase handsome things; but he was no more conscious, individually, of social pressure than he admitted the existence of such a thing as an obligatory purchase. He had not only a dislike, but a sort of moral mistrust, of uncomfortable thoughts, and it was both uncomfortable and slightly contemptible to feel obliged to square oneself with a standard. One's standard was the ideal of one's own good-humoured prosperity, the prosperity which enabled one to give as well as take. To expand, without bothering about it – without shiftless timidity on one side, or loquacious eagerness on the other – to the full compass of what he would have called a 'pleasant' experience, was Newman's most definite programme of life. He had always hated to hurry to catch railroad trains, and yet he had always caught them; and just so an undue solicitude for 'culture' seemed a sort of silly dawdling at the station, a proceeding properly confined to women, foreigners, and other unpractical persons. All this admitted, Newman enjoyed his journey, when once he had fairly entered the current, as profoundly as the most zealous *dilettante*. One's theories, after all, matter little; it is one's humour that is the great thing. Our friend was intelligent, and he could not help that. He lounged through Belgium and Holland and the Rhine-land, through Switzerland and Northern Italy, planning about nothing, but seeing everything. The guides and *valets de place** found him an excellent subject. He was always approachable, for he was much addicted to standing about in the vestibules and porticoes of inns, and he availed himself little of the opportunities for impressive seclusion which are so liberally offered in Europe to gentlemen who travel with long purses. When an excursion, a church, a gallery, a ruin was proposed to him, the first thing Newman usually did, after surveying his postulant in silence, from head to foot, was to sit down at a little table and order something to drink. The cicerone, during this process, usually retreated to a respectful distance; otherwise I am not sure that Newman would not have bidden him sit down and have a glass also, and tell him as an honest fellow whether his church or his gallery was really worth a man's trouble. At last he rose and stretched his long legs, beckoned to the man of monuments, looked at his watch, and fixed his eye on his adversary. 'What is it?' he asked. 'How far?' And whatever the answer was, although he seemed to hesitate, he never declined. He stepped into an open cab, made his conductor sit beside him to answer questions, bade the driver go fast (he had a particular aversion to slow driving), and rolled, in all probability through a dusty suburb, to the goal of his pilgrimage. If the goal was a disappointment, if the church was meagre, or the ruin a heap of rubbish, Newman never protested or berated his cicerone; he looked with an impartial eye upon great monuments and small, made the guide recite his lesson, listened to it religiously, asked if there was nothing else to be seen in the neighbourhood, and drove back again at a rattling pace. It is to be feared that his perception of the difference between good architecture and bad was not acute, and that he might some-times have been seen gazing with culpable serenity at inferior productions. Ugly churches were a part of his pastime in Europe, as well as beautiful ones, and his tour was altogether a pastime. But there is sometimes nothing like the imagination of those people who have none, and Newman, now and then, in an unguided stroll in a foreign city, before some lonely, sad-towered church, or some angular image of one who had rendered civic service in an unknown past, had felt a singular inward tremor. It was not an excitement or a perplexity; it was a placid, fathomless sense of diversion.

He encountered by chance in Holland a young American, with whom, for a time, he formed a sort of traveller's partnership. They were men of a very different cast, but each, in his way, was so good a fellow that, for a few weeks at least, it seemed something of a pleasure to share the chances of the road. Newman's comrade, whose name was Babcock, was a young Unitarian minister; a small, spare, neatly-attired man, with a strikingly candid physiognomy. He was a native of Dorchester, Massachusetts, and had spiritual charge of a small congregation in another suburb of the New England metropolis.* His digestion was weak, and he lived chiefly on Graham bread and hominy – a regimen to which he was so much attached that his tour seemed to him destined to be blighted when, on landing on the Continent, he found that these delicacies did not flourish under the *table d'hôte** system. In Paris he had purchased a bag of hominy at an establishment which called itself an American Agency,* and at which the New York illustrated papers were also to be procured, and he had carried it about with him, and shown extreme serenity and fortitude in the somewhat delicate position of having his hominy prepared for him and served at anomalous hours, at the hotels he successively visited. Newman had once spent a morning, in the course of business, at Mr Babcock's birthplace, and, for reasons too recondite to unfold, his visit there always assumed in his mind a jocular cast. To carry out his joke, which certainly seems poor so long as it is not explained, he used often to address his companion as 'Dorchester'. Fellow-travellers very soon grow intimate; but it is highly improbable that at home these extremely dissimilar characters would have found any very convenient points of contact. They were, indeed, as different as possible. Newman, who never reflected on such matters, accepted the situation with great equanimity, but Babcock used to meditate over it privately;

used often, indeed, to retire to his room early in the evening for the express purpose of considering it conscientiously and impartially. He was not sure that it was a good thing for him to associate with our hero, whose way of taking life was so little his own. Newman was an excellent, generous fellow; Mr Babcock sometimes said to himself that he was a *noble* fellow, and, certainly, it was impossible not to like him. But would it not be desirable to try to exert an influence upon him, to try to quicken his moral life and sharpen his sense of duty? He liked everything, he accepted everything, he found amusement in everything; he was not discriminating, he had not a high tone. The young man from Dorchester accused Newman of a fault which he considered very grave, and which he did his best to avoid: what he would have called a want of 'moral reaction'. Poor Mr Babcock was extremely fond of pictures and churches, and carried Mrs Jameson's works* about in his trunk; he delighted in aesthetic analysis, and received peculiar impressions from everything he saw. But nevertheless in his secret soul he detested Europe, and he felt an irritating need to protest against Newman's gross intellectual hospitality. Mr Babcock's moral *malaise*, I am afraid, lay deeper than where any definition of mine can reach it. He mistrusted the European temperament, he suffered from the European climate, he hated the European dinner-hour; European life seemed to him unscrupulous and impure. And yet he had an exquisite sense of beauty; and as beauty was often inextricably associated with the above displeasing conditions, as he wished, above all, to be just and dispassionate, and as he was, furthermore, extremely devoted to 'culture', he could not bring himself to decide that Europe was utterly bad. But he thought it was very bad indeed, and his quarrel with Newman was that this unregulated epicure had a sadly insufficient perception of the bad. Babcock himself really knew as little about the bad, in any quarter of the world, as a nursing infant; his most vivid realisation of evil had been the discovery that one of his college classmates, who was studying architecture in Paris, had a love affair with a young woman who did not expect him to marry her. Babcock had related this incident to Newman, and our hero had applied an epithet of an unflattering sort to the young girl. The next day his companion asked him whether he was very sure he had used exactly the right word to characterise the young architect's mistress.

Newman stared and laughed. 'There are a great many words to express that idea,' he said; 'you can take your choice!'

'Oh, I mean,' said Babcock, 'was she possibly not to be considered in a different light? Don't you think she *really* expected him to marry her?'

'I am sure I don't know,' said Newman. 'Very likely she did; I have no doubt she is a grand woman.' And he began to laugh again.

'I didn't mean that either,' said Babcock; 'I was only afraid that I might have seemed yesterday not to remember – not to consider; well, I think I will write to Percival about it.'

And he had written to Percival (who answered him in a really impudent fashion), and he had reflected that it was, somehow, raw and reckless in Newman to assume in that off-hand manner that the young woman in Paris might be 'grand'. The brevity of Newman's judgments very often shocked and discomposed him. He had a way of damning people without farther appeal, or of pronouncing them capital company in the face of uncomfortable symptoms, which seemed unworthy of a man whose conscience had been properly cultivated. And yet poor Babcock liked him, and remembered that even if he was sometimes perplexing and painful, this was not a reason for giving him up. Goethe recommended seeing human nature in the most various forms,* and Mr Babcock thought Goethe perfectly splendid. He often tried, in odd half hours of conversation, to infuse into Newman a little of his own spiritual starch, but Newman's personal texture was too loose to admit of stiffening. His mind could no more hold principles than a sieve can hold water. He admired principles extremely, and thought Babcock a mighty fine little fellow for having so many. He accepted all that his high-strung companion offered him, and put them away in what he supposed to be a very safe place; but poor Babcock never afterwards recognised his gifts among the articles that Newman had in daily use.

They travelled together through Germany and into Switzerland, where for three or four weeks they trudged over passes and lounged upon blue lakes. At last they crossed the Simplon* and made their way to Venice. Mr Babcock had become gloomy and even a trifle irritable; he seemed moody, absent, preoccupied; he got his plans into a tangle, and talked one moment of doing one thing and the next of doing another. Newman led his

usual life, made acquaintances, took his ease in the galleries and
churches, spent an unconscionable amount of time in strolling
in the Piazza San Marco, bought a great many bad pictures, and
for a fortnight enjoyed Venice grossly. One evening, coming
back to his inn, he found Babcock waiting for him in the little
garden beside it. The young man walked up to him, looking
very dismal, thrust out his hand, and said with solemnity that
he was afraid they must part. Newman expressed his surprise
and regret, and asked why a parting had become necessary.
'Don't be afraid I'm tired of you,' he said.

'You are not tired of me?' demanded Babcock, fixing him
with his clear grey eye.

'Why the deuce should I be? You are a very plucky fellow.
Besides, I don't grow tired of things.'

'We don't understand each other,' said the young minister.

'Don't I understand you?' cried Newman. 'Why, I hoped I
did. But what if I don't; where's the harm?'

'I don't understand *you*,' said Babcock. And he sat down and
rested his head on his hand, and looked up mournfully at his
immeasurable friend.

'Oh Lord, I don't mind that!' cried Newman, with a laugh.

'But it's very distressing to me. It keeps me in a state of unrest.
It irritates me; I can't settle anything. I don't think it's good for
me.'

'You worry too much; that's what's the matter with you,' said
Newman.

'Of course it must seem so to you. You think I take things too
hard, and I think you take things too easily. We can never
agree.'

'But we have agreed very well all along.'

'No, I haven't agreed,' said Babcock, shaking his head. 'I am
very uncomfortable. I ought to have separated from you a
month ago.'

'Oh, horrors! I'll agree to anything!' cried Newman.

Mr Babcock buried his head in both hands. At last, looking
up, 'I don't think you appreciate my position,' he said. 'I try to
arrive at the truth about everything. And then you go too fast.
For me, you are too passionate, too extravagant. I feel as if I
ought to go over all this ground we have traversed again, by
myself, alone. I am afraid I have made a great many mistakes.'

'Oh, you needn't give so many reasons,' said Newman. 'You are simply tired of my company. You have a good right to be.'

'No, no, I am not tired!' cried the pestered young divine. 'It is very wrong to be tired.'

'I give it up!' laughed Newman. 'But of course it will never do to go on making mistakes. Go your way, by all means. I shall miss you; but you have seen I make friends very easily. You will be lonely yourself; but drop me a line, when you feel like it, and I will wait for you anywhere.'

'I think I will go back to Milan. I am afraid I didn't do justice to Luini.'*

'Poor Luini!' said Newman.

'I mean that I am afraid I over-estimated him. I don't think that he is a painter of the first rank.'

'Luini?' Newman exclaimed; 'why, he's enchanting – he's magnificent! There is something in his genius that is like a beautiful woman. It gives one the same feeling.'

Mr Babcock frowned and winced. And it must be added that this was, for Newman, an unusually metaphysical flight; but in passing through Milan he had taken a great fancy to the painter. 'There you are again!' said Mr Babcock. 'Yes, we had better separate.' And on the morrow he retraced his steps and proceeded to tone down his impressions of the great Lombard artist.

A few days afterwards Newman received a note from his late companion which ran as follows:

MY DEAR MR NEWMAN – I am afraid that my conduct at Venice, a week ago, seemed to you strange and ungrateful, and I wish to explain my position, which, as I said at the time, I do not think you appreciate. I had long had it on my mind to propose that we should part company, and this step was not really so abrupt as it seemed. In the first place, you know, I am travelling in Europe on funds supplied by my congregation, who kindly offered me a vacation and an opportunity to enrich my mind with the treasures of nature and art in the Old World. I feel, therefore, as if I ought to use my time to the very best advantage. I have a high sense of responsibility. You appear to care only for the pleasure of the hour, and you give yourself up to it with a violence which I confess I am not able to emulate. I feel as if I must arrive at some conclusion and fix my belief on certain points. Art and life seem to me intensely serious things, and in our travels in Europe we should especially remember the immense seriousness of Art. You seem to hold that if a thing amuses you for the moment, that is all you need ask for it; and your relish for mere amusement is also much higher than mine. You put, moreover, a kind of reckless confidence into your pleasure which at times, I confess, has seemed to me – shall I say it? – almost cynical. Your way at any rate is not my way, and it is unwise that we should attempt any longer to pull together. And yet, let me add, that I know there is a great deal to be said for your way; I have felt its attraction, in your society, very strongly. But for this I should have left you long ago. But I was so perplexed. I hope I have not done wrong. I feel as if I had a great deal of lost time to make up. I beg you take all this as I mean it, which, Heaven knows, is not invidiously. I have a great personal esteem for you, and hope that some day, when I have recovered my balance, we shall meet again. I hope you will continue to enjoy your travels; only *do* remember that Life and Art *are* extremely serious. Believe me your sincere friend and well-wisher,   BENJAMIN BABCOCK

P.S. – I am greatly perplexed by Luini.

This letter produced in Newman's mind a singular mixture of exhilaration and awe. At first, Mr Babcock's tender conscience seemed to him a capital farce, and his travelling back to Milan only to get into a deeper muddle appeared, as the reward of his pedantry, exquisitely and ludicrously just. Then Newman reflected that these are mighty mysteries; that possibly he himself was indeed that baleful and barely mentionable thing, a cynic, and that his manner of considering the treasures of art and the privileges of life was probably very base and immoral. Newman had a great contempt for immorality, and that evening, for a good half hour, as he sat watching the star-sheen on the warm Adriatic, he felt rebuked and depressed. He was at a loss how to answer Babcock's letter. His good nature checked his resenting the young minister's lofty admonitions, and his tough, inelastic sense of humour forbade his taking them seriously. He wrote no answer at all, but a day or two afterward he found in a curiosity-shop a grotesque little statuette in ivory, of the sixteenth century, which he sent off to Babcock without a commentary. It repre-sented a gaunt, ascetic-looking monk, in a tattered gown and cowl, kneeling with clasped hands and pulling a portentously long face. It was a wonderfully delicate piece of carving, and in a moment, through one of the rents of his gown, you espied a fat capon hung round the monk's waist. In Newman's intention what did the figure symbolise? Did it mean that he was going to try to be as 'high-toned' as the monk looked at first, but that he feared he should succeed no better than the friar, on a closer inspection, proved to have done? It is not supposable that he intended a satire upon Babcock's own asceticism, for this would have been a truly cynical stroke. He made his late companion, at any rate, a very valuable little present.

Newman, on leaving Venice, went through the Tyrol to Vienna, and then returned westward, through Southern Germany. The autumn found him at Baden-Baden, where he spent several weeks. The place was charming, and he was in no hurry to depart; besides, he was looking about him and deciding what to do for the winter. His summer had been very full, and as he sat under the great trees beside the miniature river that trickles past the Baden flower-beds, he slowly rummaged it over. He had seen and done a great deal, enjoyed and observed a great deal; he felt older, and yet he felt younger too. He remembered Mr Babcock and his desire to form conclusions, and he remembered also that he had profited very little by his friend's exhortation to cultivate the same respectable habit. Could he not scrape together a few conclusions? Baden-Baden was the prettiest place he had seen yet, and orchestral music in the evening, under the stars, was decidedly a great institution. This was one of his conclusions! But he went on to reflect that he had done very wisely to pull up stakes and come abroad; this seeing of the world was a very interesting thing. He had learned a great deal; he couldn't say just what, but he had it there under his hat-band. He had done what he wanted; he had seen the great things, and he had given his mind a chance to 'improve', if it would. He cheerfully believed that it had improved. Yes, this seeing of the world was very pleasant, and he would willingly do a little more of it. Thirty-six years old as he was, he had a handsome stretch of life before him yet, and he need not begin to count his weeks. Where should he take the world next? I have said he remembered the eyes of the lady whom he had found standing in Mrs Tristram's drawing-room; four months had elapsed, and he had not forgotten them yet. He had looked – he had made a point of looking – into a great many other eyes in the interval, but the only ones he thought of now were Madame de Cintré's. If he wanted to see more of the world, should he find it in Madame de Cintré's eyes? He would certainly find something there, call it this world or the next. Throughout these rather formless meditations he sometimes thought of his past life and the long array of years (they had begun so early) during which he had had nothing in his head but 'enterprise'. They seemed far away now, for his present attitude was more than a holiday, it was almost a rupture. He had told Tristram that the pendulum was swinging back, and it appeared that the back-ward swing had not yet ended. Still 'enterprise', which was over in the other quarter, wore to his mind a different aspect at different hours. In its train a thousand forgotten episodes came trooping back into his memory. Some of them he looked complacently enough in the face; from some he averted his head. They were old efforts, old exploits, antiquated examples of 'smartness' and sharpness. Some of them, as he looked at them, he felt decidedly proud of; he admired himself as if he had been looking at another man. And, in fact, many of the qualities that make a great deed were there; the decision, the resolution, the courage, the celerity, the clear eye, and the strong hand. Of certain other achievements it would be going too far to say that he was ashamed of them, for Newman had never had a stomach for dirty work. He was blessed with a natural impulse to disfigure with a direct, unreasoning blow the comely visage of temptation. And, certainly, in no man could a want of integrity have been less excusable. Newman knew the crooked from the straight at a glance, and the former had cost him, first and last, a great many moments of lively disgust. But none the less some of his memories seemed to wear at present a rather graceless and sordid mien, and it struck him that if he had never done anything very ugly, he had never, on the other hand, done anything particularly beautiful. He had spent his years in the unremitting effort to add thousands to thousands, and, now that he stood well outside of it, the business of money-getting appeared extremely dry and sterile. It is very well to sneer at money-getting after you have filled your pockets, and Newman, it may be said, should have begun somewhat earlier to moralise thus delicately. To this it may be answered that he might have made another fortune, if he chose; and we ought to add that he was not exactly moralising. It had come back to him simply that what he had been looking at all the summer was a very rich and beautiful world, and that it had not all been made by sharp railroad men and stock-brokers.

During his stay at Baden-Baden he received a letter from Mrs Tristram, scolding him for the scanty tidings he had sent to his friends of the Avenue d'Iéna, and begging to be definitely informed that he had not concocted any horrid scheme for wintering in outlying regions, but was coming back sanely and promptly to the most comfortable city in the world. Newman's answer ran as follows:

I supposed you knew I was a miserable letter-writer, and didn't expect anything of me. I don't think I have written twenty letters of pure friendship in my whole life; in America I conducted my correspondence altogether by telegrams. This is a letter of pure friendship; you have got hold of a curiosity, and I hope you will value it. You want to know everything that has happened to me these three months. The best way to tell you, I think, would be to send you my half-dozen guide-books, with my pencil-marks in the margin. Wherever you find a scratch, or a cross, or a 'Beautiful!' or a 'So true!' or a 'Too thin!' you may know that I have had a sensation of some sort or other. That has been about my history, ever since I left you. Belgium, Holland, Switzerland, Germany, Italy – I have been through the whole list, and I don't think I am any the worse for it. I know more about Madonnas and church-steeples than I supposed any man could. I have seen some very pretty things, and shall perhaps talk them over this winter, by your fireside. You see, my face is not altogether set against Paris. I have had all kinds of plans and visions, but your letter has blown most of them away. 'L'appétit vient en mangeant,'* says the French proverb, and I find that the more I see of the world the more I want to see. Now that I am in the shafts,* why shouldn't I trot to the end of the course? Sometimes I think of the far East, and keep rolling the names of Eastern cities under my tongue; Damascus and Bagdad, Medina and Mecca. I spent a week last month in the company of a returned missionary, who told me I ought to be ashamed to be loafing about Europe when there are such big things to be seen out there. I do want to explore, but I think I would rather explore over in the Rue de l'Université. Do you ever hear from that pretty lady? If you can get her to promise she will be at home the next time I call, I will go back to Paris straight. I am more than ever in the state of mind I told you about that evening; I want a first-class wife. I have kept an eye on all the pretty girls I have come across this summer, but none of them came up to my notion, or anywhere near it. I should have enjoyed all this a thousand times more if I had had the lady just mentioned by my side. The nearest approach to her was a Unitarian minister from Boston, who very soon demanded a separation, for incompatibility of temper. He told me I was low-minded, immoral, a devotee of 'art for art'* – whatever that is: all of which greatly afflicted me, for he was really a sweet little fellow. But shortly afterwards I met an Englishman, with whom I struck up an acquaintance which at first seemed to promise well – a very bright man, who writes in the London papers and knows Paris nearly as well as Tristram. We knocked about for a week together, but he very soon gave me up in disgust. I was too virtuous by half; I was too stern a moralist. He told me, in a friendly way, that I was cursed with a conscience; that I judged things like a Methodist and talked about them like an old lady. This was rather bewildering. Which of my two critics was I to believe? I didn't worry about it, and very soon made up my mind they were both idiots. But there is one thing in which no one will ever have the impudence to pretend I am wrong; that is, in being your faithful friend,

C. N.

CHAPTER 6

Newman gave up Damascus and Bagdad and returned to Paris before the autumn was over. He established himself in some rooms selected for him by Tom Tristram, in accordance with the latter's estimate of what he called his social position. When Newman learned that his social position was to be taken into account, he professed himself utterly incompetent, and begged Tristram to relieve him of the care. 'I didn't know I had a social position,' he said, 'and if I have, I haven't the smallest idea what it is. Isn't a social position knowing some two or three thousand people and inviting them to dinner? I know you and your wife and little old Mr Nioche, who gave me French lessons last spring. Can I invite you to dinner to meet each other? If I can, you must come tomorrow.'

'That is not very grateful to me,' said Mrs Tristram, 'who introduced you last year to every creature I know.'

'So you did; I had quite forgotten. But I thought you wanted me to forget,' said Newman, with that tone of simple deliberateness which frequently marked his utterance, and which an observer would not have known whether to pronounce a somewhat mysteriously humorous affectation of ignorance or a modest aspiration to knowledge; 'you told me you disliked them all.'

'Ah, the way you remember what I say is at least very flattering. But in future,' added Mrs Tristram, 'pray forget all the wicked things and remember only the good ones. It will be easily done, and it will not fatigue your memory. But I forewarn you that if you trust my husband to pick out your rooms, you are in for something hideous.'

'Hideous, darling?' cried Tristram.

'Today I must say nothing wicked; otherwise I should use stronger language.'

'What do you think she would say, Newman?' asked Tristram. 'If she really tried, now? She can express displeasure, volubly, in two or three languages; that's what it is to be intellectual. It gives her the start of me completely, for I can't swear, for the life of me, except in English. When I get mad I have to fall back on our dear old mother tongue. There's nothing like it, after all.'

Newman declared that he knew nothing about tables and chairs, and that he would accept, in the way of a lodging, with his eyes shut, anything that Tristram should offer him. This was partly pure veracity on our hero's part, but it was also partly charity. He knew that to pry about and look at rooms, and make people open windows, and poke into sofas with his cane, and gossip with landladies, and ask who lived above and who below – he knew that this was of all pastimes the dearest to Tristram's heart, and he felt the more disposed to put it in his way as he was conscious that, as regards his obliging friend, he had suffered the warmth of ancient good-fellowship somewhat to abate. Besides, he had no taste for upholstery; he had even no very exquisite sense of comfort or convenience. He had a relish for luxury and splendour, but it was satisfied by rather gross contrivances. He scarcely knew a hard chair from a soft one, and he possessed a talent for stretching his legs which quite dispensed with adventitious facilities. His idea of comfort was to inhabit very large rooms, have a great many of them, and be conscious of their possessing a number of patented mechanical devices – half of which he should never have occasion to use. The apartments should be light and brilliant and lofty; he had once said that he liked rooms in which you wanted to keep your hat on. For the rest, he was satisfied with the assurance of any respectable person that everything was 'handsome'. Tristram accordingly secured for him an apartment to which this epithet might be lavishly applied. It was situated on the Boulevard Haussmann,* on a first-floor, and consisted of a series of rooms, gilded from floor to ceiling a foot thick, draped in various light shades of satin, and chiefly furnished with mirrors and clocks. Newman thought them magnificent, thanked Tristram heartily, immediately took possession, and had one of his trunks standing for three months in his drawing-room.

One day Mrs Tristram told him that her beautiful friend, Madame de Cintré, had returned from the country; that she had met her three days before, coming out of the Church of St Sulpice;* she herself having journeyed to that distant quarter in quest of an obscure lace-mender, of whose skill she had heard high praise.

'And how were those eyes?' Newman asked.

'Those eyes were red with weeping, if you please!' said Mrs Tristram. 'She had been to confession.'

'It doesn't tally with your account of her,' said Newman, 'that she should have sins to confess.'

'They were not sins; they were sufferings.'

'How do you know that?'

'She asked me to come and see her; I went this morning.'

'And what does she suffer from?'

'I didn't ask her. With her, somehow, one is very discreet. But I guessed, easily enough. She suffers from her wicked old mother and her Grand Turk* of a brother. They persecute her. But I can almost forgive them, because, as I told you, she is a saint, and a persecution is all that she needs to bring out her saintliness and make her perfect.'

'That's a comfortable theory for her. I hope you will never

impart it to the old folks. Why does she let them bully her? Is she not her own mistress?'

'Legally, yes, I suppose; but morally, no. In France you must never say Nay to your mother, whatever she requires of you. She may be the most abominable old woman in the world, and make your life a purgatory; but after all she is *ma mère*,* and you have no right to judge her. You have simply to obey. The thing has a fine side to it. Madame de Cintré bows her head and folds her wings.'

'Can't she at least make her brother leave off?'

'Her brother is the *chef de la famille*, as they say; he is the head of the clan. With those people the family is everything; you must act, not for your own pleasure, but for the advantage of the family.'

'I wonder what *my* family would like me to do!' exclaimed Tristram.

'I wish you had one!' said his wife.

'But what do they want to get out of that poor lady?' Newman asked.

'Another marriage. They are not rich, and they want to bring more money into the family.'

'There's your chance, my boy!' said Tristram.

'And Madame de Cintré objects,' Newman continued.

'She has been sold once; she naturally objects to being sold again. It appears that the first time they made rather a poor bargain; M. de Cintré left a scanty property.'

'And to whom do they want to marry her now?'

'I thought it best not to ask; but you may be sure it is to some horrid old nabob,* or to some dissipated little duke.'

'There's Mrs Tristram, as large as life!' cried her husband. 'Observe the richness of her imagination. She has not asked a single question – it's vulgar to ask questions – and yet she knows everything. She has the history of Madame de Cintré's marriage at her fingers' ends. She has seen the lovely Claire on her knees, with loosened tresses and streaming eyes, and the rest of them standing over her with spikes and goads and red-hot irons, ready to come down on her if she refuses the tipsy duke. The simple truth is that they have made a fuss about her milliner's bill or refused her an opera-box.'

Newman looked from Tristram to his wife with a certain mistrust in each direction. 'Do you really mean,' he asked of

Mrs Tristram, 'that your friend is being forced into an unhappy marriage?'

'I think it extremely probable. Those people are very capable of that sort of thing.'

'It is like something in a play,' said Newman; 'that dark old house over there looks as if wicked things had been done in it, and might be done again.'

'They have a still darker old house in the country, Madame de Cintré tells me, and there, during the summer, this scheme must have been hatched.'

'*Must* have been; mind that!' said Tristram.

'After all,' suggested Newman, after a silence, 'she may be in trouble about something else.'

'If it is something else, then it is something worse,' said Mrs Tristram, with rich decision.

Newman was silent awhile, and seemed lost in meditation. 'Is it possible,' he asked at last, 'that they do that sort of thing over here? that helpless women are bullied into marrying men they hate?'

'Helpless women, all over the world, have a hard time of it,' said Mrs Tristram. 'There is plenty of bullying everywhere.'

'A great deal of that kind goes on in New York,' said Tristram. 'Girls are bullied or coaxed or bribed, or all three together, into marrying nasty fellows. There is no end of that always going on in the Fifth Avenue, and other bad things besides. The Mysteries of the Fifth Avenue!* Someone ought to show them up.'

'I don't believe it!' said Newman, very gravely. 'I don't believe that, in America, girls are ever subjected to compulsion. I don't believe there have been a dozen cases of it since the country began.'

'Listen to the voice of the spread eagle!'* cried Tristram.

'The spread eagle ought to use his wings,' said Mrs Tristram. 'Fly to the rescue of Madame de Cintré!'

'To her rescue?'

'Pounce down, seize her in your talons, and carry her off. Marry her yourself.'

Newman, for some moments, answered nothing; but presently, 'I should suppose she had heard enough of marrying,' he said. 'The kindest way to treat her would be to admire her, and yet never to speak of it. But that sort of thing is infamous,' he added; 'it makes me feel savage to hear of it.'

He heard of it, however, more than once afterward. Mrs Tristram again saw Madame de Cintré, and again found her looking very sad. But on these occasions there had been no tears; her beautiful eyes were clear and still. 'She is cold, calm, and hopeless,' Mrs Tristram declared, and she added that on her mentioning that her friend Mr Newman was again in Paris and was faithful in his desire to make Madame de Cintré's acquaintance, this lovely woman had found a smile in her despair, and declared that she was sorry to have missed his visit in the spring and that she hoped he had not lost courage. 'I told her something about you,' said Mrs Tristram.

'That's a comfort,' said Newman, placidly. 'I like people to know about me.'

A few days after this, one dusky autumn afternoon, he went again to the Rue de l'Université. The early evening had closed in as he applied for admittance at the stoutly guarded Hôtel de Bellegarde. He was told that Madame de Cintré was at home; he crossed the court, entered the farther door, and was conducted through a vestibule, vast, dim, and cold, up a broad stone staircase with an ancient iron balustrade, to an apartment on the second-floor. Announced and ushered in, he found himself in a sort of panelled boudoir, at one end of which a lady and gentleman were seated before the fire. The gentleman was smoking a cigarette; there was no light in the room save that of a couple of candles and the glow from the hearth. Both persons rose to welcome Newman, who, in the firelight, recognised Madame de Cintré. She gave him her hand with a smile which seemed in itself an illumination, and, pointing to her companion, said softly, 'My brother.' The gentleman offered Newman a frank, friendly greeting, and our hero then perceived him to be the young man who had spoken to him in the court of the hotel on his former visit and who had struck him as a good fellow.

'Mrs Tristram has spoken to me a great deal of you,' said Madame de Cintré gently, as she resumed her former place.

Newman, after he had seated himself, began to consider what, in truth, was his errand. He had an unusual, unexpected sense of having wandered into a strange corner of the world. He was not given, as a general thing, to anticipating danger, or forecasting disaster, and he had had no social tremors on this particular

occasion. He was not timid and he was not impudent. He felt
too kindly toward himself to be the one, and too good-naturedly
toward the rest of the world to be the other. But his native
shrewdness sometimes placed his ease of temper at its mercy;
with every disposition to take things simply, it was obliged to
perceive that some things were not so simple as others. He felt
as one does in missing a step, in an ascent, where one expected
to find it. This strange, pretty woman, sitting in fireside talk
with her brother, in the grey depths of her inhospitable-looking
house – what had he to say to her? She seemed enveloped in a
sort of fantastic privacy; on what grounds had he pulled away
the curtain? For a moment he felt as if he had plunged into some
medium as deep as the ocean, and as if he must exert himself to
keep from sinking. Meanwhile he was looking at Madame de
Cintré, and she was settling herself in her chair and drawing in
her long dress and turning her face towards him. Their eyes met;
a moment afterwards she looked away and motioned to her
brother to put a log on the fire. But the moment, and the glance
which traversed it, had been sufficient to relieve Newman of the
first and the last fit of personal embarrassment he was ever to
know. He performed the movement which was so frequent with
him, and which was always a sort of symbol of his taking
mental possession of a scene – he extended his legs. The
impression Madame de Cintré had made upon him on their first
meeting came back in an instant; it had been deeper than he
knew. She was pleasing, she was interesting; he had opened a
book and the first lines held his attention.

She asked him several questions: how lately he had seen Mrs
Tristram, how long he had been in Paris, how long he expected
to remain there, how he liked it. She spoke English without an
accent, or rather with that distinctively British accent which, on
his arrival in Europe, had struck Newman as an altogether
foreign tongue, but which, in women, he had come to like
extremely. Here and there Madame de Cintré's utterance had a
faint shade of strangeness, but at the end of ten minutes
Newman found himself waiting for these soft roughnesses. He
enjoyed them and he marvelled to see that gross thing, error,
brought down to so fine a point.

'You have a beautiful country,' said Madame de Cintré,
presently.

'Oh, magnificent!' said Newman. 'You ought to see it.'

'I shall never see it,' said Madame de Cintré with a smile.

'Why not?' asked Newman.

'I don't travel; especially so far.'

'But you go away sometimes; you are not always here?'

'I go away in summer, a little way, to the country.'

Newman wanted to ask her something more, something personal, he hardly knew what. 'Don't you find it rather – rather quiet here?' he said; 'so far from the street?' Rather 'gloomy', he was going to say, but he reflected that that would be impolite.

'Yes, it is very quiet,' said Madame de Cintré; 'but we like that.'

'Ah, you like that,' repeated Newman slowly.

'Besides, I have lived here all my life.'

'Lived here all your life,' said Newman, in the same way.

'I was born here, and my father was born here before me, and my grandfather, and my great-grandfathers. Were they not, Valentin?' and she appealed to her brother.

'Yes, it's a family habit to be born here!' the young man said with a laugh, and rose and threw the remnant of his cigarette into the fire, and then remained leaning against the chimney-piece. An observer would have perceived that he wished to take a better look at Newman, whom he covertly examined, while he stood, stroking his moustache.

'Your house is tremendously old, then,' said Newman.

'How old is it, brother?' asked Madame de Cintré.

The young man took the two candles from the mantelshelf, lifted one high in each hand, and looked up toward the cornice of the room, above the chimney-piece. This latter feature of the apartment was of white marble, and in the familiar rococo style of the last century; but above it was a panelling of an earlier date, quaintly carved, painted white, and gilded here and there. The white had turned to yellow, and the gilding was tarnished. On the top, the figures ranged themselves into a sort of shield, on which an armorial device was cut. Above it, in relief, was a date – 1627.* 'There you have it,' said the young man. 'That is old or new, according to your point of view.'

'Well, over here,' said Newman, 'one's point of view gets shifted round considerably.' And he threw back his head and looked about the room. 'Your house is of a very curious style of architecture,' he said.

'Are you interested in architecture?' asked the young man at the chimney-piece.

'Well, I took the trouble, this summer,' said Newman, 'to examine – as well as I can calculate – some four hundred and seventy churches. Do you call that interested?'

'Perhaps you are interested in theology,' said the young man.

'Not particularly. Are you a Roman Catholic, madam?' And he turned to Madame de Cintré.

'Yes, sir,' she answered, gravely.

Newman was struck with the gravity of her tone; he threw back his head and began to look round the room again. 'Had you never noticed that number up there?' he presently asked.

She hesitated a moment, and then, 'In former years,' she said.

Her brother had been watching Newman's movement. 'Perhaps you would like to examine the house,' he said.

Newman slowly brought down his eyes and looked at him; he had a vague impression that the young man at the chimney-piece was inclined to irony. He was a handsome fellow, his face wore a smile, his moustachios were curled up at the ends, and there was a little dancing gleam in his eye. 'Damn his French impudence!' Newman was on the point of saying to himself. 'What the deuce is he grinning at?' He glanced at Madame de Cintré; she was sitting with her eyes fixed on the floor. She raised them, they met his, and she looked at her brother. Newman turned again to this young man and observed that he strikingly resembled his sister. This was in his favour, and our hero's first impression of the Count Valentin, moreover, had been agreeable. His mistrust expired, and he said he would be very glad to see the house.

The young man gave a frank laugh, and laid his hand on one of the candlesticks. 'Good, good!' he exclaimed. 'Come, then.'

But Madame de Cintré rose quickly and grasped his arm. 'Ah, Valentin!' she said. 'What do you mean to do?'

'To show Mr Newman the house. It will be very amusing.'

She kept her hand on his arm and turned to Newman with a smile. 'Don't let him take you,' she said; 'you will not find it amusing. It is a musty old house like any other.'

'It is full of curious things,' said the count, resisting. 'Besides, I want to do it; it is a rare chance.'

'You are very wicked, brother,' Madame de Cintré answered.

'Nothing venture, nothing have!' cried the young man. 'Will you come?'

Madame de Cintré stepped toward Newman, gently clasping her hands and smiling softly. 'Would you not prefer my society, here, by my fire, to stumbling about dark passages after my brother?'

'A hundred times!' said Newman. 'We will see the house some other day.'

The young man put down his candlestick with mock solemnity, and shaking his head, 'Ah, you have defeated a great scheme, sir!' he said.

'A scheme? I don't understand,' said Newman.

'You would have played your part in it all the better. Perhaps some day I shall have a chance to explain it.'

'Be quiet, and ring for the tea,' said Madame de Cintré.

The young man obeyed, and presently a servant brought in the tea, placed the tray on a small table, and departed. Madame de Cintré, from her place, busied herself with making it. She had but just begun, when the door was thrown open and a lady rushed in, making a loud rustling sound. She stared at Newman, gave a little nod and a 'Monsieur!' and then quickly approached Madame de Cintré and presented her forehead to be kissed. Madame de Cintré saluted her, and continued to make tea. The newcomer was young and pretty, it seemed to Newman; she wore her bonnet and cloak, and a train of royal proportions. She began to talk rapidly in French. 'Oh, give me some tea, my beautiful one, for the love of God! I'm exhausted, mangled, massacred.' Newman found himself quite unable to follow her; she spoke much less distinctly than M. Nioche.

'That is my sister-in-law,' said the Count Valentin, leaning towards him.

'She is very pretty,' said Newman.

'Exquisite,' answered the young man, and this time, again, Newman suspected him of irony.

His sister-in-law came round to the other side of the fire with her cup of tea in her hand, holding it out at arm's-length, so that she might not spill it on her dress, and uttering little cries of alarm. She placed the cup on the mantelshelf and began to unpin her veil and pull off her gloves, looking meanwhile at Newman.

'Is there anything I can do for you, my dear lady?' the Count Valentin asked, in a sort of mock-caressing tone.

'Present monsieur,' said his sister-in-law.

The young man answered, 'Mr Newman!'

'I can't curtsy to you, monsieur, or I shall spill my tea,' said the lady. 'So Claire receives strangers, like that?' she added in a low voice, in French, to her brother-in-law.

'Apparently!' he answered, with a smile. Newman stood a moment, and then he approached Madame de Cintré. She looked up at him as if she were thinking of something to say. But she seemed to think of nothing; so she simply smiled. He sat down near her and she handed him a cup of tea. For a few moments they talked about that, and meanwhile he looked at her. He remembered what Mrs Tristram had told him of her 'perfection', and of her having, in combination, all the brilliant things that he dreamed of finding. This made him observe her not only without mistrust, but without uneasy conjectures; the presumption, from the first moment he looked at her, had been in her favour. And yet, if she was beautiful, it was not a dazzling beauty. She was tall and moulded in long lines; she had thick, fair hair, a wide forehead, and features with a sort of harmonious irregularity. Her clear grey eyes were strikingly expressive; they were both gentle and intelligent, and Newman liked them immensely; but they had not those depths of splendour – those many-coloured rays – which illumine the brow of famous beauties. Madame de Cintré was rather thin, and she looked younger than probably she was. In her whole person there was something both youthful and subdued, slender and yet ample, tranquil yet shy; a mixture of immaturity and repose, of innocence and dignity. What had Tristram meant, Newman wondered, by calling her proud? She was certainly not proud now, to him; or if she was, it was of no use, it was lost upon him; she must pile it up higher if she expected him to mind it. She was a beautiful woman, and it was very easy to get on with her. Was she a countess, a *marquise*, a kind of historical formation? Newman, who had rarely heard these words used, had never been at pains to attach any particular image to them; but they occurred to him now and seemed charged with a sort of melodious meaning. They signified something fair and softly bright, that had easy motions and spoke very agreeably.

'Have you many friends in Paris; do you go out?' asked Madame de Cintré, who had at last thought of something to say.

'Do you mean do I dance, and all that?'

'Do you go *dans le monde*,* as we say?'

'I have seen a good many people. Mrs Tristram has taken me about. I do whatever she tells me.'

'By yourself, you are not fond of amusements?'

'Oh yes, of some sorts. I am not fond of dancing, and that sort of thing; I am too old and sober. But I want to be amused; I came to Europe for that.'

'But you can be amused in America, too.'

'I couldn't; I was always at work. But, after all, that was my amusement.'

At this moment Madame de Bellegarde came back for another cup of tea, accompanied by the Count Valentin. Madame de Cintré, when she had served her, began to talk again with Newman, and recalling what he had last said, 'In your own country you were very much occupied?' she asked.

'I was in business. I have been in business since I was fifteen years old.'

'And what was your business?' asked Madame de Bellegarde, who was decidedly not so pretty as Madame de Cintré.

'I have been in everything,' said Newman. 'At one time I sold leather; at one time I manufactured wash-tubs.'

Madame de Bellegarde made a little grimace. 'Leather? I don't like that. Wash-tubs are better. I prefer the smell of soap. I hope at least they made your fortune.' She rattled this off with the air of a woman who had the reputation of saying everything that came into her head, and with a strong French accent.

Newman had spoken with cheerful seriousness, but Madame de Bellegarde's tone made him go on, after a meditative pause, with a certain light grimness of jocularity. 'No, I lost money on wash-tubs, but I came out pretty square on leather.'

'I have made up my mind, after all,' said Madame de Bellegarde, 'that the great point is – how do you call it? – to come out square. I am on my knees to money; I don't deny it. If you have it, I ask no questions. For that I am a real democrat – like you, monsieur. Madame de Cintré is very proud; but I find that one gets much more pleasure in this sad life if one doesn't look too close.'

'Just Heaven, dear madam, how you go at it,' said the Count Valentin, lowering his voice.

'He's a man one can speak to, I suppose, since my sister

receives him,' the lady answered. 'Besides, it's very true; those are my ideas.'

'Ah, you call them ideas,' murmured the young man.

'But Mrs Tristram told me you had been in the army – in your war,' said Madame de Cintré.

'Yes, but that is not business!' said Newman.

'Very true!' said M. de Bellegarde. 'Otherwise perhaps I should not be penniless.'

'Is it true,' asked Newman in a moment, 'that you are so proud? I had already heard it.'

Madame de Cintré smiled. 'Do you find me so?'

'Oh,' said Newman, 'I am no judge. If you are proud with me, you will have to tell me. Otherwise I shall not know it.'

Madame de Cintré began to laugh. 'That would be pride in a sad position!' she said.

'It would be partly,' Newman went on, 'because I shouldn't want to know it. I want you to treat me well.'

Madame de Cintré, whose laugh had ceased, looked at him with her head half averted, as if she feared what he was going to say.

'Mrs Tristram told you the literal truth,' he went on; 'I want very much to know you. I didn't come here simply to call today; I came in the hope that you might ask me to come again.'

'Oh, pray come often,' said Madame de Cintré.

'But will you be at home?' Newman insisted. Even to himself he seemed a trifle 'pushing', but he was, in truth, a trifle excited.

'I hope so!' said Madame de Cintré.

Newman got up. 'Well, we shall see,' he said, smoothing his hat with his coat-cuff.

'Brother,' said Madame de Cintré, 'invite Mr Newman to come again.'

The Count Valentin looked at our hero from head to foot with his peculiar smile, in which impudence and urbanity seemed perplexingly commingled. 'Are you a brave man?' he asked, eyeing him askance.

'Well, I hope so,' said Newman.

'I rather suspect so. In that case, come again.'

'Ah, what an invitation!' murmured Madame de Cintré, with something painful in her smile.

'Oh, I want Mr Newman to come – particularly,' said the young man. 'It will give me great pleasure. I shall be desolate if

I miss one of his visits. But I maintain he must be brave. A stout heart, sir!' And he offered Newman his hand.

'I shall not come to see you; I shall come to see Madame de Cintré,' said Newman.

'You will need all the more courage.'

'Ah, Valentin!' said Madame de Cintré, appealingly.

'Decidedly,' cried Madame de Bellegarde, 'I am the only person here capable of saying something polite! Come to see me; you will need no courage,' she said.

Newman gave a laugh which was not altogether an assent, and took his leave. Madame de Cintré did not take up her sister's challenge to be gracious, but she looked with a certain troubled air at the retreating guest.

CHAPTER 7

One evening, very late, about a week after his visit to Madame de Cintré, Newman's servant brought him a card. It was that of young M. de Bellegarde. When, a few moments later, he went to receive his visitor, he found him standing in the middle of his great gilded parlour and eyeing it from cornice to carpet. M. de Bellegarde's face, it seemed to Newman, expressed a sense of lively entertainment. 'What the devil is he laughing at now?' our hero asked himself. But he put the question without acrimony, for he felt that Madame de Cintré's brother was a good fellow, and he had a presentiment that on this basis of good fellowship they were destined to understand each other. Only, if there was anything to laugh at, he wished to have a glimpse of it too.

'To begin with,' said the young man, as he extended his hand, 'have I come too late?'

'Too late for what?' asked Newman.

'To smoke a cigar with you.'

'You would have to come early to do that,' said Newman. 'I don't smoke.'

'Ah, you are a strong man!'

'But I keep cigars,' Newman added. 'Sit down.'

'Surely, I may not smoke here,' said M. de Bellegarde.

'What is the matter? Is the room too small?'

'It is too large. It is like smoking in a ball-room, or a church.'

'That is what you were laughing at just now?' Newman asked; 'the size of my room?'

'It is not size only,' replied M. de Bellegarde, 'but splendour, and harmony, and beauty of detail. It was the smile of admiration.'

Newman looked at him a moment, and then, 'So it *is* very ugly?' he inquired.

'Ugly, my dear sir? It is magnificent.'

'That is the same thing, I suppose,' said Newman. 'Make yourself comfortable. Your coming to see me, I take it, is an act of friendship. You were not obliged to. Therefore, if anything around here amuses you, it will be all in a pleasant way. Laugh as loud as you please; I like to see my visitors cheerful. Only, I must make this request: that you explain the joke to me as soon as you can speak. I don't want to lose anything, myself.'

M. de Bellegarde stared, with a look of unresentful perplexity. He laid his hand on Newman's sleeve and seemed on the point of saying something, but he suddenly checked himself, leaned back in his chair, and puffed at his cigar. At last, however, breaking silence, 'Certainly,' he said, 'my coming to see you is an act of friendship. Nevertheless I was in a measure obliged to do so. My sister asked me to come, and a request from my sister is, for me, a law. I was near you, and I observed lights in what I supposed were your rooms. It was not a ceremonious hour for making a call, but I was not sorry to do something that would show I was not performing a mere ceremony.'

'Well, here I am as large as life,' said Newman, extending his legs.

'I don't know what you mean,' the young man went on, 'by giving me unlimited leave to laugh. Certainly I am a great laugher, and it is better to laugh too much than too little. But it is not in order that we may laugh together – or separately – that I have, I may say, sought your acquaintance. To speak with almost impudent frankness, you interest me!' All this was uttered by M. de Bellegarde with the modulated smoothness of the man of the world, and, in spite of his excellent English, of the Frenchman; but Newman, at the same time that he sat noting its harmonious flow, perceived that it was not mere mechanical urbanity. Decidedly, there was something in his visitor that he liked. M. de Bellegarde was a foreigner to his finger-tips, and if Newman had met him on a Western prairie he would have felt it proper to address him with a 'How-d'ye-do, Mosseer?' But there was something in his physiognomy which seemed to cast a sort of aerial bridge over the impassable gulf produced by difference of race. He was below the middle height, and robust and agile in figure. Valentin de Bellegarde, Newman afterwards learned, had a mortal dread of the robustness overtaking the agility; he was afraid of growing stout; he was too short, as he said, to afford a belly. He rode and fenced and practised gymnastics with unremitting zeal, and if you greeted him with a 'How well you are looking!' he started and turned pale. In your *well* he read a grosser monosyllable. He had a round head, high above the ears, a crop of hair at once dense and silky, a broad, low forehead, a short nose, of the ironical and inquiring rather than of the dogmatic or sensitive cast, and a moustache as delicate as that of a page in a romance. He resembled his sister not in feature, but in the expression of his clear bright eye, completely void of introspection, and in the way he smiled. The great point in his face was that it was intensely alive – frankly, ardently, gallantly alive. The look of it was like a bell, of which the handle might have been in the young man's soul: at a touch of the handle it rang with a loud silver sound. There was something in his quick, light brown eye which assured you that he was not economising his conscious-ness. He was not living in a corner of it to spare the furniture of the rest. He was squarely encamped in the centre, and he was keeping open house. When he smiled, it was like the movement of a person who in emptying a cup turns it upside down: he gave you the last drop of his jollity. He inspired Newman with something of the same kindness that our hero used to feel in his earlier years for those of his companions who could perform strange and clever tricks – make their joints crack in queer places or whistle at the back of their mouths.

'My sister told me,' M. de Bellegarde continued, 'that I ought to come and remove the impression that I had taken such great pains to produce upon you; the impression that I am a lunatic. Did it strike you that I behaved very oddly the other day?'

'Rather so,' said Newman.

'So my sister tells me.' And M. de Bellegarde watched his host for a moment through his smoke-wreaths. 'If that is the case, I

think we had better let it stand. I didn't try to make you think I
was a lunatic, at all; on the contrary, I wanted to produce a
favourable impression. But if, after all, I made a fool of myself,
it was the intention of Providence. I should injure myself by
protesting too much, for I should seem to set up a claim for
wisdom which, in the sequel of our acquaintance, I could by no
means justify. Set me down as a lunatic with intervals of sanity.'

'Oh, I guess you know what you are about,' said Newman.

'When I am sane, I am very sane; that I admit,' M. de
Bellegarde answered. 'But I didn't come here to talk about
myself. I should like to ask you a few questions. You allow me?'

'Give me a specimen,' said Newman.

'You live here all alone?'

'Absolutely. With whom should I live?'

'For the moment,' said M. de Bellegarde with a smile, 'I am
asking questions, not answering them. You have come to Paris
for your pleasure?'

Newman was silent awhile. Then, at last, 'Everyone asks me
that!' he said with his mild slowness. 'It sounds so awfully
foolish.'

'But at any rate you had a reason.'

'Oh, I came for my pleasure!' said Newman. 'Though it is
foolish, it is true.'

'And you are enjoying it?'

Like any other good American, Newman thought it as well
not to truckle to the foreigner. 'Oh, so-so,' he answered.

M. de Bellegarde puffed his cigar again in silence. 'For myself,'
he said at last, 'I am entirely at your service. Anything I can do
for you I shall be very happy to do. Call upon me at your
convenience. Is there anyone you desire to know – anything you
wish to see? It is a pity you should not enjoy Paris.'

'Oh, I do enjoy it!' said Newman, good-naturedly. 'I'm much
obliged to you.'

'Honestly speaking,' M. de Bellegarde went on, 'there is
something absurd to me in hearing myself make you these offers.
They represent a great deal of good-will, but they represent little
else. You are a successful man and I am a failure, and it's a
turning of the tables to talk as if I could lend you a hand.'

'In what way are you a failure?' asked Newman.

'Oh, I'm not a tragical failure!' cried the young man with a
laugh. 'I have not fallen from a height, and my fiasco has made

no noise. You, evidently, are a success. You have made a
fortune, you have built up an edifice, you are a financial,
commercial power, you can travel about the world until you
have found a soft spot, and lie down in it with the consciousness
of having earned your rest. Is not that true? Well, imagine the
exact reverse of all that, and you have me. I have done nothing
– I can do nothing!'

'Why not?'

'It's a long story. Some day I will tell you. Meanwhile, I'm
right, eh? You are a success? You have made a fortune? It's
none of my business, but, in short, you are rich?'

'That's another thing that it sounds foolish to say,' said
Newman. 'Hang it, no man is rich!'

'I have heard philosophers affirm,' laughed M. de Bellegarde,
'that no man was poor; but your formula strikes me as an
improvement. As a general thing, I confess, I don't like successful
people, and I find clever men who have made great fortunes very
offensive. They tread on my toes; they make me uncomfortable.
But as soon as I saw you, I said to myself, "Ah, there is a man
with whom I shall get on. He has the good-nature of success
and none of the *morgue*;* he has not our confoundedly irritable
French vanity." In short, I took a fancy to you. We are very
different, I'm sure; I don't believe there is a subject on which we
think or feel alike. But I rather think we shall get on, for there is
such a thing, you know, as being too different to quarrel.'

'Oh, I never quarrel,' said Newman.

'Never? Sometimes it's a duty – or at least it's a pleasure. Oh,
I have had two or three delicious quarrels in my day!' and M.
de Bellegarde's handsome smile assumed, at the memory of these
incidents, an almost voluptuous intensity.

With the preamble embodied in his share of the foregoing
fragment of dialogue, he paid our hero a long visit; as the two
men sat with their heels on Newman's glowing hearth, they
heard the small hours of the morning striking larger from a far-
off belfry. Valentin de Bellegarde was, by his own confession, at
all times a great chatterer, and on this occasion he was evidently
in a particularly loquacious mood. It was a tradition of his race
that people of its blood always conferred a favour by their
smiles, and as his enthusiasms were as rare as his civility was
constant, he had a double reason for not suspecting that his
friendship could ever be importunate. Moreover, the flower of

an ancient stem as he was, tradition (since I have used the word) had in his temperament nothing of disagreeable rigidity. It was muffled in sociability and urbanity, as an old dowager in her laces and strings of pearls. Valentin was what is called in France a *gentilhomme*,* of the purest source, and his rule of life, so far as it was definite, was to play the part of a *gentilhomme*. This, it seemed to him, was enough to occupy comfortably a young man of ordinary good parts. But all that he was he was by instinct and not by theory, and the amiability of his character was so great that certain of the aristocratic virtues, which in some aspects seem rather brittle and trenchant, acquired in his application of them an extreme geniality. In his younger years he had been suspected of low tastes, and his mother had greatly feared he would make a slip in the mud of the highway and bespatter the family shield. He had been treated, therefore, to more than his share of schooling and drilling, but his instructors had not succeeded in mounting him upon stilts. They could not spoil his safe spontaneity, and he remained the least cautious and the most lucky of young nobles. He had been tied with so short a rope in his youth that he had now a mortal grudge against family discipline. He had been known to say, within the limits of the family, that, light-headed as he was, the honour of the name was safer in his hands than in those of some of its other members, and that if a day ever came to try it, they should see. His talk was an odd mixture of almost boyish garrulity and of the reserve and discretion of the man of the world, and he seemed to Newman, as afterwards young members of the Latin races often seemed to him, now amusingly juvenile and now appallingly mature. In America, Newman reflected, lads of twenty-five and thirty have old heads and young hearts, or at least young morals; here they have young heads and very aged hearts, morals the most grizzled and wrinkled.

'What I envy you is your liberty,' observed M. de Bellegarde, 'your wide range, your freedom to come and go, your not having a lot of people, who take themselves awfully seriously, expecting something of you. I live,' he added with a sigh, 'beneath the eyes of my admirable mother.'

'It is your own fault; what is to hinder you ranging?' said Newman.

'There is a delightful simplicity in that remark! Everything is to hinder me. To begin with, I have not a penny.'

'I had not a penny when I began to range.'

'Ah, but your poverty was your capital. Being an American, it was impossible you should remain what you were born, and being born poor – do I understand it? – it was therefore inevitable that you should become rich. You were in a position that makes one's mouth water; you looked round you and saw a world full of things you had only to step up to and take hold of. When I was twenty, I looked around me and saw a world with everything ticketed "Hands off!" and the deuce of it was that the ticket seemed meant only for me. I couldn't go into business, I couldn't make money, because I was a Bellegarde. I couldn't go into politics, because I was a Bellegarde – the Bellegardes don't recognise the Bonapartes.* I couldn't go into literature, because I was a dunce. I couldn't marry a rich girl, because no Bellegarde had ever married a *roturière*,* and it was not proper that I should begin. We shall have to come to it, yet. Marriageable heiresses, *de notre bord*,* are not to be had for nothing; it must be name for name, and fortune for fortune. The only thing I could do was to go and fight for the Pope. That I did, punctiliously, and received an apostolic flesh-wound at Castelfidardo. It did neither the Holy Father nor me any good, that I could see. Rome was doubtless a very amusing place in the days of Caligula, but it has sadly fallen off since. I passed three years in the Castle of St Angelo,* and then came back to secular life.'

'So you have no profession – you do nothing?' said Newman.

'I do nothing! I am supposed to amuse myself, and, to tell the truth, I have amused myself. One can, if one knows how. But you can't keep it up for ever. I am good for another five years, perhaps, but I foresee that after that I shall lose my appetite. Then what shall I do? I think I shall turn monk. Seriously, I think I shall tie a rope round my waist and go into a monastery. It was an old custom, and the old customs were very good. People understood life quite as well as we do. They kept the pot boiling till it cracked, and then they put it on the shelf altogether.'

'Are you very religious?' asked Newman, in a tone which gave the inquiry a grotesque effect.

M. de Bellegarde evidently appreciated the comical element in the question, but he looked at Newman a moment with extreme soberness. 'I am a very good Catholic. I respect the Church. I adore the blessed Virgin. I fear the Devil.'

'Well, then,' said Newman, 'you are very well fixed. You have got pleasure in the present and religion in the future; what do you complain of?'

'It's a part of one's pleasure to complain. There is something in your own circumstances that irritates me. You are the first man I have ever envied. It's singular, but so it is. I have known many men who besides any factitious advantages that I may possess, had money and brains into the bargain; but somehow they have never disturbed my good-humour. But you have got something that I should have liked to have. It is not money, it is not even brains – though no doubt yours are excellent. It is not your six feet of height, though I should have rather liked to be a couple of inches taller. It's a sort of air you have of being thoroughly at home in the world. When I was a boy, my father told me that it was by such an air as that that people recognised a Bellegarde. He called my attention to it. He didn't advise me to cultivate it; he said that as we grew up it always came of itself. I supposed it had come to me, because I think I have always had the feeling. My place in life was made for me, and it seemed easy to occupy it. But you who, as I understand it, have made your own place, you who, as you told us the other day, have manufactured wash-tubs – you strike me, somehow, as a man who stands at his ease, who looks at things from a height. I fancy you going about the world like a man travelling on a railroad in which he owns a large amount of stock. You make me feel as if I had missed something. What is it?'

'It is the proud consciousness of honest toil – of having manufactured a few wash-tubs,' said Newman, at once jocose and serious.

'Oh no; I have seen men who had done even more, men who had made not only wash-tubs, but soap – strong-smelling yellow soap, in great bars; and they never made me the least uncomfortable.'

'Then it's the privilege of being an American citizen,' said Newman. 'That sets a man up.'

'Possibly,' rejoined M. de Bellegarde. 'But I am forced to say that I have seen a great many American citizens who didn't seem at all set up or in the least like large stockholders. I never envied them. I rather think the thing is an accomplishment of your own.'

'Oh, come,' said Newman, 'you will make me proud!'

'No, I shall not. You have nothing to do with pride, or with humility – that is a part of this easy manner of yours. People are proud only when they have something to lose, and humble when they have something to gain.'

'I don't know what I have to lose,' said Newman, 'but I certainly have something to gain.'

'What is it?' asked his visitor.

Newman hesitated awhile. 'I will tell you when I know you better.'

'I hope that will be soon! Then, if I can help you to gain it, I shall be happy.'

'Perhaps you may,' said Newman.

'Don't forget, then, that I am your servant,' M. de Bellegarde answered; and shortly afterwards he took his departure.

During the next three weeks Newman saw Bellegarde several times, and without formally swearing an eternal friendship the two men established a sort of comradeship. To Newman, Bellegarde was the ideal Frenchman, the Frenchman of tradition and romance, so far as our hero was acquainted with these mystical influences. Gallant, expansive, amusing, more pleased himself with the effect he produced than those (even when they were well pleased) for whom he produced it; a master of all the distinctively social virtues and a votary of all agreeable sensations; a devotee of something mysterious and sacred to which he occasionally alluded in terms more ecstatic even than those in which he spoke of the last pretty woman, and which was simply the beautiful though somewhat superannuated image of *honour*; he was irresistibly entertaining and enlivening; and he formed a character to which Newman was as capable of doing justice when he had once been placed in contact with it, as he was unlikely, in musing upon the possible mixtures of our human ingredients, mentally to have foreshadowed it. Bellegarde did not in the least cause him to modify his needful premise that all Frenchmen are of a frothy and imponderable substance; he simply reminded him that light materials may be beaten up into a most agreeable compound. No two companions could be more different, but their differences made a capital basis for a friendship of which the distinctive characteristic was that it was extremely amusing to each.

Valentin de Bellegarde lived in the basement of an old house in the Rue d'Anjou St Honoré, and his small apartments lay between the court of the house and an old garden which spread itself behind it – one of those large, sunless, humid gardens into which you look unexpectingly in Paris from back windows, wondering how among the grudging habitations they find their space. When Newman returned Bellegarde's visit, he hinted that *his* lodging was at least as much a laughing matter as his own. But its oddities were of a different cast from those of our hero's gilded saloons on the Boulevard Haussmann: the place was low, dusky, contracted, and crowded with curious bric-à-brac. Bellegarde, penniless patrician as he was, was an insatiable collector, and his walls were covered with rusty arms and ancient panels and platters, his doorways draped in faded tapestries, his floors muffled in the skins of beasts. Here and there was one of those uncomfortable tributes to elegance in which the upholsterer's art, in France, is so prolific; a curtained recess with a sheet of looking-glass in which, among the shadows, you could see nothing; a divan on which, for its festoons and furbelows, you could not sit: a fireplace draped, flounced, and frilled to the complete exclusion of fire. The young man's possessions were in picturesque disorder, and his apartment was pervaded by the odour of cigars, mingled with perfumes more inscrutable. Newman thought it a damp, gloomy place to live in, and was puzzled by the obstructive and fragmentary character of the furniture.

Bellegarde, according to the custom of his country, talked very generously about himself, and unveiled the mysteries of his private history with an unsparing hand. Inevitably, he had a vast deal to say about women, and he used frequently to indulge in sentimental and ironical apostrophes to these authors of his joys and woes. 'Oh, the women, the women, and the things they have made me do!' he would exclaim with a lustrous eye. '*C'est égal*,* of all the follies and stupidities I have committed for them I would not have missed one!' On this subject Newman maintained an habitual reserve; to expatiate largely upon it had always seemed to him a proceeding vaguely analogous to the cooing of pigeons and the chatterings of monkeys, and even inconsistent with a fully-developed human character. But

Bellegarde's confidences greatly amused him, and rarely displeased him, for the generous young Frenchman was not a cynic.
'I really think,' he had once said, 'that I am not more depraved
than most of my contemporaries. They are tolerably depraved,
my contemporaries!' He said wonderfully pretty things about
his female friends, and, numerous and various as they had been,
declared that on the whole there was more good in them than
harm. 'But you are not to take that as advice,' he added. 'As an
authority I am very untrustworthy. I'm prejudiced in their
favour; I'm an *idealist*!' Newman listened to him with his
impartial smile, and was glad, for his own sake, that he had fine
feelings; but he mentally repudiated the idea of a Frenchman
having discovered any merit in the amiable sex which he himself
did not suspect. M. de Bellegarde, however, did not confine his
conversation to the autobiographical channel; he questioned our
hero largely as to the events of his own life, and Newman told
him some better stories than any that Bellegarde carried in his
budget. He narrated his career, in fact, from the beginning,
through all its variations, and whenever his companion's credulity, or his habits of gentility, appeared to protest, it amused him
to heighten the colour of the episode. Newman had sat with
Western humorists in knots, round cast-iron stoves, and seen
'tall' stories grow taller without toppling over, and his own
imagination had learned the trick of piling up consistent wonders. Bellegarde's regular attitude at last became that of laughing
self-defence; to maintain his reputation as an all-knowing
Frenchman, he doubted of everything, wholesale. The result of
this was that Newman found it impossible to convince him of
certain time-honoured verities.

'But the details don't matter,' said M. de Bellegarde. 'You
have evidently had some surprising adventures; you have seen
some strange sides of life, you have revolved to and fro over a
whole continent as I walk up and down the Boulevard. You are
a man of the world with a vengeance! You have spent some
deadly dull hours, and you have done some extremely disagreeable things: you have shovelled sand, as a boy, for supper, and
you have eaten roast dog in a gold-diggers' camp. You have
stood casting up figures for ten hours at a time, and you have
sat through Methodist sermons for the sake of looking at a
pretty girl in another pew. All that is rather stiff, as we say. But
at any rate you have done something and you are something;

you have used your will and you have made your fortune. You have not stupefied yourself with debauchery and you have not mortgaged your fortune to social conveniences. You take things easily, and you have fewer prejudices even than I, who pretend to have none, but who in reality have three or four. Happy man, you are strong and you are free. But what the deuce,' demanded the young man in conclusion, 'do you propose to do with such advantages? Really to use them you need a better world than this. There is nothing worth your while here.'

'Oh, I think there is something,' said Newman.

'What is it?'

'Well,' murmured Newman, 'I will tell you some other time!'

In this way our hero delayed from day to day broaching a subject which he had very much at heart. Meanwhile, however, he was growing practically familiar with it; in other words, he had called again, three times, on Madame de Cintré. On only two of these occasions had he found her at home, and on each of them she had other visitors. Her visitors were numerous and extremely loquacious, and they exacted much of their hostess's attention. She found time, however, to bestow a little of it on Newman, in an occasional vague smile, the very vagueness of which pleased him, allowing him as it did to fill it out mentally, both at the time and afterwards, with such meanings as most pleased him. He sat by without speaking, looking at the entrances and exits, the greetings and chatterings, of Madame de Cintré's visitors. He felt as if he were at the play, and as if his own speaking would be an interruption; sometimes he wished he had a book to follow the dialogue; he half expected to see a woman in a white cap and pink ribbons* come and offer him one for two francs. Some of the ladies looked at him very hard – or very soft, as you please; others seemed profoundly unconscious of his presence. The men only looked at Madame de Cintré. This was inevitable; for whether one called her beautiful or not, she entirely occupied and filled one's vision, just as an agreeable sound fills one's ear. Newman had but twenty distinct words with her, but he carried away an impression to which solemn promises could not have given a higher value. She was part of the play that he was seeing acted, quite as much as her companions; but how she filled the stage, and how much better she did it! Whether she rose or seated herself; whether she went with her departing friends to the door and lifted up the heavy curtain as they passed out, and stood an instant looking after them and giving them the last nod; or whether she leaned back in her chair with her arms crossed and her eyes resting, listening and smiling; she gave Newman the feeling that he should like to have her always before him, moving slowly to and fro along the whole scale of expressive hospitality. If it might be *to* him, it would be well; if it might be *for* him, it would be still better! She was so tall and yet so light, so active and yet so still, so elegant and yet so simple, so frank and yet so mysterious! It was the mystery – it was what she was off the stage, as it were – that interested Newman most of all. He could not have told you what warrant he had for talking about mysteries; if it had been his habit to express himself in poetic figures he might have said that in observing Madame de Cintré he seemed to see the vague circle which sometimes accompanies the partly-filled disc of the moon. It was not that she was reserved; on the contrary, she was as frank as flowing water. But he was sure she had qualities which she herself did not suspect.

He had abstained for several reasons from saying some of these things to Bellegarde. One reason was that before proceeding to any act he was always circumspect, conjectural, contemplative; he had little eagerness, as became a man who felt that whenever he really began to move he walked with long steps. And then it simply pleased him not to speak – it occupied him, it excited him. But one day Bellegarde had been dining with him, at a restaurant, and they had sat long over their dinner. On rising from it, Bellegarde proposed that, to help them through the rest of the evening, they should go and see Madame Dandelard. Madame Dandelard was a little Italian lady who had married a Frenchman who proved to be a rake and a brute and the torment of her life. Her husband had spent all her money, and then, lacking the means of obtaining more expensive pleasures, had taken, in his duller hours, to beating her. She had a blue spot* somewhere, which she showed to several persons, including Bellegarde. She had obtained a separation from her husband, collected the scraps of her fortune (they were very meagre) and come to live in Paris, where she was staying at a *hôtel garni*.* She was always looking for an apartment, and visiting inquiringly, those of other people. She was very pretty, very childlike, and she made very extraordinary remarks. Bellegarde had made her acquaintance, and the source of his interest in her was, according to his own declaration, a curiosity as to what would become of her. 'She is poor, she is pretty, and she is silly,' he said; 'it seems to me she can go only one way. It's a pity, but it can't be helped. I will give her six months. She has nothing to fear from me, but I am watching the process. I am curious to see just how things will go. Yes, I know what you are going to say: this horrible Paris hardens one's heart. But it quickens one's wits, and it ends by teaching one a refinement of observation! To see this little woman's little drama play itself out, now, is, for me, an intellectual pleasure.'

'If she is going to throw herself away,' Newman had said, 'you ought to stop her.'

'Stop her? How stop her?'

'Talk to her; give her some good advice.'

Bellegarde laughed. 'Heaven deliver us both! Imagine the situation! Go and advise her yourself.'

It was after this that Newman had gone with Bellegarde to see Madame Dandelard. When they came away, Bellegarde reproached his companion. 'Where was your famous advice?' he asked. 'I didn't hear a word of it.'

'Oh, I give it up,' said Newman, simply.

'Then you are as bad as I!' said Bellegarde.

'No, because I don't take an "intellectual pleasure" in her prospective adventures. I don't in the least want to see her going down hill. I had rather look the other way. But why,' he asked, in a moment, 'don't you get your sister to go and see her?'

Bellegarde stared. 'Go and see Madame Dandelard – my sister?'

'She might talk to her to very good purpose.'

Bellegarde shook his head with sudden gravity. 'My sister can't see that sort of person. Madame Dandelard is nothing at all; they would never meet.'

'I should think,' said Newman, 'that your sister might see whom she pleased.' And he privately resolved that after he knew her a little better, he would ask Madame de Cintré to go and talk to the foolish little Italian lady.

After his dinner with Bellegarde, on the occasion I have mentioned, he demurred to his companion's proposal that they should go again and listen to Madame Dandelard describe her sorrows and her bruises. 'I have something better in mind,' he said; 'come home with me and finish the evening before my fire.'

Bellegarde always welcomed the prospect of a long stretch of conversation, and before long the two men sat watching the great blaze which scattered its scintillations over the high adornments of Newman's ballroom.

CHAPTER 8

'Tell me something about your sister,' Newman began, abruptly.

Bellegarde turned and gave him a quick look. 'Now that I think of it, you have never yet asked me a question about her.'

'I know that very well.'

'If it is because you don't trust me, you are very right,' said Bellegarde. 'I can't talk of her rationally. I admire her too much.'

'Talk of her as you can,' rejoined Newman. 'Let yourself go.'

'Well, we are very good friends; we are such a brother and sister as have not been seen since Orestes and Electra.* You have seen her; you know what she is: tall, thin, light, imposing, and gentle, half a *grande dame** and half an angel; a mixture of pride and humility, of the eagle and the dove. She looks like a statue which had failed as stone, resigned itself to its grave defects, and come to life as flesh and blood, to wear white capes and long trains.* All I can say is that she really possesses every merit that her face, her glance, her smile, the tone of her voice, lead you to expect; it is saying a great deal. As a general thing, when a woman seems very charming, I should say "Beware!" But in proportion as Claire seems charming you may fold your arms and let yourself float with the current; you are safe. She is so good! I have never seen a woman half so perfect or so complete. She has everything; that is all I can say about her. There!' Bellegarde concluded: 'I told you I should rhapsodise.'

Newman was silent awhile, as if he were turning over his companion's words. 'She is very good, eh?' he repeated at last.

'Divinely good!'

'Kind, charitable, gentle, generous?'

'Generosity itself; kindness double-distilled!'

'Is she clever!'

'She is the most intelligent woman I know. Try her, some day, with something difficult, and you will see.'

'Is she fond of admiration?'

'*Parbleu!*'* cried Bellegarde; 'what woman is not?'

'Ah, when they are too fond of admiration they commit all kinds of follies to get it.'

'I did not say she was too fond!' Bellegarde exclaimed. 'Heaven forbid I should say anything so idiotic. She is not *too* anything! If I were to say she was ugly, I should not mean she was too ugly. She is fond of pleasing, and if you are pleased she is grateful. If you are not pleased, she lets it pass and thinks the worse neither of you nor of herself. I imagine, though, she hopes the saints in heaven are, for I am sure she is incapable of trying to please by any means of which they would disapprove.'

'Is she grave or gay?' asked Newman.

'She is both; not alternately, for she is always the same. There is gravity in her gaiety, and gaiety in her gravity. But there is no reason why she should be particularly gay.'

'Is she unhappy?'

'I won't say that, for unhappiness is according as one takes things, and Claire takes them according to some receipt communicated to her by the Blessed Virgin in a vision. To be unhappy is to be disagreeable, which, for her, is out of the question. So she has arranged her circumstances so as to be happy in them.'

'She is a philosopher,' said Newman.

'No, she is simply a very nice woman.'

'Her circumstances, at any rate, have been disagreeable?'

Bellegarde hesitated a moment – a thing he very rarely did. 'Oh, my dear fellow, if I go into the history of my family I shall give you more than you bargain for.'

'No, on the contrary, I bargain for that,' said Newman.

'We shall have to appoint a special séance, then, beginning early. Suffice it for the present that Claire has not slept on roses. She made, at eighteen, a marriage that was expected to be brilliant, but that turned out like a lamp that goes out; all smoke and bad smell. M. de Cintré was sixty years old, and an odious old gentleman. He lived, however, but a short time, and after his death his family pounced upon his money, brought a lawsuit against his widow, and pushed things very hard. Their case was a good one, for M. de Cintré, who had been trustee for some of his relatives, appeared to have been guilty of some very irregular practices. In the course of the suit some revelations were made as to his private history which my sister found so displeasing that she ceased to defend herself and washed her hands of the property. This required some pluck, for she was between two fires, her husband's family opposing her and her own family forcing her. My mother and my brother wished her to cleave to what they regarded as her rights. But she resisted firmly, and at last bought her freedom – obtained my mother's assent to dropping the suit at the price of a promise.'

'What was the promise?'

'To do anything else, for the next ten years, that was asked of her – anything, that is, but marry.'

'She had disliked her husband very much?'

'No one knows how much!'

'The marriage had been made in your horrible French way,' Newman continued, 'made by the two families without her having any voice?'

'It was a chapter for a novel. She saw M. de Cintré for the first time a month before the wedding, after everything, to the minutest detail, had been arranged. She turned white when she looked at him, and white she remained till her wedding-day. The evening before the ceremony she swooned away, and she spent the whole night in sobs. My mother sat holding her two hands, and my brother walked up and down the room. I declared it was revolting, and told my sister publicly that if she would refuse downright, I would stand by her. I was told to go about my business, and she became Comtesse de Cintré.'

'Your brother,' said Newman reflectively, 'must be a very nice young man.'

'He is very nice, though he is not young. He is upwards of fifty; fifteen years my senior. He has been a father to my sister and me. He is a very remarkable man; he has the best manners in France. He is extremely clever; indeed he is very learned. He is writing a history of The Princesses of France who never Married.' This was said by Bellegarde with extreme gravity, looking straight at Newman, and with an eye that betokened no mental reservation; or that, at least, almost betokened none.

Newman perhaps discovered there what little there was, for he presently said: 'You don't love your brother.'

'I beg your pardon,' said Bellegarde ceremoniously; 'well-bred people always love their brothers.'

'Well, I don't love him, then!' Newman answered.

'Wait till you know him!' rejoined Bellegarde, and this time he smiled.

'Is your mother also very remarkable?' Newman asked, after a pause.

'For my mother,' said Bellegarde, now with intense gravity, 'I have the highest admiration. She is a very extraordinary woman. You cannot approach her without perceiving it.'

'She is the daughter, I believe, of an English nobleman.'

'Of the Earl of St Dunstan's.'

'Is the Earl of St Dunstan's a very old family?'

'So-so; the sixteenth century. It is on my father's side that we go back – back, back, back. The family antiquaries themselves lose breath. At last they stop, panting and fanning themselves, somewhere in the ninth century, under Charlemagne. That is where we begin.'

'There is no mistake about it?' said Newman.

'I'm sure I hope not. We have been mistaken at least for several centuries.'

'And you have always married into old families?'

'As a rule; though in so long a stretch of time there have been some exceptions. Three or four Bellegardes, in the seventeenth and eighteenth centuries, took wives out of the *bourgeoisie** – married lawyers' daughters.'

'A lawyer's daughter; that's very bad, is it?' asked Newman.

'Horrible! one of us, in the Middle Ages, did better: he married a beggar-maid, like King Cophetua.* That was really better; it was like marrying a bird or a monkey; one didn't have to think about her family at all. Our women have always done well; they have never even gone into the *petite noblesse.** There is, I believe, not a case on record of a misalliance among the women.'

Newman turned this over awhile, and then at last he said: 'You offered, the first time you came to see me, to render me any service you could. I told you that some time I would mention something you might do. Do you remember?'

'Remember? I have been counting the hours.'

'Very well; here's your chance. Do what you can to make your sister think well of me.'

Bellegarde stared, with a smile. 'Why, I'm sure she thinks as well of you as possible, already.'

'An opinion founded on seeing me three or four times? That is putting me off with very little. I want something more. I have been thinking of it a good deal, and at last I have decided to tell you. I should like very much to marry Madame de Cintré.'

Bellegarde had been looking at him with quickened expectancy, and with the smile with which he had greeted Newman's allusion to his promised request. At this last announcement he continued to gaze; but his smile went through two or three curious phases. It felt, apparently, a momentary impulse to broaden; but this it immediately checked. Then it remained for some instants taking counsel with itself, at the end of which it decreed a retreat. It slowly effaced itself and left a look of seriousness modified by the desire not to be rude. Extreme surprise had come into the Count Valentin's face; but he had reflected that it would be uncivil to leave it there. And yet, what the deuce was he to do with it? He got up, in his agitation, and stood before the chimney-piece, still looking at Newman. He was a longer time thinking what to say than one would have expected.

'If you can't render me the service I ask,' said Newman, 'say it out!'

'Let me hear it again, distinctly,' said Bellegarde. 'It's very important, you know. I shall plead your cause with my sister, because you want – you want to marry her? That's it, eh?'

'Oh, I don't say plead my cause, exactly; I shall try and do that myself. But say a good word for me, now and then – let her know that you think well of me.'

At this, Bellegarde gave a little light laugh.

'What I want chiefly, after all,' Newman went on, 'is just to let you know what I have in mind. I suppose that is what you expect, isn't it? I want to do what is customary over here. If there is anything particular to be done, let me know and I will do it. I wouldn't for the world approach Madame de Cintré without all the proper forms. If I ought to go and tell your mother, why I will go and tell her. I will go and tell your brother, even. I will go and tell anyone you please. As I don't know anyone else, I begin by telling you. But that, if it is a social obligation, is a pleasure as well.'

'Yes, I see – I see,' said Bellegarde, lightly stroking his chin.

'You have a very right feeling about it, but I'm glad you have begun with me.' He paused, hesitated, and then turned away and walked slowly the length of the room. Newman got up and stood leaning against the mantelshelf, with his hands in his pockets, watching Bellegarde's promenade. The young Frenchman came back and stopped in front of him. 'I give it up,' he said; 'I will not pretend I am not surprised. I am – hugely! *Ouf!** It's a relief.'

'That sort of news is always a surprise,' said Newman. 'No matter what you have done, people are never prepared. But if you are so surprised, I hope at least you are pleased.'

'Come!' said Bellegarde. 'I am going to be tremendously frank. I don't know whether I am pleased or horrified.'

'If you are pleased, I shall be glad,' said Newman, 'and I shall be – encouraged. If you are horrified, I shall be sorry, but I shall not be discouraged. You must make the best of it.'

'That is quite right – that is your only possible attitude. You are perfectly serious?'

'Am I a Frenchman, that I should not be?' asked Newman. 'But why is it, by-the-bye, that you should be horrified?'

Bellegarde raised his hand to the back of his head and rubbed his hair quickly up and down, thrusting out the tip of his tongue as he did so. 'Why, you are not noble, for instance,' he said.

'The devil I am not!' exclaimed Newman.

'Oh,' said Bellegarde, a little more seriously, 'I did not know you had a title.'

'A title? What do you mean by a title?' asked Newman. 'A count, a duke, a marquis? I don't know anything about that, I don't know who is and who is not. But I say I am noble. I don't exactly know what you mean by it, but it's a fine word and a fine idea; I put in a claim to it.'

'But what have you to show, my dear fellow; what proofs?'

'Anything you please! But you don't suppose I am going to undertake to prove that I am noble. It is for you to prove the contrary.'

'That's easily done. You have manufactured wash-tubs.'

Newman stared a moment. 'Therefore I am not noble? I don't see it. Tell me something I have *not* done – something I cannot do.'

'You cannot marry a woman like Madame de Cintré for the asking.'

'I believe you mean,' said Newman slowly, 'that I am not good enough.'

'Brutally speaking – yes!'

Bellegarde had hesitated a moment, and while he hesitated Newman's attentive glance had grown somewhat eager. In answer to these last words he for a moment said nothing. He simply blushed a little. Then he raised his eyes to the ceiling and stood looking at one of the rosy cherubs that was painted upon it. 'Of course I don't expect to marry any woman for the asking,' he said at last; 'I expect first to make myself acceptable to her. She must like me, to begin with. But that I am not good enough to make a trial is rather a surprise.'

Bellegarde wore a look of mingled perplexity, sympathy, and amusement. 'You should not hesitate, then, to go up tomorrow and ask a duchess to marry you?'

'Not if I thought she would suit me. But I am very fastidious; she might not at all.'

Bellegarde's amusement began to prevail. 'And you should be surprised if she refused you?'

Newman hesitated a moment. 'It sounds conceited to say Yes; but, nevertheless, I think I should. For I should make a very handsome offer.'

'What would it be?'

'Everything she wishes. If I get hold of a woman that comes up to my standard, I shall think nothing too good for her. I have been a long time looking, and I find such women are rare. To combine the qualities I require seems to be difficult, but when the difficulty is vanquished it deserves a reward. My wife shall have a good position, and I am not afraid to say that I shall be a good husband.'

'And these qualities that you require – what are they?'

'Goodness, beauty, intelligence, a fine education, personal elegance – everything, in a word, that makes a splendid woman.'

'And noble birth, evidently,' said Bellegarde.

'Oh, throw that in, by all means, if it's there. The more the better!'

'And my sister seems to you to have all these things?'

'She is exactly what I have been looking for. She is my dream realised.'

'And you would make her a very good husband?'

'That is what I wanted you to tell her.'

Bellegarde laid his hand on his companion's arm a moment, looked at him with his head on one side, from head to foot, and then, with a loud laugh, and shaking the other hand in the air, turned away. He walked again the length of the room, and again he came back and stationed himself in front of Newman. 'All this is very interesting – it is very curious. In what I said just now I was speaking, not for myself, but for my traditions, my superstitions. For myself, really, your proposal tickles me. It startled me at first, but the more I think of it the more I see in it. It's no use attempting to explain anything; you won't understand me. After all, I don't see why you need; it's no great loss.'

'Oh, if there is anything more to explain, try it! I want to proceed with my eyes open. I will do my best to understand.'

'No,' said Bellegarde, 'it's disagreeable to me; I give it up. I liked you the first time I saw you, and I will abide by that. It would be quite odious for me to come talking to you as if I could patronise you. I have told you before that I envy you; *vous m'imposez,** as we say. I didn't know you much until within five minutes. So we will let things go, and I will say nothing to you that, if our positions were reversed, you would not say to me.'

I do not know whether, in renouncing the mysterious opportunity to which he alluded, Bellegarde felt that he was doing something very generous. If so, he was not rewarded; his generosity was not appreciated. Newman quite failed to recognise the young Frenchman's power to wound his feelings, and he had now no sense of escaping or coming off easily. He did not thank his companion even with a glance. 'My eyes are open, though,' he said, 'so far as that you have practically told me that your family and your friends will turn up their noses at me. I have never thought much about the reasons that make it proper for people to turn up their noses, and so I can only decide the question off-hand. Looking at it in that way I can't see anything in it. I simply think, if you want to know, that I'm as good as the best. Who the best are, I don't pretend to say. I have never thought much about that either. To tell the truth, I have always had rather a good opinion of myself; a man who is successful can't help it. But I will admit that I was conceited. What I don't say Yes to is that I don't stand high – as high as any one else. This is a line of speculation I should not have chosen, but you must remember you began it yourself. I should never have dreamed that I was on the defensive, or that I had to justify myself; but if your people will have it so, I will do my best.'

'But you offered, awhile ago, to make your court, as we say, to my mother and my brother.'

'Damn it!' cried Newman, 'I want to be polite.'

'Good!' rejoined Bellegarde; 'this will go far, it will be very entertaining. Excuse my speaking of it in that cold-blooded fashion, but the matter must, of necessity, be for me something of a spectacle. It's positively exciting. But apart from that I sympathise with you, and I shall be actor, so far as I can, as well as spectator. You are a capital fellow; I believe in you and I back you. The simple fact that you appreciate my sister will serve as the proof I was asking for. All men are equal – especially men of taste!'

'Do you think,' asked Newman presently, 'that Madame de Cintré is determined not to marry?'

'That is my impression. But that is not against you; it's for you to make her change her mind.'

'I am afraid it will be hard,' said Newman gravely.

'I don't think it will be easy. In a general way I don't see why a widow should ever marry again. She has gained the benefits of matrimony – freedom and consideration – and she has got rid of the drawbacks. Why should she put her head into the noose again? Her usual motive is ambition; if a man can offer her a great position, make her a princess or an ambassadress, she may think the compensation sufficient.'

'And – in that way – is Madame de Cintré ambitious?'

'Who knows?' said Bellegarde, with a profound shrug. 'I don't pretend to say all that she is or all that she is not. I think she might be touched by the prospect of becoming the wife of a great man. But in a certain way, I believe, whatever she does will be the *improbable*. Don't be too confident, but don't absolutely doubt. Your best chance for success will be precisely in being, to her mind, unusual, unexpected, original. Don't try to be any one else; be simply yourself, out and out. Something or other can't fail to come of it; I am very curious to see what.'

'I am much obliged to you for your advice,' said Newman. 'And,' he added, with a smile, 'I am glad, for your sake, I am going to be so amusing.'

'It will be more than amusing,' said Bellegarde; 'it will be inspiring. I look at it from my point of view, and you from yours. After all, anything for a change! And only yesterday I was yawning so as to dislocate my jaw, and declaring that there was nothing new under the sun! If it isn't new to see you come into the family as a suitor, I am very much mistaken. Let me say that, my dear fellow; I won't call it anything else, bad or good; I will simply call it *new*.' And overcome with a sense of the novelty thus foreshadowed, Valentin de Bellegarde threw himself into a deep arm-chair before the fire, and with a fixed intense smile, seemed to read a vision of it in the flame of the logs. After awhile he looked up. 'Go ahead, my boy; you have my good wishes,' he said. 'But it is really a pity you don't understand me, that you don't know just what I am doing.'

'Oh,' said Newman laughing, 'don't do anything wrong. Leave me to myself, rather, or defy me, out and out. I wouldn't lay any load on your conscience.'

Bellegarde sprang up again; he was evidently excited; there was a warmer spark even than usual in his eye. 'You never will understand – you never will know,' he said; 'and if you succeed, and I turn out to have helped you, you will never be grateful, not as I shall deserve you should be. You will be an excellent fellow always, but you will not be grateful. But it doesn't matter, for I shall get my own fun out of it.' And he broke into an extravagant laugh. 'You look puzzled,' he added; 'you look almost frightened.'

'It *is* a pity,' said Newman, 'that I don't understand you. I shall lose some very good jokes.'

'I told you, you remember, that we were very strange people,' Bellegarde went on. 'I give you warning again. We are! My mother is strange, my brother is strange, and I verily believe that I am stranger than either. You will even find my sister a little strange. Old trees have crooked branches, old houses have queer cracks, old races have odd secrets. Remember that we are eight hundred years old!'

'Very good,' said Newman; 'that's the sort of thing I came to Europe for. You come into my programme.'

'*Touchez-là*,* then,' said Bellegarde, putting out his hand. 'It's a bargain: I accept you; I espouse your cause. It's because I like you, in a great measure; but that is not the only reason.' And he stood holding Newman's hand and looking at him askance.

'What is the other one?'

'I am in the Opposition. I dislike someone else.'

'Your brother?' asked Newman, in his unmodulated voice.

Bellegarde laid his finger upon his lips with a whispered *hush!* 'Old races have strange secrets!' he said. 'Put yourself into motion, come and see my sister, and be assured of my sympathy!' And on this he took his leave.

Newman dropped into a chair before his fire, and sat a long time staring into the blaze.

CHAPTER 9

He went to see Madame de Cintré the next day, and was informed by the servant that she was at home. He passed as usual up the large cold staircase, and through a spacious vestibule above, where the walls seemed all composed of small door panels, touched with long-faded gilding; whence he was ushered into the sitting-room in which he had already been received. It was empty, and the servant told him that Madame la Comtesse would presently appear. He had time, while he waited, to wonder whether Bellegarde had seen his sister since the evening before, and whether in this case he had spoken to her of their talk. In this case Madame de Cintré's receiving him was an encouragement. He felt a certain trepidation as he reflected that she might come in with the knowledge of his supreme admiration and of the project he had built upon it in her eyes; but the feeling was not disagreeable. Her face could wear no look that would make it less beautiful, and he was sure beforehand that however she might take the proposal he had in reserve, she would not take it in scorn or in irony. He had a feeling that if she could only read the bottom of his heart, and measure the extent of his good-will toward her, she would be entirely kind.

She came in at last, after so long an interval that he wondered whether she had been hesitating. She smiled with her usual frankness, and held out her hand; she looked at him straight with her soft and luminous eyes, and said, without a tremor in her voice, that she was glad to see him, and that she hoped he was well. He found in her what he had found before – that faint perfume of a personal shyness worn away by contact with the world, but the more perceptible the more closely you approached her. This lingering diffidence seemed to give a peculiar value to what was definite and assured in her manner; it made it seem like an accomplishment, a beautiful talent, something that one might compare to an exquisite touch in a pianist. It was, in fact, Madame de Cintré's 'authority', as they say of artists, that especially impressed and fascinated Newman; he always came back to the feeling that when he should complete himself by taking a wife, that was the way he should like his wife to interpret him to the world. The only trouble, indeed, was that when the instrument was so perfect it seemed to interpose too much between you and the genius that used it. Madame de Cintré gave Newman the sense of an elaborate education, of her having passed through mysterious ceremonies and processes of culture in her youth, of her having been fashioned and made flexible to certain exalted social needs. All this, as I have affirmed, made her seem rare and precious – a very expensive article, as he would have said, and one which a man with an ambition to have everything about him of the best would find it highly agreeable to possess. But looking at the matter with an eye to private felicity, Newman wondered where, in so exquisite a compound, nature and art showed their dividing line. Where did the special intention separate from the habit of good manners? Where did urbanity end and sincerity begin? Newman asked himself these questions even while he stood ready to accept the admired object in all its complexity; he felt that he could do so in profound security, and examine its mechanism afterwards, at leisure.

'I am very glad to find you alone,' he said. 'You know I have never had such good luck before.'

'But you have seemed before very well contented with your luck,' said Madame de Cintré. 'You have sat and watched my visitors with an air of quiet amusement. What have you thought of them?'

'Oh, I have thought the ladies were very elegant and very graceful, and wonderfully quick at repartee. But what I have chiefly thought has been that they only help me to admire you.' This was not gallantry on Newman's part – an art in which he was quite unversed. It was simply the instinct of the practical man, who had quite made up his mind what he wanted, and was now beginning to take active steps to obtain it.

Madame de Cintré started slightly, and raised her eyebrows; she had evidently not expected so fervid a compliment. 'Oh, in that case,' she said, with a laugh, 'your finding me alone is not good luck for me. I hope some one will come in quickly.'

'I hope not,' said Newman. 'I have something particular to say to you. Have you seen your brother?'

'Yes; I saw him an hour ago.'

'Did he tell you that he had seen me last night?'

'He said so.'

'And did he tell you what we had talked about?'

Madame de Cintré hesitated a moment. As Newman asked these questions she had grown a little pale, as if she regarded what was coming as necessary, but not as agreeable. 'Did you give him a message to me?' she asked.

'It was not exactly a message – I asked him to render me a service.'

'The service was to sing your praises, was it not?' And she accompanied this question with a little smile, as if to make it easier to herself.

'Yes, that is what it really amounts to,' said Newman. 'Did he sing my praises?'

'He spoke very well of you. But when I know that it was by your special request, of course I must take his eulogy with a grain of salt.'

'Oh, that makes no difference,' said Newman. 'Your brother would not have spoken well of me unless he believed what he was saying. He is too honest for that.'

'Are you very deep?' said Madame de Cintré. 'Are you trying to please me by praising my brother? I confess it is a good way.'

'For me, any way that succeeds will be good. I will praise your brother all day, if that will help me. He is a noble little fellow. He has made me feel, in promising to do what he can to help me, that I can depend upon him.'

'Don't make too much of that,' said Madame de Cintré. 'He can help you very little.'

'Of course I must work my way myself. I know that very well; I only want a chance to. In consenting to see me, after what he told you, you almost seem to be giving me a chance.'

'I am seeing you,' said Madame de Cintré, slowly and gravely, 'because I promised my brother I would.'

'Blessings on your brother's head!' cried Newman. 'What I told him last evening was this: that I admired you more than any woman I had ever seen, and that I should like immensely to make you my wife.' He uttered these words with great directness and firmness, and without any sense of confusion. He was full of his idea, he had completely mastered it, and he seemed to look down on Madame de Cintré, with all her gathered elegance, from the height of his bracing good conscience. It is probable that this particular tone and manner were the very best he could have hit upon. Yet the light, just visibly forced smile, with which his companion had listened to him died away, and she sat looking at him with her lips parted and her face as solemn as a tragic mask. There was evidently something very painful to her in the scene to which he was subjecting her, and yet her impatience of it found no angry voice. Newman wondered whether he was hurting her; he could not imagine why the liberal devotion he meant to express should be disagreeable. He got up and stood before her, leaning one hand on the chimney-piece. 'I know I have seen you very little to say this,' he said, 'so little that it may make what I say seem disrespectful. That is my misfortune! I could have said it the first time I saw you. Really, I had seen you before; I had seen you in imagination; you seemed almost an old friend. So what I say is not mere gallantry and compliments and nonsense – I can't talk that way, I don't know how, and I wouldn't to you if I could. It's as serious as such words can be. I feel as if I knew you and knew what a beautiful admirable woman you are. I shall know better perhaps, some day, but I have a general notion now. You are just the woman I have been looking for, except that you are far more perfect. I won't make any protestations and vows, but you can trust me. It is very soon, I know, to say all this; it is almost offensive. But why not gain time if one can? And if you want time to reflect – of course you do – the sooner you begin the better for me. I don't know what you think of me; but there is no great mystery about me; you see what I am. Your brother told me that my antecedents and occupations were against me; that your family stands somehow on a higher level than I do. That is an idea which, of course, I don't understand and don't accept. But you don't care anything about that. I can assure you that I am a very solid fellow, and that if I give my mind to it I can arrange things so that in a very few years I shall not need to waste time in explaining who I am and what I am. You will decide for yourself whether you like me or not. What there is you see before you. I honestly believe I have no hidden vices or nasty tricks. I am kind, kind, kind! Everything that a man can give a woman I will give you. I have a large fortune, a very large fortune; some day, if you will allow me, I will go into details. If you want brilliancy, everything in the way of brilliancy that money can give you, you shall have. And as regards anything you may give up, don't take for granted too much that its place cannot be filled. Leave that to me; I'll take care of you; I shall know what you need. Energy and ingenuity can arrange everything. I'm a strong man! There, I have said what I had on my heart! It was better to get it off. I am very sorry if it's disagreeable to you; but think how much better it is that things should be clear. Don't answer me now, if you don't wish it. Think about it; think about it as slowly as you please. Of course I hav'n't said, I can't say, half I mean, especially about my admiration for you. But take a favourable view of me; it will only be just.'

During this speech, the longest that Newman had ever made, Madame de Cintré kept her gaze fixed upon him, and it expanded at the last into a sort of fascinated stare. When he ceased speaking she lowered her eyes and sat for some moments looking down and straight before her. Then she slowly rose to her feet, and a pair of exceptionally keen eyes would have perceived that she was trembling a little in the movement. She still looked extremely serious. 'I am very much obliged to you for your offer,' she said. 'It seems very strange, but I am glad you spoke without waiting any longer. It is better the subject should be dismissed. I appreciate all you say; you do me great honour. But I have decided not to marry.'

'Oh, don't say that!' cried Newman, in a tone absolutely *naif**
from its pleading and caressing cadence. She had turned away, and it made her stop a moment with her back to him. 'Think better of that. You are too young, too beautiful, too much made to be happy and to make others happy. If you are afraid of losing your freedom, I can assure you that this freedom here, this life you now lead, is a dreary bondage to what I will offer you. You shall do things that I don't think you have ever thought of. I will take you to live anywhere in the wide world

that you propose. Are you unhappy? You give me a feeling that
you *are* unhappy. You have no right to be, or to be made so.
Let me come in and put an end to it.'

Madame de Cintré stood there a moment longer, looking
away from him. If she was touched by the way he spoke, the
thing was conceivable. His voice, always very mild and interrogative, gradually became as soft and as tenderly argumentative
as if he had been talking to a much-loved child. He stood
watching her, and she presently turned round again, but this
time she did not look at him, and she spoke with a quietness in
which there was a visible trace of effort.

'There are a great many reasons why I should not marry,' she
said, 'more than I can explain to you. As for my happiness, I am
very happy. Your offer seems strange to me, for more reasons
also than I can say. Of course you have a perfect right to make
it. But I cannot accept it – it is impossible. Please never speak of
this matter again. If you cannot promise me this, I must ask you
not to come back.'

'Why is it impossible?' Newman demanded. 'You may think
it is, at first, without its really being so. I didn't expect you to be
pleased at first, but I do believe that if you will think of it a
good while, you may be satisfied.'

'I don't know you,' said Madame de Cintré. 'Think how little
I know you.'

'Very little, of course, and therefore I don't ask for your
ultimatum on the spot. I only ask you not to say No, and to let
me hope. I will wait as long as you desire. Meanwhile you can
see more of me and know me better, look at me as a possible
husband – as a candidate – and make up your mind.'

Something was going on, rapidly, in Madame de Cintré's
thoughts; she was weighing a question there, beneath Newman's
eyes, weighing it and deciding it. 'From the moment I don't very
respectfully beg you to leave the house and never return,' she
said, 'I listen to you, I seem to give you hope. I *have* listened to
you – against my judgment. It is because you are eloquent. If I
had been told this morning that I should consent to consider
you as a possible husband, I should have thought my informant
a little crazy. I *am* listening to you, you see!' And she threw her
hands out for a moment and let them drop with a gesture in
which there was just the slightest expression of appealing
weakness.

'Well, as far as saying goes, I have said everything,' said Newman. 'I believe in you, without restriction, and I think all the good of you that it is possible to think of a human creature. I firmly believe that in marrying me you will be *safe*. As I said just now,' he went on with a smile, 'I have no bad ways. I can *do* so much for you. And if you are afraid that I am not what you have been accustomed to, not refined and delicate and punctilious, you may easily carry that too far. I *am* delicate! You shall see!'

Madame de Cintré walked some distance away, and paused before a great plant, an azalea, which was flourishing in a porcelain tub before her window. She plucked off one of the flowers and, twisting it in her fingers, retraced her steps. Then she sat down in silence, and her attitude seemed to be a consent that Newman should say more.

'Why should you say it is impossible you should marry?' he continued. 'The only thing that could make it really impossible would be your being already married. Is it because you have been unhappy in marriage? That is all the more reason. Is it because your family exert a pressure upon you, interfere with you, annoy you? That is still another reason; you ought to be perfectly free, and marriage will make you so. I don't say anything against your family – understand that!' added Newman, with an eagerness which might have made a perspicacious observer smile. 'Whatever way you feel toward them is the right way, and anything that you should wish me to do to make myself agreeable to them I will do as well as I know how. Depend upon that!'

Madame de Cintré rose again and came toward the fireplace, near which Newman was standing. The expression of pain and embarrassment had passed out of her face, and it was illuminated with something which, this time at least, Newman need not have been perplexed whether to attribute to habit or to intention, to art or to nature. She had the air of a woman who had stepped across the frontier of friendship and, looking round her, finds the region vast. A certain checked and controlled exaltation seemed mingled with the usual level radiance of her glance. 'I will not refuse to see you again,' she said, 'because much of what you have said has given me pleasure. But I will see you only on this condition: that you say nothing more in the same way for a long time.'

'For how long?'

'For six months. It must be a solemn promise.'

'Very well; I promise.'

'Good-bye, then,' she said, and extended her hand.

He held it a moment, as if he were going to say something more. But he only looked at her; then he took his departure.

That evening, on the Boulevard, he met Valentin de Belle-garde. After they had exchanged greetings, Newman told him that he had seen Madame de Cintré a few hours before.

'I know it,' said Bellegarde. 'I dined in the Rue de l'Université.' And then, for some moments, both men were silent. Newman wished to ask Bellegarde what visible impression his visit had made, and the Count Valentin had a question of his own. Bellegarde spoke first.

'It's none of my business, but what the deuce did you say to my sister?'

'I am willing to tell you,' said Newman, 'that I made her an offer of marriage.'

'Already!' And the young man gave a whistle. ' "Time is money!" Is that what you say in America? And Madame de Cintré?' he added, with an interrogative inflection.

'She did not accept my offer.'

'She couldn't, you know, in that way.'

'But I'm to see her again,' said Newman.

'Oh the strangeness of woman!' exclaimed Bellegarde. Then he stopped, and held Newman off at arms'-length. 'I look at you with respect!' he exclaimed. 'You have achieved what we call a personal success! Immediately, now, I must present you to my brother.'

'Whenever you please!' said Newman.

CHAPTER 10

Newman continued to see his friends the Tristrams with a good deal of frequency, though, if you had listened to Mrs Tristram's account of the matter, you would have supposed that they had been cynically repudiated for the sake of grander acquaintance.

'We were all very well so long as we had no rivals – we were better than nothing. But now that you have become the fashion, and have your pick every day of three invitations to dinner, we are tossed into the corner. I am sure it is very good of you to come and see us once a month; I wonder you don't send us your cards in an envelope. When you do, pray have them with black edges; it will be for the death of my last illusion.' It was in this incisive strain that Mrs Tristram moralised over Newman's so-called neglect, which was in reality a most exemplary constancy. Of course she was joking, but there was always something ironical in her jokes, as there was always something jocular in her gravity.

'I know no better proof that I have treated you very well,' Newman had said, 'than the fact that you make so free with my character. Familiarity breeds contempt; I have made myself too cheap. If I had a little proper pride I would stay away awhile, and when you asked me to dinner say I was going to the Princess Borealska's. But I have not any pride where my pleasure is concerned, and to keep you in the humour to see me – if you must see me only to call me bad names – I will agree to anything you choose; I will admit that I am the biggest snob in Paris.' Newman, in fact, had declined an invitation personally given by the Princess Borealska, an inquiring Polish lady to whom he had been presented, on the ground that on that particular day he always dined at Mrs Tristram's; and it was only a tenderly perverse theory of his hostess of the Avenue d'Iéna that he was faithless to his early friendships. She needed the theory to explain a certain moral irritation by which she was often visited; though, if this explanation was unsound, a deeper analyst than I must give the right one. Having launched our hero upon the current which was bearing him so rapidly along, she appeared but half-pleased at its swiftness. She had succeeded too well; she had played her game too cleverly, and she wished to mix up the cards. Newman had told her, in due season, that her friend was 'satisfactory'. The epithet was not romantic, but Mrs Tristram had no difficulty in perceiving that, in essentials, the feeling which lay beneath it was. Indeed, the mild expansive brevity with which it was uttered, and a certain look, at once appealing and inscrutable, that issued from Newman's half-closed eyes as he leaned his head against the back of his chair, seemed to her the most eloquent attestation of a mature sentiment that she had

ever encountered. Newman was, according to the French
phrase,* only abounding in her own sense, but his temperate
raptures exerted a singular effect upon that ardour which she
herself had so freely manifested a few months before. She now
seemed inclined to take a purely critical view of Madame de
Cintré, and wished to have it understood that she did not in the
least answer for her being a compendium of all the virtues. 'No
woman was ever so good as that woman seems,' she said.
Remember what Shakespeare calls Desdemona:* "a supersubtle
Venetian". Madame de Cintré is a supersubtle Parisian. She is a
charming woman, and she has five hundred merits; but you had
better keep that in mind.' Was Mrs Tristram simply finding out
that she was jealous of her dear friend on the other side of the
Seine, and that in undertaking to provide Newman with an ideal
wife she had counted too much on her own disinterestedness?
We may be permitted to doubt it. The inconsistent little lady of
the Avenue d'Iéna had an insuperable need of changing her
place, intellectually. She had a lively imagination, and she was
capable, at certain times, of imagining the direct reverse of her
most cherished beliefs, with a vividness more intense than that
of conviction. She got tired of thinking aright; but there was no
serious harm in it, as she got equally tired of thinking wrong. In
the midst of her mysterious perversities she had admirable
flashes of justice. One of these occurred when Newman related
to her that he had made a formal proposal to Madame de
Cintré. He repeated in a few words what he had said, and in a
great many what she had answered. Mrs Tristram listened with
extreme interest.

'But after all,' said Newman, 'there is nothing to congratulate
me upon. It is not a triumph.'

'I beg your pardon,' said Mrs Tristram; 'it is a great triumph.
It is a great triumph that she did not silence you at the first
word, and request you never to speak to her again.'

'I don't see that,' observed Newman.

'Of course you don't; heaven forbid you should! When I told
you to go your own way and do what came into your head, I
had no idea you would go over the ground so fast. I never
dreamed you would offer yourself after five or six morning-
calls. As yet, what had you done to make her like you? You had
simply sat – not very straight – and stared at her. But she does
like you.'

'That remains to be seen.'

'No, that is proved. What will come of it remains to be seen. That you should propose to marry her, without more ado, could never have come into her head. You can form very little idea of what passed through her mind as you spoke; if she ever really marries you, the affair will be characterised by the usual justice of all human things towards women. You will think you take generous views of her; but you will never begin to know through what a strange sea of feeling she passed before she accepted you. As she stood there in front of you the other day, she plunged into it. She said, "Why not?" to something which, a few hours earlier, had been inconceivable. She turned about on a thousand gathered prejudices and traditions as on a pivot, and looked where she had never looked hitherto. When I think of it – when I think of Claire de Cintré and all that she represents, there seems to me something very fine in it. When I recommended you to try your fortune with her I of course thought well of you, and in spite of your sins I think so still. But I confess I don't see quite what you are and what you have done, to make such a woman do this sort of thing for you.'

'Oh, there is something very fine in it!' said Newman, with a laugh, repeating her words. He took an extreme satisfaction in hearing that there was something fine in it. He had not the least doubt of it himself, but he had already begun to value the world's admiration of Madame de Cintré, as adding to the prospective glory of possession.

It was immediately after this conversation that Valentin de Bellegarde came to conduct his friend to the Rue de l'Université to present him to the other members of his family. 'You are already introduced,' he said, 'and you have begun to be talked about. My sister has mentioned your successive visits to my mother, and it was an accident that my mother was present at none of them. I have spoken of you as an American of immense wealth, and the best fellow in the world, who is looking for something very superior in the way of a wife.'

'Do you suppose,' asked Newman, 'that Madame de Cintré has related to your mother the last conversation I had with her?'

'I am very certain that she has not; she will keep her own counsel. Meanwhile you must make your way with the rest of the family. Thus much is known about you; you have made a great fortune in trade; you are a little eccentric; and you frankly admire our dear Claire. My sister-in-law, whom you remember seeing in Madame de Cintré's sitting-room, took, it appears, a fancy to you; she has described you as having *beaucoup de cachet.** My mother, therefore, is curious to see you.'

'She expects to laugh at me, eh?' said Newman.

'She never laughs. If she does not like you, don't hope to purchase favour by being amusing. Take warning by me!'

This conversation took place in the evening, and half an hour later Valentin ushered his companion into an apartment of the house of the Rue de l'Université into which he had not yet penetrated, the salon of the dowager Marquise de Bellegarde. It was a vast high room, with elaborate and ponderous mould- ings, painted a whitish grey, along the upper portion of the walls and the ceiling; with a great deal of faded and carefully- repaired tapestry in the doorways and chair-backs; a Turkey carpet* in light colours, still soft and deep, in spite of great antiquity, on the floor; and portraits of each of Madame de Bellegarde's children, at the age of ten, suspended against an old screen of red silk. The room was illumined, exactly enough for conversation, by half-a-dozen candles, placed in odd corners, at a great distance apart. In a deep arm-chair, near the fire, sat an old lady in black; at the other end of the room another person was seated at the piano, playing a very expressive waltz. In this latter person Newman recognised the young Marquise de Bellegarde.

Valentin presented his friend, and Newman walked up to the old lady by the fire and shook hands with her. He received a rapid impression of a white, delicate, aged face, with a high forehead, a small mouth, and a pair of cold blue eyes which had kept much of the freshness of youth. Madame de Bellegarde looked hard at him, and returned his handshake with a sort of British positiveness which reminded him that she was the daughter of the Earl of St Dunstan's. Her daughter-in-law stopped playing and gave him an agreeable smile. Newman sat down and looked about him, while Valentin went and kissed the hand of the young marquise.

'I ought to have seen you before,' said Madame de Bellegarde. 'You have paid several visits to my daughter.'

'Oh yes,' said Newman, smiling; 'Madame de Cintré and I are old friends by this time.'

'You have gone fast,' said Madame de Bellegarde.

'Not so fast as I should like,' said Newman bravely.

'Oh, you are very ambitious,' answered the old lady.

'Yes, I confess I am,' said Newman, smiling.

Madame de Bellegarde looked at him with her cold fine eyes, and he returned her gaze, reflecting that she was a possible adversary and trying to take her measure. Their eyes remained in contact for some moments. Then Madame de Bellegarde looked away, and without smiling: 'I am very ambitious, too,' she said.

Newman felt that taking her measure was not easy; she was a formidable, inscrutable little woman. She resembled her daughter, and yet she was utterly unlike her. The colouring in Madame de Cintré was the same, and the high delicacy of her brow and nose was hereditary. But her face was a larger and freer copy, and her mouth in especial a happy divergence from that conservative orifice, a little pair of lips at once plump and pinched, that looked, when closed, as if they could not open wider than to swallow a gooseberry or to emit an 'Oh dear, no!' which probably had been thought to give the finishing touch to the aristocratic prettiness of the Lady Emmeline Atheling* as represented, forty years before, in several Books of Beauty.* Madame de Cintré's face had, to Newman's eye, a range of expression as delightfully vast as the wind-streaked, cloud-flecked distance on a Western prairie. But her mother's white, intense, respectable countenance, with its formal gaze, and its circumscribed smile, suggested a document signed and sealed; a thing of parchment, ink, and ruled lines. 'She is a woman of conventions and proprieties,' he said to himself as he looked at her; 'her world is the world of things immutably decreed. But how she is at home in it, and what a paradise she finds it! She walks about in it as if it were a blooming park, a Garden of Eden; and when she sees "This is genteel", or "This is improper", written on a milestone she stops ecstatically, as if she were listening to a nightingale or smelling a rose.' Madame de Bellegarde wore a little black velvet hood tied under her chin, and she was wrapped in an old black cashmere shawl.

'You are an American?' she said presently. 'I have seen several Americans.'

'There are several in Paris,' said Newman jocosely.

'Oh, really?' said Madame de Bellegarde. 'It was in England I saw these, or somewhere else; not in Paris. I think it must have been in the Pyrenees, many years ago. I am told your ladies are very pretty. One of these ladies was very pretty! such a wonderful complexion! She presented me a note of introduction from someone – I forget whom – and she sent with it a note of her own. I kept her letter a long time afterwards, it was so strangely expressed. I used to know some of the phrases by heart. But I have forgotten them now, it is so many years ago. Since then I have seen no more Americans. I think my daughter-in-law has; she is a great gad-about, she sees everyone.'

At this the younger lady came rustling forward, pinching in a very slender waist, and casting idly preoccupied glances over the front of her dress, which was apparently designed for a ball. She was, in a singular way, at once ugly and pretty; she had protuberant eyes, and lips that were strangely red. She reminded Newman of his friend, Mademoiselle Nioche; this was what that much-obstructed young lady would have liked to be. Valentin de Bellegarde walked behind her at a distance, hopping about to keep off the far-spreading train of her dress.

'You ought to show more of your shoulders behind,' he said, very gravely. 'You might as well wear a standing ruff as such a dress as that.'

The young woman turned her back to the mirror over the chimney-piece, and glanced behind her, to verify Valentin's assertion. The mirror descended low, and yet it reflected nothing but a large unclad flesh surface. The young marquise put her hands behind her and gave a downward pull to the waist of her dress. 'Like that, you mean?' she asked.

'That is a little better,' said Bellegarde, in the same tone, 'but it leaves a good deal to be desired.'

'Oh, I never go to extremes,' said his sister-in-law. And then, turning to Madame de Bellegarde: 'What were you calling me just now, madame?'

'I called you a gad-about,' said the old lady. 'But I might call you something else, too.'

'A gad-about? What an ugly word? What does it mean?'

'A very beautiful person,' Newman ventured to say, seeing that it was in French.

'That is a pretty compliment but a bad translation,' said the young marquise. And then, looking at him a moment: 'Do you dance?'

'Not a step.'

'You are very wrong,' she said simply. And with another look at her back in the mirror she turned away.

'Do you like Paris?' asked the old lady, who was apparently wondering what was the proper way to talk to an American.

'Yes, rather,' said Newman. And then he added, with a friendly intonation: 'Don't you?'

'I can't say I know it. I know my house – I know my friends – I don't know Paris.'

'Oh, you lose a great deal,' said Newman sympathetically.

Madame de Bellegarde stared; it was presumably the first time she had been condoled with on her losses.

'I am content with what I have,' she said, with dignity.

Newman's eyes, at this moment, were wandering round the room, which struck him as rather sad and shabby; passing from the high casements, with their small thickly-framed panes, to the sallow tints of two or three portraits in pastel, of the last century, which hung between them. He ought obviously to have answered that the contentment of his hostess was quite natural – she had a great deal; but the idea did not occur to him during the pause of some moments which followed.

'Well, my dear mother,' said Valentin, coming and leaning against the chimney-piece, 'what do you think of my dear friend Newman? Is he not the excellent fellow I told you?'

'My acquaintance with Mr Newman has not gone very far,' said Madame de Bellegarde. 'I can as yet only appreciate his great politeness.'

'My mother is a great judge of these matters,' said Valentin to Newman. 'If you have satisfied her, it is a triumph.'

'I hope I shall satisfy you, some day,' said Newman, looking at the old lady. 'I have done nothing yet.'

'You must not listen to my son; he will bring you into trouble. He is a sad scatterbrain.'

'Oh, I like him – I like him,' said Newman genially.

'He amuses you, eh?'

'Yes, perfectly.'

'Do you hear that, Valentin?' said Madame de Bellegarde. 'You amuse Mr Newman.'

'Perhaps we shall all come to that?' Valentin exclaimed.

'You must see my other son,' said Madame de Bellegarde. 'He is much better than this one. But he will not amuse you.'

'I don't know – I don't know!' murmured Valentin reflectively. 'But we shall very soon see. Here comes *Monsieur mon frère*.'*

The door had just opened to give ingress to a gentleman who stepped forward and whose face Newman remembered. He had been the author of our hero's discomfiture the first time he tried to present himself to Madame de Cintré. Valentin de Bellegarde went to meet his brother, looked at him a moment, and then, taking him by the arm, led him up to Newman.

'This is my excellent friend Mr Newman,' he said very blandly. 'You must know him.'

'I am delighted to know Mr Newman,' said the marquis, with a low bow, but without offering his hand.

'He is the old woman at second-hand,' Newman said to himself, as he returned M. de Bellegarde's greeting. And this was the starting-point of a speculative theory, in his mind, that the late marquis had been a very amiable foreigner, with an inclination to take life easily and a sense that it was difficult for the husband of the stilted little lady by the fire to do so. But if he had taken little comfort in his wife he had taken much in his two younger children, who were after his own heart, while Madame de Bellegarde had paired with her eldest-born.

'My brother has spoken to me of you,' said M. de Bellegarde; 'and as you are also acquainted with my sister, it was time we should meet.' He turned to his mother and gallantly bent over her hand, touching it with his lips, and then he assumed an attitude before the chimney-piece. With his long lean face, his high-bridged nose, and his small opaque eyes, he looked much like an Englishman. His whiskers were fair and glossy, and he had a large dimple, of unmistakable British origin, in the middle of his handsome chin. He was 'distinguished' to the tips of his polished nails, and there was not a movement of his fine perpendicular person that was not noble and majestic. Newman had never yet been confronted with such an incarnation of the art of taking oneself seriously; he felt a sort of impulse to step backward, as you do to get a view of a great façade.

'Urbain,' said young Madame de Bellegarde, who had apparently been waiting for her husband to take her to her ball, 'I call your attention to the fact that I am dressed.'

'That is a good idea,' murmured Valentin.

'I am at your orders, my dear friend,' said M. de Bellegarde.

'Only, you must allow me first the pleasure of a little conversation with Mr Newman.'

'Oh, if you are going to a party, don't let me keep you,' objected Newman. 'I am very sure we shall meet again. Indeed, if you would like to converse with me I will gladly name an hour.' He was eager to make it known that he would readily answer all questions and satisfy all exactions.

M. de Bellegarde stood in a well-balanced position before the fire, caressing one of his fair whiskers with one of his white hands, and looking at Newman, half askance, with eyes from which a particular ray of observation made its way through a general meaningless smile. 'It is very kind of you to make such an offer,' he said. 'If I am not mistaken, your occupations are such as to make your time precious. You are in – a – as we say, *dans les affaires.*'

'In business, you mean? Oh no, I have thrown business overboard for the present. I am "loafing", as *we* say. My time is quite my own.'

'Ah, you are taking a holiday,' rejoined M. de Bellegarde. ' "Loafing." Yes, I have heard that expression.'

'Mr Newman is American,' said Madame de Bellegarde.

'My brother is a great ethnologist,' said Valentin.

'An ethnologist?' said Newman. 'Ah, you collect negroes' skulls, and that sort of thing.'

The marquis looked hard at his brother, and began to caress his other whisker. Then, turning to Newman, with sustained urbanity: 'You are travelling for your pleasure?' he asked.

'Oh, I am knocking about to pick up one thing and another. Of course I get a good deal of pleasure out of it.'

'What especially interests you?' inquired the marquis.

'Well, everything interests me,' said Newman. 'I am not particular. Manufactures are what I care most about.'

'That has been your specialty?'

'I can't say I have had any specialty. My specialty has been to make the largest possible fortune in the shortest possible time.' Newman made this last remark very deliberately; he wished to open the way, if it were necessary, to an authoritative statement of his means.

M. de Bellegarde laughed agreeably. 'I hope you have succeeded,' he said.

'Yes, I have made a fortune in a reasonable time. I am not so old, you see.'

'Paris is a very good place to spend a fortune. I wish you great enjoyment of yours.' And M. de Bellegarde drew forth his gloves and began to put them on.

Newman for a few moments watched him sliding his white hands into the white kid, and as he did so his feelings took a singular turn. M. de Bellegarde's good wishes seemed to descend out of the white expanse of his sublime serenity with the soft scattered movement of a shower of snow-flakes. Yet Newman was not irritated; he did not feel that he was being patronised; he was conscious of no especial impulse to introduce a discord into so noble a harmony. Only he felt himself suddenly in personal contact with the forces with which his friend Valentin had told him that he would have to contend, and he became sensible of their intensity. He wished to make some answering manifestations, to stretch himself out at his own length, to sound a note at the uttermost end of *his* scale. It must be added that if this impulse was not vicious or malicious, it was by no means void of humorous expectancy. Newman was quite as ready to give play to that loosely-adjusted smile of his, if his hosts should happen to be shocked, as he was far from deliberately planning to shock them.

'Paris is a very good place for idle people,' he said, 'or it is a very good place if your family has been settled here for a long time, and you have made acquaintances and got your relations round you; or if you have got a big house like this, and a wife and children and mother and sister, and everything comfortable. I don't like that way of living all in rooms next door to each other. But I am not an idler. I try to be, but I can't manage it; it goes against the grain. My business habits are too deep-seated. Then, I hav'n't any house to call my own, or anything in the way of a family. My sisters are five thousand miles away, my mother died when I was a youngster, and I hav'n't any wife; I wish I had! So, you see, I don't exactly know what to do with myself. I am not fond of books, as you are, sir, and I get tired of dining out and going to the opera. I miss my business activity. You see, I began to earn my living when I was almost a baby, and until a few months ago I have never had my hand off the plow. Elegant leisure comes hard.'

This speech was followed by a profound silence of some

moments, on the part of Newman's entertainers. Valentin stood looking at him fixedly, with his hands in his pockets, and then he slowly, with a half-sidling motion, went out of the room. The marquis continued to draw on his gloves and to smile benignantly.

'You began to earn your living when you were a mere baby?' said the marquise.

'Hardly more – a small boy.'

'You say you are not fond of books,' said M. de Bellegarde; 'but you must do yourself the justice to remember that your studies were interrupted early.'

'That is very true; on my tenth birthday I stopped going to school. I thought it was a grand way to keep it. But I picked up some information afterwards,' said Newman, reassuringly.

'You have some sisters?' asked old Madame de Bellegarde.

'Yes, two sisters. Splendid women!'

'I hope that for them the hardships of life commenced less early.'

'They married very early, if you call that a hardship, as girls do in our Western country. One of them is married to the owner of the largest india-rubber house in the West.'

'Ah, you make houses also of india-rubber?' inquired the marquise.

'You can stretch them as your family increases,' said young Madame de Bellegarde, who was muffling herself in a long white shawl.

Newman indulged in a burst of hilarity, and explained that the house in which his brother-in-law lived was a large wooden structure, but that he manufactured and sold india-rubber on a colossal scale.

'My children have some little india-rubber shoes which they put on when they go to play in the Tuileries* in damp weather,' said the young marquise. 'I wonder whether your brother-in-law made them?'

'Very likely,' said Newman; 'if he did, you may be very sure that they are well made.'

'Well, you must not be discouraged,' said M. de Bellegarde, with vague urbanity.

'Oh, I don't mean to be. I have a project which gives me plenty to think about, and that is an occupation.' And then Newman was silent a moment, hesitating, yet thinking rapidly;

he wished to make his point, and yet to do so forced him to speak out in a way that was disagreeable to him. Nevertheless he continued, addressing himself to old Madame de Bellegarde, 'I will tell you my project; perhaps you can help me. I want to take a wife.'

'It is a very good project, but I am no matchmaker,' said the old lady.

Newman looked at her an instant, and then, with perfect sincerity: 'I should have thought you were,' he declared.

Madame de Bellegarde appeared to think him too sincere. She murmured something sharply in French, and fixed her eyes on her son. At this moment the door of the room was thrown open, and with a rapid step Valentin reappeared.

'I have a message for you,' he said to his sister-in-law. 'Claire bids me to request you not to start for your ball. She will go with you.'

'Claire will go with us!' cried the young marquise. '*En voilà, du nouveau!*'*

'She has changed her mind; she decided half an hour ago, and she is sticking the last diamond into her hair!' said Valentin.

'What has taken possession of my daughter?' demanded Madame de Bellegarde sternly. 'She has not been into the world these three years. Does she take such a step at half an hour's notice and without consulting me?'

'She consulted me, dear mother, five minutes since,' said Valentin, 'and I told her that such a beautiful woman – she is beautiful, you will see – had no right to bury herself alive.'

'You should have referred Claire to her mother, my brother,' said M. de Bellegarde, in French. 'This is very strange.'

'I refer her to the whole company!' said Valentin. 'Here she comes!' and he went to the open door, met Madame de Cintré on the threshold, took her by the hand, and led her into the room. She was dressed in white; but a long blue cloak, which hung almost to her feet, was fastened across her shoulders by a silver clasp. She had tossed it back, however, and her long white arms were uncovered. In her dense fair hair there glittered a dozen diamonds. She looked serious and, Newman thought, rather pale; but she glanced round her, and, when she saw him, smiled and put out her hand. He thought her tremendously handsome. He had a chance to look at her full in the face, for she stood a moment in the centre of the room, hesitating, apparently, what she should do, without meeting his eyes. Then she went up to her mother, who sat in her deep chair by the fire, looking at Madame de Cintré almost fiercely. With her back turned to the others, Madame de Cintré held her cloak apart to show her dress.

'What do you think of me?' she asked.

'I think you are audacious,' said the marquise. 'It was but three days ago, when I asked you, as a particular favour to myself, to go to the Duchess de Lusignan's, that you told me you were going nowhere, and that one must be consistent. Is this your consistency? Why should you distinguish Madame Robineau? Who is it you wish to please tonight?'

'I wish to please myself, dear mother,' said Madame de Cintré. And she bent over and kissed the old lady.

'I don't like surprises, my sister,' said Urbain de Bellegarde; 'especially when one is on the point of entering a drawing-room.'

Newman at this juncture felt inspired to speak. 'Oh, if you are going into a room with Madame de Cintré, you needn't be afraid of being noticed yourself?'

M. de Bellegarde turned to his sister with a smile too intense to be easy. 'I hope you appreciate a compliment that is paid you at your brother's expense,' he said. 'Come, come, madam.' And offering Madame de Cintré his arm he led her rapidly out of the room. Valentin rendered the same service to young Madame de Bellegarde, who had apparently been reflecting on the fact that the ball-dress of her sister-in-law was much less brilliant than her own, and yet had failed to derive absolute comfort from the reflection. With a farewell smile she sought the complement of her consolation in the eyes of the American visitor, and perceiving in them a certain mysterious brilliancy, it is not improbable that she may have flattered herself she had found it.

Newman, left alone with old Madame de Bellegarde, stood before her a few moments in silence. 'Your daughter is very beautiful,' he said, at last.

'She is very strange,' said Madame de Bellegarde.

'I am glad to hear it,' Newman rejoined, smiling. 'It makes me hope.'

'Hope what?'

'That she will consent, some day, to marry me.'

The old lady rose slowly to her feet. 'That really is your project, then?'

'Yes; will you favour it?'

'Favour it?' Madame de Bellegarde looked at him a moment and then shook her head. 'No!' she said softly.

'Will you suffer it then? Will you let it pass?'

'You don't know what you ask. I am a very proud and meddlesome old woman.'

'Well, I am very rich,' said Newman.

Madame de Bellegarde fixed her eyes on the floor, and Newman thought it probable she was weighing the reasons in favour of resenting the brutality of this remark. But at last looking up, she said simply: 'How rich?'

Newman expressed his income in a round number which had the magnificent sound that large aggregations of dollars put on when they are translated into francs. He added a few remarks of a financial character, which completed a sufficiently striking presentment of his resources.

Madame de Bellegarde listened in silence. 'You are very frank,' she said finally. 'I will be the same. I would rather favour you, on the whole, than suffer you. It will be easier.'

'I am thankful for any terms,' said Newman. 'But, for the present, you have suffered me long enough. Good-night!' And he took his leave.

CHAPTER 11

Newman, on his return to Paris, had not resumed the study of French conversation with M. Nioche; he found that he had too many other uses for his time. M. Nioche, however, came to see him very promptly; having learned his whereabouts by a mysterious process to which his patron never obtained the key. The shrunken little capitalist repeated his visit more than once. He seemed oppressed by a humiliating sense of having been overpaid, and wished apparently to redeem his debt by the offer of grammatical and statistical information in small instalments. He wore the same decently melancholy aspect as a few months before; a few months more or less of brushing could make little difference in the antique lustre of his coat and hat. But the poor old man's spirit was a trifle more threadbare; it seemed to have received some hard rubs during the summer. Newman inquired with interest about Mademoiselle Noémie; and M. Nioche, at first, for answer, simply looked at him in lachrymose silence.

'Don't ask me, sir,' he said at last. 'I sit and watch her, but I can do nothing.'

'Do you mean that she misconducts herself?'

'I don't know, I am sure. I can't follow her. I don't understand her. She has something in her head; I don't know what she is trying to do. She is too deep for me.'

'Does she continue to go to the Louvre? Has she made any of those copies for me?'

'She goes to the Louvre, but I see nothing of the copies. She has something on her easel; I suppose it is one of the pictures you ordered. Such a magnificent order ought to give her fairy-fingers. But she is not in earnest. I can't say anything to her; I am afraid of her. One evening, last summer, when I took her to walk in the Champs Élysées, she said some things to me that frightened me.'

'What were they?'

'Excuse an unhappy father from telling you,' said M. Nioche, unfolding his calico pocket-handkerchief.

Newman promised himself to pay Mademoiselle Noémie another visit at the Louvre. He was curious about the progress of his copies, but it must be added that he was still more curious about the progress of the young lady herself. He went one afternoon to the great museum, and wandered through several of the rooms in fruitless quest of her. He was bending his steps to the long hall of the Italian masters,* when suddenly he found himself face to face with Valentin de Bellegarde. The young Frenchman greeted him with ardour, and assured him that he was a godsend. He himself was in the worst of humours and he wanted someone to contradict.

'In a bad humour among all these beautiful things?' said Newman. 'I thought you were so fond of pictures, especially the old black ones. There are two or three here that ought to keep you in spirits.'

'Oh, today,' answered Valentin, 'I am not in a mood for pictures, and the more beautiful they are the less I like them.

Their great staring eyes and fixed positions irritate me. I feel as if I were at some big dull party, in a room full of people I shouldn't wish to speak to. What should I care for their beauty? It's a bore, and, worse still, it's a reproach. I have a great many *ennuis*;* I feel vicious.'

'If the Louvre has so little comfort for you, why in the world did you come here?' Newman asked.

'That is one of my *ennuis*. I came to meet my cousin – a dreadful English cousin, a member of my mother's family – who is in Paris for a week for her husband, and who wishes me to point out the "principal beauties". Imagine a woman who wears a green crape bonnet in December and has straps sticking out of the ankles of her interminable boots! My mother begged I would do something to oblige them. I have undertaken to play *valet de place* this afternoon. They were to have met me here at two o'clock, and I have been waiting for them twenty minutes. Why doesn't she arrive? She has at least a pair of feet to carry her. I don't know whether to be furious at their playing me false, or delighted to have escaped them.'

'I think in your place I would be furious,' said Newman, 'because they may arrive yet, and then your fury will still be of use to you. Whereas if you were delighted and they were afterwards to turn up, you might not know what to do with your delight.'

'You give me excellent advice, and I already feel better. I will be furious; I will let them go to the deuce and I myself will go with you – unless by chance you too have a rendezvous.'

'It is not exactly a rendezvous,' said Newman. 'But I have in fact come to see a person, not a picture.'

'A woman, presumably?'

'A young lady.'

'Well,' said Valentin, 'I hope for you with all my heart that she is not clothed in green tulle and that her feet are not too much out of focus.'

'I don't know much about her feet, but she has very pretty hands.'

Valentin gave a sigh. 'And on that assurance I must part with you?'

'I am not certain of finding my young lady,' said Newman, 'and I am not quite prepared to lose your company on the chance. It does not strike me as particularly desirable to introduce you to her, and yet I should rather like to have your opinion of her.'

'Is she pretty?'

'I guess you will think so.'

Bellegarde passed his arm into that of his companion. 'Conduct me to her on the instant! I should be ashamed to make a pretty woman wait for my verdict.'

Newman suffered himself to be gently propelled in the direction in which he had been walking, but his step was not rapid. He was turning something over in his mind. The two men passed into the long gallery of the Italian masters, and Newman, after having scanned for a moment its brilliant vista, turned aside into the smaller apartment devoted to the same school, on the left.* It contained very few persons, but at the farther end of it sat Mademoiselle Nioche, before her easel. She was not at work; her palette and brushes had been laid down beside her, her hands were folded in her lap, and she was leaning back in her chair and looking intently at two ladies on the other side of the hall, who, with their backs turned to her, had stopped before one of the pictures. These ladies were apparently persons of high fashion; they were dressed with great splendour, and their long silken trains and furbelows were spread over the polished floor. It was at their dresses Mademoiselle Noémie was looking, though what she was thinking of I am unable to say. I hazard the supposition that she was saying to herself that to be able to drag such a train over a polished floor was a felicity worth any price. Her reflections, at any rate, were disturbed by the advent of Newman and his companion. She glanced at them quickly, and then, colouring a little, rose and stood before her easel.

'I came here on purpose to see you,' said Newman in his bad French, offering to shake hands. And then, like a good American, he introduced Valentin formally: 'Allow me to make you acquainted with the Comte Valentin de Bellegarde.'

Valentin made a bow which must have seemed to Mademoiselle Noémie quite in harmony with the impressiveness of his title, but the graceful brevity of her own response made no concession to underbred surprise. She turned to Newman, putting up her hands to her hair and smoothing its delicately-felt roughness. Then, rapidly, she turned the canvas that was on her easel over upon its face. 'You have not forgotten me?' she asked.

'I shall never forget you,' said Newman. 'You may be sure of that.'

'Oh,' said the young girl, 'there are a great many different ways of remembering a person.' And she looked straight at Valentin de Bellegarde, who was looking at her as a gentleman may when a 'verdict' is expected of him.

'Have you painted anything for me?' said Newman. 'Have you been industrious?'

'No, I have done nothing.' And taking up her palette, she began to mix her colours at hazard.

'But your father tells me you have come here constantly.'

'I have nowhere else to go! Here, all summer, it was cool, at least.'

'Being here, then,' said Newman, 'you might have tried something.'

'I told you before,' she answered softly, 'that I don't know how to paint.'

'But you have something charming on your easel, now,' said Valentin, 'if you would only let me see it.'

She spread out her two hands, with the fingers expanded, over the back of the canvas – those hands which Newman had called pretty, and which, in spite of several paint-stains, Valentin could now admire. 'My painting is not charming,' she said.

'It is the only thing about you that is not, then, mademoiselle,' quoth Valentin gallantly.

She took up her little canvas and silently passed it to him. He looked at it, and in a moment she said, 'I am sure you are a judge.'

'Yes,' he answered, 'I am.'

'You know, then, that that is very bad.'

'*Mon Dieu!*'* said Valentin, shrugging his shoulders, 'let us distinguish.'

'You know that I ought not to attempt to paint,' the young girl continued.

'Frankly, then, mademoiselle, I think you ought not.'

She began to look at the dresses of the two splendid ladies again – a point on which, having risked one conjecture, I think I may risk another. While she was looking at the ladies she was seeing Valentin de Bellegarde. He, at all events, was seeing her. He put down the roughly-besmeared canvas and addressed a little click with his tongue, accompanied by an elevation of the eyebrows, to Newman.

'Where have you been all these months?' asked Mademoiselle Noémie of our hero. 'You took those great journeys, you amused yourself well?'

'Oh yes,' said Newman, 'I amused myself well enough.'

'I am very glad,' said Mademoiselle Noémie with extreme gentleness; and she began to dabble in her colours again. She was singularly pretty, with the look of serious sympathy that she threw into her face.

Valentin took advantage of her downcast eyes to telegraph again to his companion. He renewed his mysterious physiognomical play, making at the same time a rapid tremulous movement in the air with his fingers. He was evidently finding Mademoiselle Noémie extremely interesting; the blue devils* had departed, leaving the field clear.

'Tell me something about your travels,' murmured the young girl.

'Oh, I went to Switzerland – to Geneva, and Zermatt, and Zürich, and all those places, you know; and down to Venice, and all through Germany, and down the Rhine, and into Holland and Belgium – the regular round. How do you say that in French – the regular round?' Newman asked of Valentin.

Mademoiselle Nioche fixed her eyes an instant on Bellegarde, and then with a little smile: 'I don't understand, monsieur,' she said, 'when he says so much at once. Would you be so good as to translate?'

'I would rather talk to you out of my own head,' Valentin declared.

'No,' said Newman gravely, still in his bad French, 'you must not talk to Mademoiselle Nioche, because you say discouraging things. You ought to tell her to work, to persevere.'

'And we French, mademoiselle,' said Valentin, 'are accused of being false flatterers!'

'I don't want any flattery, I want only the truth. But I know the truth.'

'All I say is that I suspect there are some things that you can do better than paint,' said Valentin.

'I know the truth – I know the truth,' Mademoiselle Noémie repeated. And, dipping a brush into a clot of red paint, she drew a great horizontal daub across her unfinished picture.

'What is that?' asked Newman.

Without answering, she drew another long crimson daub, in a vertical direction, down the middle of her canvas, and so, in a moment, completed the rough indication of a cross. 'It is the sign of the truth,' she said at last.

The two men looked at each other, and Valentin indulged in another flash of physiognomical eloquence. 'You have spoiled your picture,' said Newman.

'I know that very well. It was the only thing to do with it. I had sat looking at it all day without touching it. I had begun to hate it. It seemed to me something was going to happen.'

'I like it better that way than as it was before,' said Valentin. 'Now it is more interesting. It tells a story. Is it for sale, mademoiselle?'

'Everything I have is for sale,' said Mademoiselle Noémie.

'How much is this thing?'

'Ten thousand francs,' said the young girl, without a smile.

'Everything that Mademoiselle Nioche may do at present is mine in advance,' said Newman. 'It makes part of an order I gave her some months ago. So you can't have this.'

'Monsieur will lose nothing by it,' said the young girl, looking at Valentin. And she began to put up her utensils.

'I shall have gained a charming memory,' said Valentin. 'You are going away? your day is over?'

'My father is coming to fetch me,' said Mademoiselle Noémie.

She had hardly spoken when, through the door behind her, which opens on one of the great white stone staircases of the Louvre,* M. Nioche made his appearance. He came in with his usual patient shuffle, and he made a low salute to the two gentlemen who were standing before his daughter's easel. Newman shook his hand with muscular friendliness, and Valentin returned his greeting with extreme deference. While the old man stood waiting for Noémie to make a parcel of her implements, he let his mild oblique gaze hover towards Bellegarde, who was watching Mademoiselle Noémie put on her bonnet and mantle. Valentin was at no pains to disguise his scrutiny. He looked at a pretty girl as he would have listened to a piece of music. Attention, in each case, was simple good manners. M. Nioche at last took his daughter's paint-box in one hand and the bedaubed canvas, after giving it a solemn puzzled stare, in the other, and led the way to the door. Mademoiselle

Noémie made the young men the salute of a duchess, and followed her father.

'Well,' said Newman, 'what do you think of her?'

'She is very remarkable. *Diable, diable, diable!*'* repeated M. de Bellegarde, reflectively; 'she is very remarkable.'

'I am afraid she is a sad little adventuress,' said Newman.

'Not a little one – a great one. She has the material.' And Valentin began to walk away slowly, looking vaguely at the pictures on the walls, with a thoughtful illumination in his eye. Nothing could have appealed to his imagination more than the possible adventures of a young lady endowed with the 'material' of Mademoiselle Nioche. 'She is very interesting,' he went on. 'She is a beautiful type.'

'A beautiful type? What the deuce do you mean?' asked Newman.

'I mean from the artistic point of view. She is an artist – outside of her painting, which obviously is execrable.'

'But she is not beautiful. I don't even think her very pretty.'

'She is quite pretty enough for her purposes, and it is a face and figure in which everything tells. If she were prettier she would be less intelligent, and her intelligence is half of her charm.'

'In what way,' asked Newman, who was much amused at his companion's immediate philosophisation of Mademoiselle Nioche, 'does her intelligence strike you as so remarkable?'

'She has taken the measure of life, and she has determined to *be* something – to succeed at any cost. Her painting, of course, is a mere trick to gain time. She is waiting for her chance; she wishes to launch herself, and to do it well. She knows her Paris. She is one of fifty thousand, so far as the mere ambition goes; but I am very sure that in the way of resolution and capacity she is a rarity. And in one gift – perfect heartlessness – I will warrant she is unsurpassed. She has not as much heart as will go on the point of a needle. That is an immense virtue. Yes, she is one of the celebrities of the future.'

'Heaven help us!' said Newman, 'how far the artistic point of view may take a man! But in this case I must request that you don't let it take you too far. You have learned a wonderful deal about Mademoiselle Noémie in a quarter of an hour. Let that suffice; don't follow up your researches.'

'My dear fellow,' cried Bellegarde, with warmth, 'I hope I have too good manners to intrude.'

'You are not intruding. The girl is nothing to me. In fact, I rather dislike her. But I like her poor old father, and for his sake I beg you to abstain from any attempt to verify your theories.'

'For the sake of that seedy old gentleman who came to fetch her?' demanded Valentin, stopping short. And on Newman's assenting, 'Ah no, ah no,' he went on with a smile. 'You are quite wrong, my dear fellow; you needn't mind him.'

'I verily believe that you are accusing the poor gentleman of being capable of rejoicing in his daughter's dishonour.'

'*Voyons!*' said Valentin; 'who is he? what is he?'

'He is what he looks like: as poor as a rat, but very high-toned.'

'Exactly. I noticed him perfectly; be sure I do him justice. He has had losses, *des malheurs,** as we say. He is very low-spirited, and his daughter is too much for him. He is the pink of respectability, and he has sixty years of honesty on his back. All this I perfectly appreciate. But I know my fellow-men and my fellow-Parisians, and I will make a bargain with you.' Newman gave ear to his bargain and he went on. 'He would rather his daughter were a good girl than a bad one, but if the worst comes to the worst, the old man will not do what Virginius* did. Success justifies everything. If Mademoiselle Noémie makes a figure, her papa will feel – well, we will call it relieved. And she will make a figure. The old gentleman's future is assured.'

'I don't know what Virginius did, but M. Nioche will shoot Miss Noémie,' said Newman. 'After that, I suppose his future will be assured in some snug prison.'

'I am not a cynic; I am simply an observer,' Valentin rejoined. 'Mademoiselle Noémie interests me; she is extremely remarkable. If there is a good reason, in honour or decency, for dismissing her from my thoughts forever, I am perfectly willing to do it. Your estimate of the papa's sensibilities is a good reason until it is invalidated. I promise you not to look at the young girl again until you tell me that you have changed your mind about the papa. When he has given distinct proof of being a philosopher, you will raise your interdict. Do you agree to that?'

'Do you mean to bribe him?'

'Oh, you admit, then, that he is bribable? No, he would ask

too much, and it would not be exactly fair. I mean simply to wait. You will continue, I suppose, to see this interesting couple, and you will give me the news yourself.'

'Well,' said Newman, 'if the old man turns out a humbug, you may do what you please. I wash my hands of the matter. For the girl herself, you may be at rest. I don't know what harm she may do to me, but I certainly can't hurt her. It seems to me,' said Newman, 'that you are very well matched. You are both hard cases, and M. Nioche and I, I believe, are the only virtuous men to be found in Paris.'

Soon after this M. de Bellegarde, in punishment for his levity, received a stern poke in the back from a pointed instrument. Turning quickly round he found the weapon to be a parasol wielded by a lady in a green gauze bonnet. Valentin's English cousins had been drifting about unpiloted, and evidently deemed that they had a grievance. Newman left him to their mercies, but with a boundless faith in his power to plead his cause.

CHAPTER 12

Three days after his introduction to the family of Madame de Cintré, Newman, coming in toward evening, found upon his table the card of the Marquis de Bellegarde. On the following day he received a note informing him that the Marquise de Bellegarde would be grateful for the honour of his company at dinner.

He went, of course, though he had to break another engagement to do it. He was ushered into the room in which Madame de Bellegarde had received him before, and here he found his venerable hostess, surrounded by her entire family. The room was lighted only by the crackling fire, which illumined the very small pink slippers of a lady who, seated in a low chair, was stretching out her toes before it. This lady was the younger Madame de Bellegarde. Madame de Cintré was seated at the other end of the room, holding a little girl against her knee, the child of her brother Urbain, to whom she was apparently relating a wonderful story. Valentin was sitting on a puff close to his sister-in-law, into whose ear he was certainly distilling the finest nonsense. The marquis was stationed before the fire, with his head erect and his hands behind him, in an attitude of formal expectancy.

Old Madame de Bellegarde stood up to give Newman her greeting, and there was that in the way she did so which seemed to measure narrowly the extent of her condescension. 'We are all alone, you see; we have asked no one else,' she said austerely.

'I am very glad you didn't; this is much more sociable,' said Newman. 'Good evening, sir,' and he offered his hand to the marquis.

M. de Bellegarde was affable, but in spite of his dignity he was restless. He began to pace up and down the room, he looked out of the long windows, he took up books and laid them down again. Young Madame de Bellegarde gave Newman her hand without moving and without looking at him.

'You may think that is coldness,' exclaimed Valentin; 'but it is not, it is warmth. It shows she is treating you as an intimate. Now she detests me, and yet she is always looking at me.'

'No wonder I detest you if I am always looking at you?' cried the lady. 'If Mr Newman does not like my way of shaking hands, I will do it again.'

But this charming privilege was lost upon our hero, who was already making his way across the room to Madame de Cintré. She looked at him as she shook hands, but she went on with the story she was telling her little niece. She had only two or three phrases to add, but they were apparently of great moment. She deepened her voice, smiling as she did so, and the little girl gazed at her with round eyes.

'But in the end the young prince married the beautiful Florabella,' said Madame de Cintré, 'and carried her off to live with him in the Land of the Pink Sky. There she was so happy that she forgot all her troubles, and went out to drive every day of her life in an ivory coach drawn by five hundred white mice. Poor Florabella,' she explained to Newman, 'had suffered terribly.'

'She had had nothing to eat for six months,' said little Blanche.

'Yes, but when the six months were over, she had a plum-cake as big as that ottoman,' said Madame de Cintré. 'That quite set her up again.'

'What a checkered career!' said Newman. 'Are you very fond

of children?' He was certain that she was, but he wished to make her say it.

'I like to talk with them,' she answered; 'we can talk with them so much more seriously than with grown persons. That is great nonsense that I have been telling Blanche, but it is a great deal more serious than most of what we say in society.'

'I wish you would talk to me, then, as if I were Blanche's age,' said Newman laughing. 'Were you happy at your ball the other night?'

'Ecstatically!'

'Now you are talking the nonsense that we talk in society,' said Newman. 'I don't believe that.'

'It was my own fault if I was not happy. The ball was very pretty, and everyone very amiable.'

'It was on your conscience,' said Newman, 'that you had annoyed your mother and your brother.'

Madame de Cintré looked at him a moment without answering. 'That is true,' she replied at last. 'I had undertaken more than I could carry out. I have very little courage; I am not a heroine.' She said this with a certain soft emphasis; but then, changing her tone: 'I could never have gone through the sufferings of the beautiful Florabella,' she added, 'not even for her prospective rewards.'

Dinner was announced, and Newman betook himself to the side of old Madame de Bellegarde. The dining-room, at the end of a cold corridor, was vast and sombre; the dinner was simple and delicately excellent. Newman wondered whether Madame de Cintré had had something to do with ordering the repast, and greatly hoped she had. Once seated at table, with the various members of the ancient house of Bellegarde around him, he asked himself the meaning of his position. Was the old lady responding to his advances? Did the fact that he was a solitary guest augment his credit or diminish it? Were they ashamed to show him to other people, or did they wish to give him a sign of sudden adoption into their last reserve of favour? Newman was on his guard; he was watchful and conjectural; and yet at the same time he was vaguely indifferent. Whether they gave him a long rope or a short one he was there now, and Madame de Cintré was opposite to him. She had a tall candlestick on each side of her; she would sit there for the next hour, and that was enough. The dinner was extremely solemn and measured; he wondered whether this was always the state of things in 'old families'. Madame de Bellegarde held her head very high, and fixed her eyes, which looked peculiarly sharp in her little finely-wrinkled white face, very intently upon the table-service. The marquis appeared to have decided that the fine arts offered a safe subject of conversation, as not leading to startling personal revelations. Every now and then, having learned from Newman that he had been through the museums of Europe, he uttered some polished aphorism upon the flesh-tints of Rubens and the good-taste of Sansovino.* His manners seemed to indicate a fine nervous dread that something disagreeable might happen if the atmosphere were not purified by allusions of a thoroughly superior cast. 'What under the sun is the man afraid of?' Newman asked himself. 'Does he think I am going to offer to swap jack-knives with him?' It was useless to shut his eyes to the fact that the marquis was profoundly disagreeable to him. He had never been a man of strong personal aversions; his nerves had not been at the mercy of the mystical qualities of his neighbours. But here was a man towards whom he was irresistibly in opposition; a man of forms and phrases and postures; a man full of possible impertinences and treacheries. M. de Bellegarde made him feel as if he were standing barefooted on a marble floor; and yet, to gain his desire, Newman felt perfectly able to stand. He wondered what Madame de Cintré thought of his being accepted, if accepted it was. There was no judging from her face, which expressed simply the desire to be gracious in a manner which should require as little explicit recognition as possible. Young Madame de Bellegarde had always the same manners; she was always preoccupied, distracted, listening to everything and hearing nothing, looking at her dress, her rings, her finger-nails, seeming rather bored, and yet puzzling you to decide what was her ideal of social diversion. Newman was enlightened on this point later. Even Valentin did not quite seem master of his wits; his vivacity was fitful and forced, yet Newman observed that in the lapses of his talk he appeared excited. His eyes had an intenser spark than usual. The effect of all this was that Newman, for the first time in his life, was not himself; that he measured his movements, and counted his words, and resolved that if the occasion demanded that he should appear to have swallowed a ramrod, he would meet the emergency.

After dinner M. de Bellegarde proposed to his guest that they should go into the smoking-room, and he led the way toward a small somewhat musty apartment, the walls of which were ornamented with old hangings of stamped leather and trophies of rusty arms. Newman refused a cigar, but he established himself upon one of the divans, while the marquis puffed his own weed before the fireplace, and Valentin sat looking through the light fumes of a cigarette from one to the other.

'I can't keep quiet any longer,' said Valentin, at last. 'I must tell you the news and congratulate you. My brother seems unable to come to the point; he revolves around his announcement like the priest around the altar. You are accepted as a candidate for the hand of our sister.'

'Valentin, be a little proper!' murmured the marquis, with a look of the most delicate irritation contracting the bridge of his high nose.

'There has been a family council,' the young man continued; 'my mother and Urbain have put their heads together, and even my testimony has not been altogether excluded. My mother and the marquis sat at a table covered with green cloth; my sister-in-law and I were on a bench against the wall. It was like a committee at the Corps Législatif.* We were called up, one after the other, to testify. We spoke of you very handsomely. Madame de Bellegarde said that if she had not been told who you were, she would have taken you for a duke – an American duke, the Duke of California. I said that I could warrant you grateful for the smallest favours – modest, humble, unassuming. I was sure that you would know your own place always, and never give us occasion to remind you of certain differences. After all, you couldn't help it if you were not a duke. There were none in your country; but if there had been, it was certain that, smart and active as you are, you would have got the pick of the titles. At this point I was ordered to sit down, but I think I made an impression in your favour.'

M. de Bellegarde looked at his brother with dangerous coldness, and gave a smile as thin as the edge of a knife. Then he removed a spark of cigar-ash from the sleeve of his coat; he fixed his eyes for a while on the cornice of the room, and at last he inserted one of his white hands into the breast of his waistcoat. 'I must apologise to you for the deplorable levity of my brother,' he said, 'and I must notify you that this is probably not the last time that his want of tact will cause you serious embarrassment.'

'No, I confess I have no tact,' said Valentin. 'Is your embarrassment really painful, Newman? The marquis will put you right again; his own touch is deliciously delicate.'

'Valentin, I am sorry to say,' the marquis continued, 'has never possessed the tone, the manner, that belong to a young man in his position. It has been a great affliction to his mother, who is very fond of the old traditions. But you must remember that he speaks for no one but himself.'

'Oh, I don't mind him, sir,' said Newman good-humouredly. 'I know what he amounts to.'

'In the good old times,' said Valentin, 'marquises and counts used to have their appointed fools and jesters, to crack jokes for them. Nowadays we see a great strapping democrat keeping a count about him to play the fool. It's a good situation, but I certainly am very degenerate.'

M. de Bellegarde fixed his eyes for some time on the floor. 'My mother informed me,' he said presently, 'of the announcement that you made to her the other evening.'

'That I desired to marry your sister?' said Newman.

'That you wished to arrange a marriage,' said the marquis slowly, 'with my sister, the Comtesse de Cintré. The proposal was serious, and required, on my mother's part, a great deal of reflection. She naturally took me into her counsels, and I gave my most zealous attention to the subject. There was a great deal to be considered; more than you appear to imagine. We have viewed the question on all its faces, we have weighed one thing against another. Our conclusion has been that we favour your suit. My mother has desired me to inform you of our decision. She will have the honour of saying a few words to you on the subject herself. Meanwhile, by us, the heads of the family, you are accepted.'

Newman got up and came nearer to the marquis. 'You will do nothing to hinder me, and all you can to help me, eh?'

'I will recommend my sister to accept you.'

Newman passed his hand over his face, and pressed it for a moment upon his eyes. This promise had a great sound, and yet the pleasure he took in it was embittered by his having to stand there so and receive his passport from M. de Bellegarde. The idea of having this gentleman mixed up with his wooing and wedding was more and more disagreeable to him. But Newman had resolved to go through the mill, as he imaged it, and he would not cry out at the first turn of the wheel. He was silent awhile, and then he said, with a certain dryness which Valentin told him afterwards had a very grand air: 'I am much obliged to you.'

'I take note of the promise,' said Valentin, 'I register the vow.'

M. de Bellegarde began to gaze at the cornice again; he apparently had something more to say. 'I must do my mother the justice,' he resumed, 'I must do myself the justice, to say that our decision was not easy. Such an arrangement was not what we had expected. The idea that my sister should marry a gentleman – ah – in business, was something of a novelty.'

'So I told you, you know,' said Valentin, raising his finger at Newman.

'The novelty has not quite worn away, I confess,' the marquis went on; 'perhaps it never will, entirely. But possibly that is not altogether to be regretted,' and he gave his thin smile again. 'It may be that the time has come when we should make some concession to novelty. There had been no novelties in our house for a great many years. I made the observation to my mother, and she did me the honour to admit that it was worthy of attention.'

'My dear brother,' interrupted Valentin, 'is not your memory just here leading you the least bit astray? Our mother is, I may say, distinguished for her small respect for abstract reasoning. Are you very sure that she replied to your striking proposition in the gracious manner you describe? You know how terribly incisive she is sometimes. Didn't she, rather, do you the honour to say: "A fiddlestick for your phrases! There are better reasons than that?"'

'Other reasons were discussed,' said the marquis, without looking at Valentin, but with an audible tremor in his voice; 'some of them possibly were better. We are conservative, Mr Newman, but we are not also bigots. We judged the matter liberally. We have no doubt that everything will be comfortable.'

Newman had stood listening to these remarks with his arms folded and his eyes fastened upon M. de Bellegarde. 'Comfortable?' he said, with a sort of grim flatness of intonation. 'Why shouldn't we be comfortable? If you are not, it will be your own fault; I have everything to make *me* so.'

'My brother means that with the lapse of time you may get used to the change,' and Valentin paused, to light another cigarette.

'What change?' asked Newman, in the same tone.

'Urbain,' said Valentin, very gravely, 'I am afraid that Mr Newman does not quite realise the change. We ought to insist upon that.'

'My brother goes too far,' said M. de Bellegarde. 'It is his fatal want of tact again. It is my mother's wish, and mine, that no such allusions should be made. Pray never make them yourself. We prefer to assume that the person accepted as the possible husband of my sister is one of ourselves, and that he should have no explanations to make. With a little discretion on both sides, everything, I think, will be easy. That is exactly what I wished to say – that we quite understand what we have undertaken, and that you may depend upon our adhering to our resolution.'

Valentin shook his hands in the air and then buried his face in them. 'I have less tact than I might have, no doubt; but oh, my brother, if you knew what you yourself were saying!' And he went off into a long laugh.

M. de Bellegarde's face flushed a little, but he held his head higher, as if to repudiate this concession to vulgar perturbability. 'I am sure you understand me,' he said to Newman.

'Oh no, I don't understand you at all,' said Newman. 'But you needn't mind that. I don't care. In fact, I think I had better not understand you. I might not like it. That wouldn't suit me at all, you know. I want to marry your sister, that's all; to do it as quickly as possible, and to find fault with nothing. I don't care how I do it. I am not marrying you, you know, sir. I have got my leave, and that is all I want.'

'You had better receive the last word from my mother,' said the marquis.

'Very good; I will go and get it,' said Newman; and he prepared to return to the drawing-room.

M. de Bellegarde made a motion for him to pass first, and when Newman had gone out he shut himself into the room with Valentin. Newman had been a trifle bewildered by the audacious irony of the younger brother, and he had not needed its aid to point the moral of M. de Bellegarde's transcendent patronage. He had wit enough to appreciate the force of that civility which consists in calling your attention to the impertinences it spares you. But he had felt warmly the delicate sympathy with himself that underlay Valentin's fraternal irreverence, and he was most unwilling that his friend should pay a tax upon it. He paused a moment in the corridor, after he had gone a few steps, expecting to hear the resonance of M. de Bellegarde's displeasure; but he detected only a perfect stillness. The stillness itself seemed a trifle portentous; he reflected, however, that he had no right to stand listening, and he made his way back to the salon. In his absence several persons had come in. They were scattered about the room in groups, two or three of them having passed into a small boudoir, next to the drawing-room, which had now been lighted and opened. Old Madame de Bellegarde was in her place by the fire, talking to a very old gentleman in a wig and a profuse white neckcloth of the fashion of 1820. Madame de Cintré was bending a listening head to the historic confidences of an old lady who was presumably the wife of the old gentleman in the neckcloth, an old lady in a red satin dress and an ermine cape, who wore across her forehead a band with a topaz set in it. Young Madame de Bellegarde, when Newman came in, left some people among whom she was sitting, and took the place that she had occupied before dinner. Then she gave a little push to the puff that stood near her, and by a glance at Newman seemed to indicate that she had placed it in position for him. He went and took possession of it; the marquis's wife amused and puzzled him.

'I know your secret,' she said, in her bad but charming English; 'you need make no mystery of it. You wish to marry my sister-in-law. *C'est un beau choix.** A man like you ought to marry a tall thin woman. You must know that I have spoken in your favour; you owe me a famous taper!'*

'You have spoken to Madame de Cintré?' said Newman.

'Oh no, not that. You may think it strange, but my sister-in-law and I are not so intimate as that. No; I spoke to my husband and my mother-in-law; I said I was sure we could do what we chose with you.'

'I am much obliged to you,' said Newman, laughing; 'but you can't.'

'I know that very well; I didn't believe a word of it. But I wanted you to come into the house; I thought we should be friends.'

'I am very sure of it,' said Newman.

'Don't be too sure. If you like Madame de Cintré so much, perhaps you will not like me. We are as different as blue and pink. But you and I have something in common. I have come into this family by marriage; you want to come into it in the same way.'

'Oh no, I don't!' interrupted Newman. 'I only want to take Madame de Cintré out of it.'

'Well, to cast your nets you have to go into the water. Our positions are alike; we shall be able to compare notes. What do you think of my husband? It's a strange question, isn't it? But I shall ask you some stranger ones yet.'

'Perhaps a stranger one will be easier to answer,' said Newman. 'You might try me.'

'Oh, you get off very well; the old Comte de la Rochefidèle, yonder, couldn't do it better. I told them that if we only gave you a chance you would be a perfect *talon rouge*.* I know something about men. Besides, you and I belong to the same camp. I am a ferocious democrat. By birth I am *vieille roche*;* a good little bit of the history of France is the history of my family. Oh, you never heard of us, of course! *Ce que c'est que la gloire!** We are much better than the Bellegardes, at any rate. But I don't care a pin for my pedigree; I want to belong to my time. I'm a revolutionist, a radical, a child of the age! I am sure I go beyond you. I like clever people, wherever they come from, and I take my amusement wherever I find it. I don't pout at the Empire;* here all the world pouts at the Empire. Of course I have to mind what I say; but I expect to take my revenge with you.' Madame de Bellegarde discoursed for some time longer in this sympathetic strain, with an eager abundance which seemed to indicate that her opportunities for revealing her esoteric philosophy were indeed rare. She hoped that Newman would never be afraid of her, however he might be with the others, for, really, she went very far indeed. 'Strong people' – *les gens forts* – were in her opinion equal, all the world over. Newman listened to her with an attention at once beguiled and irritated. He wondered what the deuce she, too, was driving at, with her hope that he would not be afraid of her and her protestations of equality. In so far as he could understand her, she was wrong; a silly rattling woman was certainly not the equal of a sensible man, preoccupied with an ambitious passion. Madame de

Bellegarde stopped suddenly, and looked at him sharply, shaking her fan. 'I see you don't believe me,' she said, 'you are too much on your guard. You will not form an alliance, offensive or defensive? You are very wrong; I could help you.'

Newman answered that he was very grateful and that he would certainly ask for help; she should see. 'But first of all,' he said, 'I must help myself.' And he went to join Madame de Cintré.

'I have been telling Madame de la Rochefidèle that you are an American,' she said, as he came up. 'It interests her greatly. Her father went over with the French troops to help you in your battles in the last century, and she has always, in consequence, wanted greatly to see an American. But she has never succeeded till tonight. You are the first – to her knowledge – that she has ever looked at.'

Madame de la Rochefidèle had an aged cadaverous face, with a falling of the lower jaw which prevented her from bringing her lips together, and reduced her conversation to a series of impressive but inarticulate gutturals. She raised an antique eyeglass, elaborately mounted in chased silver, and looked at Newman from head to foot. Then she said something to which he listened deferentially, but which he completely failed to understand.

'Madame de la Rochefidèle says that she is convinced that she must have seen Americans without knowing it,' Madame de Cintré explained. Newman thought it probable she had seen a great many things without knowing it; and the old lady, again addressing herself to utterance, declared – as interpreted by Madame de Cintré – that she wished she had known it.

At this moment the old gentleman who had been talking to the elder Madame de Bellegarde drew near, leading the marquise on his arm. His wife pointed out Newman to him, apparently explaining his remarkable origin. M. de la Rochefidèle, whose old age was rosy and rotund, spoke very neatly and clearly; almost as prettily, Newman thought, as M. Nioche. When he had been enlightened, he turned to Newman with an inimitable elderly grace.

'Monsieur is by no means the first American that I have seen,' he said. 'Almost the first person I ever saw – to notice him – was an American.'

'Ah!' said Newman, sympathetically.

'The great Dr Franklin,' said M. de la Rochefidèle. 'Of course I was very young. He was received very well in our *monde*.'

'Not better than Mr Newman,' said Madame de Bellegarde. 'I beg he will offer me his arm into the other room. I could have offered no higher privilege to Dr Franklin.'

Newman, complying with Madame de Bellegarde's request, perceived that her two sons had returned to the drawing-room. He scanned their faces an instant for traces of the scene that had followed his separation from them, but the marquis seemed neither more nor less frigidly grand than usual, and Valentin was kissing ladies' hands with at least his habitual air of self-abandonment to the act. Madame de Bellegarde gave a glance at her eldest son, and by the time she had crossed the threshold of her boudoir he was at her side. The room was now empty and offered a sufficient degree of privacy. The old lady disengaged herself from Newman's arm and rested her hand on the arm of the marquis; and in this position she stood a moment, holding her head high and biting her small under-lip. I am afraid the picture was lost upon Newman, but Madame de Bellegarde was, in fact, at this moment a striking image of the dignity which – even in the case of a little time-shrunken old lady – may reside in the habit of unquestioned authority and the absoluteness of a social theory favourable to yourself.

'My son has spoken to you as I desired,' she said, 'and you understand that we shall not interfere. The rest will lie with yourself.'

'M. de Bellegarde told me several things I didn't understand,' said Newman, 'but I made out that. You will leave me an open field. I am much obliged.'

'I wish to add a word that my son probably did not feel at liberty to say,' the marquise rejoined. 'I must say it for my own peace of mind. We are stretching a point; we are doing you a great favour.'

'Oh, your son said it very well; didn't you?' said Newman.

'Not so well as my mother,' declared the marquis.

'I can only repeat – I am much obliged.'

'It is proper I should tell you,' Madame de Bellegarde went on, 'that I am very proud, and that I hold my head very high. I may be wrong, but I am too old to change. At least I know it, and I don't pretend to anything else. Don't flatter yourself that my daughter is not proud. She is proud in her own way – a somewhat different way from mine. You will have to make your terms with that. Even Valentin is proud, if you touch the right spot – or the wrong one. Urbain is proud – that you see for yourself. Sometimes I think he is a little too proud; but I wouldn't change him. He is the best of my children; he cleaves to his old mother. But I have said enough to show you that we are all proud together. It is well that you should know the sort of people you have come among.'

'Well,' said Newman, 'I can only say, in return, that I am *not* proud; I shan't mind you! But you speak as if you intended to be very disagreeable.'

'I shall not enjoy having my daughter marry you, and I shall not pretend to enjoy it. If you don't mind that, so much the better.'

'If you stick to your own side of the contract we shall not quarrel; that is all I ask of you,' said Newman. 'Keep your hands off, and give me an open field. I am very much in earnest, and there is not the slightest danger of my getting discouraged or backing out. You will have me constantly before your eyes; if you don't like it, I am sorry for you. I will do for your daughter, if she will accept me, everything that a man can do for a woman. I am happy to tell you that, as a promise – a pledge. I consider that on your side you make me an equal pledge. You will not back out, eh?'

'I don't know what you mean by "backing out", said the marquise. 'It suggests a movement of which I think no Bellegarde has ever been guilty.'

'Our word is our word,' said Urbain. 'We have given it.'

'Well, now,' said Newman, 'I am very glad you are so proud; it makes me believe you will keep it.'

The marquise was silent a moment, and then, suddenly, 'I shall always be polite to you, Mr Newman,' she declared, 'but, decidedly, I shall never like you.'

'Don't be too sure,' said Newman, laughing.

'I am so sure that I will ask you to take me back to my arm-chair without the least fear of having my sentiments modified by the service you render me.' And Madame de Bellegarde took his arm, and returned to the salon and to her customary place.

M. de la Rochefidèle and his wife were preparing to take their leave, and Madame de Cintré's interview with the mumbling old lady was at an end. She stood looking about her, asking herself,

apparently, to whom she should next speak, when Newman
came up to her.

'Your mother has given me leave – very solemnly – to come
here often,' he said. 'I mean to come often.'

'I shall be glad to see you,' she answered simply. And then, in
a moment: 'You probably think it very strange that there should
be such a solemnity – as you say – about your coming.'

'Well, yes; I do, rather.'

'Do you remember what my brother Valentin said, the first
time you came to see me – that we were a strange, strange
family?'

'It was not the first time I came, but the second,' said
Newman.

'Very true. Valentin annoyed me at the time; but now I know
you better, I may tell you he was right. If you come often, you
will see!' and Madame de Cintré turned away.

Newman watched her awhile, talking with other people, and
then he took his leave. He shook hands last with Valentin de
Bellegarde, who came out with him to the top of the staircase.
'Well, you have got your permit,' said Valentin. 'I hope you
liked the process.'

'I like your sister more than ever. But don't worry your
brother any more, for my sake,' Newman added. 'I don't mind
him. I am afraid he came down on you in the smoking-room,
after I went out.'

'When my brother comes down on me,' said Valentin, 'he
falls hard. I have a peculiar way of receiving him. I must say,' he
continued, 'that they came up to the mark much sooner than I
expected. I don't understand it; they must have had to turn the
screw pretty tight. It's a tribute to your millions.'

'Well, it's the most precious one they have ever received,' said
Newman.

He was turning away when Valentin stopped him, looking at
him with a brilliant softly-cynical glance. 'I should like to know
whether, within a few days, you have seen your venerable friend
M. Nioche.'

'He was yesterday at my rooms,' Newman answered.

'What did he tell you?'

'Nothing particular.'

'You didn't see the muzzle of a pistol sticking out of his
pocket?'

'What are you driving at?' Newman demanded. 'I thought he seemed rather cheerful, for him.'

Valentin broke into a laugh. 'I am delighted to hear it! I win my bet. Mademoiselle Noémie has thrown her cap over the mill,* as we say. She has left the paternal domicile. She is launched! And M. Nioche is rather cheerful – *for him!* Don't brandish your tomahawk at that rate; I have not seen her nor communicated with her since that day at the Louvre. Andromeda has found another Perseus* than I. My information is exact; on such matters it always is. I suppose that now you will raise your protest?'

'My protest be hanged!' murmured Newman, disgustedly.

But his tone found no echo in that in which Valentin, with his hand on the door, to return to his mother's apartment, exclaimed: 'But I shall see her now! She is very remarkable – she is very remarkable!'

CHAPTER 13

Newman kept his promise, or his menace, of going often to the Rue de l'Université, and during the next six weeks he saw Madame de Cintré more times than he could have numbered. He flattered himself that he was not in love, but his biographer may be supposed to know better. He claimed, at least, none of the exemptions and emoluments of the romantic passion. Love, he believed, made a fool of a man, and his present emotion was not folly but wisdom – wisdom sound, serene, well-directed. What he felt was an intense all-consuming tenderness, which had for its object an extraordinarily graceful and delicate, and at the same time impressive woman, who lived in a large grey house on the left bank of the Seine. This tenderness turned very often into a positive heartache; a sign in which, certainly, Newman ought to have read the appellation which science has conferred upon his sentiment. When the heart has a heavy weight upon it, it hardly matters whether the weight be of gold or of lead; when, at any rate, happiness passes into that place in which it becomes identical with pain, a man may admit that the reign of wisdom is temporarily suspended. Newman wished Madame de Cintré so well that nothing he could think of doing for her in the future rose to the high standard which his present mood had set itself. She seemed to him so felicitous a product of nature and circumstance, that his invention, musing on future combinations, was constantly catching its breath with the fear of stumbling into some brutal compression or mutilation of her beautiful personal harmony. This is what I mean by Newman's tenderness: Madame de Cintré pleased him so, exactly as she was, that his desire to interpose between her and the troubles of life had the quality of a young mother's eagerness to protect the sleep of her first-born child. Newman was simply charmed, and he handled his charm as if it were a music-box which would stop if one shook it. There can be no better proof of the hankering epicure that is hidden in every man's temperament, waiting for a signal from some divine confederate that he may safely peep out. Newman at last was enjoying, purely, freely, deeply. Certain of Madame de Cintré's personal qualities – the luminous sweetness of her eyes, the delicate mobility of her face, the deep liquidity of her voice – filled all his consciousness. A rose-crowned Greek of old, gazing at a marble goddess with his whole bright intellect resting satisfied in the act, could not have been a more complete embodiment of the wisdom that loses itself in the enjoyment of quiet harmonies.

He made no violent love to her – no sentimental speeches. He never trespassed on what she had made him understand was for the present forbidden ground. But he had, nevertheless, a comfortable sense that she knew better from day to day how much he admired her. Though in general he was no great talker, he talked much, and he succeeded perfectly in making her say many things. He was not afraid of boring her, either by his discourse or by his silence; and whether or no he did occasionally bore her, it is probable that on the whole she liked him only the better for his absence of embarrassed scruples. Her visitors, coming in often while Newman sat there, found a tall, lean, silent man, in a half-lounging attitude, who laughed out sometimes when no one had meant to be droll, and remained grave in the presence of calculated witticisms, for the appreciation of which he had apparently not the proper culture.

It must be confessed that the number of subjects upon which Newman had no ideas was extremely large, and it must be added that as regards those subjects upon which he was without ideas he was also perfectly without words. He had little of the small change of conversation, and his stock of ready-made formulas and phrases was the scantiest. On the other hand he had plenty of attention to bestow, and his estimate of the importance of a topic did not depend upon the number of clever things he could say about it. He himself was almost never bored, and there was no man with whom it would have been a greater mistake to suppose that silence meant displeasure. What it was that entertained him during some of his speechless sessions I must, however, confess myself unable to determine. We know in a general way that a great many things which were old stories to a great many people had the charm of novelty to him, but a complete list of his new impressions would probably contain a number of surprises for us. He told Madame de Cintré a hundred long stories; he explained to her, in talking of the United States, the working of various local institutions and mercantile customs. Judging by the sequel, she was interested, but one would not have been sure of it beforehand. As regards her own talk, Newman was very sure himself that she herself enjoyed it: this was as a sort of amendment to the portrait that Mrs Tristram had drawn of her. He discovered that she had naturally an abundance of gaiety. He had been right at first in saying she was shy; her shyness, in a woman whose circumstances and tranquil beauty afforded every facility for well-mannered hardihood, was only a charm the more. For Newman it had lasted some time, and even when it went it left something behind it which for awhile performed the same office. Was this the tearful secret of which Mrs Tristram had had a glimpse, and of which, as of her friend's reserve, her high-breeding, and her profundity, she had given a sketch of which the outlines were, perhaps, rather too heavy? Newman supposed so, but he found himself wondering less every day what Madame de Cintré's secrets might be, and more convinced that secrets were, in themselves, hateful things to her. She was a woman for the light, not for the shade; and her natural line was not picturesque reserve and mysterious melancholy, but frank, joyous, brilliant action, with just so much meditation as was necessary, and not a grain more. To this, apparently, he had succeeded in bringing her back. He felt, himself, that he was an antidote to oppressive secrets; what he offered her was, in fact, above all things a vast sunny immunity from the need of having any. He often passed his evenings, when Madame de Cintré had so appointed it, at the chilly fireside of Madame de Bellegarde, contenting himself with looking across the room, through narrowed eyelids, at his mistress, who always made a point, before her family, of talking to someone else. Madame de Bellegarde sat by the fire convers-ing neatly and coldly with whomsoever approached her, and glancing round the room with her slowly-restless eye, the effect of which, when it lighted upon him, was to Newman's sense identical with that of a sudden spurt of damp air. When he shook hands with her he always asked her with a laugh whether she could 'stand him' another evening, and she replied, without a laugh, that, thank God, she had always been able to do her duty. Newman, talking once of the marquise to Mrs Tristram, said that after all it was very easy to get on with her; it always was easy to get on with out-and-out rascals.

'And is it by that elegant term,' said Mrs Tristram, 'that you designate the Marquise de Bellegarde?'

'Well,' said Newman, 'she is wicked, she is an old sinner.'

'What is her crime?' asked Mrs Tristram.

'I shouldn't wonder if she had murdered someone – all from a sense of duty, of course.'

'How can you be so dreadful?' sighed Mrs Tristram.

'I am not dreadful. I am speaking of her favourably.'

'Pray what will you say when you want to be severe?'

'I shall keep my severity for someone else – for the marquis. There's a man I can't swallow, mix the drink as I will.'

'And what has *he* done?'

'I can't quite make out; it is something dreadfully bad, something mean and underhand, and not redeemed by audacity, as his mother's misdemeanours may have been. If he has never committed murder, he has at least turned his back and looked the other way while someone else was committing it.'

In spite of this invidious hypothesis, which must be taken for nothing more than an example of the capricious play of 'Ameri-can humour', Newman did his best to maintain an easy and friendly style of communication with M. de Bellegarde. So long as he was in personal contact with people, he disliked extremely to have anything to forgive them, and he was capable of a good deal of unsuspected imaginative effort (for the sake of his own personal comfort) to assume for the time that they were good fellows. He did his best to treat the marquis as one; he believed honestly, moreover, that he could not, in reason, be such a confounded fool as he seemed. Newman's familiarity was never importunate; his sense of human equality was not an aggressive taste or an aesthetic theory, but something as natural and organic as a physical appetite which had never been put on a scanty allowance, and consequently was innocent of ungraceful eagerness. His tranquil unsuspectingness of the relativity of his own place in the social scale was probably irritating to M. de Bellegarde, who saw himself reflected in the mind of his potential brother-in-law in a crude and colourless form, unpleasantly dissimilar to the impressive image projected upon his own intellectual mirror. He never forgot himself for an instant, and replied to what he must have considered Newman's 'advances' with mechanical politeness. Newman, who was constantly forgetting himself, and indulging in an unlimited amount of irresponsible inquiry and conjecture, now and then found himself confronted by the conscious ironical smile of his host. What the deuce M. de Bellegarde was smiling at he was at a loss to divine. M. de Bellegarde's smile may be supposed to have been, for himself, a compromise between a great many emotions. So long as he smiled he was polite, and it was proper he should be polite. A smile, moreover, committed him to nothing more than politeness, and left the degree of politeness agreeably vague. A smile, too, was neither dissent – which was too serious – nor agreement, which might have brought on terrible complications. And then a smile covered his own personal dignity, which in this critical situation he was resolved to keep immaculate; it was quite enough that the glory of his house should pass into eclipse. Between him and Newman, his whole manner seemed to declare, that there could be no interchange of opinion; he was holding his breath so as not to inhale the odour of democracy. Newman was far from being versed in European politics, but he liked to have a general idea of what was going on about him, and he accordingly asked M. de Bellegarde several times what he thought of public affairs. M. de Bellegarde answered with suave concision that he thought as ill of them as possible, that they were going from bad to worse, and that the age was rotten to its core. This gave Newman, for the moment, an almost kindly feeling for the marquis; he pitied a man for whom the world was so cheerless a place, and the next time he saw M. de

Bellegarde he attempted to call his attention to some of the brilliant features of the time. The marquis presently replied that he had but a single political conviction, which was enough for him: he believed in the divine right of Henry of Bourbon, Fifth of his name,* to the throne of France. Newman stared, and after this he ceased to talk politics with M. de Bellegarde. He was not horrified nor scandalised, he was not even amused; he felt as he should have felt if he had discovered in M. de Bellegarde a taste for certain oddities of diet; an appetite, for instance, for fish-bones or nutshells. Under these circumstances, of course, he would never have broached dietary questions with him.

One afternoon, on his calling on Madame de Cintré, Newman was requested by the servant to wait a few moments, as his hostess was not at liberty. He walked about the room awhile, taking up her books, smelling her flowers, and looking at her prints and photographs (which he thought prodigiously pretty), and at last he heard the opening of a door to which his back was turned. On the threshold stood an old woman whom he remembered to have met several times in entering and leaving the house. She was tall and straight, and dressed in black, and she wore a cap which, if Newman had been initiated into such mysteries, would have been a sufficient assurance that she was not a Frenchwoman; a cap of pure British composition. She had a pale, decent, depressed-looking face, and a clear, dull, English eye. She looked at Newman a moment, both intently and timidly, and then she dropped a short, straight English curtsy.

'Madame de Cintré begs you will kindly wait,' she said. 'She has just come in; she will soon have finished dressing.'

'Oh, I will wait as long as she wants,' said Newman. 'Pray tell her not to hurry.'

'Thank you, sir,' said the woman softly; and then, instead of retiring with the message, she advanced into the room. She looked about her for a moment, and presently went to the table and began to arrange certain books and knick-knacks. Newman was struck with the high respectability of her appearance; he was afraid to address her as a servant. She busied herself for some moments with putting the table in order and pulling the curtains straight, while Newman walked slowly to and fro. He perceived at last, from her reflection in the mirror, as he was passing, that her hands were idle and that she was looking at him intently. She evidently wished to say something, and Newman perceiving it, helped her to begin.

'You are English?' he asked.

'Yes, sir, please,' she answered quickly and softly; 'I was born in Wiltshire.'

'And what do you think of Paris?'

'Oh, I don't think of Paris, sir,' she said, in the same tone. 'It is so long since I have been here.'

'Ah, you have been here very long?'

'It is more than forty years, sir. I came over with Lady Emmeline.'

'You mean with old Madame de Bellegarde?'

'Yes, sir. I came with her when she was married. I was my lady's own woman.'

'And you have been with her ever since?'

'I have been in the house ever since. My lady has taken a younger person. You see I am very old. I do nothing regular now. But I keep about.'

'You look very strong and well,' said Newman, observing the erectness of her figure, and a certain venerable rosiness in her cheek.

'Thank God I am not ill, sir; I hope I know my duty too well to go panting and coughing about the house. But I am an old woman, sir, and it is as an old woman that I venture to speak to you.'

'Oh, speak out,' said Newman, curiously. 'You needn't be afraid of me.'

'Yes, sir. I think you are kind. I have seen you before.'

'On the stairs, you mean?'

'Yes, sir. When you have been coming to see the countess. I have taken the liberty of noticing that you come often.'

'Oh yes; I come very often,' said Newman, laughing. 'You need not have been very wide awake to notice that.'

'I have noticed it with pleasure, sir,' said the ancient tire-woman* gravely. And she stood looking at Newman with a strange expression of face. The old instinct of deference and humility was there; the habit of decent self-effacement and knowledge of her 'own place'. But there mingled with it a certain mild audacity, born of the occasion and of a sense, probably, of Newman's unprecedented approachableness, and, beyond this, a vague indifference to the old proprieties; as if my lady's own woman had at last begun to reflect that, since my lady had taken another person, she had a slight reversionary property in herself.

'You take a great interest in the family?' said Newman.

'A deep interest, sir. Especially in the countess.'

'I am glad of that,' said Newman. And in a moment he added, smiling: 'So do I!'

'So I supposed, sir. We can't help noticing these things and having our ideas; can we, sir?'

'You mean as a servant?' said Newman.

'Ah, there it is, sir. I am afraid that when I let my thoughts meddle with such matters I am no longer a servant. But I am so devoted to the countess; if she were my own child I couldn't love her more. That is how I come to be so bold, sir. They say you want to marry her.'

Newman eyed his interlocutress and satisfied himself that she was not a gossip, but a zealot; she looked anxious, appealing, discreet. 'It is quite true,' he said. 'I want to marry Madame de Cintré.'

'And to take her away to America?'

'I will take her wherever she wants to go.'

'The farther away the better, sir!' exclaimed the old woman with sudden intensity. But she checked herself, and, taking up a paper-weight in mosaic, began to polish it with her black apron. 'I don't mean anything against the house or the family, sir. But I think a great change would do the poor countess good. It is very sad here.'

'Yes, it's not very lively,' said Newman. 'But Madame de Cintré is gay herself.'

'She is everything that is good. You will not be vexed to hear that she has been gayer for a couple of months past than she had been in many a day before.'

Newman was delighted to gather this testimony to the prosperity of his suit, but he repressed all violent marks of elation. 'Has Madame de Cintré been in bad spirits before this?' he asked.

'Poor lady, she had good reason. M. de Cintré was no husband for a sweet young lady like that. And then, as I say, it has been a sad house. It is better, in my humble opinion, that she were out of it. So, if you will excuse me for saying so, I hope she will marry you.'

'I hope she will!' said Newman.

'But you must not lose courage, sir, if she doesn't make up her mind at once. That is what I wanted to beg of you, sir. Don't give it up, sir. You will not take it ill if I say it's a great risk for any lady at any time; all the more when she has got rid of one bad bargain. But if she can marry a good, kind, respectable gentleman, I think she had better make up her mind to it. They speak very well of you, sir, in the house, and, if you will allow me to say so, I like your face. You have a very different appearance from the late count; he wasn't five feet high. And they say your fortune is beyond everything. There's no harm in that. So I beseech you to be patient, sir, and bide your time. If I don't say this to you, sir, perhaps no one will. Of course it is not for me to make any promises. I can answer for nothing. But I think your chance is not so bad, sir. I am nothing but a weary old woman in my quiet corner, but one woman understands another, and I think I make out the countess. I received her in my arms when she came into the world, and her first wedding-day was the saddest of my life. She owes it to me to show me another and a brighter one. If you will hold firm, sir – and you look as if you would – I think we may see it.'

'I am much obliged to you for your encouragement,' said Newman heartily. 'One can't have too much. I mean to hold firm. And if Madame de Cintré marries me, you must come and live with her.'

The old woman looked at him strangely, with her soft lifeless eyes. 'It may seem a heartless thing to say, sir, when one has been forty years in a house, but I may tell you that I should like to leave this place.'

'Why, it's just the time to say it,' said Newman fervently. 'After forty years one wants a change.'

'You are very kind, sir;' and this faithful servant dropped another curtsy and seemed disposed to retire. But she lingered a moment, and gave a timid joyless smile. Newman was disappointed, and his fingers stole half shyly half irritably into his waistcoat-pocket. His informant noticed the movement. 'Thank God I am not a Frenchwoman,' she said. 'If I were, I would tell you with a brazen simper, old as I am, that if you please, monsieur, my information is worth something. Let me tell you so in my own decent English way. It *is* worth something.'

'How much, please?' said Newman.

'Simply this: a promise not to hint to the countess that I have said these things.'

'If that is all, you have it,' said Newman.

'That is all, sir. Thank you, sir. Good-day, sir.' And having once more slid down telescope-wise into her scanty petticoats, the old woman departed. At the same moment Madame de Cintré came in by an opposite door. She noticed the movement of the other *portière** and asked Newman who had been entertaining him.

'The British female!' said Newman. 'An old lady in a black dress and a cap, who curtsies up and down, and expresses herself ever so well.'

'An old lady who curtsies and expresses herself? . . . Ah, you mean poor Mrs Bread. I happen to know that you have made a conquest of her.'

'Mrs Cake, she ought to be called,' said Newman. 'She is very sweet. She is a delicious old woman.'

Madame de Cintré looked at him a moment. 'What can she have said to you? She is an excellent creature, but we think her rather dismal.'

'I suppose,' Newman answered presently, 'that I like her because she has lived near you so long. Since your birth, she told me.'

'Yes,' said Madame de Cintré, simply; 'she is very faithful; I can trust her.'

Newman had never made any reflections to this lady upon her mother and her brother Urbain; had given no hint of the impression they made upon him. But, as if she had guessed his thoughts, she seemed careful to avoid all occasion for making him speak of them. She never alluded to her mother's domestic decrees; she never quoted the opinions of the marquis. They had talked, however, of Valentin, and she had made no secret of her extreme affection for her younger brother. Newman listened sometimes with a certain harmless jealousy; he would have liked to divert some of her tender allusions to his own credit. Once Madame de Cintré told him, with a little air of triumph, about something that Valentin had done which she thought very much to his honour. It was a service he had rendered to an old friend of the family; something more 'serious' than Valentin was usually supposed capable of being. Newman said he was glad to hear of it, and then began to talk about something which lay upon his own heart. Madame de Cintré listened, but after awhile she said: 'I don't like the way you speak of my brother Valentin.' Hereupon Newman, surprised, said that he had never spoken of him but kindly.

'It is too kindly,' said Madame de Cintré. 'It is a kindness that costs nothing; it is the kindness you show to a child. It is as if you didn't respect him.'

'Respect him? Why, I think I do.'

'You think? If you are not sure, it is no respect.'

'Do you respect him?' said Newman. 'If you do, I do.'

'If one loves a person, that is a question one is not bound to answer,' said Madame de Cintré.

'You should not have asked it of me, then. I am very fond of your brother.'

'He amuses you. But you would not like to resemble him.'

'I shouldn't like to resemble anyone. It is hard enough work resembling oneself.'

'What do you mean,' asked Madame de Cintré, 'by resembling oneself?'

'Why, doing what is expected of one. Doing one's duty.'

'But that is only when one is very good.'

'Well, a great many people are good,' said Newman. 'Valentin is quite good enough for me.'

Madame de Cintré was silent for a short time. 'He is not good enough for me,' she said at last. 'I wish he would do something.'

'What can he do?' asked Newman.

'Nothing. Yet he is very clever.'

'It is a proof of cleverness,' said Newman, 'to be happy without doing anything.'

'I don't think Valentin is happy, in reality. He is clever, generous, brave – but what is there to show for it? To me there is something sad in his life, and sometimes I have a sort of foreboding about him. I don't know why, but I fancy he will have some great trouble – perhaps an unhappy end.'

'Oh, leave him to me,' said Newman jovially. 'I will watch over him and keep harm away.'

One evening, in Madame de Bellegarde's salon, the conversation had flagged most sensibly. The marquis walked up and down in silence, like a sentinel at the door of some smooth-fronted citadel of the proprieties; his mother sat staring at the fire; young Madame de Bellegarde worked at an enormous band of tapestry. Usually there were three or four visitors, but on this occasion a violent storm sufficiently accounted for the absence of even the most devoted habitués. In the long silences the howling of the wind and the beating of the rain were distinctly audible. Newman sat perfectly still, watching the clock, determined to stay till the stroke of eleven, but not a moment longer. Madame de Cintré had turned her back to the circle, and had been standing for some time within the uplifted curtain of a window, with her forehead against the pane, gazing out into the deluged darkness. Suddenly she turned round toward her sister-in-law.

'For heaven's sake,' she said, with peculiar eagerness, 'go to the piano and play something.'

Madame de Bellegarde held up her tapestry and pointed to a little white flower. 'Don't ask me to leave this. I am in the midst of a masterpiece. My flower is going to smell very sweet; I am putting in the smell with this gold-coloured silk. I am holding my breath; I can't leave off. Play something yourself.'

'It is absurd for me to play when you are present,' said Madame de Cintré. But the next moment she went to the piano and began to strike the keys with vehemence. She played for some time, rapidly and brilliantly; when she stopped, Newman went to the piano and asked her to begin again. She shook her head, and, on his insisting, she said: 'I have not been playing for you; I have been playing for myself.' She went back to the window again and looked out, and shortly afterwards left the room. When Newman took leave, Urbain de Bellegarde accompanied him, as he always did, just three steps down the staircase. At the bottom stood a servant with his overcoat. He had just put it on when he saw Madame de Cintré coming towards him across the vestibule.

'Shall you be at home on Friday?' Newman asked.

She looked at him a moment before answering his question. 'You don't like my mother and my brother,' she said.

He hesitated a moment, and then he said softly: 'No.'

She laid her hand on the balustrade and prepared to ascend the stairs, fixing her eyes on the first step.

'Yes, I shall be at home on Friday,' and she passed up the wide dusky staircase.

On the Friday, as soon as he came in, she asked him to please to tell her why he disliked her family.

'Dislike your family?' he exclaimed. 'That has a horrid sound. I didn't say so, did I? I didn't mean it, if I did.'

'I wish you would tell me what you think of them,' said Madame de Cintré.

'I don't think of any of them but you.'

'That is because you dislike them. Speak the truth; you can't offend me.'

'Well, I don't exactly love your brother,' said Newman. 'I remember now. But what is the use of my saying so? I had forgotten it.'

'You are too good-natured,' said Madame de Cintré, gravely. Then, as if to avoid the appearance of inviting him to speak ill of the marquis, she turned away, motioning him to sit down.

But he remained standing before her and said presently: 'What is of much more importance is that they don't like me.'

'No – they don't,' she said.

'And don't you think they are wrong?' Newman asked. 'I don't believe I am a man to dislike.'

'I suppose that a man who may be liked, may also be disliked. And my brother – my mother,' she added, 'have not made you angry?'

'Yes, sometimes.'

'You have never shown it.'

'So much the better.'

'Yes, so much the better. They think they have treated you very well.'

'I have no doubt they might have handled me much more roughly,' said Newman. 'I am much obliged to them. Honestly.'

'You are generous,' said Madame de Cintré. 'It's a disagreeable position.'

'For them, you mean. Not for me.'

'For me,' said Madame de Cintré.

'Not when their sins are forgiven!' said Newman. 'They don't think I am as good as they are. I do. But we shan't quarrel about it.'

'I can't even agree with you without saying something that has a disagreeable sound. The presumption was against you. That you probably don't understand.'

Newman sat down and looked at her for some time. 'I don't think I really understand it. But when you say it, I believe it.'

'That's a poor reason,' said Madame de Cintré, smiling.

'No, it's a very good one. You have a high spirit, a high standard; but with you it's all natural and unaffected; you don't seem to have stuck your head into a vice,* as if you were sitting for the photograph of propriety. You think of me as a fellow who has had no idea in life but to make money and drive sharp bargains. That's a fair description of me, but it is not the whole story. A man ought to care for something else, though I don't know exactly what. I cared for money-making, but I never cared particularly for the money. There was nothing else to do, and it was impossible to be idle. I have been very easy to others, and to myself. I have done most of the things that people asked me – I don't mean rascals. As regards your mother and your brother,' Newman added, 'there is only one point upon which I feel that I might quarrel with them. I don't ask them to sing my praises to you, but I ask them to let you alone. If I thought they talked ill of me to you, I should come down upon them.'

'They have let me alone, as you say. They have not talked ill of you.'

'In that case,' cried Newman, 'I declare they are only too good for this world!'

Madame de Cintré appeared to find something startling in his exclamation. She would, perhaps, have replied, but at this moment the door was thrown open, and Urbain de Bellegarde stepped across the threshold. He appeared surprised at finding Newman, but his surprise was but a momentary shadow across the surface of an unwonted joviality. Newman had never seen the marquis so exhilarated; his pale unlighted countenance had a sort of thin transfiguration. He held open the door for someone else to enter, and presently appeared old Madame de Bellegarde, leaning on the arm of a gentleman whom Newman had not seen before. He had already risen, and Madame de Cintré rose, as she always did before her mother. The marquis, who had greeted Newman almost genially, stood apart, slowly rubbing his hands. His mother came forward with her companion. She gave a majestic little nod at Newman, and then she released the strange gentleman, that he might make his bow to her daughter.

'My daughter,' she said, 'I have brought you an unknown relative, Lord Deepmere. Lord Deepmere is our cousin, but he has done only today what he ought to have done long ago – come to make our acquaintance.'

Madame de Cintré smiled, and offered Lord Deepmere her

hand. 'It is very extraordinary,' said this noble laggard, 'but this is the first time that I have ever been in Paris for more than three or four weeks.'

'And how long have you been here now?' asked Madame de Cintré.

'Oh, for the last two months,' said Lord Deepmere.

These two remarks might have constituted an impertinence; but a glance at Lord Deepmere's face would have satisfied you, as it apparently satisfied Madame de Cintré, that they constituted only a *naïveté*. When his companions were seated, Newman, who was out of the conversation, occupied himself with observing the newcomer. Observation, however, as regards Lord Deepmere's person, had no great range. He was a small meagre man, of some three-and-thirty years of age, with a bald head, a short nose, and no front teeth in the upper jaw; he had round, candid, blue eyes, and several pimples on his chin. He was evidently very shy, and he laughed a great deal, catching his breath with an odd startling sound, as the most convenient imitation of repose. His physiognomy denoted great simplicity, a certain amount of brutality, and a probable failure in the past to profit by rare educational advantages. He remarked that Paris was awfully jolly, but that for real, thorough-paced entertainment it was nothing to Dublin. He even preferred Dublin to London. Had Madame de Cintré ever been to Dublin? They must all come over there some day, and he would show them some Irish sport. He always went to Ireland for the fishing, and he came to Paris for the new Offenbach* things. They always brought them out in Dublin, but he couldn't wait. He had been nine times to hear La Pomme de Paris.* Madame de Cintré, leaning back, with her arms folded, looked at Lord Deepmere with a more visibly puzzled face than she usually showed to society. Madame de Bellegarde, on the other hand, wore a fixed smile. The marquis said that among light operas his favourite was the 'Gazza Ladra'.* The marquise then began a series of inquiries about the duke and the cardinal, the old countess and Lady Barbara, after listening to which, and to Lord Deepmere's somewhat irreverent responses, for a quarter of an hour, Newman rose to take his leave. The marquis went with him three steps into the hall.

'Is he Irish?' asked Newman, nodding in the direction of the visitor.

'His mother was the daughter of Lord Finucane,' said the marquis; 'he has great Irish estates. Lady Bridget, in the complete absence of male heirs, either direct or collateral – a most extraordinary circumstance – came in for everything. But Lord Deepmere's title is English, and his English property is immense. He is a charming young man.'

Newman answered nothing, but he detained the marquis as the latter was beginning gracefully to recede. 'It is a good time for me to thank you,' he said, 'for sticking so punctiliously to our bargain, for doing so much to help me on with your sister.'

The marquis stared. 'Really, I have done nothing that I can boast of,' he said.

'Oh, don't be modest,' Newman answered, laughing. 'I can't flatter myself that I am doing so well simply by my own merit. And thank your mother for me, too!' And he turned away, leaving M. de Bellegarde looking after him.

CHAPTER 14

The next time Newman came to the Rue de l'Université he had the good fortune to find Madame de Cintré alone. He had come with a definite intention, and he lost no time in executing it. She wore, moreover, a look which he eagerly interpreted as expectancy.

'I have been coming to see you for six months, now,' he said, 'and I have never spoken to you a second time of marriage. That was what you asked me; I obeyed. Could any man have done better?'

'You have acted with great delicacy,' said Madame de Cintré.

'Well, I am going to change now,' said Newman. 'I don't mean that I am going to be indelicate; but I am going to go back to where I began. I *am* back there. I have been all round the circle. Or rather, I have never been away from there. I have never ceased to want what I wanted then. Only now I am more sure of it, if possible; I am more sure of myself, and more sure of you. I know you better, though I don't know anything I didn't believe three months ago. You are everything – you are beyond everything – I can imagine or desire. You know me now; you *must* know me. I won't say that you have seen the best – but you have seen the worst. I hope you have been thinking all this while. You must have seen that I was only waiting; you can't suppose that I was changing. What will you say to me, now? Say that everything is clear and reasonable, and that I have been very patient and considerate, and deserve my reward. And then give me your hand. Madame de Cintré, do that. Do it.'

'I knew you were only waiting,' she said; 'and I was very sure this day would come. I have thought about it a great deal. At first I was half afraid of it. But I am not afraid of it now.' She paused a moment, and then she added: 'It's a relief.'

She was sitting on a low chair, and Newman was on an ottoman, near her. He leaned a little and took her hand, which for an instant she let him keep. 'That means that I have not waited for nothing,' he said. She looked at him for a moment, and he saw her eyes fill with tears. 'With me,' he went on, 'you will be as safe – as safe' – and even in his ardour he hesitated a moment for a comparison – 'as safe,' he said, with a kind of simple solemnity, 'as in your father's arms.'

Still she looked at him and her tears increased. Then, abruptly, she buried her face on the cushioned arm of the sofa beside her chair, and broke into noiseless sobs. 'I am weak – I am weak,' he heard her say.

'All the more reason why you should give yourself up to me,' he answered. 'Why are you troubled? There is nothing here that should trouble you. I offer you nothing but happiness. Is that so hard to believe?'

'To you everything seems so simple,' she said, raising her head. 'But things are not so. I like you extremely. I liked you six months ago, and now I am sure of it, as you say you are sure. But it is not easy, simply for that, to decide to marry you. There are a great many things to think about.'

'There ought to be only one thing to think about – that we love each other,' said Newman. And as she remained silent he quickly added: 'Very good; if you can't accept that, don't tell me so.'

'I should be very glad to think of nothing,' she said at last; 'not to think at all; only to shut both my eyes and give myself up. But I can't. I'm cold, I'm old, I'm a coward; I never supposed

I should marry again, and it seems to me very strange I should ever have listened to you. When I used to think, as a girl, of what I should do if I were to marry freely by my own choice, I thought of a very different man from you.'

'That's nothing against me,' said Newman, with an immense smile; 'your taste was not formed.'

His smile made Madame de Cintré smile. 'Have you formed it?' she asked. And then she said, in a different tone: 'Where do you wish to live?'

'Anywhere in the wide world you like. We can easily settle that.'

'I don't know why I ask you,' she presently continued. 'I care very little. I think if I were to marry you I could live almost anywhere. You have some false ideas about me; you think that I need a great many things – that I must have a brilliant worldly life. I am sure you are prepared to take a great deal of trouble to give me such things. But that is very arbitrary; I have done nothing to prove that.' She paused again, looking at him, and her mingled sound and silence were so sweet to him that he had no wish to hurry her, any more than he would have had a wish to hurry a golden sunrise. 'Your being so different, which at first seemed a difficulty, a trouble, began one day to seem to me a pleasure, a great pleasure. I was glad you were different. And yet, if I had said so, no one would have understood me; I don't mean simply to my family.'

'They would have said I was a queer monster, eh?' said Newman.

'They would have said I could never be happy with you – you were too different; and I would have said it was just *because* you were so different that I might be happy. But they would have given better reasons than I. My only reason – ' and she paused again.

But this time, in the midst of his golden sunrise, Newman felt the impulse to grasp at a rosy cloud. 'Your only reason is that you love me!' he murmured, with an eloquent gesture, and for want of a better reason Madame de Cintré reconciled herself to this one.

Newman came back the next day, and in the vestibule, as he entered the house, he encountered his friend Mrs Bread. She was wandering about in honourable idleness, and when his eyes fell upon her she delivered him one of her curtsies. Then turning to the servant who had admitted him, she said, with the combined majesty of her native superiority and of a rugged English accent: 'You may retire; I will have the honour of conducting monsieur.' In spite of this combination, however, it appeared to Newman that her voice had a slight quaver, as if the tone of command were not habitual to it. The man gave her an impertinent stare, but he walked slowly away, and she led Newman upstairs. At half its course the staircase gave a bend, forming a little platform. In the angle of the wood stood an indifferent statue of an eighteenth-century nymph, simpering, sallow, and cracked. Here Mrs Bread stopped and looked with shy kindness at her companion.

'I know the good news, sir,' she murmured.

'You have a good right to be first to know it,' said Newman. 'You have taken such a friendly interest.'

Mrs Bread turned away and began to blow the dust off the statue, as if this might be mockery.

'I suppose you want to congratulate me,' said Newman. 'I am greatly obliged.' And then he added: 'You gave me much pleasure the other day.'

She turned round, apparently reassured. 'You are not to think that I have been told anything,' she said; 'I have only guessed. But when I looked at you, as you came in, I was sure I had guessed aright.'

'You are very sharp,' said Newman. 'I am sure that in your quiet way you see everything.'

'I am not a fool, sir, thank God. I have guessed something else beside,' said Mrs Bread.

'What's that?'

'I needn't tell you that, sir; I don't think you would believe it. At any rate it wouldn't please you.'

'Oh, tell me nothing but what will please me,' laughed Newman. 'That is the way you began.'

'Well, sir, I suppose you won't be vexed to hear that the sooner everything is over the better.'

'The sooner we are married, you mean? The better for me, certainly.'

'The better for everyone.'

'The better for you, perhaps. You know you are coming to live with us,' said Newman.

'I am extremely obliged to you, sir, but it is not of myself I was thinking. I only wanted, if I might take the liberty, to recommend you to lose no time.'

'Whom are you afraid of?'

Mrs Bread looked up the staircase and then down, and then she looked at the undusted nymph, as if she possibly had sentient ears. 'I am afraid of everyone,' she said.

'What an uncomfortable state of mind!' said Newman. 'Does "everyone" wish to prevent my marriage?'

'I am afraid of already having said too much,' Mrs Bread replied. 'I won't take it back, but I won't say any more. And she took her way up the staircase again and led him into Madame de Cintré's salon.

Newman indulged in a brief and silent imprecation when he found that Madame de Cintré was not alone. With her sat her mother, and in the middle of the room stood young Madame de Bellegarde, in her bonnet and mantle. The old marquise, who was leaning back in her chair with a hand clasping the knob of each arm, looked at him fixedly, without moving. She seemed barely conscious of his greeting; she appeared to be musing intently. Newman said to himself that her daughter had been announcing her engagement, and that the old lady found the morsel hard to swallow. But Madame de Cintré, as she gave him her hand, gave him also a look by which she appeared to mean that he should understand something. Was it a warning or a request? Did she wish to enjoin speech or silence? He was puzzled, and young Madame de Bellegarde's pretty grin gave him no information.

'I have not told my mother,' said Madame de Cintré, abruptly, looking at him.

'Told me what?' demanded the marquise. 'You tell me too little; you should tell me everything.'

'That is what I do,' said Madame Urbain, with a little laugh.

'Let *me* tell your mother,' said Newman.

The old lady stared at him again, and then turned to her daughter. 'You are going to marry him?' she cried softly.

'*Oui, ma mère*,'* said Madame de Cintré.

'Your daughter has consented, to my great happiness,' said Newman.

'And when was this arrangement made?' asked Madame de Bellegarde. 'I seem to be picking up the news by chance!'

'My suspense came to an end yesterday,' said Newman.

'And how long was mine to have lasted?' said the marquise to her daughter. She spoke without irritation; with a sort of cold noble displeasure.

Madame de Cintré stood silent, with her eyes on the ground. 'It is over now,' she said.

'Where is my son – where is Urbain?' asked the marquise. 'Send for your brother and inform him.'

Young Madame de Bellegarde laid her hand on the bell-rope. 'He was to make some visits with me, and I was to go and knock – very softly, very softly – at the door of his study. But he can come to me!' She pulled the bell, and in a few moments Mrs Bread appeared, with a face of calm inquiry.

'Send for your brother,' said the old lady.

But Newman felt an irresistible impulse to speak, and to speak in a certain way. 'Tell the marquis we want him,' he said to Mrs Bread, who quietly retired.

Young Madame de Bellegarde went to her sister-in-law and embraced her. Then she turned to Newman, with an intense smile. 'She is charming. I congratulate you.'

'I congratulate you, sir,' said Madame de Bellegarde, with extreme solemnity. 'My daughter is an extraordinarily good woman. She may have faults, but I don't know them.'

'My mother does not often make jokes,' said Madame de Cintré; 'but when she does they are terrible.'

'She is ravishing,' the Marquise Urbain resumed, looking at her sister-in-law, with her head on one side. 'Yes, I congratulate you.'

Madame de Cintré turned away, and, taking up a piece of tapestry, began to ply the needle. Some minutes of silence elapsed, which were interrupted by the arrival of M. de Belle-garde. He came in with his hat in his hand, gloved, and was followed by his brother Valentin, who appeared to have just entered the house. M. de Bellegarde looked around the circle and greeted Newman with his usual finely-measured courtesy. Valentin saluted his mother and his sisters, and, as he shook hands with Newman, gave him a glance of acute interrogation.

'*Arrivez donc, messieurs!*'* cried young Madame de Belle-garde. 'We have great news for you.'

'Speak to your brother, my daughter,' said the old lady.

Madame de Cintré had been looking at her tapestry. She raised her eyes to her brother. 'I have accepted Mr Newman.'

'Your sister has consented,' said Newman. 'You see, after all, I knew what I was about.'

'I am charmed!' said M. de Bellegarde, with superior benignity.

'So am I,' said Valentin to Newman. 'The marquis and I are charmed. I can't marry, myself, but I can understand it. I can't stand on my head, but I can applaud a clever acrobat. My dear sister, I bless your union.'

The marquis stood looking for awhile into the crown of his hat. 'We have been prepared,' he said at last, 'but it is inevitable that in the face of the event one should experience a certain emotion.' And he gave a most unhilarious smile.

'I feel no emotion that I was not perfectly prepared for,' said his mother.

'I can't say that for myself,' said Newman, smiling, but differently from the marquis. 'I am happier than I expected to be. I suppose it's the sight of your happiness!'

'Don't exaggerate that,' said Madame de Bellegarde, getting up and laying her hand upon her daughter's arm. 'You can't expect an honest old woman to thank you for taking away her beautiful only daughter.'

'You forget me, dear madame,' said the young marquise, demurely.

'Yes, she is very beautiful,' said Newman.

'And when is the wedding, pray?' asked young Madame de Bellegarde; 'I must have a month to think over a dress.'

'That must be discussed,' said the marquise.

'Oh, we will discuss it, and let you know!' Newman exclaimed.

'I have no doubt we shall agree,' said Urbain.

'If you don't agree with Madame de Cintré, you will be very unreasonable.'

'Come, come, Urbain,' said young Madame de Bellegarde. 'I must go straight to my tailor's.'

The old lady had been standing with her hand on her daughter's arm, looking at her fixedly. She gave a little sigh and murmured, 'No, I did *not* expect it! You are a fortunate man,' she added, turning to Newman, with an expressive nod.

'Oh, I know that!' he answered. 'I feel tremendously proud. I feel like crying it on the housetops – like stopping people in the street to tell them.'

Madame de Bellegarde narrowed her lips. 'Pray don't,' she said.

'The more people that know it, the better,' Newman declared. 'I haven't yet announced it here, but I telegraphed it this morning to America.'

'Telegraphed it to America?' the old lady murmured.

'To New York, to St Louis, and to San Francisco; those are the principal cities, you know. Tomorrow I shall tell my friends here.'

'Have you many?' asked Madame de Bellegarde, in a tone of which I am afraid that Newman but partly measured the impertinence.

'Enough to bring me a great many handshakes and congratulations. To say nothing,' he added, in a moment, 'of those I shall receive from your friends.'

'They will not use the telegraph,' said the marquise, taking her departure.

M. de Bellegarde, whose wife, her imagination having apparently taken flight to the tailor's, was fluttering her silken wings in emulation, shook hands with Newman, and said, with a more persuasive accent than the latter had ever heard him use: 'You may count upon me.' Then his wife led him away.

Valentin stood looking from his sister to our hero.

'I hope you have both reflected seriously,' he said.

Madame de Cintré smiled. 'We have neither your powers of reflection nor your depth of seriousness; but we have done our best.'

'Well, I have a great regard for each of you,' Valentin continued. 'You are charming young people. But I am not satisfied, on the whole, that you belong to that small and superior class – that exquisite group – composed of persons who are worthy to remain unmarried. These are rare souls; they are the salt of the earth. But I don't mean to be invidious; the marrying people are often very nice.'

'Valentin holds that women should marry, and that men should not,' said Madame de Cintré. 'I don't know how he arranges it.'

'I arrange it by adoring you, my sister,' said Valentin, ardently. 'Good-bye.'

'Adore someone whom you can marry,' said Newman. 'I will arrange that for you some day. I foresee that I am going to turn apostle.'

Valentin was on the threshold; he looked back a moment, with a face that had turned grave. 'I adore someone I can't marry!' he said. And he dropped the *portière* and departed.

'They don't like it,' said Newman, standing alone before Madame de Cintré.

'No,' she said, after a moment; 'they don't like it.'

'Well, now, do you mind that?' asked Newman.

'Yes!' she said, after another interval.

'That's a mistake.'

'I can't help it. I should prefer that my mother were pleased.'

'Why the deuce,' demanded Newman, 'is she not pleased? She gave you leave to marry me.'

'Very true; I don't understand it. And yet I do "mind it", as you say. You will call it superstitious.'

'That will depend upon how much you let it bother you. Then I shall call it an awful bore.'

'I will keep it to myself,' said Madame de Cintré. 'It shall not bother you.' And they then talked of their marriage-day, and Madame de Cintré assented unreservedly to Newman's desire to have it fixed for an early date.

Newman's telegrams were answered with interest. Having despatched but three electric missives, he received no less than eight gratulatory bulletins in return. He put them into his pocket-book, and the next time he encountered old Madame de Bellegarde drew them forth and displayed them to her. This, it must be confessed, was a slightly malicious stroke; the reader must judge in what degree the offence was venial. Newman knew that the marquise disliked his telegrams, though he could see no sufficient reason for it. Madame de Cintré, on the other hand, liked them; and, most of them being of a humorous cast, laughed at them immoderately, and inquired into the character of their authors. Newman, now that his prize was gained, felt a peculiar desire that his triumph should be manifest. He more than suspected that the Bellegardes were keeping quiet about it, and allowing it, in their select circle, but a limited resonance; and it pleased him to think that if he were to take the trouble he might, as he phrased it, break all the windows. No man likes being repudiated, and yet Newman, if he was not flattered, was not exactly offended. He had not this good excuse for his somewhat aggressive impulse to promulgate his felicity; his sentiment was of another quality. He wanted for once to make the heads of the house of Bellegarde *feel* him; he knew not when he should have another chance. He had had for the past six months a sense of the old lady and her son looking straight over his head, and he was now resolved that they should toe a mark which he would give himself the satisfaction of drawing.

'It is like seeing a bottle emptied when the wine is poured too slowly,' he said to Mrs Tristram. 'They make me want to joggle their elbows and force them to spill their wine.'

To this Mrs Tristram answered that he had better leave them alone, and let them do things in their own way. 'You must make allowances for them,' she said. 'It is natural enough that they should hang fire a little. They thought they accepted you when you made your application; but they are not people of imagination, they could not project themselves into the future, and now they will have to begin again. But they *are* people of honour, and they will do whatever is necessary.'

Newman spent a few moments in narrow-eyed meditation.

'I am not hard on them,' he presently said; 'and to prove it I will invite them all to a festival.'

'To a festival?'

'You have been laughing at my great gilded rooms all winter; I will show you that they are good for something. I will give a party. What is the grandest thing one can do here? I will hire all the great singers from the opera, and all the first people from the Théâtre Française, and I will give an entertainment.'

'And whom will you invite?'

'You, first of all. And then the old lady and her son. And then everyone among her friends whom I have met at her house or elsewhere, everyone who has shown me the minimum of politeness, every duke of them and his wife. And then all my friends, without exception – Miss Kitty Upjohn, Miss Dora Finch; General Packard, C. P. Hatch, and all the rest. And everyone shall know what it is about; that is, to celebrate my engagement to the Countess de Cintré. What do you think of the idea?'

'I think it is odious!' said Mrs Tristram. And then in a moment: 'I think it is delicious!'

The very next evening Newman repaired to Madame de Bellegarde's salon, where he found her surrounded by her

children, and invited her to honour his poor dwelling by her
presence on a certain evening a fortnight distant.

The marquise stared a moment. 'My dear sir,' she cried, 'what
do you want to do to me?'

'To make you acquainted with a few people, and then to place
you in a very easy chair and ask you to listen to Madame
Frezzolini's singing.'*

'You mean to give a concert?'

'Something of that sort.'

'And to have a crowd of people?'

'All my friends, and I hope some of yours and your daughter's.
I want to celebrate my engagement.'

It seemed to Newman that Madame de Bellegarde turned
pale. She opened her fan, a fine old painted fan of the last
century, and looked at the picture, which represented a *fête
champêtre* * – a lady with a guitar, singing, and a group of
dancers round a garlanded Hermes.

'We go out so little,' murmured the marquis, 'since my poor
father's death.'

'But *my* dear father is still alive, my friend,' said his wife. 'I
am only waiting for my invitation to accept it,' and she glanced
with amiable confidence at Newman. 'It will be magnificent; I
am very sure of that.'

I am sorry to say, to the discredit of Newman's gallantry, that
this lady's invitation was not then and there bestowed; he was
giving all his attention to the old marquise. She looked up at last
smiling. 'I can't think of letting you offer me a fête,'* she said,
'until I have offered you one. We want to present you to our
friends; we will invite them all. We have it very much at heart.
We must do things in order. Come to me about the 25th; I will
let you know the exact day immediately. We shall not have
anyone so fine as Madame Frezzolini, but we shall have some
very good people. After that you may talk of your own fête.'
The old lady spoke with a certain quick eagerness, smiling more
agreeably as she went on.

It seemed to Newman a handsome proposal, and such propos-
als always touched the sources of his good-nature. He said to
Madame de Bellegarde that he should be glad to come on the
25th or any other day, and that it mattered very little whether
he met his friends at her house or at his own. I have said that
Newman was observant, but it must be admitted that on this

occasion he failed to notice a certain delicate glance which passed between Madame de Bellegarde and the marquis, and which we may presume to have been a commentary upon the innocence displayed in that latter clause of his speech.

Valentin de Bellegarde walked away with Newman that evening, and when they had left the Rue de l'Université some distance behind them he said reflectively: 'My mother is very strong – very strong.' Then in answer to an interrogative movement of Newman's he continued: 'She was driven to the wall; but you would never have thought it. Her fête of the 25th was an invention of the moment. She had no idea whatever of giving a fête, but finding it the only issue from your proposal, she looked straight at the dose – excuse the expression – and bolted it, as you saw, without winking. She is very strong.'

'Dear me!' said Newman, divided between relish and compassion. 'I don't care a straw for her fête; I am willing to take the will for the deed.'

'No, no,' said Valentin, with a little inconsequent touch of family pride. 'The thing will be done now, and done handsomely.'

CHAPTER 15

Valentin de Bellegarde's announcement of the secession of Mademoiselle Nioche from her father's domicile, and his irreverent reflections upon the attitude of this anxious parent in so grave a catastrophe, received a practical commentary in the fact that M. Nioche was slow to seek another interview with his late pupil. It had cost Newman some disgust to be forced to assent to Valentin's somewhat cynical interpretation of the old man's philosophy, and, though circumstances seemed to indicate that he had not given himself up to a noble despair, Newman thought it very possible he might be suffering more keenly than was apparent. M. Nioche had been in the habit of paying him a respectful little visit every two or three weeks, and his absence might be a proof quite as much of extreme depression as of a desire to conceal the success with which he had patched up his sorrow. Newman presently learned from Valentin several details touching this new phase of Mademoiselle Noémie's career.

'I told you she was remarkable,' this unshrinking observer declared, 'and the way she has managed this performance proves it. She has had other chances, but she was resolved to take none but the best. She did you the honour to think for awhile that you might be such a chance. You were not; so she gathered up her patience and waited awhile longer. At last her occasion came along, and she made her move with her eyes wide open. I am very sure she had no innocence to lose, but she had all her respectability. Dubious little damsel as you thought her, she had kept a firm hold of that; nothing could be proved against her, and she was determined not to let her reputation go till she had got her equivalent. About her equivalent she had high ideas. Apparently her ideal has been satisfied. It is fifty years old, bald-headed, and deaf, but it is very easy about money.'

'And where in the world,' asked Newman, 'did you pick up this valuable information?'

'In conversation. Remember my frivolous habits. In conversation with a young woman engaged in the humble trade of glove-cleaner, who keeps a small shop in the Rue St Roch. M. Nioche lives in the same house, up six pair of stairs, across the court, in and out of whose ill-swept doorway Miss Noémie has been flitting for the last five years. The little glove-cleaner was an old acquaintance; she used to be the friend of a friend of mine, who has married and dropped such friends. I often saw her in his society. As soon as I espied her behind her clear little windowpane, I recollected her. I had on a spotlessly fresh pair of gloves, but I went in and held up my hands, and said to her: "Dear mademoiselle, what will you ask me for cleaning these?" "Dear count," she answered immediately, "I will clean them for you for nothing." She had instantly recognised me, and I had to hear her history for the last six years. But after that, I put her upon that of her neighbours. She knows and admires Noémie, and she told me what I have just repeated.'

A month elapsed without M. Nioche reappearing, and Newman, who every morning read two or three suicides in the *Figaro*,* began to suspect that, mortification proving stubborn, he had sought a balm for his wounded pride in the waters of the Seine. He had a note of M. Nioche's address in his pocket-book, and finding himself one day in the *quartier*, he determined, in so

far as he might, to clear up his doubts. He repaired to the house
in the Rue St Roch which bore the recorded number, and
observed in a neighbouring basement, behind a dangling row of
neatly inflated gloves,* the attentive physiognomy of Bellegarde's informant – a sallow person in a dressing-gown – peering
into the street as if she were expecting that amiable nobleman
to pass again. But it was not to her that Newman applied; he
simply asked of the portress if M. Nioche were at home. The
portress replied, as the portress invariably replies, that her lodger
had gone out barely three minutes before; but then, through the
little square hole of her lodge-window taking the measure of
Newman's fortunes, and seeing them, by an unspecified process,
refresh the dry places of servitude to occupants of fifth floors on
courts, she added that M. Nioche would have had just time to
reach the Café de la Patrie, round the second corner to the left,
at which establishment he regularly spent his afternoons.
Newman thanked her for the information, took the second
turning to the left, and arrived at the Café de la Patrie. He felt a
momentary hesitation to go in; was it not rather mean to 'follow
up' poor old Nioche at that rate? But there passed across his
vision an image of a haggard little septuagenarian taking measured sips of a glass of sugar and water, and finding them quite
impotent to sweeten his desolation. He opened the door and
entered, perceiving nothing at first but a dense cloud of tobacco-
smoke. Across this, however, in a corner, he presently descried
the figure of M. Nioche, stirring the contents of a deep glass,
with a lady seated in front of him. The lady's back was turned
to Newman, but M. Nioche very soon perceived and recognised
his visitor. Newman had gone toward him, and the old man
rose slowly, gazing at him with a more blighted expression even
than usual.
  'If you are drinking hot punch,' said Newman, 'I suppose you
are not dead. That's all right. Don't move.'
  M. Nioche stood staring, with a fallen jaw, not daring to put
out his hand. The lady, who sat facing him, turned round in her
place and glanced upward with a spirited toss of her head,
displaying the agreeable features of his daughter. She looked at
Newman sharply, to see how he was looking at her, then – I
don't know what she discovered – she said graciously: 'How
d'ye do, monsieur? won't you come into our little corner?'

'Did you come – did you come after *me*?' asked M. Nioche, very softly.

'I went to your house to see what had become of you. I thought you might be sick,' said Newman.

'It is very good of you, as always,' said the old man. 'No, I am not well. Yes, I am *seek*.'

'Ask monsieur to sit down,' said Mademoiselle Nioche. 'Garçon,* bring a chair.'

'Will you do us the honour to *seat*?' said M. Nioche, timorously, and with a double foreignness of accent.

Newman said to himself that he had better see the thing out, and he took a chair at the end of the table, with Mademoiselle Nioche on his left and her father on the other side. 'You will take something, of course,' said Miss Noémie, who was sipping a glass of madeira. Newman said that he believed not, and then she turned to her papa with a smile. 'What an honour, eh? he has come only for us.' M. Nioche drained his pungent glass at a long draught, and looked out from eyes more lachrymose in consequence. 'But you didn't come for me, eh?' Mademoiselle Noémie went on. 'You didn't expect to find me here?'

Newman observed the change in her appearance. She was very elegant, and prettier than before; she looked a year or two older, and it was noticeable that, to the eye, she had only gained in respectability. She looked 'lady-like'. She was dressed in quiet colours, and she wore her expensively unobtrusive toilet with a grace that might have come from years of practice. Her present self-possession and *aplomb* struck Newman as really infernal, and he inclined to agree with Valentin de Bellegarde that the young lady was very remarkable. 'No, to tell the truth, I didn't come for you,' he said, 'and I didn't expect to find you. I was told,' he added in a moment, 'that you had left your father.'

'*Quelle horreur!*'* cried Mademoiselle Nioche, with a smile. 'Does one leave one's father? You have the proof of the contrary.'

'Yes, convincing proof,' said Newman, glancing at M. Nioche. The old man caught his glance obliquely, with his faded deprecating eye, and then, lifting his empty glass, pretended to drink again.

'Who told you that?' Noémie demanded. 'I know very well. It was M. de Bellegarde. Why don't you say yes? You are not polite.'

'I am embarrassed,' said Newman.

'I set you a better example. I know M. de Bellegarde told you. He knows a great deal about me – or he thinks he does. He has taken a great deal of trouble to find out, but half of it isn't true. In the first place, I haven't left my father; I am much too fond of him. Isn't it so, little father? M. de Bellegarde is a charming young man; it is impossible to be cleverer. I know a good deal about him too; you can tell him that when you next see him.'

'No,' said Newman, with a sturdy grin; 'I won't carry any messages for you.'

'Just as you please,' said Mademoiselle Nioche. 'I don't depend upon you, nor does M. de Bellegarde either. He is very much interested in me; he can be left to his own devices. He is a contrast to you.'

'Oh, he is a great contrast to me, I have no doubt,' said Newman. 'But I don't exactly know how you mean it.'

'I mean it in this way. First of all, he never offered to help me to a *dot* and a husband.' And Mademoiselle Nioche paused, smiling. 'I won't say that is in his favour, for I do you justice. What led you, by the way, to make me such a queer offer? You didn't care for me.'

'Oh yes, I did,' said Newman.

'How so?'

'It would have given me real pleasure to see you married to a respectable young fellow.'

'With six thousand francs of income!' cried Mademoiselle Nioche. 'Do you call that caring for me? I'm afraid you know little about women. You were not *galant*;* you were not what you might have been.'

Newman flushed, a trifle fiercely. 'Come!' he exclaimed, 'that's rather strong. I had no idea I had been so shabby.'

Mademoiselle Nioche smiled as she took up her muff. 'It is something, at any rate, to have made you angry.'

Her father had leaned both his elbows on the table, and his head, bent forward, was supported in his hands, the thin white fingers of which were pressed over his ears. In this position he was staring fixedly at the bottom of his empty glass, and Newman supposed he was not hearing. Mademoiselle Noémie buttoned her furred jacket and pushed back her chair, casting a glance charged with the consciousness of an expensive appearance first down over her flounces and then up at Newman.

'You had better have remained an honest girl,' Newman said quietly.

M. Nioche continued to stare at the bottom of his glass, and his daughter got up, still bravely smiling. 'You mean that I look so much like one? That's more than most women do nowadays. Don't judge me yet awhile,' she added. 'I mean to succeed; that's what I mean to do. I leave you; I don't mean to be seen in cafés, for one thing. I can't think what you want of my poor father; he's very comfortable now. It isn't his fault either. *Au revoir,** little father.' And she tapped the old man on the head with her muff. Then she stopped a minute, looking at Newman. 'Tell M. de Bellegarde, when he wants news of me, to come and get it from *me!*' And she turned and departed, the white-aproned waiter, with a bow, holding the door wide open for her.

M. Nioche sat motionless, and Newman hardly knew what to say to him. The old man looked dismally foolish. 'So you determined not to shoot her, after all,' Newman said presently.

M. Nioche, without moving, raised his eyes and gave him a long peculiar look. It seemed to confess everything, and yet not to ask for pity, nor to pretend, on the other hand, to a rugged ability to do without it. It might have expressed the state of mind of an innocuous insect, flat in shape, and conscious of the impending pressure of a boot-sole, and reflecting that he was perhaps too flat to be crushed. M. Nioche's gaze was a profession of moral flatness. 'You despise me terribly,' he said, in the weakest possible voice.

'Oh no,' said Newman; 'it is none of my business. It's a good plan to take things easily.'

'I made you too many fine speeches,' M. Nioche added. 'I meant them at the time.'

'I am sure I am very glad you didn't shoot her,' said Newman. 'I was afraid you might have shot yourself. That is why I came to look you up.' And he began to button his coat.

'Neither,' said M. Nioche. 'You despise me, and I can't explain to you. I hoped I shouldn't see you again.'

'Why, that's rather shabby,' said Newman. 'You shouldn't drop your friends that way. Besides, the last time you came to see me I thought you particularly jolly.'

'Yes, I remember,' said M. Nioche musingly; 'I was in a fever. I didn't know what I said, what I did. It was delirium.'

'Ah well, you are quieter now.'

M. Nioche was silent a moment. 'As quiet as the grave,' he whispered softly.

'Are you very unhappy?' asked Newman.

M. Nioche rubbed his forehead slowly, and even pushed back his wig a little, looking askance at his empty glass. 'Yes – yes. But that's an old story. I have always been unhappy. My daughter does what she will with me. I take what she gives me, good or bad. I have no spirit, and when you have no spirit you must keep quiet. I shan't trouble you any more.'

'Well,' said Newman, rather disgusted at the smooth operation of the old man's philosophy, 'that's as you please.'

M. Nioche seemed to have been prepared to be despised, but nevertheless he made a feeble movement of appeal from Newman's faint praise. 'After all,' he said, 'she is my daughter, and I can still look after her. If she will do wrong, why she will. But there are many different paths, there are degrees. I can give her the benefit – give her the benefit' – and M. Nioche paused, staring vaguely at Newman, who began to suspect that his brain had softened – 'the benefit of my experience,' M. Nioche added.

'Your experience?' inquired Newman, both amused and amazed.

'My experience of business,' said M. Nioche gravely.

'Ah yes,' said Newman, laughing, 'that will be a great advantage to her!' And then he said good-bye, and offered the poor foolish old man his hand.

M. Nioche took it and leaned back against the wall, holding it a moment and looking up at him. 'I suppose you think my wits are going,' he said. 'Very likely; I have always a pain in my head. That's why I can't explain, I can't tell you. And she's so strong, she makes me walk as she will, anywhere! But there's this – there's this.' And he stopped, still staring up at Newman. His little white eyes expanded and glittered for a moment like those of a cat in the dark. 'It's not as it seems. I haven't forgiven her. Oh no!'

'That's right; don't,' said Newman. 'She's a bad case.'

'It's horrible, it's terrible,' said M. Nioche; 'but do you want to know the truth? I hate her! I take what she gives me, and I hate her more. Today she brought me three hundred francs; they are here in my waistcoat-pocket. Now I hate her almost cruelly. No, I haven't forgiven her.'

'Why did you accept the money?' Newman asked.

'If I hadn't,' said M. Nioche, 'I should have hated her still more. That's what misery is. No, I haven't forgiven her.'

'Take care you don't hurt her!' said Newman, laughing again. And with this he took his leave. As he passed along the glazed side of the café, on reaching the street, he saw the old man motioning the waiter, with a melancholy gesture, to replenish his glass.

One day, a week after his visit to the Café de la Patrie, he called upon Valentin de Bellegarde, and by good fortune found him at home. Newman spoke of his interview with M. Nioche and his daughter, and said he was afraid Valentin had judged the old man correctly. He had found the couple hobnobbing together in amity; the old gentleman's rigour was purely theoretic. Newman confessed that he was disappointed; he should have expected to see M. Nioche take high ground.

'High ground, my dear fellow,' said Valentin, laughing; 'there is no high ground for him to take. The only perceptible eminence in M. Nioche's horizon is Montmartre,* which is not an edifying quarter. You can't go mountaineering in a flat country.'

'He remarked, indeed,' said Newman, 'that he had not forgiven her. But she'll never find it out.'

'We must do him the justice to suppose he doesn't like the thing,' Valentin rejoined. 'Mademoiselle Nioche is like the great artists whose biographies we read, who at the beginning of their career have suffered opposition in the domestic circle. Their vocation has not been recognised by their families, but the world has done it justice. Mademoiselle Nioche has a vocation.'

'Oh, come,' said Newman impatiently, 'you take the little baggage too seriously.'

'I know I do; but when one has nothing to think about, one must think of little baggages. I suppose it is better to be serious about light things than not to be serious at all. This little baggage entertains me.'

'Oh, she has discovered that. She knows you have been hunting her up and asking questions about her. She is very much tickled by it. That's rather annoying.'

'Annoying, my dear fellow,' laughed Valentin; 'not the least!'

'Hanged if I should want to have a greedy little adventuress like that know I was giving myself such pains about her!' said Newman.

'A pretty woman is always worth one's pains,' objected

Valentin. 'Mademoiselle Nioche is welcome to be tickled by my curiosity, and to know that I am tickled that she is tickled. She is not so much tickled, by the way.'

'You had better go and tell her,' Newman rejoined. 'She gave me a message for you of some such drift.'

'Bless your quiet imagination,' said Valentin, 'I have been to see her – three times in five days. She is a charming hostess; we talk of Shakespeare and the musical-glasses.* She is extremely clever and a very curious type; not at all coarse or wanting to be coarse – determined not to be. She means to take very good care of herself. She is extremely perfect; she is as hard and clear-cut as some little figure of a sea-nymph in an antique intaglio,* and I will warrant that she has not a grain more of sentiment or heart than if she were scooped out of a big amethyst. You can't scratch her even with a diamond. Extremely pretty – really, when you know her, she is wonderfully pretty – intelligent, determined, ambitious, unscrupulous, capable of looking at a man strangled without changing colour, she is, upon my honour, extremely entertaining.'

'It's a fine list of attractions,' said Newman; 'they would serve as a police-detective's description of a favourite criminal. I should sum them up by another word than "entertaining".'

'Why, that is just the word to use. I don't say she is laudable or lovable. I don't want her as my wife or my sister. But she is a very curious and ingenious piece of machinery; I like to see it in operation.'

'Well, I have seen some very curious machines, too,' said Newman; 'and once, in a needle factory, I saw a gentleman from the city, who had stepped too near one of them, picked up as neatly as if he had been prodded by a fork, swallowed down straight, and ground into small pieces.'

Re-entering his domicile, late in the evening, three days after Madame de Bellegarde had made her bargain with him – the expression is sufficiently correct – touching the entertainment at which she was to present him to the world, he found on his table a card of goodly dimensions bearing an announcement that this lady would be at home on the 27th of the month, at ten o'clock in the evening. He stuck it into the frame of his mirror and eyed it with some complacency; it seemed an agreeable emblem of triumph, documentary evidence that his prize was gained. Stretched out on a chair, he was looking at it lovingly, when Valentin de Bellegarde was shown into the room. Valentin's glance presently followed the direction of Newman's, and he perceived his mother's invitation.

'And what have they put into the corner?' he asked. Not the customary "music", "dancing", or "*tableaux vivants*"?* They ought at least to put "An American".'

'Oh, there are to be several of us,' said Newman. 'Mrs Tristram told me today that she had received a card and sent an acceptance.'

'Ah, then, with Mrs Tristram and her husband you will have support. My mother might have put on her card "Three Americans". But I suspect you will not lack amusement. You will see a great many of the best people in France. I mean the long pedigrees and the high noses, and all that. Some of them are awful idiots; I advise you to take them up cautiously.'

'Oh, I guess I shall like them,' said Newman. 'I am prepared to like everyone and everything in these days; I am in high good-humour.'

Valentin looked at him a moment in silence, and then dropped himself into a chair with an unwonted air of weariness. 'Happy man!' he said with a sigh. 'Take care you don't become offensive.'

'If anyone chooses to take offence, he may. I have a good conscience,' said Newman.

'So you are really in love with my sister?'

'Yes, sir!' said Newman, after a pause.

'And she also?'

'I guess she likes me,' said Newman.

'What is the witchcraft you have used?' Valentin asked. 'How do *you* make love?'

'Oh, I haven't any general rules,' said Newman. 'In any way that seems acceptable.'

'I suspect that, if one knew it,' said Valentin, laughing, 'you are a terrible customer. You walk in seven-league boots.'

'There is something the matter with you tonight,' Newman said in response to this. 'You are vicious. Spare me all discordant sounds until after my marriage. Then, when I have settled down for life, I shall be better able to take things as they come.'

'And when does your marriage take place?'

'About six weeks hence.'

Valentin was silent awhile, and then he said: 'And you feel very confident about the future?'

'Confident. I knew what I wanted, exactly, and I know what I have got.'

'You are sure you are going to be happy?'

'Sure?' said Newman. 'So foolish a question deserves a foolish answer. Yes!'

'You are not afraid of anything?'

'What should I be afraid of? You can't hurt me unless you kill me by some violent means. That I should indeed consider a tremendous sell. I want to live and I mean to live. I can't die of illness, I am too ridiculously tough; and the time for dying of old age won't come round yet awhile. I can't lose my wife, I shall take too good care of her. I may lose my money, or a large part of it; but that won't matter, for I shall make twice as much again. So what have I to be afraid of?'

'You are not afraid it may be rather a mistake for an American man of business to marry a French countess?'

'For the countess, possibly; but not for the man of business, if you mean me! But my countess shall not be disappointed; I answer for her happiness!' And as if he felt the impulse to celebrate his happy certitude by a bonfire, he got up to throw a couple of logs upon the already blazing hearth. Valentin watched for a few moments the quickened flame, and then, with his head leaning on his hand, gave a melancholy sigh. 'Got a headache?' Newman asked.

'*Je suis triste*,' said Valentin, with Gallic simplicity.

'You are sad, eh? Is it about the lady you said the other night that you adored and that you couldn't marry?'

'Did I really say that? It seemed to me afterwards that the words had escaped me. Before Claire it was bad taste. But I felt gloomy as I spoke, and I feel gloomy still. Why did you ever introduce me to that girl?'

'Oh, it's Noémie, is it? Lord deliver us! You don't mean to say you are lovesick about her?'

'Lovesick, no; it's not a grand passion. But the cold-blooded little demon sticks in my thoughts; she has bitten me with those even little teeth of hers; I feel as if I might turn rabid and do something crazy in consequence. It's very low; it's disgustingly low. She's the most mercenary little jade* in Europe. Yet she really affects my peace of mind; she is always running in my

head. It's a striking contrast to your noble and virtuous attach-
ment – a vile contrast! It is rather pitiful that it should be the
best I am able to do for myself at my present respectable age. I
am a nice young man, eh, *en somme?** You can't warrant my
future, as you do your own.'

'Drop that girl, short,' said Newman; 'don't go near her again,
and your future will do. Come over to America and I will get
you a place in a bank.'

'It is easy to say drop her,' said Valentin, with a light laugh.
'You can't drop a pretty woman like that. One must be polite,
even with Noémie. Besides, I'll not have her suppose I am afraid
of her.'

'So, between politeness and vanity, you will get deeper into
the mud? Keep them both for something better. Remember, too,
that I didn't want to introduce you to her; you insisted. I had a
sort of uneasy feeling about it.'

'Oh, I don't reproach you,' said Valentin. 'Heaven forbid! I
wouldn't for the world have missed knowing her. She is really
extraordinary. The way she has already spread her wings is
amazing. I don't know when a woman has amused me more.
But excuse me,' he added in an instant; 'she doesn't amuse you,
at second hand, and the subject is an impure one. Let us talk of
something else.' Valentin introduced another topic, but within
five minutes Newman observed that, by a bold transition, he
had reverted to Mademoiselle Nioche, and was giving pictures
of her manners and quoting specimens of her *mots*.* These were
very witty, and, for a young woman who six months before had
been painting the most artless madonnas, startlingly cynical. But
at last, abruptly, he stopped, became thoughtful, and for some
time afterwards said nothing. When he rose to go it was evident
that his thoughts were still running upon Mademoiselle Nioche.
'Yes, she's a frightful little monster!' he said.

The next ten days were the happiest that Newman had ever known. He saw Madame de Cintré every day, and never saw either old Madame de Bellegarde or the elder of his prospective brothers-in-law. Madame de Cintré at last seemed to think it becoming to apologise for their never being present. 'They are much taken up,' she said, 'with doing the honours of Paris to Lord Deepmere.' There was a smile in her gravity as she made this declaration, and it deepened as she added: 'He is our seventh cousin, you know, and blood is thicker than water. And then, he is so interesting!' And with this she laughed.

Newman met young Madame de Bellegarde two or three times, always roaming about with graceful vagueness, as if in search of an unattainable ideal of amusement. She always reminded him of a painted perfume-bottle with a crack in it; but he had grown to have a kindly feeling for her, based on the fact of her owing conjugal allegiance to Urbain de Bellegarde. He pitied M. de Bellegarde's wife, especially since she was a silly, thirstily-smiling little brunette, with a suggestion of an unregulated heart. The small marquise sometimes looked at him with an intensity too marked not to be innocent, for coquetry is more finely shaded. She apparently wanted to ask him something or tell him something; he wondered what it was. But he was shy of giving her an opportunity, because, if her communication bore upon the aridity of her matrimonial lot, he was at a loss to see how he could help her. He had a fancy, however, of her coming up to him some day and saying (after looking round behind her) with a little passionate hiss: 'I know you detest my husband; let me have the pleasure of assuring you for once you are right. Pity a poor woman who is married to a clock-image in *papier-mâché*!'* Possessing, however, in default of a competent knowledge of the principles of etiquette, a very downright sense of the 'meanness' of certain actions, it seemed to him to belong to his position to keep on his guard; he was not going to put it into the power of these people to say that in their house he had done anything unpleasant. As it was, Madame de Bellegarde used to give him news of the dress she meant to wear at his wedding, and which had not yet, in her creative imagination, in spite of many interviews with the tailor, resolved itself into its composite totality. 'I told you pale blue bows on the sleeves, at the elbows,' she said. 'But today I don't see my blue bows at all. I don't know what has become of them. Today I see pink – a tender pink. And then I pass through strange dull phases in which neither blue nor pink says anything to me. And yet I must have the bows.'

'Have them green or yellow,' said Newman.

'*Malheureux!*'* the little marquise would cry. 'Green bows would break your marriage – your children would be illegitimate!'*

Madame de Cintré was calmly happy before the world, and Newman had the felicity of fancying that before him, when the world was absent, she was almost agitatedly happy. She said very tender things. 'I take no pleasure in you. You never give me a chance to scold you, to correct you. I bargained for that; I expected to enjoy it. But you won't do anything dreadful; you are dismally inoffensive. It is very stupid; there is no excitement for me; I might as well be marrying someone else.'

'I am afraid it's the worst I can do,' Newman would say in answer to this. 'Kindly overlook the deficiency.' He assured her that he, at least, would never scold her; she was perfectly satisfactory. 'If you only knew,' he said, 'how exactly you are what I coveted! And I am beginning to understand why I coveted it; the having it makes all the difference that I expected. Never was a man so pleased with his good fortune. You have been holding your head for a week past just as I wanted my wife to hold hers. You say just the things I want her to say. You walk about the room just as I want her to walk. You have just the taste in dress that I want her to have. In short, you come up to the mark; and, I can tell you, my mark was high.'

These observations seemed to make Madame de Cintré rather grave. At last she said: 'Depend upon it, I don't come up to the mark; your mark is too high. I am not all that you suppose; I am a much smaller affair. She is a magnificent woman, your ideal. Pray, how did she come to such perfection?'

'She was never anything else,' Newman said.

'I really believe,' Madame de Cintré went on, 'that she is better than my own ideal. Do you know that is a very handsome compliment? Well, sir, I will make her my own!'

Mrs Tristram came to see her dear Claire after Newman had announced his engagement, and she told our hero the next day that his good fortune was simply absurd. 'For the ridiculous part of it is,' she said, 'that you are evidently going to be as happy as if you were marrying Miss Smith or Miss Thompson. I call it a brilliant match for you, but you get brilliancy without paying any tax upon it. Those things are usually a compromise, but here you have everything, and nothing crowds anything else out. You will be brilliantly happy as well.' Newman thanked her for her pleasant encouraging way of saying things; no woman could encourage or discourage better. Tristram's way of saying things was different; he had been taken by his wife to call upon Madame de Cintré, and he gave an account of the expedition.

'You don't catch me giving an opinion on your countess this time,' he said; 'I put my foot in it once. That's a d——d underhand thing to do, by the way – coming round to sound a fellow upon the woman you are going to marry. You deserve anything you get. Then of course you rush and tell her, and she takes care to make it pleasant for the poor spiteful wretch the first time he calls. I will do you the justice to say, however, that you don't seem to have told Madame de Cintré; or, if you have, she's uncommonly magnanimous. She was very nice; she was tremendously polite. She and Lizzie sat on the sofa, pressing each other's hands and calling each other *chère belle*,* and Madame de Cintré sent me with every third word a magnificent smile, as if to give me to understand that I too was a handsome dear. She quite made up for past neglect, I assure you; she was very pleasant and sociable. Only in an evil hour it came into her head to say that she must present us to her mother – her mother wished to know your friends. I didn't want to know her mother, and I was on the point of telling Lizzie to go in alone and let me wait for her outside. But Lizzie, with her usual infernal ingenuity, guessed my purpose and reduced me by a glance of her eye. So they marched off arm-in-arm, and I followed as I could. We found the old lady in her arm-chair, twiddling her aristocratic thumbs. She looked at Lizzie from head to foot; but at that game Lizzie, to do her justice, was a match for her. My wife told her we were great friends of Mr Newman. The marquise stared a moment, and then said: "Oh, Mr Newman! My daughter has made up her mind to marry a Mr Newman." Then Madame de Cintré began to fondle Lizzie again, and said it was this dear lady that had planned the match and brought them together.

"Oh, 'tis you I have to thank for my American son-in-law," the old lady said to Mrs Tristram. "It was a very clever thought of yours. Be sure of my gratitude." And then she began to look at me, and presently said: "Pray, are you engaged in some species of manufacture?" I wanted to say that I manufactured broom-sticks for old witches to ride on, but Lizzie got in ahead of me. "My husband, Madame la Marquise," she said, "belongs to that unfortunate class of persons who have no profession and no business, and do very little good in the world." To get her poke at the old woman she didn't care where she shoved me. "Dear me," said the marquise, "we all have our duties." "I am sorry mine compel me to take leave of you," said Lizzie. And we bundled out again. But you have a mother-in-law, in all the force of the term.'

'Oh,' said Newman, 'my mother-in-law desires nothing better than to let me alone.'

Betimes, on the evening of the 27th, he went to Madame de Bellegarde's ball. The old house in the Rue de l'Université looked strangely brilliant. In the circle of light projected from the outer gate a detachment of the populace stood watching the carriages roll in; the court was illumined with flaring torches and the portico carpeted with crimson. When Newman arrived there were but a few people present. The marquise and her two daughters were at the top of the staircase, where the sallow old nymph in the angle peeped out from a bower of plants. Madame de Bellegarde, in purple and fine laces; looked like an old lady painted by Vandyke;* Madame de Cintré was dressed in white. The old lady greeted Newman with majestic formality, and, looking round her, called several of the persons who were standing near. They were elderly gentlemen, of what Valentin de Bellegarde had designated as the high-nosed category; two or three of them wore cordons and stars. They approached with measured alertness, and the marquise said that she wished to present them to Mr Newman, who was going to marry her daughter. Then she introduced successively three dukes, three counts, and a baron. These gentlemen bowed and smiled most agreeably, and Newman indulged in a series of impartial hand shakes, accompanied by a 'Happy to make your acquaintance, sir'. He looked at Madame de Cintré, but she was not looking at him. If his personal self-consciousness had been of a nature to make him constantly refer to her, as the critic before whom,

in company, he played his part, he might have found it a
flattering proof of her confidence that he never caught her eyes
resting upon him. It is a reflection Newman did not make, but
we may nevertheless risk it, that in spite of this circumstance she
probably saw every movement of his little finger. Young
Madame de Bellegarde was dressed in an audacious toilet of
crimson crape, bestrewn with huge silver moons – thin crescents
and full discs.*

'You don't say anything about my dress,' she said to Newman.

'I feel,' he answered, 'as if I were looking at you through a
telescope. It is very strange.'

'If it is strange it matches the occasion. But I am not a
heavenly body.'

'I never saw the sky at midnight that particular shade of
crimson,' said Newman.

'That is my originality; anyone could have chosen blue. My
sister-in-law would have chosen a lovely shade of blue, with a
dozen little delicate moons. But I think crimson is much more
amusing. And I give my idea, which is moonshine.'

'Moonshine and bloodshed,' said Newman.

'A murder by moonlight,' laughed Madame de Bellegarde.
'What a delicious idea for a toilet! To make it complete, there is
a dagger of diamonds, you see, stuck into my hair. But here
comes Lord Deepmere,' she added in a moment; 'I must find out
what he thinks of it.' Lord Deepmere came up, looking very red
in the face, and laughing. 'Lord Deepmere can't decide which he
prefers, my sister-in-law or me,' said Madame de Bellegarde.
'He likes Claire because she is his cousin, and me because I am
not. But he has no right to make love to Claire, whereas I am
perfectly *disponible*.* It is very wrong to make love to a woman
who is engaged, but it is very wrong not to make love to a
woman who is married.'

'Oh, it's very jolly making love to married women,' said Lord
Deepmere, 'because they can't ask you to marry them.'

'Is that what the others do – the spinsters?' Newman inquired.

'Oh dear yes,' said Lord Deepmere; 'in England all the girls
ask a fellow to marry them.'

'And a fellow brutally refuses,' said Madame de Bellegarde.

'Why, really, you know, a fellow can't marry any girl that
asks him,' said his lordship.

'Your cousin won't ask you. She is going to marry Mr Newman.'

'Oh, that's a very different thing!' laughed Lord Deepmere.

'You would have accepted *her*, I suppose. That makes me hope that after all you prefer me.'

'Oh, when things are nice I never prefer one to the other,' said the young Englishman. 'I take them all.'

'Ah, what a horror! I won't be taken in that way; I must be kept apart,' cried Madame de Bellegarde. 'Mr Newman is much better; he knows how to choose. Oh, he chooses as if he were threading a needle. He prefers Madame de Cintré to any conceivable creature or thing.'

'Well, you can't help my being her cousin,' said Lord Deepmere to Newman, with candid hilarity.

'Oh no, I can't help that,' said Newman, laughing back; 'neither can she!'

'And you can't help my dancing with her,' said Lord Deepmere, with sturdy simplicity.

'I could prevent that only by dancing with her myself,' said Newman. 'But unfortunately I don't know how to dance.'

'Oh, you may dance without knowing how; may you not, milord?' said Madame de Bellegarde. But to this Lord Deepmere replied that a fellow ought to know how to dance if he didn't want to make an ass of himself; and at this same moment Urbain de Bellegarde joined the group, slow-stepping and with his hands behind him.

'This is a very splendid entertainment,' said Newman cheerfully. 'The old house looks very bright.'

'If *you* are pleased, we are content,' said the marquis, lifting his shoulders and bending them forward.

'Oh, I suspect everyone is pleased,' said Newman. 'How can they help being pleased when the first thing they see as they come in is your sister, standing there as beautiful as an angel?'

'Yes, she is very beautiful,' rejoined the marquis solemnly. 'But that is not so great a source of satisfaction to other people, naturally, as to you.'

'Yes, I am satisfied, marquis, I am satisfied,' said Newman, with his protracted enunciation. 'And now tell me,' he added, looking round, 'who some of your friends are.'

M. de Bellegarde looked about him in silence, with his head bent and his hand raised to his lower lip, which he slowly rubbed. A stream of people had been pouring into the salon in which Newman stood with his host, the rooms were filling up and the spectacle had become brilliant. It borrowed its splendour chiefly from the shining shoulders and profuse jewels of the women, and from the voluminous elegance of their dresses. There were no uniforms, as Madame de Bellegarde's door was inexorably closed against the myrmidons of the upstart power which then ruled the fortunes of France, and the great company of smiling and chattering faces was not graced by any very frequent suggestions of harmonious beauty. It is a pity, neverthe-less, that Newman had not been a physiognomist, for a great many of the faces were irregularly agreeable, expressive, and suggestive. If the occasion had been different they would hardly have pleased him; he would have thought the women not pretty enough and the men too smirking; but he was now in a humour to receive none but agreeable impressions, and he looked no more narrowly than to perceive that everyone was brilliant, and to feel that the sum of their brilliancy was a part of his credit. 'I will present you to some people,' said M. de Bellegarde after awhile. 'I will make a point of it, in fact. You will allow me?'

'Oh, I will shake hands with anyone you want,' said Newman. 'Your mother just introduced me to half-a-dozen old gentlemen. Take care you don't pick up the same parties again.'

'Who are the gentlemen to whom my mother presented you?'

'Upon my word, I forget them,' said Newman, laughing. 'The people here look very much alike.'

'I suspect they have not forgotten you,' said the marquis, and he began to walk through the rooms. Newman, to keep near him in the crowd, took his arm; after which, for some time, the marquis walked straight along, in silence. At last, reaching the farther end of the suite of reception-rooms, Newman found himself in the presence of a lady of monstrous proportions, seated in a very capacious arm-chair, with several persons standing in a semicircle round her. This little group had divided as the marquis came up, and M. de Bellegarde stepped forward and stood for an instant silent and obsequious, with his hat raised to his lips, as Newman had seen some gentlemen stand in churches as soon as they entered their pews. The lady, indeed, bore a very fair likeness to a reverend effigy in some idolatrous shrine. She was monumentally stout and imperturbably serene. Her aspect was to Newman almost formidable; he had a troubled consciousness of a triple chin, a small piercing eye, a vast expanse of uncovered bosom, a nodding and twinkling tiara of plumes and gems, and an immense circumference of satin petticoat. With her little circle of beholders this remarkable woman reminded him of the Fat Lady at a fair. She fixed her small, unwinking eyes at the newcomers.

'Dear duchess,' said the marquis, 'let me present you our good friend Mr Newman, of whom you have heard us speak. Wishing to make Mr Newman known to those who are dear to us, I could not possibly fail to begin with you.'

'Charmed, dear friend; charmed, monsieur,' said the duchess in a voice which, though small and shrill, was not disagreeable, while Newman executed his obeisance. 'I came on purpose to see monsieur. I hope he appreciates the compliment. You have only to look at me to do so, sir,' she continued, sweeping her person with a much-encompassing glance. Newman hardly knew what to say, though it seemed that to a duchess who joked about her corpulence one might say almost anything. On hearing that the duchess had come on purpose to see Newman, the gentlemen who surrounded her turned a little and looked at him with sympathetic curiosity. The marquis with supernatural gravity mentioned to him the name of each, while the gentleman who bore it bowed; they were all what are called in France *beaux noms.** 'I wanted extremely to see you,' the duchess went on. '*C'est positif.** In the first place, I am very fond of the person you are going to marry; she is the most charming creature in France. Mind you treat her well, or you shall hear some news of me. But you look as if you were good. I am told you are very remarkable. I have heard all sorts of extraordinary things about you. *Voyons*, are they true?'

'I don't know what you can have heard,' said Newman.

'Oh, you have your *légende.** We have heard that you have had a career the most chequered, the most *bizarre.** What is that about your having founded a city some ten years ago in the great West, a city which contains today half a million of inhabitants? Isn't it half a million, messieurs? You are exclusive proprietor of this flourishing settlement, and are consequently fabulously rich, and you would be richer still if you didn't grant lands and houses free of rent to all newcomers who will pledge themselves never to smoke cigars. At this game, in three years, we are told, you are going to be made president of America.'

The duchess recited this amusing 'legend' with a smooth self-possession which gave the speech, to Newman's mind, the air of being a bit of amusing dialogue in a play, delivered by a veteran comic actress. Before she had ceased speaking he had burst into loud, irrepressible laughter. 'Dear duchess, dear duchess,' the marquis began to murmur, soothingly. Two or three persons came to the door of the room to see who was laughing at the duchess. But the lady continued with the soft, serene assurance of a person who, as a duchess, was certain of being listened to, and, as a garrulous woman, was independent of the pulse of her auditors. 'But I know you are very remarkable. You must be, to have endeared yourself to this good marquis and to his admirable mother. They don't bestow their esteem on all the world. They are very exacting. I myself am not very sure at this hour of really possessing it. Eh, Bellegarde? To please you, I see, one must be an American millionaire. But your real triumph, my dear sir, is pleasing the countess; she is as difficult as a princess in a fairy tale. Your success is a miracle. What is your secret? I don't ask you to reveal it before all these gentlemen, but come and see me some day and give me a specimen of your talents.'

'The secret is with Madame de Cintré,' said Newman. 'You must ask her for it. It consists in her having a great deal of charity.'

'Very pretty!' said the duchess. 'That's a very nice specimen, to begin with. What, Bellegarde, are you already taking monsieur away?'

'I have a duty to perform, dear friend,' said the marquis, pointing to the other groups.

'Ah, for you I know what that means. Well, I have seen monsieur; that is what I wanted. He can't persuade me that he isn't very clever. Farewell.'

As Newman passed on with his host, he asked who the duchess was. 'The greatest lady in France,' said the marquis. M. de Bellegarde then presented his prospective brother-in-law to some twenty other persons of both sexes, selected apparently for their typically august character. In some cases this character was written in a good round hand upon the countenance of the wearer; in others Newman was thankful for such help as his companion's impressively brief intimation contributed to the discovery of it. There were large, majestic men, and small, demonstrative men; there were ugly ladies in yellow lace and quaint jewels, and pretty ladies with white shoulders from which jewels and everything else were absent. Everyone gave Newman extreme attention, everyone smiled, everyone was charmed to make his acquaintance, everyone looked at him with that soft hardness of good society which puts out its hand but keeps its fingers closed over the coin. If the marquis was going about as a bear-leader,* if the fiction of Beauty and the Beast was supposed to have found its companion-piece, the general impression appeared to be that the bear was a very fair imitation of humanity. Newman found his reception among the marquis's friends very 'pleasant'; he could not have said more for it. It was pleasant to be treated with so much explicit politeness; it was pleasant to hear neatly-turned civilities, with a flavour of wit, uttered from beneath carefully-shaped moustaches; it was pleasant to see clever Frenchwomen – they all seemed clever – turn their backs to their partners to get a good look at the strange American whom Claire de Cintré was to marry, and reward the object of the exhibition with a charming smile. At last, as he turned away from a battery of smiles and other amenities, Newman caught the eye of the marquis looking at him heavily; and thereupon, for a single instant, he checked himself. 'Am I behaving like a d——d fool?' he asked himself. 'Am I stepping about like a terrier on his hind legs?' At this moment he perceived Mrs Tristram at the other side of the room, and he waved his hand in farewell to M. de Bellegarde and made his way toward her.

'Am I holding my head too high?' he asked. 'Do I look as if I had the lower end of a pulley fastened to my chin?'

'You look like all happy men, very ridiculous,' said Mrs Tristram. 'It's the usual thing, neither better nor worse. I have been watching you for the last ten minutes, and I have been watching M. de Bellegarde. He doesn't like it.'

'The more credit to him for putting it through,' replied Newman. 'But I shall be generous. I shan't trouble him any more. But I am very happy. I can't stand still here. Please to take my arm and we will go for a walk.'

He led Mrs Tristram through all the rooms. There were a great many of them, and, decorated for the occasion and filled with a stately crowd, their somewhat tarnished nobleness recovered its lustre. Mrs Tristram, looking about her, dropped a series of softly-incisive comments upon her fellow-guests. But

Newman made vague answers; he hardly heard her; his thoughts were elsewhere. They were lost in a cheerful sense of success, of attainment and victory. His momentary care as to whether he looked like a fool passed away, leaving him simply with a rich contentment. He had got what he wanted. The savour of success had always been highly agreeable to him, and it had been his fortune to know it often. But it had never before been so sweet, been associated with so much that was brilliant and suggestive and entertaining. The lights, the flowers, the music, the crowd, the splendid women, the jewels, the strangeness even of the universal murmur of a clever foreign tongue, were all a vivid symbol and assurance of his having grasped his purpose and forced along his groove. If Newman's smile was larger than usual, it was not tickled vanity that pulled the strings; he had no wish to be shown with the finger or to achieve a personal success. If he could have looked down at the scene, invisible, from a hole in the roof, he would have enjoyed it quite as much. It would have spoken to him about his own prosperity and deepened that easy feeling about life to which, sooner or later, he made all experience contribute. Just now the cup seemed full.

'It is a very pretty party,' said Mrs Tristram, after they had walked awhile. 'I have seen nothing objectionable except my husband leaning against the wall and talking to an individual whom I suppose he takes for a duke, but whom I more than suspect to be the functionary who attends to the lamps. Do you think you could separate them? Knock over a lamp!'

I doubt whether Newman, who saw no harm in Tristram's conversing with an ingenious mechanic, would have complied with this request; but at this moment Valentin de Bellegarde drew near. Newman, some weeks previously, had presented Madame de Cintré's youngest brother to Mrs Tristram, for whose merits Valentin professed a discriminating relish and to whom he had paid several visits.

'Did you ever read Keats's "Belle Dame sans Merci"?'* asked Mrs Tristram. 'You remind me of the hero of the ballad:

> 'Oh, what can ail thee, knight-at-arms,
> Alone and palely loitering?'

'If I am alone, it is because I have been deprived of your society,' said Valentin. 'Besides, it is good manners for no man except Newman to look happy. This is all to his address. It is not for you and me to go before the curtain.'

'You promised me last spring,' said Newman to Mrs Tristram, 'that six months from that time I should get into a monstrous rage. It seems to me the time's up, and yet the nearest I can come to doing anything rough now is to offer you a *café glacé*.'*

'I told you we should do things grandly,' said Valentin. 'I don't allude to the *cafés glacés*. But everyone is here, and my sister told me just now that Urbain had been adorable.'

'He's a good fellow, he's a good fellow,' said Newman. 'I love him as a brother. That reminds me that I ought to go and say something polite to your mother.'

'Let it be something very polite indeed,' said Valentin. 'It may be the last time you will feel so much like it!'

Newman walked away, almost disposed to clasp old Madame de Bellegarde round the waist. He passed through several rooms and at last found the old marquise in the first saloon, seated on a sofa, with her young kinsman, Lord Deepmere, beside her. The young man looked somewhat bored; his hands were thrust into his pockets and his eyes were fixed upon the toes of his shoes, his feet being thrust out in front of him. Madame de Bellegarde appeared to have been talking to him with some intensity and to be waiting for an answer to what she had said, or for some sign of the effect of her words. Her hands were folded in her lap, and she was looking at his lordship's simple physiognomy with an air of politely suppressed irritation.

Lord Deepmere looked up as Newman approached, met his eyes, and changed colour.

'I am afraid I disturb an interesting interview,' said Newman.

Madame de Bellegarde rose, and her companion rising at the same time, she put her hand into his arm. She answered nothing for an instant, and then, as he remained silent, she said with a smile: 'It would be polite for Lord Deepmere to say it was very interesting.'

'Oh, I'm not polite!' cried his lordship. 'But it *was* interesting.'

'Madame de Bellegarde was giving you some good advice, eh?' said Newman; 'toning you down a little?'

'I was giving him some excellent advice,' said the marquise, fixing her fresh cold eyes upon our hero. 'It's for him to take it.'

'Take it, sir, take it!' Newman exclaimed. 'Any advice the marquise gives you tonight must be good; for tonight, marquise, you must speak from a cheerful, comfortable spirit, and that makes good advice. You see everything going on so brightly and successfully round you. Your party is magnificent; it was a very happy thought. It is much better than that thing of mine would have been.'

'If you are pleased I am satisfied,' said Madame de Bellegarde. 'My desire was to please you.'

'Do you want to please me a little more?' said Newman. 'Just drop our lordly friend; I am sure he wants to be off and shake his heels a little. Then take my arm and walk through the rooms.'

'My desire was to please you,' the old lady repeated. And she liberated Lord Deepmere, Newman rather wondering at her docility. 'If this young man is wise,' she added, 'he will go and find my daughter and ask her to dance.'

'I have been endorsing your advice,' said Newman, bending over her and laughing, 'I suppose I must swallow that!'

Lord Deepmere wiped his forehead and departed, and Madame de Bellegarde took Newman's arm. 'Yes, it's a very pleasant, sociable entertainment,' the latter declared, as they proceeded on their circuit. 'Everyone seems to know everyone and to be glad to see everyone. The marquis has made me acquainted with ever so many people, and I feel quite like one of the family. It's an occasion,' Newman continued, wanting to say something thoroughly kind and comfortable, 'that I shall always remember, and remember very pleasantly.'

'I think it is an occasion that we shall none of us forget,' said the marquise, with her pure, neat enunciation.

People made way for her as she passed, others turned round and looked at her, and she received a great many greetings and pressings of the hand, all of which she accepted with the most delicate dignity. But though she smiled upon everyone, she said nothing until she reached the last of the rooms, where she found her elder son. Then, 'This is enough, sir,' she declared with measured softness to Newman, and turned to the marquis. He put out both his hands and took both hers, drawing her to a seat with an air of the tenderest veneration. It was a most harmonious family group, and Newman discreetly retired. He moved through the rooms for some time longer, circulating freely, overtopping most people by his great height, renewing acquaintance with some of the groups to which Urbain de

Bellegarde had presented him, and expending generally the
surplus of his equanimity. He continued to find it all extremely
agreeable; but the most agreeable things have an end, and the
revelry on this occasion began to deepen to a close. The music
was sounding its ultimate strains and people were looking for
the marquise, to make their farewells. There seemed to be some
difficulty in finding her, and Newman heard a report that she
had left the ball, feeling faint. 'She has succumbed to the
emotions of the evening,' he heard a lady say. 'Poor, dear
marquise; I can imagine all that they may have been for her!'

But he learned immediately afterwards that she had recovered
herself and was seated in an arm-chair near the doorway,
receiving parting compliments from great ladies who insisted
upon her not rising. He himself set out in quest of Madame de
Cintré. He had seen her move past him many times in the rapid
circles of a waltz, but in accordance with her explicit instructions
he had exchanged no words with her since the beginning of the
evening. The whole house having been thrown open, the apartments of the *rez-de-chaussée** were also accessible, though a
smaller number of persons had gathered there. Newman wandered through them, observing a few scattered couples to whom
this comparative seclusion appeared grateful, and reached a
small conservatory which opened into the garden. The end of
the conservatory was formed by a clear sheet of glass, unmasked
by plants, and admitting the winter starlight so directly that a
person standing there would seem to have passed into the open
air. Two persons stood there now, a lady and a gentleman; the
lady Newman, from within the room, and although she had
turned her back to it, immediately recognised as Madame de
Cintré. He hesitated as to whether he would advance, but as he
did so she looked round, feeling apparently that he was there.
She rested her eyes on him a moment, and then turned again to
her companion.

'It is almost a pity not to tell Mr Newman,' she said softly,
but in a tone that Newman could hear.

'Tell him if you like!' the gentleman answered, in the voice of
Lord Deepmere.

'Oh, tell me by all means!' said Newman, advancing.

Lord Deepmere, he observed, was very red in the face, and he
had twisted his gloves into a tight cord as if he had been
squeezing them dry. These, presumably, were tokens of violent

emotion, and it seemed to Newman that the traces of a corresponding agitation were visible in Madame de Cintré's face. The two had been talking with much vivacity. 'What I should tell you is only to my lord's credit,' said Madame de Cintré, smiling frankly enough.

'He wouldn't like it any better for that,' said my lord, with his awkward laugh.

'Come; what's the mystery?' Newman demanded. 'Clear it up. I don't like mysteries.'

'We must have some things we don't like, and go without some we do,' said the ruddy young nobleman, laughing still.

'It is to Lord Deepmere's credit, but it is not to everyone's,' said Madame de Cintré. 'So I shall say nothing about it. You may be sure,' she added; and she put out her hand to the Englishman, who took it half shyly, half impetuously. 'And now go and dance!' she said.

'Oh yes, I feel awfully like dancing!' he answered. 'I shall go and get tipsy.' And he walked away with a gloomy guffaw.

'What has happened between you?' Newman asked.

'I can't tell you – now,' said Madame de Cintré. 'Nothing that need make you unhappy.'

'Has the little Englishman been trying to make love to you?'

She hesitated, and then she uttered a grave 'No! he's a very honest little fellow.'

'But you are agitated. Something is the matter.'

'Nothing, I repeat, that need make you unhappy. My agitation is over. Some day I will tell you what it was; not now. I can't now!'

'Well, I confess,' remarked Newman, 'I don't want to hear anything unpleasant. I am satisfied with everything – most of all with you. I have seen all the ladies and talked with a great many of them; but I am satisfied with you.' Madame de Cintré covered him for a moment with her large, soft glance, and then turned her eyes away into the starry night. So they stood silent a moment, side by side. 'Say you are satisfied with me,' said Newman.

He had to wait a moment for the answer; but it came at last, low yet distinct: 'I am very happy.'

It was presently followed by a few words from another source, which made them both turn round. 'I am sadly afraid Madame de Cintré will take a chill. I have ventured to bring a shawl.'

Mrs Bread stood there softly solicitous, holding a white drapery in her hand.

'Thank you,' said Madame de Cintré, 'the sight of those cold stars gives one a sense of frost. I won't take your shawl, but we will go back into the house.'

She passed back and Newman followed her, Mrs Bread standing respectfully aside to make way for them. Newman paused an instant before the old woman, and she glanced up at him with a silent greeting. 'Oh yes,' he said, 'you must come and live with us.'

'Well then, sir, if you will,' she answered, 'you have not seen the last of me!'

CHAPTER 17

Newman was fond of music and went often to the opera. A couple of evenings after Madame de Bellegarde's ball he sat listening to 'Don Giovanni',* having in honour of this work, which he had never yet seen represented, come to occupy his orchestra-chair* before the rising of the curtain. Frequently he took a large box and invited a party of his compatriots; this was a mode of recreation to which he was much addicted. He liked making up parties of his friends and conducting them to the theatre, and taking them to drive on high drags* or to dine at remote restaurants. He liked doing things which involved his paying for people; the vulgar truth is that he enjoyed 'treating' them. This was not because he was what is called purse-proud; handling money in public was on the contrary positively disagreeable to him; he had a sort of personal modesty about it, akin to what he would have felt about making a toilet* before spectators. But just as it was a gratification to him to be handsomely dressed, just so it was a private satisfaction to him (he enjoyed it very clandestinely) to have interposed, pecuniarily, in a scheme of pleasure. To set a large group of people in motion and transport them to a distance, to have special conveyances, to charter railway-carriages and steamboats, harmonised with his relish for bold processes, and made hospitality seem more

active and more to the purpose. A few evenings before the
occasion of which I speak he had invited several ladies and
gentlemen to the opera to listen to Madame Alboni* – a party
which included Miss Dora Finch. It befell, however, that Miss
Dora Finch, sitting near Newman in the box, discoursed brilliantly, not only during the entr'actes,* but during many of the
finest portions of the performance, so that Newman had really
come away with an irritated sense that Madame Alboni had a
thin, shrill voice, and that her musical phrase was much gar-
nished with a laugh of the giggling order. After this he promised
himself to go for awhile to the opera alone.

When the curtain had fallen upon the first act of 'Don
Giovanni', he turned round in his place to observe the house.
Presently, in one of the boxes, he perceived Urbain de Bellegarde
and his wife. The little marquise was sweeping the house very
busily with a glass, and Newman, supposing that she saw him,
determined to go and bid her good-evening. M. de Bellegarde
was leaning against a column, motionless, looking straight in
front of him, with one hand in the breast of his white waistcoat
and the other resting his hat on his thigh. Newman was about
to leave his place when he noticed in that obscure region devoted
to the small boxes which in France are called, not inaptly,
'bathing-tubs', a face which even the dim light and the distance
could not make wholly indistinct. It was the face of a young and
pretty woman, and it was surmounted with a *coiffure* of pink
roses and diamonds. This person was looking round the house,
and her fan was moving to and fro with the most practised
grace; when she lowered it, Newman perceived a pair of plump
white shoulders and the edge of a rose-coloured dress. Beside
her, very close to the shoulders, and talking, apparently with an
earnestness which it pleased her scantily to heed, sat a young
man with a red face and a very low shirt-collar. A moment's
gazing left Newman with no doubts; the pretty young woman
was Noémie Nioche. He looked hard into the depths of the box,
thinking her father might perhaps be in attendance, but from
what he could see the young man's eloquence had no other
auditor. Newman at last made his way out, and in doing so he
passed beneath the *baignoire** of Mademoiselle Noémie. She
saw him as he approached, and gave him a nod and smile which
seemed meant as an assurance that she was still a good-natured
girl, in spite of her enviable rise in the world. Newman passed

into the *foyer* and walked through it. Suddenly he paused in front of a gentleman seated on one of the divans. The gentleman's elbows were on his knees; he was leaning forward and staring at the pavement, lost apparently in meditations of a somewhat gloomy cast. But in spite of his bent head Newman recognised him, and in a moment sat down beside him. Then the gentleman looked up and displayed the expressive countenance of Valentin de Bellegarde.

'What in the world are you thinking of so hard?' asked Newman.

'A subject that requires hard thinking to do it justice,' said Valentin. 'My immeasurable idiocy.'

'What is the matter now?'

'The matter now is that I am a man again, and no more a fool than usual. But I came within an inch of taking that girl *au sérieux*.'*

'You mean the young lady below stairs, in a *baignoire*, in a pink dress?' said Newman.

'Did you notice what a brilliant kind of pink it was?' Valentin inquired, by way of answer. 'It makes her look as white as new milk.'

'White or black, as you please. But you have stopped going to see her?'

'Oh, bless you, no. Why should I stop? I have changed, but she hasn't,' said Valentin. 'I see she is a vulgar little wretch, after all. But she is as amusing as ever, and one *must* be amused.'

'Well, I am glad she strikes you so unpleasantly,' Newman rejoined. 'I suppose you have swallowed all those fine words you used about her the other night. You compared her to a sapphire, or a topaz, or an amethyst – some precious stone; what was it?'

'I don't remember,' said Valentin, 'it may have been to a carbuncle!* But she won't make a fool of me now. She has no real charm. It's an awfully low thing to make a mistake about a person of that sort.'

'I congratulate you,' Newman declared, 'upon the scales having fallen from your eyes. It's a great triumph; it ought to make you feel better.'

'Yes, it makes me feel better!' said Valentin gaily. Then, checking himself, he looked askance at Newman. 'I rather think you are laughing at me. If you were not one of the family I would take it up.'

'Oh no, I'm not laughing, any more than I am one of the family. You make me feel badly. You are too clever a fellow, you are made of too good stuff, to spend your time in ups and downs over that class of goods. The idea of splitting hairs about Miss Nioche! It seems to me awfully foolish. You say you have given up taking her seriously; but you take her seriously so long as you take her at all.'

Valentin turned round in his place and looked awhile at Newman, wrinkling his forehead and rubbing his knees. '*Vous parlez d'or.** But she has wonderfully pretty arms. Would you believe I didn't know it till this evening?'

'But she is a vulgar little wretch, remember, all the same,' said Newman.

'Yes; the other day she had the bad taste to begin to abuse her father, to his face, in my presence. I shouldn't have expected it of her; it was a disappointment; heigho!'

'Why, she cares no more for her father than for her doormat,' said Newman. 'I discovered that the first time I saw her.'

'Oh, that's another affair; she may think of the poor old beggar what she pleases. But it was low in her to call him bad names; it quite threw me off. It was about a frilled petticoat that he was to have fetched from the washer-woman's; he appeared to have neglected this graceful duty. She almost boxed his ears. He stood there staring at her with his little blank eyes and smoothing his old hat with his coat-tail. At last he turned round and went out without a word. Then I told her it was in very bad taste to speak so to one's papa. She said she should be so thankful to me if I would mention it to her whenever her taste was at fault; she had immense confidence in mine. I told her I couldn't have the bother of forming her manners; I had had an idea they were already formed, after the best models. She had disappointed me. But I shall get over it,' said Valentin gaily.

'Oh, time's a great consoler!' Newman answered with humorous sobriety. He was silent a moment, and then he added in another tone: 'I wish you would think of what I said to you the other day. Come over to America with us, and I will put you in the way of doing some business. You have got a very good head if you will only use it.'

Valentin made a genial grimace. 'My head is much obliged to you. Do you mean the place in a bank?'

'There are several places, but I suppose you would consider the bank the most aristocratic.'

Valentin burst into a laugh. 'My dear fellow, at night all cats are grey! When one derogates there are no degrees.'

Newman answered nothing for a minute. Then, 'I think you will find there are degrees in success,' he said with a certain dryness.

Valentin had leaned forward again, with his elbows on his knees, and he was scratching the pavement with his stick. At last he said, looking up: 'Do you really think I ought to do something?'

Newman laid his hand on his companion's arm and looked at him a moment through sagaciously-narrowed eyelids. 'Try it and see. You are not good enough for it, but we will stretch a point.'

'Do you really think I can make some money? I should like to see how it feels to have a little.'

'Do what I tell you, and you shall be rich,' said Newman. 'Think of it.' And he looked at his watch and prepared to resume his way to Madame de Bellegarde's box.

'Upon my word I will think of it,' said Valentin. 'I will go and listen to Mozart another half hour – I can always think better to music – and profoundly meditate upon it.'

The marquis was with his wife when Newman entered their box; he was bland, remote, and correct as usual; or, as it seemed to Newman, even more than usual.

'What do you think of the opera?' asked our hero. 'What do you think of the Don?'

'We all know what Mozart is,' said the marquis; 'our impressions don't date from this evening. Mozart is youth, freshness, brilliancy, facility – a little too great facility, perhaps. But the execution is here and there deplorably rough.'

'I am very curious to see how it ends,' said Newman.

'You speak as if it were a *feuilleton* in the *Figaro*,'* observed the marquis. 'You have surely seen the opera before?'

'Never,' said Newman. 'I am sure I should have remembered it. Donna Elvira* reminds me of Madame de Cintré; I don't mean in her circumstances, but in the music she sings.'

'It is a very nice distinction,' laughed the marquis lightly.

'There is no great possibility, I imagine, of Madame de Cintré being forsaken.'

'Not much!' said Newman. 'But what becomes of the Don?'

'The devil comes down – or comes up,' said Madame de Bellegarde, 'and carries him off. I suppose Zerlina* reminds you of me.'

'I will go to the *foyer* for a few moments,' said the marquis, 'and give you a chance to say that the Commander – the man of stone* – resembles me.' And he passed out of the box.

The little marquise stared an instant at the velvet ledge of the balcony, and then murmured: 'Not a man of stone, a man of wood.' Newman had taken her husband's empty chair. She made no protest, and then she turned suddenly and laid her closed fan upon his arm. 'I am very glad you came in,' she said. 'I want to ask you a favour. I wanted to do so on Thursday, at my mother-in-law's ball, but you would give me no chance. You were in such very good spirits that I thought you might grant my little favour then; not that you look particularly doleful now. It is something you must promise me; now is the time to take you; after you are married you will be good for nothing. Come, promise!'

'I never sign a paper without reading it first,' said Newman. 'Show me your document.'

'No, you must sign with your eyes shut; I will hold your hand. Come, before you put your head into the noose. You ought to be thankful for me giving you a chance to do something amusing.'

'If it is so amusing,' said Newman, 'it will be in even better season after I am married.'

'In other words,' cried Madame de Bellegarde, 'you will not do it at all. You will be afraid of your wife.'

'Oh, if the thing is intrinsically improper,' said Newman, 'I won't go into it. If it is not, I will do it after my marriage.'

'You talk like a treatise on logic, and English logic into the bargain!' exclaimed Madame de Bellegarde. 'Promise, then, after you are married. After all, I shall enjoy keeping you to it.'

'Well, then, after I am married,' said Newman serenely.

The little marquise hesitated a moment, looking at him, and he wondered what was coming. 'I suppose you know what my life is,' she presently said. 'I have no pleasure, I see nothing, I do nothing. I live in Paris as I might live at Poitiers.* My mother-in-law calls me – what is the pretty word? – a gadabout? accuses me of going to unheard-of places, and thinks it ought to be joy enough for me to sit at home and count over my ancestors on my fingers. But why should I bother about my ancestors? I am sure they never bothered about me. I don't propose to live with a green shade on my eyes; I hold that things were made to look at. My husband, you know, has principles, and the first on the list is that the Tuileries are dreadfully vulgar. If the Tuileries are vulgar, his principles are tiresome. If I chose I might have principles quite as well as he. If they grew on one's family tree I should only have to give mine a shake to bring down a shower of the finest. At any rate, I prefer clever Bonapartes to stupid Bourbons.'

'Oh, I see; you want to go to court,' said Newman, vaguely conjecturing that she might wish him to appeal to the United States legation to smooth her way to the imperial halls.

The marquise gave a little sharp laugh. 'You are a thousand miles away. I will take care of the Tuileries myself; the day I decide to go they will be very glad to have me. Sooner or later I shall dance in an imperial quadrille. I know what you are going to say: "How will you dare?" But I *shall* dare. I am afraid of my husband; he is soft, smooth, irreproachable, everything that you know; but I am afraid of him – horribly afraid of him. And yet I shall arrive at the Tuileries. But that will not be this winter, nor perhaps next, and meantime I must live. For the moment, I want to go somewhere else; it's my dream. I want to go to the Bal Bullier.'

'To the Bal Bullier?' repeated Newman, for whom the words at first meant nothing.

'The ball in the Latin Quarter,* where the students dance with their mistresses. Don't tell me you have not heard of it.'

'Oh yes,' said Newman; 'I have heard of it; I remember now. I have even been there. And you want to go there?'

'It is silly, it is low, it is anything you please. But I want to go. Some of my friends have been, and they say it is awfully *drôle*.* My friends go everywhere; it is only I who sit moping at home.'

'It seems to me you are not at home now,' said Newman, 'and I shouldn't exactly say you were moping.'

'I am bored to death. I have been to the opera twice a week for the last eight years. Whenever I ask for anything my mouth is stopped with that: Pray, madam, haven't you an opera-box?

Could a woman of taste want more? In the first place, my opera-box was down in my *contrat*;* they have to give it to me. Tonight, for instance, I should have preferred a thousand times to go to the Palais Royal. But my husband won't go to the Palais Royal because the ladies of the court go there so much. You may imagine, then, whether he would take me to Bullier's; he says it is a mere imitation – and a bad one – of what they do at the Princess Kleinfuss's. But as I don't go to the Princess Kleinfuss's, the next best thing is to go to Bullier's. It is my dream, at any rate; it's a fixed idea. All I ask of you is to give me your arm; you are less compromising than anyone else. I don't know why, but you are. I can arrange it. I shall risk something, but that is my own affair. Besides, fortune favours the bold. Don't refuse me; it is my dream!'

Newman gave a loud laugh. It seemed to him hardly worth-while to be the wife of the Marquis de Bellegarde, a daughter of the crusaders, heiress of six centuries of glories and traditions, to have centred one's aspirations upon the sight of a couple of hundred young ladies kicking off young men's hats.* It struck him as a theme for the moralist; but he had no time to moralise upon it. The curtain rose again; M. de Bellegarde returned, and Newman went back to his seat.

He observed that Valentin de Bellegarde had taken his place in the *baignoire* of Mademoiselle Nioche, behind this young lady and her companion, where he was visible only if one carefully looked for him. In the next act Newman met him in the lobby and asked him if he had reflected upon possible emigration. 'If you really meant to meditate,' he said, 'you might have chosen a better place for it.'

'Oh, the place was not bad,' said Valentin. 'I was not thinking of that girl. I listened to the music, and without thinking of the play or looking at the stage, I turned over your proposal. At first it seemed quite fantastic. And then a certain fiddle in the orchestra – I could distinguish it – began to say as it scraped away: "Why not, why not?" And then, in that rapid movement, all the fiddles took it up, and the conductor's stick seemed to beat it in the air: "Why not, why not?" I'm sure I can't say! I don't see why not. I don't see why I shouldn't do something. It appears to me really a very bright idea. This sort of thing is certainly very stale. And then I could come back with a trunk full of dollars. Besides, I might possibly find it amusing. They

call me a *raffiné*;* who knows but that I might discover an
unsuspected charm in shop-keeping? It would really have a
certain romantic, picturesque side; it would look well in my
biography. It would look as if I were a strong man, a first-rate
man, a man who dominated circumstances.'

'Never mind how it would look,' said Newman. 'It always
looks well to have half a million of dollars. There is no reason
why you shouldn't have them if you will mind what I tell you –
I alone – and not talk to other parties.' He passed his arm into
that of his companion, and the two walked for some time up
and down one of the less frequented corridors. Newman's
imagination began to glow with the idea of converting his
bright, impracticable friend into a first-class man of business.
He felt for the moment a sort of spiritual zeal, the zeal of the
propagandist. Its ardour was in part the result of that general
discomfort which the sight of all uninvested capital produced in
him; so fine an intelligence as Bellegarde's ought to be dedicated
to high uses. The highest uses known to Newman's experience
were certain transcendent sagacities in the handling of railway
stock. And then his zeal was quickened by his personal kindness
for Valentin; he had a sort of pity for him which he was well
aware he never could have made the Comte de Bellegarde
understand. He never lost a sense of its being pitiable that
Valentin should think it a large life to revolve in varnished boots
between the Rue d'Anjou and the Rue de l'Université, taking the
Boulevard des Italiens* on the way, when over there in America
one's promenade was a continent, and one's boulevard stretched
from New York to San Francisco. It mortified him, moreover,
to think that Valentin lacked money; there was a painful
grotesqueness in it. It affected him as the ignorance of a
companion, otherwise without reproach, touching some rudi-
mentary branch of learning would have done. There were things
that one knew about as a matter of course, he would have said
in such a case. Just so, if one pretended to be easy in the world,
one had money as a matter of course; one had made it! There
was something almost ridiculously anomalous to Newman in
the sight of lively pretensions unaccompanied by large investments in railroads; though I may add that he would not have
maintained that such investments were in themselves a proper
ground for pretensions. 'I will make you do something,' he said
to Valentin; 'I will put you through. I know half-a-dozen things

in which we can make a place for you. You will see some lively work. It will take you a little while to get used to the life, but you will work in before long, and at the end of six months – after you have done a thing or two on your own account – you will like it. And then it will be very pleasant for you, having your sister over there. It will be pleasant for her to have you, too. Yes, Valentin,' continued Newman, pressing his friend's arm genially, 'I think I see just the opening for you. Keep quiet, and I'll push you right in.'

Newman pursued this favouring strain for some time longer. The two men strolled about for a quarter of an hour. Valentin listened and questioned, many of his questions making Newman laugh loud at the *naïveté* of his ignorance of the vulgar processes of money-getting; smiling himself, too, half ironical and half curious. And yet he was serious; he was fascinated by Newman's plain prose version of the legend of El Dorado.* It is true, however, that though to accept an 'opening' in an American mercantile house might be a bold, original, and in its consequences extremely agreeable thing to do, he did not quite see himself objectively doing it. So that when the bell rang to indicate the close of the entr'acte, there was a certain mock-heroism in his saying, with his brilliant smile: 'Well, then, put me through; push me in! I make myself over to you. Dip me into the pot and turn me into gold.'

They had passed into the corridor which encircled the row of *baignoires*, and Valentin stopped in front of the dusky little box in which Mademoiselle Nioche had bestowed herself, laying his hand on the door-knob. 'Oh, come, are you going back there?' asked Newman.

'*Mon Dieu, oui*,' said Valentin.

'Haven't you another place?'

'Yes, I have my usual place, in the stalls.'

'You had better go and occupy it, then.'

'I see her very well from there, too,' added Valentin serenely; 'and tonight she is worth seeing. But,' he added in a moment, 'I have a particular reason for going back just now.'

'Oh, I give you up,' said Newman. 'You are infatuated!'

'No, it is only this. There is a young man in the box whom I shall annoy by going in, and I want to annoy him.'

'I am sorry to hear it,' said Newman. 'Can't you leave the poor fellow alone?'

'No, he has given me cause. The box is not his; Noémie came in alone and installed herself. I went and spoke to her, and in a few moments she asked me to go and get her fan from the pocket of her cloak, which the *ouvreuse** had carried off. In my absence this gentleman came in and took the chair beside Noémie in which I had been sitting. My reappearance disgusted him, and he had the grossness to show it. He came within an ace of being impertinent. I don't know who he is; he is some vulgar wretch. I can't think where she picks up such acquaintances. He has been drinking, too, but he knows what he is about. Just now, in the second act, he was unmannerly again. I shall put in another appearance for ten minutes – time enough to give him an opportunity to commit himself, if he feels inclined. I really can't let the brute suppose that he is keeping me out of the box.'

'My dear fellow,' said Newman remonstrantly, 'what child's play! You are not going to pick a quarrel about that girl, I hope.'

'That girl has nothing to do with it, and I have no intention of picking a quarrel. I am not a bully nor a fire-eater.* I simply wish to make a point that a gentleman must.'

'Oh, damn your point!' said Newman. 'That is the trouble with you Frenchmen; you must be always making points. Well,' he added, 'be short. But if you are going in for this kind of thing, we must ship you off to America in advance.'

'Very good,' Valentin answered, 'whenever you please. But if I go to America, I must not let this gentleman suppose that it is to run away from him.'

And they separated. At the end of the act Newman observed that Valentin was still in the *baignoire*. He strolled into the corridor again, expecting to meet him, and when he was within a few yards of Mademoiselle Nioche's box, saw his friend pass out, accompanied by the young man who had been seated beside its fair occupant. The two gentlemen walked with some quickness of step to a distant part of the lobby, where Newman perceived them stop and stand talking. The manner of each was perfectly quiet, but the stranger, who looked flushed, had begun to wipe his face very emphatically with his pocket-handkerchief. By this time Newman was abreast of the *baignoire*; the door had been left ajar, and he could see a pink dress inside. He immediately went in. Mademoiselle Nioche turned and greeted him with a brilliant smile.

'Ah, you have at last decided to come and see me?' she exclaimed. 'You just save your politeness. You find me in a fine moment. Sit down.' There was a very becoming little flush in her cheek, and her eye had a noticeable spark. You would have said that she had received some very good news.

'Something has happened here!' said Newman, without sitting down.

'You find me in a very fine moment,' she repeated. 'Two gentlemen – one of them is M. de Bellegarde, the pleasure of whose acquaintance I owe to you – have just had words about your humble servant. Very big words too. They can't come off without crossing swords. A duel – that will give me a push!' cried Mademoiselle Noémie, clapping her little hands. '*C'est ça qui pose une femme!*'*

'You don't mean to say that Bellegarde is going to fight about *you*!' exclaimed Newman disgustedly.

'Nothing less!' and she looked at him with a hard little smile. 'No, no, you are not *galant*! And if you prevent this affair I shall owe you a grudge – and pay my debt!'

Newman uttered an imprecation which, though brief – it consisted simply of the interjection 'Oh!' followed by a geographical, or more correctly, perhaps, a theological noun in four letters* – had better not be transferred to these pages. He turned his back without more ceremony upon the pink dress and went out of the box. In the corridor he found Valentin and his companion walking towards him. The latter was thrusting a card into his waistcoat-pocket. Mademoiselle Noémie's jealous votary was a tall robust young man with a thick nose, a prominent blue eye, a Germanic physiognomy, and a massive watch-chain. When they reached the box, Valentin with an emphasised bow made way for him to pass in first. Newman touched Valentin's arm as a sign that he wished to speak with him, and Bellegarde answered that he would be with him in an instant. Valentin entered the box after the robust young man, but a couple of minutes afterwards he reappeared, largely smiling.

'She is immensely tickled,' he said. 'She says we will make her fortune. I don't want to be fatuous, but I think it is very possible.'

'So you are going to fight?' said Newman.

'My dear fellow, don't look so mortally disgusted. It was not my own choice. The thing is all arranged.'

'I told you so!' groaned Newman.

'I told *him* so,' said Valentin, smiling.

'What did he do to you?'

'My good friend, it doesn't matter what. He used an expression – I took it up.'

'But I insist upon knowing; I can't, as your elder brother, have you rushing into this sort of nonsense.'

'I am very much obliged to you,' said Valentin. 'I have nothing to conceal, but I can't go into particulars now and here.'

'We will leave this place, then. You can tell me outside.'

'Oh no, I can't leave this place; why should I hurry away? I will go to my orchestra-stall and sit out the opera.'

'You will not enjoy it; you will be preoccupied.'

Valentin looked at him a moment, coloured a little, smiled, and patted him on the arm. 'You are delightfully simple! Before an affair a man is quiet. The quietest thing I can do is to go straight to my place.'

'Ah,' said Newman, 'you want her to see you there – you and your quietness. I am not so simple! It is a poor business.'

Valentin remained, and the two men, in their respective places, sat out the rest of the performance, which was also enjoyed by Mademoiselle Nioche and her truculent admirer. At the end Newman joined Valentin again, and they went into the street together. Valentin shook his head at his friend's proposal that he should get into Newman's own vehicle, and stopped on the edge of the pavement. 'I must go off alone,' he said; 'I must look up a couple of friends who will take charge of this matter.'

'I will take charge of it,' Newman declared. 'Put it into my hands.'

'You are very kind, but that is hardly possible. In the first place, you are, as you said just now, almost my brother; you are about to marry my sister. That alone disqualifies you; it casts doubts on your impartiality. And if it didn't, it would be enough for me that I strongly suspect you of disapproving of the affair. You would try to prevent a meeting.'

'Of course I should,' said Newman. 'Whoever your friends are, I hope they will do that.'

'Unquestionably they will. They will urge that excuses be

made, proper excuses. But you would be too good-natured. You
won't do.'

Newman was silent a moment. He was keenly annoyed, but
he saw it was useless to attempt interference. 'When is this
precious performance to come off?' he asked.

'The sooner the better,' said Valentin. 'The day after
tomorrow, I hope.'

'Well,' said Newman, 'I have certainly a claim to know the
facts. I can't consent to shut my eyes to the matter.'

'I shall be most happy to tell you the facts,' said Valentin.
'They are very simple, and it will be quickly done. But now
everything depends on my putting my hands on my friends
without delay. I will jump into a cab; you had better drive to
my room and wait for me there. I will turn up at the end of an
hour.'

Newman assented protestingly, let his friend go, and then
betook himself to the picturesque little apartment in the Rue
d'Anjou. It was more than an hour before Valentin returned, but
when he did so he was able to announce that he had found one
of his desired friends, and that this gentleman had taken upon
himself the care of securing an associate. Newman had been
sitting without lights by Valentin's faded fire, upon which he
had thrown a log; the blaze played over the richly-encumbered
little sitting-room and produced fantastic gleams and shadows.
He listened in silence to Valentin's account of what had passed
between him and the gentleman whose card he had in his pocket
– M. Stanislas Kapp, of Strasbourg* – after his return to
Mademoiselle Nioche's box. This hospitable young lady had
espied an acquaintance on the other side of the house, and had
expressed her displeasure at his not having the civility to come
and pay her a visit. 'Oh, let him alone!' M. Stanislas Kapp had
hereupon exclaimed. 'There are too many people in the box
already.' And he had fixed his eyes with a demonstrative stare
upon M. de Bellegarde. Valentin had promptly retorted that if
there were too many people in the box it was easy for M. Kapp
to diminish the number. 'I shall be most happy to open the door
for *you*!' M. Kapp exclaimed. 'I shall be delighted to fling you
into the pit!' Valentin had answered. 'Oh, do make a rumpus
and get into the papers!' Miss Noémie had gleefully ejaculated.
'M. Kapp, turn him out; or, M. de Bellegarde, pitch him into
the pit, into the orchestra – anywhere! I don't care who does

which, so long as you make a scene.' Valentin answered that they would make no scene, but that the gentleman would be so good as to step into the corridor with him. In the corridor, after a brief further exchange of words, there had been an exchange of cards. M. Stanislas Kapp was very stiff. He evidently meant to force his offence home.

'The man, no doubt, was insolent,' Newman said; 'but if you hadn't gone back into the box the thing wouldn't have happened.'

'Why, don't you see,' Valentin replied, 'that the event proves the extreme propriety of my going back into the box? M. Kapp wished to provoke me; he was awaiting his chance. In such a case – that is, when he has been, so to speak, notified – a man must be on hand to receive the provocation. My not returning would simply have been tantamount to my saying to M. Stanislas Kapp: "Oh, if you are going to be disagreeable" – '

'"You must manage it by yourself; damned if I'll help you!" That would have been a thoroughly sensible thing to say. The only attraction for you seems to have been the prospect of M. Kapp's impertinence,' Newman went on. 'You told me you were not going back for that girl.'

'Oh, don't mention that girl any more,' murmured Valentin. 'She's a bore.'

'With all my heart. But if that is the way you feel about her, why couldn't you let her alone?'

Valentin shook his head with a fine smile. 'I don't think you quite understand, and I don't believe I can make you. She understood the situation; she knew what was in the air; she was watching us.'

'A cat may look at a king! What difference does that make?'

'Why, a man can't back down before a woman.'

'I don't call her a woman. You said yourself she was a stone,' cried Newman.

'Well,' Valentin rejoined, 'there is no disputing about tastes. It's a matter of feeling; it's measured by one's sense of honour.'

'Oh, confound your sense of honour!' cried Newman.

'It is vain talking,' said Valentin; 'words have passed, and the thing is settled.'

Newman turned away, taking his hat. Then pausing with his hand on the door, 'What are you going to use?' he asked.

'That is for M. Stanislas Kapp, as the challenged party, to

decide. My own choice would be a short, light sword. I handle it well. I'm an indifferent shot.'

Newman had put on his hat; he pushed it back, gently scratching his forehead high up. 'I wish it were pistols,' he said. 'I could show you how to lodge a bullet!'

Valentin broke into a laugh. 'What is it some English poet says about consistency? It's a flower, or a star, or a jewel. Yours has the beauty of all three!' But he agreed to see Newman again on the morrow, after the details of his meeting with M. Stanislas Kapp should have been arranged.

In the course of the day Newman received three lines from him, saying that it had been decided that he should cross the frontier, with his adversary, and that he was to take the night express to Geneva. He should have time, however, to dine with Newman. In the afternoon Newman called upon Madame de Cintré, but his visit was brief. She was as gracious and sympathetic as he had ever found her, but she was sad, and she confessed, on Newman's charging her with her red eyes, that she had been crying. Valentin had been with her a couple of hours before, and his visit had left her with a painful impression. He had laughed and gossiped, he had brought her no bad news, he had only been, in his manner, rather more affectionate than usual. His fraternal tenderness had touched her, and on his departure she had burst into tears. She had felt as if something strange and sad were going to happen; she had tried to reason away the fancy, and the effort had only given her a headache. Newman, of course, was perforce tongue-tied about Valentin's projected duel, and his dramatic talent was not equal to satirising Madame de Cintré's presentiment as pointedly as perfect security demanded. Before he went away he asked Madame de Cintré whether Valentin had seen his mother.

'Yes,' she said, 'but he didn't make her cry.'

It was in Newman's own apartment that Valentin dined, having brought his portmanteau,* so that he might adjourn directly to the railway. M. Stanislas Kapp had positively declined to make excuses, and he, on his side, obviously, had none to offer. Valentin had found out with whom he was dealing. M. Stanislas Kapp was the son and heir of a rich brewer of Strasbourg, a youth of a sanguineous – and sanguinary – temperament. He was making ducks and drakes* of the paternal brewery, and although he passed in a general way for a good fellow, he had already been observed to be quarrelsome after dinner. '*Que voulez-vous?*'* said Valentin. 'Brought up on beer, he can't stand champagne.' He had chosen pistols. Valentin, at dinner, had an excellent appetite; he made a point, in view of his long journey, of eating more than usual. He took the liberty of suggesting to Newman a slight modification in the composition of a certain fish-sauce; he thought it would be worth mentioning to the cook. But Newman had no thoughts for fish-sauce; he felt thoroughly discontented. As he sat and watched his amiable and clever companion going through his excellent repast with the delicate deliberation of hereditary epicurism, the folly of so charming a fellow travelling off to expose his agreeable young life for the sake of M. Stanislas and Mademoiselle Noémie struck him with intolerable force. He had grown fond of Valentin, he felt now how fond; and his sense of helplessness only increased his irritation.

'Well, this sort of thing may be all very well,' he cried at last, 'but I declare I don't see it. I can't stop you, perhaps, but at least I can protest. I do protest, violently.'

'My dear fellow, don't make a scene,' said Valentin. 'Scenes in these cases are in very bad taste.'

'Your duel itself is a scene,' said Newman; 'that's all it is! It's a wretched theatrical affair. Why don't you take a band of music with you outright? It's d——d barbarous and it's d——d corrupt, both.'

'Oh, I can't begin, at this time of day, to defend the theory of duelling,' said Valentin. 'It is our custom, and I think it is a good thing. Quite apart from the goodness of the cause in which a duel may be fought, it has a kind of picturesque charm which in this age of vile prose seems to me greatly to recommend it. It's a remnant of a higher-tempered time; one ought to cling to it. Depend upon it, a duel is never amiss.'

'I don't know what you mean by a higher-tempered time,' said Newman. 'Because your great-grandfather was an ass, is that any reason why you should be? For my part, I think we had better let our temper take care of itself; it generally seems to me quite high enough; I am not afraid of being too meek. If your great-grandfather were to make himself unpleasant to me, I think I could manage him yet.'

'My dear friend,' said Valentin, smiling, 'you can't invent

anything that will take the place of satisfaction for an insult. To demand it and to give it are equally excellent arrangements.'

'Do you call this sort of thing satisfaction?' Newman asked. 'Does it satisfy you to receive a present of the carcass of that coarse fop? does it gratify you to make him a present of yours? If a man hits you, hit him back; if a man libels you, haul him up.'

'Haul him up, into court? Oh, that is very nasty!' said Valentin.

'The nastiness is his – not yours. And for that matter, what you are doing is not particularly nice. You are too good for it. I don't say you are the most useful man in the world, or the cleverest, or the most amiable. But you are too good to go and get your throat cut for a prostitute.'

Valentin flushed a little, but he laughed. 'I shan't get my throat cut if I can help it. Moreover, one's honour hasn't two different measures. It only knows that it is hurt; it doesn't ask when, or how, or where.'

'The more fool it is!' said Newman.

Valentin ceased to laugh; he looked grave. 'I beg you not to say any more,' he said. 'If you do I shall almost fancy you don't care about – about' – and he paused.

'About what?'

'About that matter – about one's honour.'

'Fancy what you please,' said Newman. 'Fancy while you are at it that I care about *you* – though you are not worth it. But come back without damage,' he added in a moment, 'and I will forgive you. And then,' he continued, as Valentin was going: 'I will ship you straight off to America.'

'Well,' answered Valentin, 'if I am to turn over a new page, this may figure as a tail-piece* to the old.' And then he lit another cigar and departed.

'Blast that girl!' said Newman, as the door closed upon Valentin.

Newman went the next morning to see Madame de Cintré, timing his visit so as to arrive after the noonday breakfast. In the court of the *hôtel*, before the portico, stood Madame de Bellegarde's old square carriage. The servant who opened the door answered Newman's inquiry with a slightly embarrassed and hesitating murmur, and at the same moment Mrs Bread appeared in the background, dim-visaged as usual, and wearing a large black bonnet and shawl.

'What is the matter?' asked Newman. 'Is Madame la Comtesse at home, or not?'

Mrs Bread advanced, fixing her eyes upon him; he observed that she held a sealed letter, very delicately, in her fingers. 'The countess has left a message for you, sir; she has left this,' said Mrs Bread, holding out the letter, which Newman took.

'Left it? Is she out? Is she gone away?'

'She is going away, sir; she is leaving town,' said Mrs Bread.

'Leaving town!' exclaimed Newman. 'What has happened?'

'It is not for me to say, sir,' said Mrs Bread, with her eyes on the ground. 'But I thought it would come.'

'What would come, pray?' Newman demanded. He had broken the seal of the letter, but he still questioned. 'She is in the house? She is visible?'

'I don't think she expected you this morning,' the old waiting-woman replied. 'She was to leave immediately.'

'Where is she going?'

'To Fleurières.'

'To Fleurières? But surely I can see her?'

Mrs Bread hesitated a moment, and then clasping together her two hands, 'I will take you!' she said. And she led the way upstairs. At the top of the staircase she paused and fixed her dry, sad eyes upon Newman. 'Be very easy with her,' she said; 'she is most unhappy!' Then she went on to Madame de Cintré's apartment; Newman, perplexed and alarmed, followed her rapidly. Mrs Bread threw open the door, and Newman pushed back the curtain at the farther side of its deep embrasure. In the middle of the room stood Madame de Cintré; her face was pale and she was dressed for travelling. Behind her, before the fireplace, stood Urbain de Bellegarde, looking at his finger-nails;

near the marquis sat his mother, buried in an arm-chair, and with her eyes immediately fixing themselves upon Newman. He felt, as soon as he entered the room, that he was in the presence of something evil; he was startled and pained, as he would have been by a threatening cry in the stillness of the night. He walked straight to Madame de Cintré and seized her by the hand.

'What is the matter?' he asked commandingly; 'what is happening?'

Urbain de Bellegarde stared, then left his place and came and leaned upon his mother's chair, behind. Newman's sudden irruption had evidently discomposed both mother and son. Madame de Cintré stood silent, with her eyes resting upon Newman's. She had often looked at him with all her soul, as it seemed to him; but in this present gaze there was a sort of bottomless depth. She was in distress; it was the most touching thing he had ever seen. His heart rose into his throat, and he was on the point of turning to her companions with an angry challenge; but she checked him, pressing the hand that held her own.

'Something very grave has happened,' she said. 'I cannot marry you.'

Newman dropped her hand and stood staring, first at her and then at the others. 'Why not?' he asked, as quietly as possible.

Madame de Cintré almost smiled, but the attempt was strange. 'You must ask my mother, you must ask my brother.'

'Why can't she marry me?' said Newman, looking at them.

Madame de Bellegarde did not move in her place, but she was as pale as her daughter. The marquis looked down at her. She said nothing for some moments, but she kept her keen clear eyes upon Newman bravely. The marquis drew himself up and looked at the ceiling. 'It's impossible!' he said softly.

'It's improper,' said Madame de Bellegarde.

Newman began to laugh. 'Oh, you are fooling!' he exclaimed.

'My sister, you have no time; you are losing your train,' said the marquis.

'Come, is he mad?' asked Newman.

'No; don't think that,' said Madame de Cintré. 'But I am going away.'

'Where are you going?'

'To the country, to Fleurières; to be alone.'

'To leave me?' said Newman slowly.

'I can't see you, now,' said Madame de Cintré.

'*Now* – why not?'

'I am ashamed,' said Madame de Cintré simply.

Newman turned toward the marquis. 'What have you done to her – what does it mean?' he asked with the same effort at calmness, the fruit of his constant practice in taking things easily. He was excited, but excitement with him was only an intenser deliberateness; it was the swimmer stripped.

'It means that I have given you up,' said Madame de Cintré. 'It means that.'

Her face was too charged with tragic expression not fully to confirm her words. Newman was profoundly shocked, but he felt as yet no resentment against her. He was amazed, bewildered, and the presence of the old marquise and her son seemed to smite his eyes like the glare of a watchman's lantern. 'Can't I see you alone?' he asked.

'It would be only more painful. I hoped I should not see you – I should escape. I wrote to you. Good-bye.' And she put out her hand again.

Newman put both his own into his pockets. 'I will go with you,' he said.

She laid her two hands on his arm. 'Will you grant me a last request?' and as she looked at him, urging this, her eyes filled with tears. 'Let me go alone – let me go in peace. I can't call it peace – it's death. But let me bury myself. So – good-bye.'

Newman passed his hand into his hair and stood slowly rubbing his head and looking through his keenly-narrowed eyes from one to the other of the three persons before him. His lips were compressed, and the two lines which had formed themselves beside his mouth might have made it appear at a first glance that he was smiling. I have said that his excitement was an intenser deliberateness, and now he looked grimly deliberate. 'It seems very much as if you had interfered, marquis,' he said slowly. 'I thought you said you wouldn't interfere. I know you don't like me; but that doesn't make any difference. I thought you promised me you wouldn't interfere. I thought you swore on your honour that you wouldn't interfere. Don't you remember, marquis?'

The marquis lifted his eyebrows; but he was apparently determined to be even more urbane than usual. He rested his two hands upon the back of his mother's chair and bent forward, as if he were leaning over the edge of a pulpit or a lecture-desk. He did not smile, but he looked softly grave. 'Excuse me, sir,' he said, 'I assured you that I would not influence my sister's decision. I adhered, to the letter, to my engagement. Did I not, sister?'

'Don't appeal, my son,' said the marquise, 'your word is sufficient.'

'Yes – she accepted me,' said Newman. 'That is very true; I can't deny that. At least,' he added, in a different tone, turning to Madame de Cintré, 'you *did* accept me?'

Something in the tone seemed to move her strongly. She turned away, burying her face in her hands.

'But you have interfered now, haven't you?' inquired Newman of the marquis.

'Neither then nor now have I attempted to influence my sister. I used no persuasion then, I have used no persuasion today.'

'And what have you used?'

'We have used authority,' said Madame de Bellegarde in a rich, bell-like voice.

'Ah, you have used authority,' Newman exclaimed. 'They have used authority,' he went on, turning to Madame de Cintré. 'What is it? how did they use it?'

'My mother commanded,' said Madame de Cintré.

'Commanded you to give me up – I see. And you obey – I see. But why do you obey?' asked Newman.

Madame de Cintré looked across at the old marquise; her eyes slowly measured her from head to foot. 'I am afraid of my mother,' she said.

Madame de Bellegarde rose with a certain quickness, crying: 'This is a most indecent scene!'

'I have no wish to prolong it,' said Madame de Cintré; and turning to the door she put out her hand again. 'If you can pity me a little, let me go alone.'

Newman shook her hand quietly and firmly. 'I'll come down there,' he said. The *portière* dropped behind her, and Newman sank with a long breath into the nearest chair. He leaned back in it, resting his hands on the knobs of the arms and looking at Madame de Bellegarde and Urbain. There was a long silence. They stood side by side, with their heads high and their handsome eyebrows arched.

'So you make a distinction?' Newman said at last. 'You make

a distinction between persuading and commanding? It's very neat. But the distinction is in favour of commanding. That rather spoils it.'

'We have not the least objection to defining our position,' said M. de Bellegarde. 'We understand that it should not at first appear to you quite clear. We rather expect, indeed, that you should not do us justice.'

'Oh, I'll do you justice,' said Newman. 'Don't be afraid. Please proceed.'

The marquise laid her hand on her son's arm, as if to deprecate the attempt to define their position. 'It is quite useless,' she said, 'to try and arrange this matter so as to make it agreeable to you. It can never be agreeable to you. It is a disappointment, and disappointments are unpleasant. I thought it over carefully and tried to arrange it better; but I only gave myself a headache and lost my sleep. Say what we will, you will think yourself ill-treated, and you will publish your wrongs among your friends. But we are not afraid of that. Besides, your friends are not our friends, and it will not matter. Think of us as you please. I only beg you not to be violent. I have never in my life been present at a violent scene of any kind, and at my age I can't be expected to begin.'

'Is *that* all you have got to say?' asked Newman, slowly rising out of his chair. 'That's a poor show for a clever lady like you, marquise. Come, try again.'

'My mother goes to the point, with her usual honesty and intrepidity,' said the marquis, toying with his watch-guard. 'But it is perhaps well to say a little more. We of course quite repudiate the charge of having broken faith with you. We left you entirely at liberty to make yourself agreeable to my sister. We left her quite at liberty to entertain your proposal. When she accepted you we said nothing. We therefore quite observed our promise. It was only at a later stage of the affair, and on quite a different basis, as it were, that we determined to speak. It would have been better, perhaps, if we had spoken before. But really, you see, nothing has yet been done.'

'Nothing has yet been done?' Newman repeated the words, unconscious of their comical effect. He had lost the sense of what the marquis was saying; M. de Bellegarde's superior style was a mere humming in his ears. All that he understood, in his deep and simple indignation, was that the matter was not a violent joke, and that the people before him were perfectly serious. 'Do you suppose I can take this?' he asked. 'Do you suppose it can matter to me what you say? Do you suppose I can seriously listen to you? You are simply crazy!'

Madame de Bellegarde gave a rap with her fan in the palm of her hand. 'If you don't take it you can leave it, sir. It matters very little what you do. My daughter has given you up.'

'She doesn't mean it,' Newman declared after a moment.

'I think I can assure you that she does,' said the marquis.

'Poor woman, what damnable thing have you done to her?' cried Newman.

'Gently, gently!' murmured M. de Bellegarde.

'She told you,' said the old lady. 'I commanded her.'

Newman shook his head heavily. 'This sort of thing can't be, you know,' he said. 'A man can't be used in this fashion. You have got no right; you have got no power.'

'My power,' said Madame de Bellegarde, 'is in my children's obedience.'

'In their fear, your daughter said. There is something very strange in it. Why should your daughter be afraid of you?' added Newman, after looking a moment at the old lady. 'There is some foul play.'

The marquise met his gaze without flinching, and as if she did not hear or heed what he said. 'I did my best,' she said quietly. 'I could endure it no longer.'

'It was a bold experiment!' said the marquis.

Newman felt disposed to walk to him, clutch his neck with his fingers and press his windpipe with his thumb. 'I needn't tell you how you strike me,' he said, 'of course you know that. But I should think you would be afraid of your friends – all those people you introduced me to the other night. There were some very nice people among them; you may depend upon it there were some honest men and women.'

'Our friends approve us,' said M. de Bellegarde; 'there is not a family among them that would have acted otherwise. And however that may be, we take the cue from no one. The Bellegardes have been used to set the example, not to wait for it.'

'You would have waited long before anyone would have set you such an example as this,' exclaimed Newman. 'Have I done anything wrong?' he demanded. 'Have I given you reason to

change your opinion? Have you found out anything against me?
I can't imagine.'

'Our opinion,' said Madame de Bellegarde, 'is quite the same
as at first – exactly. We have no ill-will towards yourself; we are
very far from accusing you of misconduct. Since your relations
with us began you have been, I frankly confess, less – less
peculiar than I expected. It is not your disposition that we object
to, it is your antecedents. We really cannot reconcile ourselves
to a commercial person. We fancied in an evil hour that we
could; it was a great misfortune. We determined to persevere to
the end, and to give you every advantage. I was resolved that
you should have no reason to accuse me of a want of loyalty.
We let the thing certainly go very far – we introduced you to
our friends. To tell the truth, it was that, I think, that broke me
down. I succumbed to the scene that took place on Thursday
night in these rooms. You must excuse me if what I say is
disagreeable to you, but we cannot release ourselves without an
explanation.'

'There can be no better proof of our good faith,' said the
marquis, 'than our committing ourselves to you in the eyes of
the world the other evening. We endeavoured to bind ourselves
– to tie our hands, as it were.'

'But it was that,' added his mother, 'that opened our eyes and
broke our bonds. We should have been most uncomfortable!
You know,' she added in a moment, 'that you were forewarned.
I told you we were very proud.'   ·

Newman took up his hat and began mechanically to smooth
it; the very fierceness of his scorn kept him from speaking. 'You
are not proud enough,' he observed at last.

'In all this matter,' said the marquis, smiling, 'I really see
nothing but our humility.'

'Let us have no more discussion than is necessary,' resumed
Madame de Bellegarde. 'My daughter told you everything when
she said she gave you up.'

'I am not satisfied about your daughter,' said Newman; 'I
want to know what you did to her. It is all very easy talking
about authority and saying you commanded her. She didn't
accept me blindly, and she wouldn't have given me up blindly.
Not that I believe yet she has really given me up; she will talk it
over with me. But you have frightened her, you have bullied her,
you have *hurt* her. What was it you did to her?'

'I did very little!' said Madame de Bellegarde, in a tone which gave Newman a chill when he afterwards remembered it.

'Let me remind you that we offered you these explanations,' the marquis observed, 'with the express understanding that you should abstain from violence of language.'

'I am not violent,' Newman answered, 'it is you who are violent! But I don't know that I have much more to say to you. What you expect of me, apparently, is to go my way, thanking you for favours received, and promising never to trouble you again.'

'We expect of you to act like a clever man,' said Madame de Bellegarde. 'You have shown yourself that already, and what we have done is altogether based upon your being so. When one must submit, one must. Since my daughter absolutely withdraws, what will be the use of your making a noise?'

'It remains to be seen whether your daughter absolutely withdraws. Your daughter and I are still very good friends; nothing is changed in that. As I say, I will talk it over with her.'

'That will be of no use,' said the old lady. 'I know my daughter well enough to know that words spoken as she just now spoke to you are final. Besides, she has promised me.'

'I have no doubt her promise is worth a good deal more than your own,' said Newman; 'nevertheless I don't give her up.'

'Just as you please! But if she won't even see you – and she won't – your constancy must remain purely Platonic.'

Poor Newman was feigning a greater confidence than he felt. Madame de Cintré's strange intensity had in fact struck a chill to his heart; her face, still impressed upon his vision, had been a terribly vivid image of renunciation. He felt sick, and suddenly helpless. He turned away and stood for a moment with his hand on the door; then he faced about, and after the briefest hesitation broke out with a different accent. 'Come, think of what this must be to me, and let her alone! Why should you object to me so – what's the matter with me? I can't hurt you, I wouldn't if I could. I'm the most unobjectionable fellow in the world. What if I am a commercial person? What under the sun do you mean? A commercial person? I will be any sort of person you want. I never talk to you about business. Let her go, and I will ask no questions. I will take her away, and you shall never see me or hear of me again. I will stay in America if you like. I'll sign a paper promising never to come back to Europe! All I want is not to lose her!'

Madame de Bellegarde and her son exchanged a glance of lucid irony, and Urbain said: 'My dear sir, what you propose is hardly an improvement. We have not the slightest objection to seeing you, as an amiable foreigner, and we have every reason for not wishing to be eternally separated from my sister. We object to the marriage; and in that way,' and M. de Bellegarde gave a small, thin laugh, 'she would be more married than ever.'

'Well, then,' said Newman, 'where is this place of yours – Fleurières? I know it is near some old city on a hill.'

'Precisely, Poitiers is on a hill,' said Madame de Bellegarde. 'I don't know how old it is. We are not afraid to tell you.'

'It is Poitiers, is it? Very good,' said Newman. 'I shall immediately follow Madame de Cintré.'

'The trains after this hour won't serve you,' said Urbain.

'I shall hire a special train!'

'That will be a very silly waste of money,' said Madame de Bellegarde.

'It will be time enough to talk about waste three days hence,' Newman answered; and clapping his hat on his head, he departed.

He did not immediately start for Fleurières; he was too stunned and wounded for consecutive action. He simply walked; he walked straight before him, following the river, till he got out of the *enceinte** of Paris. He had a burning, tingling sense of personal outrage. He had never in his life received so absolute a check; he had never been pulled up, or, as he would have said, 'let down', so short; and he found the sensation intolerable; he strode along, tapping the trees and lamp-posts fiercely with his stick and inwardly raging. To lose Madame de Cintré after he had taken such jubilant and triumphant possession of her was as great an affront to his pride as it was an injury to his happiness. And to lose her by the interference and the dictation of others, by an impudent old woman and a pretentious fop stepping in with their 'authority'! It was too preposterous, it was too pitiful. Upon what he deemed the unblushing treachery of the Bellegardes, Newman wasted little thought; he consigned it, once for all, to eternal perdition. But the treachery of Madame de Cintré herself amazed and confounded him; there was a key to the mystery, of course, but he groped for it in vain. Only three days had elapsed since she stood beside him in the starlight, beautiful and tranquil as the trust with which he had inspired her, and told him that she was happy in the prospect of their marriage. What was the meaning of the change? of what infernal potion had she tasted? Poor Newman had a terrible apprehension that she had really changed. His very admiration for her attached the idea of force and weight to her rupture. But he did not rail at her as false, for he was sure she was unhappy. In his walk he had crossed one of the bridges of the Seine, and he still followed, unheedingly, the long, unbroken quay. He had left Paris behind him, and he was almost in the country; he was in the pleasant suburb of Auteuil.* He stopped at last, looked around him without seeing or caring for its pleasantness, and then slowly turned and at a slower pace retraced his steps. When he came abreast of the fantastic embankment known as the Trocadero,* he reflected, through his throbbing pain, that he was near Mrs Tristram's dwelling, and that Mrs Tristram, on particular occasions, had much of a woman's kindness in her utterance. He felt that he needed to pour out his ire, and took the road to her house. Mrs Tristram was at home and alone, and as soon as she had looked at him, on his entering the room, she told him that she knew what he had come for. Newman sat down heavily, in silence, looking at her.

'They have backed out!' she said. 'Well, you may think it strange, but I felt something the other night in the air.' Presently he told her his story; she listened, with her eyes fixed on him. When he had finished she said quietly: 'They want her to marry Lord Deepmere.' Newman stared. He did not know that she knew anything about Lord Deepmere. 'But I don't think she will,' Mrs Tristram added.

'*She* marry that poor little cub!' cried Newman. 'Oh, Lord! And yet, why did she refuse me?'

'But that isn't the only thing,' said Mrs Tristram. 'They really couldn't endure you any longer. They had overrated their courage. I must say, to give the devil his due, that there is something rather fine in that. It was your commercial quality in the abstract they couldn't swallow. That is really aristocratic. They wanted your money, but they have given you up for an idea.'

Newman frowned most ruefully, and took up his hat again. 'I

thought you would encourage me!' he said, with almost childlike sadness.

'Excuse me,' she answered very gently. 'I feel none the less sorry for you, especially as I am at the bottom of your troubles. I have not forgotten that I suggested the marriage to you. I don't believe that Madame de Cintré has any intention of marrying Lord Deepmere. It is true he is not younger than she, as he looks. He is thirty-three years old; I looked in the Peerage.* But no – I can't believe her so horribly, cruelly false.'

'Please say nothing against her,' said Newman.

'Poor woman, she *is* cruel. But of course you will go after her and you will plead powerfully. Do you know that as you are now,' Mrs Tristram pursued with characteristic audacity of comment, 'you are extremely eloquent, even without speaking? To resist you a woman must have a very fixed idea in her head. I wish I had done you a wrong, that you might come to me in that fine fashion! But go to Madame de Cintré at any rate, and tell her that she is a puzzle even to me. I am very curious to see how far family discipline will go.'

Newman sat awhile longer, leaning his elbows on his knees and his head in his hands, and Mrs Tristram continued to temper charity with philosophy, and compassion with criticism. At last she inquired: 'And what does the Count Valentin say to it?' Newman started; he had not thought of Valentin and his errand on the Swiss frontier since the morning. The reflection made him restless again, and he took his leave. He went straight to his apartment, where, upon the table of the vestibule, he found a telegram. It ran (with the date and place) as follows: 'I am seriously ill; please to come to me as soon as possible. V. B.' Newman groaned at this miserable news, and at the necessity of deferring his journey to the Château de Fleurières. But he wrote to Madame de Cintré these few lines; they were all he had time for:

> I don't give you up, and I don't really believe you give me up. I don't understand it, but we shall clear it up together. I can't follow you today, as I am called to see a friend at a distance who is very ill, perhaps dying. But I shall come to you as soon as I can leave my friend. Why shouldn't I say that he is your brother? – C.N.

After this he had only time to catch the night-express to Geneva.

Newman possessed a remarkable talent for sitting still when it was necessary, and he had an opportunity to use it on his journey to Switzerland. The successive hours of the night brought him no sleep; but he sat motionless in his corner of the railway-carriage, with his eyes closed, and the most observant of his fellow-travellers might have envied him his apparent slumber. Toward morning slumber really came, as an effect of mental rather than of physical fatigue. He slept for a couple of hours, and at last, waking, found his eyes resting upon one of the snow-powdered peaks of the Jura,* behind which the sky was just reddening with the dawn. But he saw neither the cold mountain nor the warm sky; his consciousness began to throb again, on the very instant, with a sense of his wrong. He got out of the train half an hour before it reached Geneva, in the cold morning twilight, at the station indicated in Valentin's telegram. A drowsy station-master was on the platform with a lantern, and the hood of his overcoat over his head, and near him stood a gentleman who advanced to meet Newman. This personage was a man of forty, with a tall lean figure, a sallow face, a dark eye, a neat moustache, and a pair of fresh gloves. He took off his hat, looking very grave, and pronounced Newman's name. Our hero assented and said: 'You are M. de Bellegarde's friend?'

'I unite with you in claiming that sad honour,' said the gentleman. 'I had placed myself at M. de Bellegarde's service in this melancholy affair, together with M. de Grosjoyaux, who is now at his bedside. M. de Grosjoyaux, I believe, has had the honour of meeting you in Paris, but as he is a better nurse than I he remained with our poor friend. Bellegarde has been eagerly expecting you.'

'And how is Bellegarde?' said Newman. 'He was badly hit?'

'The doctor has condemned him; we brought a surgeon with us. But he will die in the best sentiments. I sent last evening for the curé of the nearest French village, who spent an hour with him. The curé* was quite satisfied.'

'Heaven forgive us!' groaned Newman. 'I would rather the doctor were satisfied! And can he see me – shall he know me?'

'When I left him, half an hour ago, he had fallen asleep, after a feverish, wakeful night. But we shall see.' And Newman's companion proceeded to lead the way out of the station to the village, explaining as he went that the little party was lodged in the humblest of Swiss inns, where, however, they had succeeded in making M. de Bellegarde much more comfortable than could at first have been expected. 'We are old companions-in-arms,' said Valentin's second; 'it is not the first time that one of us has helped the other to lie easily. It is a very nasty wound, and the nastiest thing about it is that Bellegarde's adversary was no shot. He put his bullet where he could. It took it into its head to walk straight into Bellegarde's left side, just below the heart.'

As they picked their way in the grey, deceptive dawn, between the manure-heaps of the village street, Newman's new acquaintance narrated the particulars of the duel. The conditions of the meeting had been that if the first exchange of shots should fail to satisfy one of the two gentlemen, a second should take place. Valentin's first bullet had done exactly what Newman's companion was convinced he had intended it to do; it had grazed the arm of M. Stanislas Kapp, just scratching the flesh. M. Kapp's own projectile, meanwhile, had passed at ten good inches from the person of Valentin. The representatives of M. Stanislas had demanded another shot, which was granted. Valentin had then fired aside and the young Alsatian had done effective execution. 'I saw, when we met him on the ground,' said Newman's informant, 'that he was not going to be *commode*.* It is a kind of bovine temperament.' Valentin had immediately been installed at the inn, and M. Stanislas and his friends had withdrawn to regions unknown. The police authorities of the canton* had waited upon the party at the inn, had been extremely majestic, and had drawn up a long *procès-verbal*;* but it was probable that they would wink at so very gentlemanly a bit of bloodshed. Newman asked whether a message had not been sent to Valentin's family, and learned that up to a late hour on the preceding evening Valentin had opposed it. He had refused to believe his wound was dangerous. But after his interview with the curé he had consented, and a telegram had been despatched to his mother. 'But the marquise had better hurry,' said Newman's conductor.

'Well, it's an abominable affair!' said Newman. 'That's all I have got to say!' To say this, at least, in a tone of infinite disgust, was an irresistible need.

'Ah, you don't approve?' questioned his conductor, with curious urbanity.

'Approve?' cried Newman. 'I wish that when I had him there, night before last, I had locked him up in my *cabinet de toilette*!'*

Valentin's late second opened his eyes, and shook his head up and down two or three times, gravely, with a little flute-like whistle. But they had reached the inn, and a stout maid-servant in a night-cap was at the door with a lantern, to take Newman's travelling-bag from the porter who trudged behind him. Valentin was lodged on the ground-floor at the back of the house, and Newman's companion went along a stone-faced passage and softly opened a door. Then he beckoned to Newman, who advanced and looked into the room, which was lighted by a single shaded candle. Beside the fire sat M. de Grosjoyaux asleep in his dressing-gown – a little plump fair man whom Newman had seen several times in Valentin's company. On the bed lay Valentin, pale and still, with his eyes closed – a figure very shocking to Newman, who had seen it hitherto awake to its finger-tips. M. de Grosjoyaux's colleague pointed to an open door beyond, and whispered that the doctor was within, keeping guard. So long as Valentin slept, or seemed to sleep, of course Newman could not approach him; so our hero withdrew for the present, committing himself to the care of the half-waked *bonne*.* She took him to a room above-stairs, and introduced him to a bed on which a magnified bolster, in yellow calico, figured as a counterpane. Newman lay down, and, in spite of his counterpane, slept for three or four hours. When he awoke, the morning was advanced and the sun was filling his window, and he heard, outside of it, the clucking of hens.

While he was dressing there came to his door a messenger from M. de Grosjoyaux and his companion, proposing that he should breakfast with them. Presently he went downstairs to the little stone-paved dining-room, where the maid-servant, who had taken off her night-cap, was serving the repast. M. de Grosjoyaux was there, surprisingly fresh for a gentleman who had been playing sick nurse half the night, rubbing his hands and watching the breakfast-table attentively. Newman renewed acquaintance with him, and learned that Valentin was still sleeping; the surgeon, who had had a fairly tranquil night, was at present sitting with him. Before M. de Grosjoyaux's associate reappeared, Newman learned that his name was M. Ledoux, and that Bellegarde's acquaintance with him dated from the days when they served together in the Pontifical Zouaves.* M. Ledoux was the nephew of a distinguished Ultramontane bishop. At last the bishop's nephew came in with a toilet in which an ingenious attempt at harmony with the peculiar situation was visible, and with a gravity tempered by a decent deference to the best breakfast that the Croix Helvétique* had ever set forth. Valentin's servant, who was allowed only in scanty measure the honour of watching with his master, had been lending a light Parisian hand in the kitchen. The two Frenchmen did their best to prove that if circumstances might overshadow, they could not really obscure the national talent for conversation, and M. Ledoux delivered a neat little eulogy on poor Bellegarde, whom he pronounced the most charming Englishman he had ever known.

'Do you call him an Englishman?' Newman asked.

M. Ledoux smiled a moment and then made an epigram. '*C'est plus qu'un Anglais – c'est un Anglomane!*'* Newman said soberly that he had never noticed it; and M. de Grosjoyaux remarked that it was really too soon to deliver a funeral oration upon poor Bellegarde. 'Evidently,' said M. Ledoux. 'But I couldn't help observing this morning to Mr Newman that when a man has taken such excellent measures for his salvation as our dear friend did last evening, it seems almost a pity he should put it in peril again by returning to the world.' M. Ledoux was a great Catholic, and Newman thought him a queer mixture. His countenance, by daylight, had a sort of amiably saturnine cast; he had a very large thin nose, and looked like a Spanish picture. He appeared to think duelling a very perfect arrangement, provided, if one should get hit, one could promptly see the priest. He seemed to take a great satisfaction in Valentin's interview with the curé, and yet his conversation did not at all indicate a sanctimonious habit of mind. M. Ledoux had evidently a high sense of the becoming, and was prepared to be urbane and tasteful on all points. He was always furnished with a smile (which pushed his moustache up under his nose) and an explanation. *Savoir-vivre* – knowing how to live – was his specialty, in which he included knowing how to die; but, as Newman reflected, with a good deal of dumb irritation, he seemed disposed to delegate to others the application of his learning on this latter point. M. de Grosjoyaux was of quite

another complexion, and appeared to regard his friend's theological unction as the sign of an inaccessibly superior mind. He
was evidently doing his utmost, with a kind of jovial tenderness,
to make life agreeable to Valentin to the last, and help him as
little as possible to miss the Boulevard des Italiens; but what
chiefly occupied his mind was the mystery of a bungling brewer's
son making so neat a shot. He himself could snuff a candle, &c.,
and yet he confessed that he could not have done better than
this. He hastened to add that on the present occasion he would
have made a point of not doing so well. It was not an occasion
for that sort of murderous work, *que diable!** He would have
picked out some quiet fleshy spot and just tapped it with a
harmless ball. M. Stanislas Kapp had been deplorably heavy-
handed; but really, when the world had come to that pass that
one granted a meeting to a brewer's son! ... This was M. de
Grosjoyaux's nearest approach to a generalisation. He kept
looking through the window, over the shoulder of M. Ledoux,
at a slender tree which stood at the end of a lane, opposite to
the inn, and seemed to be measuring its distance from his
extended arm and secretly wishing that, since the subject had
been introduced, propriety did not forbid a little speculative
pistol-practice.

Newman was in no humour to enjoy good company. He
could neither eat nor talk; his soul was sore with grief and
anger, and the weight of his double sorrow was intolerable. He
sat with his eyes fixed upon his plate, counting the minutes,
wishing at one moment that Valentin would see him and leave
him free to go in quest of Madame de Cintré and his lost
happiness, and mentally calling himself a vile brute the next, for
the impatient egotism of the wish. He was very poor company,
himself, and even his acute preoccupation and his general lack
of the habit of pondering the impression he produced did not
prevent him from reflecting, that his companions must be
puzzled to see how poor Bellegarde came to take such a fancy
to this taciturn Yankee that he must needs have him at his
death-bed. After breakfast he strolled forth alone into the village
and looked at the fountain, the geese, the open barn doors, the
brown, bent old women, showing their hugely-darned stocking-
heels at the ends of their slowly-clicking sabots,* and the
beautiful view of snowy Alp and purple Jura at either end of the
little street. The day was brilliant; early spring was in the air

and sunshine, and the winter's damp was trickling out of the
cottage eaves. It was birth and brightness for all nature, even for
chirping chickens and waddling goslings, and it was to be death
and burial for poor, foolish, generous, delightful Bellegarde.
Newman walked as far as the village church, and went into the
small graveyard beside it, where he sat down and looked at the
awkward tablets which were planted around. They were all
sordid and hideous, and Newman could feel nothing but the
hardness and coldness of death. He got up and came back to the
inn, where he found M. Ledoux having coffee and a cigarette at
a little green table which he had caused to be carried into the
small garden. Newman, learning that the doctor was still sitting
with Valentin, asked M. Ledoux if he might not be allowed to
relieve him; he had a great desire to be useful to his poor friend.
This was easily arranged; the doctor was very glad to go to bed.
He was a youthful and rather jaunty practitioner, but he had a
clever face, and the ribbon of the Legion of Honour in his
button-hole; Newman listened attentively to the instructions he
gave him before retiring, and took mechanically from his hand
a small volume which the surgeon recommended as a help to
wakefulness, and which turned out to be an old copy of 'Les
Liaisons Dangereuses'.*

Valentin was still lying with his eyes closed, and there was no
visible change in his condition. Newman sat down near him,
and for a long time narrowly watched him. Then his eyes
wandered away with his thoughts upon his own situation, and
rested upon the chain of the Alps, disclosed by the drawing of
the scant white cotton curtain of the window, through which
the sunshine passed and lay in squares upon the red-tiled floor.
He tried to interweave his reflections with hope, but he only half
succeeded. What had happened to him seemed to have, in its
violence and audacity, the force of a real calamity – the strength
and insolence of Destiny herself. It was unnatural and monstrous, and he had no arms against it. At last a sound struck
upon the stillness, and he heard Valentin's voice.

'It can't be about *me* you are pulling that long face!' He
found, when he turned, that Valentin was lying in the same
position; but his eyes were open, and he was even trying to
smile. It was with a very slender strength that he returned the
pressure of Newman's hand. 'I have been watching you for a
quarter of an hour,' Valentin went on; 'you have been looking

as black as thunder. You are greatly disgusted with me, I see.
Well, of course! So am I!'

'Oh, I shall not scold you,' said Newman. 'I feel too badly.
And how are you getting on?'

'Oh, I'm getting off! They have quite settled that; haven't
they?'

'That's for you to settle; you can get well if you try,' said
Newman with resolute cheerfulness.

'My dear fellow, how can I try? Trying is violent exercise, and
that sort of thing isn't in order for a man with a hole in his side
as big as your hat, that begins to bleed if he moves a hair's-
breadth. I knew you would come,' he continued; 'I knew I
should wake up and find you here; so I'm not surprised. But last
night I was very impatient. I didn't see how I could keep still
until you came. It was a matter of keeping still, just like this; as
still as a mummy in his case. You talk about trying; I tried that!
Well, here I am yet – these twenty hours. It seems like twenty
days.' Bellegarde talked slowly and feebly, but distinctly enough.
It was visible, however, that he was in extreme pain, and at last
he closed his eyes. Newman begged him to remain silent and
spare himself; the doctor had left urgent orders. 'Oh,' said
Valentin, 'let us eat and drink, for tomorrow – tomorrow'* –
and he paused again. 'No, not tomorrow, perhaps, but today. I
can't eat and drink, but I can talk. What's to be gained, at this
pass, by renun – renunciation? I mustn't use such big words. I
was always a chatterer; Lord, how I have talked in my day!'

'That's a reason for keeping quiet now,' said Newman. 'We
know how well you talk, you know.'

But Valentin, without heeding him, went on in the same weak
dying drawl. 'I wanted to see you because you have seen my
sister. Does she know – will she come?'

Newman was embarrassed. 'Yes, by this time she must know.'

'Didn't you tell her?' Valentin asked. And then, in a moment:
'Didn't you bring me any message from her?' His eyes rested
upon Newman's with a certain soft keenness.

'I didn't see her after I got your telegram,' said Newman. 'I
wrote to her.'

'And she sent you no answer?'

Newman was obliged to reply that Madame de Cintré had
left Paris. 'She went yesterday to Fleurières.'

'Yesterday – to Fleurières? Why did she go to Fleurières?

What day is this? What day was yesterday? Ah, then I shan't see her,' said Valentin sadly. 'Fleurières is too far!' And then he closed his eyes again. Newman sat silent, summoning pious invention to his aid, but he was relieved at finding that Valentin was apparently too weak to reason or to be curious. Bellegarde, however, presently went on. 'And my mother – and my brother – will they come? Are they at Fleurières?'

'They were in Paris, but I didn't see them, either,' Newman answered. 'If they received your telegram in time, they will have started this morning. Otherwise they will be obliged to wait for the night-express, and they will arrive at the same hour as I did.'

'They won't thank me – they won't thank me,' Valentin murmured. 'They will pass an atrocious night, and Urbain doesn't like the early morning air. I don't remember ever in my life to have seen him before noon – before breakfast. No one ever saw him. We don't know how he is then. Perhaps he's different. Who knows? Posterity, perhaps, will know. That's the time he works, in his *cabinet*,* at the history of the Princesses. But I had to send for them – hadn't I? And then I want to see my mother sit there where you sit, and say good-bye to her. Perhaps, after all, I don't know her, and she will have some surprise for me. Don't think you know her yet, yourself; perhaps, she may surprise *you*. But if I can't see Claire, I don't care for anything. I have been thinking of it – and in my dreams, too. Why did she go to Fleurières today? She never told me. What has happened? Ah, she ought to have guessed I was here – this way. It is the first time in her life she ever disappointed me. Poor Claire!'

'You know we are not man and wife quite yet – your sister and I,' said Newman. 'She doesn't yet account to me for all her actions.' And, after a fashion, he smiled.

Valentin looked at him a moment. 'Have you quarrelled?'

'Never, never, never!' Newman exclaimed.

'How happily you say that!' said Valentin. 'You are going to be happy – *va!*'* In answer to this stroke of irony, none the less powerful for being so unconscious, all poor Newman could do was to give a helpless and transparent stare. Valentin continued to fix him with his own rather over-bright gaze, and presently he said: 'But something *is* the matter with you. I watched you just now; you haven't a bridegroom's face.'

'My dear fellow,' said Newman, 'how can I show *you* a

bridegroom's face? If you think I enjoy seeing you lie there and
not being able to help you – '

'Why, you are just the man to be cheerful; don't forfeit your
rights! I'm a proof of your wisdom. When was a man ever
gloomy when he could say: "I told you so?" You told me so,
you know. You did what you could about it. You said some
very good things; I have thought them over. But, my dear friend,
I was right, all the same. This is the regular way.'

'I didn't do what I ought,' said Newman. 'I ought to have
done something else.'

'For instance?'

'Oh, something or other. I ought to have treated you as a
small boy.'

'Well, I'm a very small boy, now,' said Valentin. 'I'm rather
less than an infant. An infant is helpless, but it's generally voted
promising. I'm not promising, eh? Society can't lose a less
valuable member.'

Newman was strongly moved. He got up and turned his back
upon his friend and walked away to the window, where he
stood looking out, but only vaguely seeing. 'No, I don't like the
look of your back,' Valentin continued. 'I have always been an
observer of backs; yours is quite out of sorts.'

Newman returned to his bedside and begged him to be quiet.
'Be quiet and get well,' he said. 'That's what you must do. Get
well and help me.'

'I told you you were in trouble! How can I help you?' Valentin
asked.

'I'll let you know when you are better. You were always
curious; there is something to get well for!' Newman answered,
with resolute animation.

Valentin closed his eyes and lay a long time without speaking.
He seemed even to have fallen asleep. But at the end of half an
hour he began to talk again. 'I am rather sorry about that place
in the bank. Who knows but that I might have become another
Rothschild?* But I wasn't meant for a banker; bankers are not
so easy to kill. Don't you think I have been very easy to kill? It's
not like a serious man. It's really very mortifying. It's like telling
your hostess you must go, when you count upon her begging
you to stay, and then finding she does no such thing. "Really –
so soon? You've only just come!" Life doesn't make me any
such polite little speech.'

Newman for some time said nothing, but at last he broke out. 'It's a bad case – it's a bad case – it's the worst case I ever met. I don't want to say anything unpleasant, but I can't help it. I've seen men dying before – and I've seen men shot. But it always seemed more natural; they were not so clever as you. Damnation – damnation! You might have done something better than this. It's about the meanest winding-up of a man's affairs that I can imagine!'

Valentin feebly waved his hand to and fro. 'Don't insist – don't insist! It is mean – decidedly mean. For you see at the bottom – down at the bottom, in a little place as small as the end of a wine-funnel – I agree with you!'

A few moments after this the doctor put his head through the half-opened door, and, perceiving that Valentin was awake, came in and felt his pulse. He shook his head and declared that he had talked too much – ten times too much. 'Nonsense!' said Valentin; 'a man sentenced to death can never talk too much. Have you never read an account of an execution in a newspaper? Don't they always set a lot of people at the prisoner – lawyers, reporters, priests – to make him talk? But it's not Mr Newman's fault; he sits there as mum as a death's-head.'

The doctor observed that it was time his patient's wound should be dressed again; MM. de Grosjoyaux and Ledoux, who had already witnessed this delicate operation, taking Newman's place as assistants. Newman withdrew and learned from his fellow-watchers that they had received a telegram from Urbain de Bellegarde to the effect that their message had been delivered in the Rue de l'Université too late to allow him to take the morning train, but that he would start with his mother in the evening. Newman wandered away into the village again, and walked about restlessly for two or three hours. The day seemed terribly long. At dusk he came back and dined with the doctor and M. Ledoux. The dressing of Valentin's wound had been a very critical operation; the doctor didn't really see how he was to endure a repetition of it. He then declared that he must beg of Mr Newman to deny himself for the present the satisfaction of sitting with M. de Bellegarde; more than anyone else, apparently, he had the flattering but inconvenient privilege of exciting him. M. Ledoux, at this, swallowed a glass of wine in silence; he must have been wondering what the deuce Bellegarde found so exciting in the American.

Newman, after dinner, went up to his room, where he sat for a long time staring at his lighted candle, and thinking that Valentin was dying downstairs. Late, when the candle had burnt low, there came a soft tap at his door. The doctor stood there with a candlestick and a shrug.

'He must amuse himself still!' said Valentin's medical adviser. 'He insists upon seeing you, and I am afraid you must come. I think, at this rate, that he will hardly outlast the night.'

Newman went back to Valentin's room, which he found lighted by a taper on the hearth. Valentin begged him to light a candle. 'I want to see your face,' he said. 'They say you excite me,' he went on, as Newman complied with this request, 'and I confess I do feel excited; but it isn't you – it's my own thoughts. I have been thinking – thinking. Sit down there and let me look at you again.' Newman seated himself, folded his arms, and bent a heavy gaze upon his friend. He seemed to be playing a part, mechanically, in a lugubrious comedy. Valentin looked at him for some time. 'Yes, this morning I was right; you have something on your mind heavier than Valentin de Bellegarde. Come, I'm a dying man and it's indecent to deceive me. Something happened after I left Paris. It was not for nothing that my sister started off at this season of the year for Fleurières. Why was it? It sticks in my crop. I have been thinking it over, and if you don't tell me I shall guess.'

'I had better not tell you,' said Newman. 'It won't do you any good.'

'If you think it will do me any good not to tell me, you are very much mistaken. There is trouble about your marriage.'

'Yes,' said Newman. 'There is trouble about my marriage.'

'Good!' And Valentin was silent again. 'They have stopped it.'

'They have stopped it,' said Newman. Now that he had spoken out, he found a satisfaction in it which deepened as he went on. 'Your mother and brother have broken faith. They have decided that it can't take place. They have decided that I am not good enough, after all. They have taken back their word. Since you insist, there it is!'

Valentin gave a sort of groan, lifted his hands a moment, and then let them drop.

'I am sorry not to have anything better to tell you about them,' Newman pursued. 'But it's not my fault. I was, indeed, very unhappy when your telegram reached me; I was quite upside down. You may imagine whether I feel any better now.'

Valentin moaned gaspingly, as if his wound were throbbing. 'Broken faith, broken faith!' he murmured. 'And my sister – my sister?'

'Your sister is very unhappy; she has consented to give me up. I don't know why. I don't know what they have done to her; it must be something pretty bad. In justice to her you ought to know it. They have made her suffer. I haven't seen her alone, but only before them! We had an interview yesterday morning. They came out flat, in so many words. They told me to go about my business. It seems to me a very bad case. I'm angry, I'm sore, I'm sick.'

Valentin lay there staring, with his eyes more brilliantly lighted, his lips soundlessly parted, and a flush of colour in his pale face. Newman had never before uttered so many words in the plaintive key, but now, in speaking to Valentin in the poor fellow's extremity, he had a feeling that he was making his complaint somewhere within the presence of the power that men pray to in trouble; he felt his out-gush of resentment as a sort of spiritual privilege.

'And Claire,' said Bellegarde, 'Claire? She has given you up?'

'I don't really believe it,' said Newman.

'No, don't believe it, don't believe it. She is gaining time; excuse her.'

'I pity her!' said Newman.

'Poor Claire!' murmured Valentin. 'But they – but they' – and he paused again. 'You saw them; they dismissed you, face to face?'

'Face to face. They were very explicit.'

'What did they say?'

'They said they couldn't stand a commercial person.'

Valentin put out his hand and laid it upon Newman's arm. 'And about their promise – their engagement with you?'

'They made a distinction. They said it was to hold good only until Madame de Cintré accepted me.'

Valentin lay staring awhile, and his flush died away. 'Don't tell me any more,' he said at last; 'I'm ashamed.'

'You? You are the soul of honour,' said Newman simply.

Valentin groaned and turned away his head. For some time nothing more was said. Then Valentin turned back again and found a certain force to press Newman's arm. 'It's very bad – very bad. When my people – when my race – come to that, it is time for me to withdraw. I believe in my sister; she will explain. Excuse her. If she can't – if she can't, forgive her. She has suffered. But for the others it is very bad – very bad. You take it very hard? No, it's a shame to make you say so.' He closed his eyes and again there was a silence. Newman felt almost awed; he had evoked a more solemn spirit than he expected. Presently Valentin looked at him again, removing his hand from his arm. 'I apologise,' he said. 'Do you understand? Here on my death-bed. I apologise for my family. For my mother. For my brother. For the ancient house of Bellegarde. *Voilà!** he added softly.

Newman for all answer took his hand and pressed it with a world of kindness. Valentin remained quiet, and at the end of half an hour the doctor softly came in. Behind him, through the half-open door, Newman saw the two questioning faces of MM. de Grosjoyaux and Ledoux. The doctor laid his hand on Valentin's wrist and sat looking at him. He gave no sign and the two gentlemen came in, M. Ledoux having first beckoned to someone outside. This was M. le Curé, who carried in his hand an object unknown to Newman, and covered with a white napkin. M. le Curé was short, round, and red: he advanced, pulling off his little black cap to Newman, and deposited his burden on the table; and then he sat down in the best arm-chair, with his hands folded across his person. The other gentlemen had exchanged glances which expressed unanimity as to the timeliness of their presence. But for a long time Valentin neither spoke nor moved. It was Newman's belief, afterwards, that M. le Curé went to sleep. At last, abruptly, Valentin pronounced Newman's name. His friend went to him, and he said in French: 'You are not alone. I want to speak to you alone.' Newman looked at the doctor, and the doctor looked at the curé, who looked back at him; and then the doctor and the curé, together, gave a shrug. 'Alone – for five minutes,' Valentin repeated. 'Please leave us.'

The curé took up his burden again and led the way out, followed by his companions. Newman closed the door behind them and came back to Valentin's bedside. Bellegarde had watched all this intently.

'It's very bad, it's very bad,' he said, after Newman had seated himself close to him. 'The more I think of it the worse it is.'

'Oh, don't think of it,' said Newman.

But Valentin went on, without heeding him. 'Even if they should come round again, the shame – the baseness – is there.'

'Oh, they won't come round!' said Newman.

'Well, you can make them.'

'Make them?'

'I can tell you something – a great secret – an immense secret. You can use it against them – frighten them, force them.'

'A secret!' Newman repeated. The idea of letting Valentin, on his death-bed, confide to him an 'immense secret' shocked him, for the moment, and made him draw back. It seemed an illicit way of arriving at information, and even had a vague analogy with listening at a keyhole. Then, suddenly, the thought of 'forcing' Madame de Bellegarde and her son became attractive, and Newman bent his head closer to Valentin's lips. For some time, however, the dying man said nothing more. He only lay and looked at his friend with his kindled, expanded, troubled eye, and Newman began to believe that he had spoken in delirium. But at last he said:

'There was something done – something done at Fleurières. It was foul play. My father – something happened to him. I don't know; I have been ashamed – afraid to know. But I know there is something. My mother knows – Urbain knows.'

'Something happened to your father?' said Newman urgently.

Valentin looked at him, still more wide-eyed. 'He didn't get well.'

'Get well of what?'

But the immense effort which Valentin had made, first to decide to utter these words, and then to bring them out, appeared to have taken his last strength. He lapsed again into silence, and Newman sat watching him. 'Do you understand?' he began again presently. 'At Fleurières. You can find out. Mrs Bread knows. Tell her I begged you to ask her. Then tell them that, and see. It may help you. If not, tell everyone. It will – it will' – here Valentin's voice sank to the feeblest murmur – 'it will avenge you!'

The words died away in a long soft groan. Newman stood up, deeply impressed, not knowing what to say; his heart was beating violently. 'Thank you,' he said at last. 'I am much obliged.' But Valentin seemed not to hear him; he remained silent, and his silence continued. At last Newman went and opened the door. M. le Curé re-entered, bearing his sacred vessel,* and followed by the three gentlemen and by Valentin's servant. It was almost processional.

CHAPTER 20

Valentin de Bellegarde died tranquilly, just as the cold faint March dawn began to illumine the faces of the little knot of friends gathered about his bedside. An hour afterwards Newman left the inn and drove to Geneva; he was naturally unwilling to be present at the arrival of Madame de Bellegarde and her first-born. At Geneva, for the moment, he remained. He was like a man who has had a fall and wants to sit still and count his bruises. He instantly wrote to Madame de Cintré, relating to her the circumstances of her brother's death – with certain exceptions – and asking her what was the earliest moment at which he might hope that she would consent to see him. M. Ledoux had told him that he had reason to know that Valentin's will – Bellegarde had a great deal of elegant personal property to dispose of – contained a request that he should be buried near his father in the churchyard of Fleurières, and Newman intended that the state of his own relations with the family should not deprive him of the satisfaction of helping to pay the last earthly honours to the best fellow in the world. He reflected that Valentin's friendship was older than Urbain's enmity, and that at a funeral it was easy to escape notice. Madame de Cintré's answer to his letter enabled him to time his arrival at Fleurières. This answer was very brief; it ran as follows:

> I thank you for your letter, and for your being with Valentin. It is a most inexpressible sorrow to me that I was not. To see you will be nothing but a distress to me; there is no need, therefore, to wait for what you call brighter days. It is all one now, and I shall have no brighter days. Come when you please; only notify me first. My brother is to be buried here on Friday, and my family is to remain.
>   – C. DE C.

As soon as he received this letter Newman went straight to Paris and to Poitiers. The journey took him far southward, through green Touraine and across the far-shining Loire, into a country where the early spring deepened about him as he went; but he had never made a journey during which he heeded less what he would have called the lay of the land. He obtained lodging at an inn at Poitiers, and the next morning drove in a couple of hours to the village of Fleurières. But here, preoccupied though he was, he could not fail to notice the picturesqueness of the place. It was what the French call a *petit bourg*;* it lay at the base of a sort of huge mound, on the summit of which stood the crumbling ruins of a feudal castle, much of whose sturdy material, as well as that of the wall which dropped along the hill, to enclose the clustered houses defensively, had been absorbed into the very substance of the village. The church was simply the former chapel of the castle, fronting upon its grass-grown court, which, however, was of generous enough width to have given up its quaintest corner to a little graveyard. Here the very headstones themselves seemed to sleep, as they slanted into the grass; the patient elbow of the rampart held them together on one side, and in front, far beneath their mossy lids, the green plains and blue distances stretched away. The way to church, up the hill, was impracticable to vehicles. It was lined with peasants two or three rows deep, who stood watching old Madame de Bellegarde slowly ascend it, on the arm of her elder son, behind the pall-bearers of the other. Newman chose to lurk among the common mourners, who murmured 'Madame la Comtesse' as a tall figure veiled in black passed before them. He stood in the dusky little church while the service was going forward, but at the dismal tomb-side, he turned away and walked down the hill. He went back to Poitiers, and spent two days in which patience and impatience were singularly commingled. On the third day he sent Madame de Cintré a note, saying that he would call upon her in the afternoon, and in accordance with this he again took his way to Fleurières. He left his vehicle at the tavern in the village street, and obeyed the simple instructions which were given him for finding the château.

'It is just beyond there,' said the landlord, and pointed to the tree-tops of the park above the opposite houses. Newman followed the first cross-road to the right – it was bordered with mouldy cottages – and in a few moments saw before him the peaked roofs of the towers. Advancing farther he found himself before a vast iron gate, rusty and closed; here he paused a moment, looking through the bars. The château was near the road; this was at once its merit and its defect; but its aspect was extremely impressive. Newman learned afterwards, from a guide-book of the province, that it dated from the time of Henry IV.* It presented to the wide paved area which preceded it, and which was edged with shabby farm-buildings, an immense façade of dark time-stained brick, flanked by two low wings, each of which terminated in a little Dutch-looking pavilion, capped with a fantastic roof. Two towers rose behind, and behind the towers was a mass of elms and beeches, now just faintly green.

But the great feature was a wide green river, which washed the foundations of the château. The building rose from an island in the circling stream, so that this formed a perfect moat, spanned by a two-arched bridge without a parapet. The dull brick walls, which here and there made a grand straight sweep, the ugly little cupolas of the wings, the deep-set windows, the long steep pinnacles of mossy slate, all mirrored themselves in the quiet water. Newman rang at the gate, and was almost frightened at the tone with which a big rusty bell above his head replied to him. An old woman came out from the gate-house and opened the creaking portal just wide enough for him to pass, and he went in, across the dry bare court and the little cracked white slabs of the causeway on the moat. At the door of the château he waited for some moments, and this gave him a chance to observe that Fleurières was not 'kept up', and to reflect that it was a melancholy place of residence. 'It looks,' said Newman to himself – and I give the comparison for what it is worth – 'like a Chinese penitentiary.' At last the door was opened by a servant whom he remembered to have seen in the Rue de l'Université. The man's dull face brightened as he perceived our hero, for Newman, for indefinable reasons, enjoyed the confidence of the liveried gentry.* The footman led the way across a great central vestibule, with a pyramid of plants in tubs in the middle, and glass doors all around, to what appeared to be the principal drawing-room of the château. Newman crossed the threshold of a room of superb proportions, which made him feel at first like a tourist with a guide-book and a cicerone awaiting a fee. But when his guide had left him alone, with the observation that he would call Madame la Comtesse, Newman perceived that the salon contained little that was remarkable, save a dark ceiling with curiously-carved rafters, some curtains of elaborate antiquated tapestry, and a dark oaken floor, polished like a mirror. He waited some minutes, walking up and down; but at length, as he turned at the end of the room, he saw that Madame de Cintré had come in by a distant door. She wore a black dress, and she stood looking at him. As the length of the immense room lay between them he had time to look at her before they met in the middle of it.

He was dismayed at the change in her appearance. Pale, heavy-browed, almost haggard, with a sort of monastic rigidity in her dress, she had little but her pure features in common with the woman whose radiant good grace he had hitherto admired. She let her eyes rest on his own, and she let him take her hand; but her eyes looked like two rainy autumn moons, and her touch was portentously lifeless.

'I was at your brother's funeral,' Newman said. 'Then I waited three days. But I could wait no longer.'

'Nothing can be lost or gained by waiting,' said Madame de Cintré. 'But it was very considerate of you to wait, wronged as you have been.'

'I'm glad you think I have been wronged,' said Newman, with that oddly humorous accent with which he often uttered words of the gravest meaning.

'Do I need to say so?' she asked. 'I don't think I have wronged, seriously, many persons; certainly not consciously. To you, to whom I have done this hard and cruel thing, the only reparation I can make is to say: "I know it, I feel it!" The reparation is pitifully small!'

'Oh, it's a great step forward!' said Newman, with a gracious smile of encouragement. He pushed a chair towards her and held it, looking at her urgently. She sat down mechanically, and he seated himself near her; but in a moment he got up, restlessly, and stood before her. She remained seated, like a troubled creature who had passed through the stage of restlessness.

'I say nothing is to be gained by my seeing you,' she went on, 'and yet I am very glad you came. Now I can tell you what I feel. It is a selfish pleasure, but it is one of the last I shall have.' And she paused, with her great misty eyes fixed upon him. 'I know how I have deceived and injured you; I know how cruel and cowardly I have been. I see it as vividly as you do – I feel it to the ends of my fingers.' And she unclasped her hands, which were locked together in her lap, lifted them, and dropped them at her side. 'Anything that you may have said of me in your angriest passion is nothing to what I have said to myself.'

'In my angriest passion,' said Newman, 'I have said nothing hard of you. The very worst thing I have said of you yet is that you are the loveliest of women.' And he seated himself before her again abruptly.

She flushed a little, but even her flush was pale. 'That is because you think I will come back. But I will not come back. It is in that hope you have come here, I know; I am very sorry for you. I would do almost anything for you. To say that, after what I have done, seems simply impudent; but what can I say that will not seem impudent? To wrong you and apologise – that is easy enough. I should not have wronged you.' She stopped a moment, looking at him, and motioned him to let her go on. 'I ought never to have listened to you at first; that was the wrong. No good could come of it. I felt it, and yet I listened; that was your fault. I liked you too much; I believed in you.'

'And don't you believe in me now?'

'More than ever. But now it doesn't matter. I have given you up.'

Newman gave a powerful thump with his clenched fist upon his knee. 'Why, why, why?' he cried. 'Give me a reason – a decent reason. You are not a child – you are not a minor, nor an idiot. You are not obliged to drop me because your mother told you to. Such a reason isn't worthy of you.'

'I know that; it's not worthy of me. But it's the only one I have to give. After all,' said Madame de Cintré, throwing out her hands, 'think me an idiot and forget me! That will be the simplest way.'

Newman got up and walked away with a crushing sense that his cause was lost, and yet with an equal inability to give up fighting. He went to one of the great windows, and looked out at the stiffly-embanked river and the formal gardens which lay beyond it. When he turned round, Madame de Cintré had risen; she stood there silent and passive. 'You are not frank,' said Newman; 'you are not honest. Instead of saying that you are imbecile, you should say that other people are wicked. Your mother and your brother have been false and cruel; they have been so to me, and I am sure they have been so to you. Why do you try to shield them? Why do you sacrifice me to them? I'm not false; I'm not cruel. You don't know what you give up; I can tell you that – you don't. They bully you and plot about you; and I – I – ' And he paused, holding out his hands. She turned away and began to leave him. 'You told me the other day that you were afraid of your mother,' he said, following her. 'What did you mean?'

Madame de Cintré shook her head. 'I remember; I was sorry afterwards.'

'You were sorry when she came down and put on the thumbscrews. In God's name, what *is* it she does to you?'

'Nothing. Nothing that you can understand. And now that I have given you up, I must not complain of her to you.'

'That's no reasoning!' cried Newman. 'Complain of her, on the contrary. Tell me all about it, frankly and trustfully, as you ought, and we will talk it over so satisfactorily that you won't give me up.'

Madame de Cintré looked down some moments, fixedly; and then, raising her eyes, she said: 'One good at least has come of this: I have made you judge me more fairly. You thought of me in a way that did me great honour; I don't know why you had taken it into your head. But it left me no loophole for escape – no chance to be the common weak creature I am. It was not my fault; I warned you from the first. But I ought to have warned you more. I ought to have convinced you that I was doomed to disappoint you. But I *was*, in a way, too proud. You see what my superiority amounts to, I hope!' she went on, raising her voice with a tremor which even then and there Newman thought beautiful. 'I am too proud to be honest, I am not too proud to be faithless. I am timid and cold and selfish. I am afraid of being uncomfortable.'

'And you call marrying me uncomfortable!' said Newman, staring.

Madame de Cintré blushed a little, and seemed to say that if begging his pardon in words was impudent, she might at least thus mutely express her perfect comprehension of his finding her conduct odious. 'It is not marrying you; it is doing all that would go with it. It's the rupture, the defiance, the insisting upon being happy in my own way. What right have I to be happy when – when – ' And she paused.

'When what?' said Newman.

'When others have been most unhappy.'

'What others?' Newman asked. 'What have you to do with any others but me? Besides, you said just now that you wanted happiness, and that you should find it by obeying your mother. You contradict yourself.'

'Yes, I contradict myself; that shows you that I am not even intelligent.'

'You are laughing at me!' cried Newman. 'You are mocking me!'

She looked at him intently, and an observer might have said that she was asking herself whether she might not most quickly end their common pain by confessing that she was mocking him. 'No; I am not,' she presently said.

'Granting that you are not intelligent,' he went on, 'that you are weak, that you are common, that you are nothing that I have believed you were – what I ask of you is not an heroic effort, it is a very common effort. There is a great deal on my side to make it easy. The simple truth is that you don't care enough about me to make it.'

'I am cold,' said Madame de Cintré. 'I am as cold as that flowing river.'

Newman gave a great rap on the floor with his stick, and a long grim laugh. 'Good, good!' he cried. 'You go altogether too far – you overshoot the mark. There isn't a woman in the world as bad as you would make yourself out. I see your game; it's what I said. You are blackening yourself to whiten others. You don't want to give me up at all; you like me – you like me. I know you do; you have shown it, and I have felt it. After that you may be as cold as you please! They have bullied you, I say; they have tortured you. It's an outrage, and I insist upon saving you from the extravagance of your own generosity. Would you chop off your hand if your mother requested it?'

Madame de Cintré looked a little frightened. 'I spoke of my mother too blindly the other day. I am my own mistress, by law and by her approval. She can do nothing to me; she has done nothing. She has never alluded to those hard words I used about her.'

'She has made you feel them; I'll promise you!' said Newman.

'It's my conscience that makes me feel them.'

'Your conscience seems to me to be rather mixed!' exclaimed Newman passionately.

'It has been in great trouble, but now it is very clear,' said Madame de Cintré. 'I don't give you up for any worldly advantage or for any worldly happiness.'

'Oh, you don't give me up for Lord Deepmere, I know,' said Newman. 'I won't pretend, even to provoke you, that I think that. But that's what your mother and your brother wanted, and your mother, at that villainous ball of hers – I liked it at the time, but the very thought of it now makes me rabid – tried to push him on to make up to you.'

'Who told you this?' said Madame de Cintré softly.

'Not Valentin. I observed it. I guessed it. I didn't know at the time that I was observing it, but it stuck in my memory. And afterwards, you recollect, I saw Lord Deepmere with you in the conservatory. You said then that you would tell me at another time what he had said to you.'

'That was before – before *this*,' said Madame de Cintré.

'It doesn't matter,' said Newman; 'and, besides, I think I know. He's an honest little Englishman. He came and told you what your mother was up to – that she wanted him to supplant me; not being a commercial person. If he would make you an offer she would undertake to bring you over and give me the slip. Lord Deepmere isn't very intellectual, so she had to spell it out to him. He said he admired you "no end", and that he wanted you to know it; but he didn't like being mixed up with that sort of underhand work, and he came to you and told tales. That was about the amount of it, wasn't it? And then you said you were perfectly happy.'

'I don't see why we should talk of Lord Deepmere,' said Madame de Cintré. 'It was not for that you came here; and about my mother, it doesn't matter what you suspect and what you know. When once my mind has been made up, as it is now, I should not discuss these things. Discussing anything, now, is very idle. We must try and live each as we can. I believe you will be happy again; even, sometimes, when you think of me. When you do so, think this – that it was not easy, and that I did the best I could. I have things to reckon with that you don't know. I mean I have feelings. I must do as they force me – I must, I must. They would haunt me otherwise,' she cried, with vehemence; 'they would kill me!'

'I know what your feelings are: they are superstitions! They are the feeling that, after all, though I *am* a good fellow, I have been in business; the feeling that your mother's looks are law and your brother's words are gospel; that you all hang together, and that it's a part of the everlasting proprieties that they should have a hand in everything you do. It makes my blood boil. That *is* cold; you are right. And what I feel here,' and Newman struck his heart and became more poetical than he knew, 'is a glowing fire!'

A spectator less preoccupied than Madame de Cintré's distracted wooer would have felt sure from the first that her appealing calm of manner was the result of violent effort, in spite of which the tide of agitation was rapidly rising. On these last words of Newman's it overflowed, though at first she spoke low, for fear of her voice betraying her. 'No, I was not right – I am not cold! I believe that if I am doing what seems so bad, it is not mere weakness and falseness. Mr Newman, it's like a religion. I can't tell you – I can't! It's cruel of you to insist. I don't see why I shouldn't ask you to believe me – and pity me. It's like a religion. There's a curse upon the house; I don't know what – I don't know why – don't ask me. We must all bear it. I have been too selfish; I wanted to escape from it. You offered me a great chance – besides my liking you. It seemed good to change completely, to break, to go away. And then I admired you. But I can't – it has overtaken and come back to me.' Her self-control had now completely abandoned her, and her words were broken with long sobs. 'Why do such dreadful things happen to us – why is my brother Valentin killed, like a beast, in the midst of his youth and his gaiety and his brightness and all that we loved him for? Why are there things I can't ask about – that I am afraid to know? Why are there places I can't look at, sounds I can't hear? Why is it given to me to choose, to decide, in a case so hard and so terrible as this? I am not meant for that – I am not made for boldness and defiance. I was made to be happy in a quiet natural way.' At this Newman gave a most expressive groan, but Madame de Cintré went on: 'I was made to do gladly and gratefully what is expected of me. My mother has always been very good to me; that's all I can say. I must not judge her; I must not criticise her. If I did, it would come back to me. I can't change!'

'No,' said Newman bitterly; '*I* must change – if I break in two in the effort!'

'You are different. You are a man; you will get over it. You have all kinds of consolation. You were born – you were trained, to changes. Besides – besides, I shall always think of you.'

'I don't care for that!' cried Newman. 'You are cruel – you are terribly cruel. God forgive you! You may have the best reasons and the finest feelings in the world; that makes no difference. You are a mystery to me; I don't see how such hardness can go with such loveliness.'

Madame de Cintré fixed him a moment with her swimming eyes. 'You believe I am hard, then?'

Newman answered her look, and then broke out: 'You are a perfect faultless creature! Stay by me!'

'Of course I am hard,' she went on. 'Whenever we give pain we are hard. And we *must* give pain; that's the world – the hateful miserable world! Ah!' and she gave a long deep sigh, 'I can't even say I am glad to have known you – though I am. That too is to wrong you. I can say nothing that is not cruel. Therefore let us part, without more of this. Good-bye!' And she put out her hand.

Newman stood and looked at it without taking it, and then raised his eyes to her face. He felt himself like shedding tears of rage. 'What are you going to do!' he asked. 'Where are you going?'

'Where I shall give no more pain and suspect no more evil. I am going out of the world.'

'Out of the world?'

'I am going into a convent.'

'Into a convent!' Newman repeated the words with the deepest dismay; it was as if she had said she was going into an hospital. 'Into a convent – *you!*'

'I told you that it was not for my worldly advantage or pleasure I was leaving you.'

But still Newman hardly understood. 'You are going to be a nun,' he went on, 'in a cell – for life – with a gown and white veil?'

'A nun – a Carmelite nun,' said Madame de Cintré. 'For life, with God's leave.'

The idea struck Newman as too dark and horrible for belief, and made him feel as he would have done if she had told him that she was going to mutilate her beautiful face, or drink some potion that would make her mad. He clasped his hands and began to tremble visibly.

'Madame de Cintré, don't, don't!' he said, 'I beseech you! On my knees, if you like, I'll beseech you.'

She laid her hand upon his arm, with a tender, pitying, almost reassuring gesture. 'You don't understand,' she said. 'You have wrong ideas. It's nothing horrible. It is only peace and safety. It is to be out of the world, where such troubles as this come to the innocent, to the best. And for life – that's the blessing of it! They can't begin again.'

Newman dropped into a chair and sat looking at her with a long inarticulate murmur. That this superb woman, in whom he had seen all human grace and household force, should turn from him and all the brightness that he offered her – him and his future and his fortune and his fidelity – to muffle herself in ascetic rags and entomb herself in a cell, was a confounding combination of the inexorable and the grotesque. As the image deepened before him the grotesque seemed to expand and overspread it; it was a reduction to the absurd of the trial to which he was subjected. 'You – you a nun!' he exclaimed; 'you with your beauty defaced – you behind locks and bars! Never, never, if I can prevent it!' And he sprang to his feet with a violent laugh.

'You can't prevent it,' said Madame de Cintré, 'and it ought – a little – to satisfy you. Do you suppose I will go on living in the world, still beside you, and yet not with you? It is all arranged. Good-bye, good-bye.'

This time he took her hand, took it in both his own. 'Forever?' he said. Her lips made an inaudible movement and his own uttered a deep imprecation. She closed her eyes, as if with the pain of hearing it; then he drew her towards him and clasped her to his breast. He kissed her white face; for an instant she resisted and for a moment she submitted; then, with force, she disengaged herself and hurried away over the long shining floor. The next moment the door closed behind him.

Newman made his way out as he could.

CHAPTER 21

There is a pretty public walk at Poitiers,* laid out upon the crest of the high hill around which the little city clusters, planted with thick trees, and looking down upon the fertile fields in which the old English princes fought for their right and held it. Newman paced up and down this quiet promenade for the greater part of the next day, and let his eyes wander over the historic prospect; but he would have been sadly at a loss to tell you afterwards whether the latter was made up of coal-fields or of vineyards. He was wholly given up to his grievance, of which reflection by no means diminished the weight. He feared that Madame de Cintré was irretrievably lost; and yet, as he would have said himself, he didn't see his way clear to giving her up. He found it impossible to turn his back upon Fleurières and its inhabitants; it seemed to him that some germ of hope or reparation must lurk there somewhere, if he could only stretch his arm out far enough to pluck it. It was as if he had his hand on a door-knob and were closing his clenched fist upon it: he had thumped, he had called, he had pressed the door with his powerful knee, and shaken it with all his strength, and dead damning silence had answered him. And yet something held him there – something hardened the grasp of his fingers. Newman's satisfaction had been too intense, his whole plan too deliberate and mature, his prospect of happiness too rich and comprehensive, for this fine moral fabric to crumble at a stroke. The very foundation seemed fatally injured, and yet he felt a stubborn desire still to try to save the edifice. He was filled with a sorer sense of wrong than he had ever known, or than he had supposed it possible he should know. To accept his injury and walk away without looking behind him was a stretch of good-nature of which he found himself incapable. He looked behind him intently and continually, and what he saw there did not assuage his resentment. He saw himself trustful, generous, liberal, patient, easy, pocketing frequent irritation and furnishing unlimited modesty. To have eaten humble pie, to have been snubbed and patronised and satirised, and have consented to take it as one of the conditions of the bargain – to have done this, and done it all for nothing, surely gave one a right to protest. And to be turned off because one was a commercial person? As if he had ever talked or dreamt of the commercial since his connection with the Bellegardes began – as if he had made the least circumstance of the commercial – as if he would not have consented to confound the commercial fifty times a day, if it might have increased by a hair's-breadth the chance of the Bellegardes' not playing him a trick! Granted that being commercial was fair ground for having a trick played upon one, how little they knew about the class so designated and its enterprising way of not standing upon trifles! It was in the light of his injury that the weight of Newman's past endurance seemed so heavy; his actual irritation had not been so great, merged as it was in his vision of the cloudless blue that overarched his immediate wooing. But now his sense of outrage was deep, rancorous, and ever present; he felt that he was a good fellow wronged. As for Madame de Cintré's conduct, it struck him with a kind of awe, and the fact that he was powerless to understand it or feel the reality of its motives only deepened the force with which he had attached himself to her. He had never let the fact of her Catholicism trouble him; Catholicism to him was nothing but a name, and to express a mistrust of the form in which her religious feelings had moulded themselves would have seemed to him on his own part a rather pretentious affectation of Protestant zeal. If such superb white flowers as that could bloom in Catholic soil, the soil was not insalubrious. But it was one thing to be a Catholic, and another to turn nun – on your hands! There was something lugubriously comical in the way Newman's thoroughly contemporaneous optimism was confronted with this dusky old-world expedient. To see a woman made for him and for motherhood to his children juggled away in this tragic travesty – it was a thing to rub one's eyes over, a nightmare, an illusion, a hoax. But the hours passed away without disproving the thing, and leaving him only the after-sense of the vehemence with which he had embraced Madame de Cintré. He remembered her words and her looks; he turned them over and tried to shake the mystery out of them, and to infuse them with an endurable meaning. What had she meant by her feeling being a kind of religion? It was the religion simply of the family laws, the religion of which her implacable little mother was the high-priestess. Twist the thing about as her generosity would, the one certain fact was that they had used force against her. Her generosity had tried to screen them, but Newman's heart rose into his throat at the thought that they should go scot-free.

The twenty-four hours wore themselves away, and the next morning Newman sprang to his feet with the resolution to return to Fleurières and demand another interview with Madame de Bellegarde and her son. He lost no time in putting it into practice. As he rolled swiftly over the excellent road in the little calèche* furnished him at the inn at Poitiers, he drew forth, as it were, from the very safe place in his mind to which he had consigned it, the last information given him by poor Valentin. Valentin had told him he could do something with it, and Newman thought it would be well to have it at hand. This was of course not the first time, lately, that Newman had given it his attention. It was information in the rough – it was dark and puzzling; but Newman was neither helpless nor afraid. Valentin had evidently meant to put him in possession of a powerful instrument, though he could not be said to have placed the handle very securely within his grasp. But if he had not really told him the secret, he had at least given him the clew to it – a clew of which that queer old Mrs Bread held the other end. Mrs Bread had always looked to Newman as if she knew secrets; and as he apparently enjoyed her esteem, he suspected she might be induced to share her knowledge with him. So long as there was only Mrs Bread to deal with, he felt easy. As to what there was to find out, he had only one fear – that it might not be bad enough. Then, with the image of the marquise and her son rose before him again, standing side by side, the old woman's hand in Urbain's arm, and the same cold unsociable fixedness in the eyes of each, he cried out to himself that the fear was groundless. There was blood in the secret at the very least! He arrived at Fleurières almost in a state of elation; he had satisfied himself, logically, that in the presence of his threat of exposure they would, as he mentally phrased it, rattle down like unwound buckets. He remembered indeed that he must first catch his hare – first ascertain what there was to expose; but after that, why shouldn't his happiness be as good as new again? Mother and son would drop their lovely victim in terror, and take to hiding, and Madame de Cintré, left to herself, would surely come back to him. Give her a chance and she would rise to the surface, return to the light. How could she fail to perceive that his house would be much the most comfortable sort of convent?

Newman, as he had done before, left his conveyance at the inn and walked the short remaining distance to the château. When he reached the gate, however, a singular feeling took possession of him – a feeling which, strange as it may seem, had its source in its unfathomable good-nature. He stood there awhile, looking through the bars of the large time-stained face of the edifice, and wondering to what crime it was that the dark old house, with its flowery name, had given convenient occasion. It had given occasion, first and last, to tyrannies and sufferings enough, Newman said to himself; it was an evil-looking place to live in. Then, suddenly, came the reflection: What a horrible rubbish-heap of iniquity to fumble in! The attitude of inquisitor turned its ignoble face, and with the same movement Newman declared that the Bellegardes should have another chance. He would appeal once more directly to their sense of fairness, and not to their fear; and if they should be accessible to reason, he need know nothing worse about them than what he already knew. That was bad enough.

The gate-keeper let him in through the same stiff crevice as before, and he passed through the court and over the little rustic bridge on the moat. The door was opened before he had reached it, and, as if to put his clemency to rout with the suggestion of a richer opportunity, Mrs Bread stood there awaiting him. Her face, as usual, looked as hopelessly blank as the tide-smoothed sea-sand, and her black garments seemed of an intenser sable. Newman had already learned that her strange inexpressiveness could be a vehicle for emotion, and he was not surprised at the muffled vivacity with which she whispered: 'I thought you would try again, sir. I was looking out for you.'

'I am glad to see you,' said Newman; 'I think you are my friend.'

Mrs Bread looked at him opaquely. 'I wish you well, sir; but it's vain wishing now.'

'You know, then, how they have treated me?'

'Oh, sir,' said Mrs Bread dryly, 'I know everything.'

Newman hesitated a moment. 'Everything?'

Mrs Bread gave him a glance somewhat more lucent. 'I know at least too much, sir.'

'One can never know too much. I congratulate you. I have

come to see Madame de Bellegarde and her son,' Newman added. 'Are they at home? If they are not, I will wait.'

'My lady is always at home,' Mrs Bread replied, 'and the marquis is mostly with her.'

'Please then tell them – one or the other, or both – that I am here and that I desire to see them.'

Mrs Bread hesitated. 'May I take a great liberty, sir?'

'You have never taken a liberty but you have justified it,' said Newman, with diplomatic urbanity.

Mrs Bread dropped her wrinkled eyelids as if she were curtsying; but the curtsy stopped there; the occasion was too grave. 'You have come to plead with them again, sir? Perhaps you don't know this – that Madame de Cintré returned this morning to Paris.'

'Ah, she's gone!' And Newman, groaning, smote the pavement with his stick.

'She has gone straight to the convent – the Carmelites they call it. I see you know, sir. My lady and the marquis take it very ill. It was only last night she told them.'

'Ah, she had kept it back, then?' cried Newman. 'Good, good! And they are very fierce?'

'They are not pleased,' said Mrs Bread. 'But they may well dislike it. They tell me it's most dreadful, sir; of all the nuns in Christendom the Carmelites are the worst. You may say they are really not human, sir; they make you give up everything – forever. And to think of *her* there! If I was one that cried, sir, I could cry.'

Newman looked at her an instant. 'We mustn't cry, Mrs Bread; we must act. Go and call them!' And he made a movement to enter farther.

But Mrs Bread gently checked him. 'May I take another liberty? I am told you were with my dearest Mr Valentin, in his last hours. If you would tell me a word about him! The poor count was my own boy, sir; for the first year of his life he was hardly out of my arms; I taught him to speak. And the count spoke so well, sir! He always spoke well to his poor old Bread. When he grew up and took his pleasure he always had a kind word for me. And to die in that wild way! They have a story that he fought with a wine merchant. I can't believe that, sir! And was he in great pain?'

'You are a wise kind old woman, Mrs Bread,' said Newman.

'I hoped I might see you with my own children in your arms. Perhaps I shall yet.' And he put out his hand. Mrs Bread looked for a moment at his open palm, and then, as if fascinated by the novelty of the gesture, extended her own ladylike fingers. Newman held her hand firmly and deliberately, fixing his eyes upon her. 'You want to know all about Mr Valentin?' he said.

'It would be a sad pleasure, sir.'

'I can tell you everything. Can you sometimes leave this place?'

'The château, sir? I really don't know. I never tried.'

'Try, then; try hard. Try this evening, at dusk. Come to me in the old ruin there on the hill, in the court before the church. I will wait for you there; I have something very important to tell you. An old woman like you can do as she pleases.'

Mrs Bread stared, wondering, with parted lips. 'Is it from the count, sir?' she asked.

'From the count – from his death-bed,' said Newman.

'I will come, then. I will be bold, for once, for *him*.'

She led Newman into the great drawing-room with which he had already made acquaintance, and retired to execute his commands. Newman waited a long time; at last he was on the point of ringing and repeating his request. He was looking round him for a bell when the marquis came in with his mother on his arm. It will be seen that Newman had a logical mind when I say that he declared to himself, in perfect good faith, as a result of Valentin's dark hints, that his adversaries looked grossly wicked. 'There is no mistake about it now,' he said to himself as they advanced. 'They're a bad lot; they have pulled off the mask.' Madame de Bellegarde and her son certainly bore in their faces the signs of extreme perturbation; they looked like people who had passed a sleepless night. Confronted, moreover, with an annoyance which they hoped they had disposed of, it was not natural that they should have any very tender glances to bestow upon Newman. He stood before them, and such eye-beams as they found available they levelled at him; Newman feeling as if the door of a sepulchre had suddenly been opened, and the damp darkness were being exhaled.

'You see I have come back,' he said. 'I have come to try again.'

'It would be ridiculous,' said M. de Bellegarde, 'to pretend that we are glad to see you or that we don't question the taste of your visit.'

'Oh, don't talk about taste,' said Newman with a laugh, 'or that will bring us round to yours! If I consulted my taste I certainly shouldn't come to see you. Besides, I will make as short work as you please. Promise me to raise the blockade – to set Madame de Cintré at liberty – and I will retire instantly.'

'We hesitated as to whether we would see you,' said Madame de Bellegarde; 'and we were on the point of declining the honour. But it seemed to me that we should act with civility, as we have always done, and I wished to have the satisfaction of informing you that there are certain weaknesses that people of our way of feeling can be guilty of but once.'

'You may be weak but once, but you will be audacious many times, madam,' Newman answered. 'I didn't come, however, for conversational purposes. I came to say this simply: That if you will write immediately to your daughter that you withdraw your opposition to her marriage, I will take care of the rest. You don't want her to turn nun – you know more about the horrors of it than I do. Marrying a commercial person is better than that. Give me a letter to her, signed and sealed, saying you retract, and that she may marry me with your blessing, and I will take it to her at the convent and bring her out. There's your chance – I call those easy terms.'

'We look at the matter otherwise, you know. We call them very hard terms,' said Urbain de Bellegarde. They had all remained standing rigidly in the middle of the room. 'I think my mother will tell you that she would rather her daughter should become Soeur Catherine* than Mrs Newman.'

But the old lady, with the serenity of supreme power, let her son make her epigrams for her. She only smiled, almost sweetly, shaking her head and repeating: 'But once, Mr Newman; but once!'

Nothing that Newman had ever seen or heard gave him such a sense of marble hardness as this movement and the tone that accompanied it. 'Could anything compel you?' he asked. 'Do you know of anything that would force you?'

'This language, sir,' said the marquis, 'addressed to people in bereavement and grief is beyond all qualification.'

'In most cases,' Newman answered, 'your objection would have some weight, even admitting that Madame de Cintré's present intentions make time precious. But I have thought of what you speak of, and I have come here today without scruple simply because I consider your brother and you two very different parties. I see no connection between you. Your brother was ashamed of you. Lying there wounded and dying, the poor fellow apologised to me for your conduct. He apologised to me for that of his mother.'

For a moment the effect of these words was as if Newman had struck a physical blow. A quick flush leaped into the faces of Madame de Bellegarde and her son, and they exchanged a glance like a twinkle of steel. Urbain uttered two words which Newman but half heard, but of which the sense came to him as it were in the reverberation of the sound, *'Le misérable!'* *

'You show little respect for the living,' said Madame de Bellegarde, 'but at least respect the dead. Don't profane – don't insult – the memory of my innocent son.'

'I speak the simple truth,' Newman declared, 'and I speak it for a purpose. I repeat it – distinctly. Your son was utterly disgusted – your son apologised.'

Urbain de Bellegarde was frowning portentously, and Newman supposed he was frowning at poor Valentin's invidious image. Taken by surprise, his scant affection for his brother had made a momentary concession to dishonour. But not for an appreciable instant did his mother lower her flag. 'You are immensely mistaken, sir,' she said. 'My son was sometimes light, but he was never indecent. He died faithful to his name.'

'You simply misunderstood him,' said the marquis, beginning to rally. 'You affirm the impossible.'

'Oh, I don't care for poor Valentin's apology,' said Newman. 'It was far more painful than pleasant to me. This atrocious thing was not his fault; he never hurt me, or anyone else; he was the soul of honour. But it shows how he took it.'

'If you wish to prove that my poor brother, in his last moments, was out of his head, we can only say that under the melancholy circumstances nothing was more possible. But confine yourself to that.'

'He was quite in his right mind,' said Newman, with gentle but dangerous doggedness; 'I have never seen him so bright and clever. It was terrible to see that witty capable fellow dying such a death. You know I was very fond of your brother. And I have further proof of his sanity,' Newman concluded.

The marquise gathered herself together majestically. 'This is too gross!' she cried. 'We decline to accept your story, sir – we repudiate it. Urbain, open the door.' She turned away, with an imperious motion to her son, and passed rapidly down the length of the room. The marquis went with her and held the door open. Newman was left standing.

He lifted his finger, as a sign to M. de Bellegarde, who closed the door behind his mother and stood waiting. Newman slowly advanced, more silent, for the moment, than life. The two men stood face to face. Then Newman had a singular sensation; he felt his sense of injury almost brimming over into jocularity. 'Come,' he said, 'you don't treat me well; at least admit that.'

M. de Bellegarde looked at him from head to foot, and then, in the most delicate best-bred voice: 'I detest you personally,' he said.

'That's the way I feel to you, but for politeness's sake I don't say it,' said Newman. 'It's singular I should want so much to be your brother-in-law, but I can't give it up. Let me try once more.' And he paused a moment. 'You have a secret – you have a skeleton in the closet.' M. de Bellegarde continued to look at him hard, but Newman could not see whether his eyes betrayed anything; the look of his eyes was always so strange. Newman paused again, and then went on. 'You and your mother have committed a crime.' At this M. de Bellegarde's eyes certainly did change; they seemed to flicker, like blown candles. Newman could see that he was profoundly startled; but there was something admirable in his self-control.

'Continue,' said M. de Bellegarde.

Newman lifted a finger and made it waver a little in the air. 'Need I continue? You are trembling.'

'Pray where did you obtain this interesting information?' M. de Bellegarde asked very softly.

'I shall be strictly accurate,' said Newman. 'I won't pretend to know more than I do. At present that is all I know. You have done something that you must hide, something that would damn you if it were known, something that would disgrace the name you are so proud of. I don't know what it is, but I can find out. Persist in your present course and I *will* find out. Change it, let your sister go in peace, and I will leave you alone. It's a bargain?'

The marquis almost succeeded in looking untroubled; the breaking up of the ice in his handsome countenance was an operation that was necessarily gradual. But Newman's mildlysyllabled argumentation seemed to press, and press, and presently he averted his eyes. He stood some moments, reflecting.

'My brother told you this,' he said, looking up.

Newman hesitated a moment. 'Yes, your brother told me.'

The marquis smiled, handsomely. 'Didn't I say that he was out of his mind?'

'He was out of his mind if I don't find out. He was very much in it if I do.'

M. de Bellegarde gave a shrug. 'Eh, sir, find out or not, as you please.'

'I don't frighten you?' demanded Newman.

'That's for you to judge.'

'No, it's for you to judge, at your leisure. Think it over, feel yourself all round. I will give you an hour or two. I can't give you more, for how do we know how fast they may be making Madame de Cintré a nun? Talk it over with your mother; let her judge whether she is frightened. I don't believe she is as easily frightened, in general, as you; but you will see. I will go and wait in the village, at the inn, and I beg you to let me know as soon as possible. Say by three o'clock. A simple *yes* or *no* on paper will do. Only, you know, in case of a *yes* I shall expect you, this time, to stick to your bargain.' And with this Newman opened the door and let himself out. The marquis did not move, and Newman, retiring, gave him another look. 'At the inn, in the village,' he repeated. Then he turned away altogether and passed out of the house.

He was extremely excited by what he had been doing, for it was inevitable that there should be a certain emotion in calling up the spectre of dishonour before a family a thousand years old. But he went back to the inn and contrived to wait there, deliberately, for the next two hours. He thought it more than probable that Urbain de Bellegarde would give no sign; for an answer to his challenge, in either sense, would be a confession of guilt. What he most expected was silence – in other words defiance. But he prayed that, as he imaged it, his shot might bring them down. It did bring, by three o'clock, a note, delivered by a footman; a note addressed in Urbain de Bellegarde's handsome English hand. It ran as follows:

I cannot deny myself the satisfaction of letting you know that I return to Paris, tomorrow, with my mother, in order that we may

see my sister and confirm her in the resolution which is the most
effectual reply to your audacious pertinacity.

                    HENRI-URBAIN DE BELLEGARDE

Newman put the letter into his pocket, and continued his
walk up and down the inn-parlour. He had spent most of his
time, for the past week, in walking up and down. He continued
to measure the length of the little *salle** of the Armes de France*
until the day began to wane, when he went out to keep his
rendezvous with Mrs Bread. The path which led up the hill to
the ruin was easy to find, and Newman in a short time had
followed it to the top. He passed beneath the rugged arch of the
castle-wall, and looked about him in the early dusk for an old
woman in black. The castle-yard was empty, but the door of the
church was open. Newman went into the little nave and of
course found a deeper dusk than without. A couple of tapers,
however, twinkled on the altar and just enabled him to perceive
a figure seated by one of the pillars. Closer inspection helped
him to recognise Mrs Bread, in spite of the fact that she was
dressed with unwonted splendour. She wore a large black silk
bonnet, with imposing bows of crape, and an old black satin
dress disposed itself in vaguely lustrous folds about her person.
She had judged it proper to the occasion to appear in her
stateliest apparel. She had been sitting with her eyes fixed upon
the ground, but when Newman passed before her she looked up
at him, and then she rose.

'Are you a Catholic, Mrs Bread?' he asked.

'No, sir; I'm a good Church of England woman, very Low,'*
she answered. 'But I thought I should be safer in here than
outside. I was never out in the evening before, sir.'

'We shall be safer,' said Newman, 'where no one can hear us.'
And he led the way back into the castle-court and then followed
a path beside the church, which he was sure must lead into
another part of the ruin. He was not deceived. It wandered
along the crest of the hill and terminated before a fragment of
wall pierced by a rough aperture which had once been a door.
Through this aperture Newman passed and found himself in a
nook peculiarly favourable to quiet conversation, as probably
many an earnest couple, otherwise assorted than our friends,
had assured themselves. The hill sloped abruptly away, and on
the remnant of its crest were scattered two or three fragments of

stone. Beneath, over the plain, lay the gathered twilight, through which, in the near distance, gleamed two or three lights from the château. Mrs Bread rustled slowly after her guide, and Newman, satisfying himself that one of the fallen stones was steady, proposed to her to sit upon it. She cautiously complied, and he placed himself upon another, near her.

CHAPTER 22

'I am very much obliged to you for coming,' Newman said. I hope it won't get you into trouble.'

'I don't think I shall be missed. My lady, in these days, is not fond of having me about her.' This was said with a certain fluttered eagerness which increased Newman's sense of having inspired the old woman with confidence.

'From the first, you know,' he answered, 'you took an interest in my prospects. You were on my side. That gratified me, I assure you. And now that you know what they have done to me, I am sure you are with me all the more.'

'They have not done well – I must say it,' said Mrs Bread. 'But you mustn't blame the poor countess; they pressed her hard.'

'I would give a million of dollars to know what they did to her!' cried Newman.

Mrs Bread sat with a dull, oblique gaze fixed upon the lights of the château. 'They worked on her feelings; they knew that was the way. She is a delicate creature. They made her feel wicked. She is only too good.'

'Ah, they made her feel wicked,' said Newman slowly; and then he repeated it. 'They made her feel wicked – they made her feel wicked.' The words seemed to him for the moment a vivid description of infernal ingenuity.

'It was because she was so good that she gave up – poor sweet lady!' added Mrs Bread.

'But she was better to them than to me,' said Newman.

'She was afraid,' said Mrs Bread, very confidently; 'she has always been afraid, or at least for a long time. That was the real trouble, sir. She was like a fair peach, I may say, with just one little speck. She had one little sad spot. You pushed her into the sunshine, sir, and it almost disappeared. Then they pulled her back into the shade and in a moment it began to spread. Before we knew it she was gone. She was a delicate creature.'

This singular attestation of Madame de Cintré's delicacy, for all its singularity, set Newman's wound aching afresh. 'I see,' he presently said; 'she knew something bad about her mother.'

'No, sir, she knew nothing,' said Mrs Bread, holding her head very stiff and keeping her eyes fixed upon the glimmering windows of the château.

'She guessed something, then, or suspected it.'

'She was afraid to know,' said Mrs Bread.

'But *you* know, at any rate,' said Newman.

She slowly turned her vague eyes upon Newman, squeezing her hands together in her lap. 'You are not quite faithful, sir. I thought it was to tell me about Mr Valentin you asked me to come here.'

'Oh, the more we talk of Mr Valentin the better,' said Newman. 'That's exactly what I want. I was with him, as I told you, in his last hour. He was in a great deal of pain, but he was quite himself. You know what that means; he was bright and lively and clever.'

'Oh, he would always be clever, sir,' said Mrs Bread. 'And did he know of your trouble?'

'Yes, he guessed it of himself.'

'And what did he say to it?'

'He said it was a disgrace to his name – but it was not the first.'

'Lord, Lord!' murmured Mrs Bread.

'He said that his mother and his brother had once put their heads together and invented something even worse.'

'You shouldn't have listened to that, sir.'

'Perhaps not. But I *did* listen, and I don't forget it. Now I want to know what it is they did.'

Mrs Bread gave a soft moan. 'And you have enticed me up into this strange place to tell you?'

'Don't be alarmed,' said Newman. 'I won't say a word that shall be disagreeable to you. Tell me as it suits you, and when it suits you. Only remember that it was Mr Valentin's last wish that you should.'

'Did he say that?'

'He said it with his last breath: "Tell Mrs Bread I told you to ask her." '

'Why didn't he tell you himself?'

'It was too long a story for a dying man; he had no breath left in his body. He could only say that he wanted me to know – that, wronged as I was, it was my right to know.'

'But how will it help you, sir?' said Mrs Bread.

'That's for me to decide. Mr Valentin believed it would, and that's why he told me. Your name was almost the last word he spoke.'

Mrs Bread was evidently awe-struck by this statement; she shook her clasped hands slowly up and down. 'Excuse me, sir,' she said, 'if I take a great liberty. Is it the solemn truth you are speaking? I *must* ask you that; must I not, sir?'

'There's no offence. It *is* the solemn truth; I solemnly swear it. Mr Valentin himself would certainly have told me more if he had been able.'

'Oh, sir, if he knew more!'

'Don't you suppose he did?'

'There's no saying what he knew about anything,' said Mrs Bread, with a mild head-shake. 'He was so mightily clever. He could make you believe he knew things that he didn't, and that he didn't know others that he had better not have known.'

'I suspect he knew something about his brother that kept the marquis civil to him,' Newman propounded; 'he made the marquis feel him. What he wanted now was to put me in his place; he wanted to give me a chance to make the marquis feel *me*.'

'Mercy on us!' cried the old waiting-woman, 'how wicked we all are!'

'I don't know,' said Newman; 'some of us are wicked, certainly. I am very angry, I am very sore, and I am very bitter, but I don't know that I am wicked. I have been cruelly injured. They have hurt me, and I want to hurt them. I don't deny that; on the contrary, I tell you plainly that that is the use I want to make of your secret.'

Mrs Bread seemed to hold her breath. 'You want to publish them – you want to shame them?'

'I want to bring them down – down, down, down! I want to turn the tables upon them – I want to mortify them as they mortified me. They took me up into a high place and made me stand there for all the world to see me, and then they stole behind me and pushed me into this bottomless pit, where I lie howling and gnashing my teeth! I made a fool of myself before all their friends; but I shall make something worse of them.'

This passionate sally, which Newman uttered with the greater fervour that it was the first time he had had a chance to say all this aloud, kindled two small sparks in Mrs Bread's fixed eyes. 'I suppose you have a right to your anger, sir; but think of the dishonour you will draw down on Madame de Cintré.'

'Madame de Cintré is buried alive,' cried Newman. 'What are honour or dishonour to her? The door of the tomb is at this moment closing behind her.'

'Yes, it is most awful,' moaned Mrs Bread.

'She has moved off, like her brother Valentin, to give me room to work. It's as if it were done on purpose.'

'Surely,' said Mrs Bread, apparently impressed by the ingenuity of this reflection. She was silent for some moments; then she added: 'And would you bring my lady before the courts?'

'The courts care nothing for my lady,' Newman replied. 'If she has committed a crime, she will be nothing for the courts but a wicked old woman.'

'And will they hang her, sir?'

'That depends upon what she has done.' And Newman eyed Mrs Bread intently.

'It would break up the family most terribly, sir!'

'It's time such a family should be broken up!' said Newman, with a laugh.

'And me at my age out of place, sir!' sighed Mrs Bread.

'Oh, I will take care of you! You shall come and live with me. You shall be my housekeeper, or anything you like. I will pension you for life.'

'Dear, dear, sir, you think of everything.' And she seemed to fall a-brooding.

Newman watched her awhile, and then he said suddenly: 'Ah, Mrs Bread, you are too fond of my lady!'

She looked at him as quickly. 'I wouldn't have you say that, sir. I don't think it any part of my duty to be fond of my lady. I have served her faithfully this many a year; but if she were to die tomorrow, I believe, before Heaven, I shouldn't shed a tear for her.' Then after a pause, 'I have no reason to love her!' Mrs

Bread added. 'The most she has done for me has been not to turn me out of the house.' Newman felt that decidedly his companion was more and more confidential – that if luxury is corrupting, Mrs Bread's conservative habits were already relaxed by the spiritual comfort of this preconcerted interview, in a remarkable locality, with a free-spoken millionaire. All his native shrewdness admonished him that his part was simply to let her take her time – let the charm of the occasion work. So he said nothing; he only looked at her kindly. Mrs Bread sat nursing her lean elbows. 'My lady once did me a great wrong,' she went on at last. 'She has a terrible tongue when she is vexed. It was many a year ago, but I have never forgotten it. I have never mentioned it to a human creature; I have kept my grudge to myself. I daresay I have been wicked, but my grudge has grown old with me. It has grown good for nothing, too, I daresay; but it has lived along, as I have lived. It will die when I die – not before!'

'And what *is* your grudge?' Newman asked.

Mrs Bread dropped her eyes and hesitated. 'If I were a foreigner, sir, I should make less of telling you; it comes harder to a decent Englishwoman. But I sometimes think I have picked up too many foreign ways. What I was telling you belongs to a time when I was much younger and very different looking to what I am now. I had a very high colour, sir, if you can believe it; indeed I was a very smart lass. My lady was younger, too, and the late marquis was youngest of all – I mean in the way he went on, sir; he had a very high spirit; he was a magnificent man. He was fond of his pleasure, like most foreigners, and it must be owned that he sometimes went rather below him to take it. My lady was often jealous, and, if you'll believe it, sir, she did me the honour to be jealous of me. One day I had a red ribbon in my cap, and my lady flew out at me and ordered me to take it off. She accused me of putting it on to make the marquis look at me. I don't know that I was impertinent, but I spoke up like an honest girl and didn't count my words. A red ribbon indeed! As if it was my ribbons the marquis looked at! My lady knew afterwards that I was perfectly respectable, but she never said a word to show that she believed it. But the marquis did!' Mrs Bread presently added: 'I took off my red ribbon and put it away in a drawer, where I have kept it to this day. It's faded, now, it's a very pale pink; but there it lies. My grudge has faded, too; the red has all gone out of it; but it lies here yet.' And Mrs Bread stroked her black satin bodice.

Newman listened with interest to this decent narrative, which seemed to have opened up the deeps of memory to his companion. Then, as she remained silent, and seemed to be losing herself in retrospective meditation upon her perfect respectability, he ventured upon a short cut to his goal. 'So Madame de Bellegarde was jealous; I see. And M. de Bellegarde admired pretty women, without distinction of class. I suppose one mustn't be hard upon him, for they probably didn't all behave so properly as you. But years afterwards it could hardly have been jealousy that turned Madame de Bellegarde into a criminal.'

Mrs Bread gave a weary sigh. 'We are using dreadful words, sir, but I don't care now. I see you have your idea, and I have no will of my own. My will was the will of my children, as I called them; but I have lost my children now. They are dead – I may say it of both of them; and what should I care for the living? What is anyone in the house to me now – what am I to them? My lady objects to me – she has objected to me these thirty years. I should have been glad to be something to young Madame de Bellegarde, though I never was nurse to the present marquis. When he was a baby I was too young; they wouldn't trust me with him. But his wife told her own maid, Mamselle Clarisse, the opinion she had of me. Perhaps you would like to hear it, sir.'

'Oh, immensely,' said Newman.

'She said that if I would sit in her children's schoolroom I should do very well for a penwiper! When things have come to that I don't think I need stand upon ceremony.'

'Decidedly not,' said Newman. 'Go on, Mrs Bread.'

Mrs Bread, however, relapsed again into troubled dumbness, and all Newman could do was to fold his arms and wait. But at last she appeared to have set her memories in order. 'It was when the late marquis was an old man and his eldest son had been two years married. It was when the time came on for marrying Mademoiselle Claire; that's the way they talk of it here, you know, sir. The marquis's health was bad; he was very much broken down. My lady had picked out M. de Cintré, for no good reason that I could see. But there are reasons, I very well know, that are beyond me, and you must be high in the world to understand them. Old M. de Cintré was very high, and my lady thought him almost as good as herself; that's saying a good deal. Mr Urbain took sides with his mother, as he always did. The trouble, I believe, was that my lady would give very little money, and all the other gentlemen asked more. It was only M. de Cintré that was satisfied. The Lord willed it he should have that one soft spot; it was the only one he had. He may have been very grand in his birth, and he certainly was very grand in his bows and speeches; but that was all the grandeur he had. I think he was like what I have heard of comedians; not that I have ever seen one. But I know he painted his face. He might paint it all he would; he could never make me like it! The marquis couldn't abide him, and declared that sooner than take such a husband as that, Mademoiselle Claire should take none at all. He and my lady had a great scene; it came even to our ears in the servants' hall. It was not their first quarrel, if the truth must be told. They were not a loving couple, but they didn't often come to words, because, I think, neither of them thought the other's doings worth the trouble. My lady had long ago got over her jealousy, and she had taken to indifference. In this, I must say, they were well matched. The marquis was very easy-going; he had a most gentlemanly temper. He got angry only once a year, but then it was very bad. He always took to bed directly afterwards. This time I speak of he took to bed as usual, but he never got up again. I'm afraid the poor gentleman was paying for his dissipation; isn't it true they mostly do, sir, when they get old? My lady and Mr Urbain kept quiet, but I know my lady wrote letters to M. de Cintré. The marquis got worse and the doctors gave him up. My lady she gave him up too, and if the truth must be told, she gave him up gladly. When once he was out of the way she could do what she pleased with her daughter, and it was all arranged that my poor innocent child should be handed over to M. de Cintré. You don't know what mademoiselle was in those days, sir; she was the sweetest young creature in France, and knew as little of what was going on around her as the lamb does of the butcher. I used to nurse the marquis, and I was always in his room. It was here at Fleurières, in the autumn. We had a doctor from Paris, who came and stayed two or three weeks in the house. Then there came two others, and there was a consultation, and these two others, as I said, declared that the marquis couldn't be saved.

After this they went off, pocketing their fees, but the other one stayed and did what he could. The marquis himself kept crying out that he wouldn't die, that he didn't want to die, that he would live and look after his daughter. Mademoiselle Claire and the viscount – that was Mr Valentin, you know – were both in the house. The doctor was a clever man – that I could see myself – and I think he believed that the marquis might get well. We took good care of him, he and I, between us, and one day, when my lady had almost ordered her mourning, my patient suddenly began to mend. He got better and better, till the doctor said he was out of danger. What was killing him was the dreadful fits of pain in his stomach. But little by little they stopped, and the poor marquis began to make his jokes again. The doctor found something that gave him great comfort – some white stuff that we kept in a great bottle on the chimney-piece. I used to give it to the marquis through a glass tube; it always made him easier. Then the doctor went away, after telling me to keep on giving him the mixture whenever he was bad. After that there was a little doctor from Poitiers, who came every day. So we were alone in the house – my lady and her poor husband and their three children. Young Madame de Bellegarde had gone away, with her little girl, to her mother's. You know she is very lively, and her maid told me that she didn't like to be where people were dying.' Mrs Bread paused a moment, and then she went on with the same quiet consistency. 'I think you have guessed, sir, that when the marquis began to turn my lady was disappointed.' And she paused again, bending upon Newman a face which seemed to grow whiter as the darkness settled down upon them.

Newman had listened eagerly – with an eagerness greater even than that with which he had bent his ear to Valentin de Bellegarde's last words. Every now and then, as his companion looked up at him, she reminded him of an ancient tabby cat, protracting the enjoyment of a dish of milk. Even her triumph was measured and decorous; the faculty of exultation had been chilled by disuse. She presently continued. 'Late one night I was sitting by the marquis in his room, the great red room in the west tower. He had been complaining a little, and I gave him a spoonful of the doctor's dose. My lady had been there in the early part of the evening; she sat for more than an hour by his bed. Then she went away and left me alone. After midnight she came back, and her eldest son was with her. They went to the bed and looked at the marquis, and my lady took hold of his hand. Then she turned to me and said he was not so well; I remember how the marquis, without saying anything, lay staring at her. I can see his white face, at this moment, in the great black square between the bed-curtains. I said I didn't think he was very bad; and she told me to go to bed – she would sit a while with him. When the marquis saw me going he gave a sort of groan, and called out to me not to leave him; but Mr Urbain opened the door for me and pointed the way out. The present marquis – perhaps you have noticed, sir – has a very proud way of giving orders, and I was there to take orders. I went to my room, but I wasn't easy; I couldn't tell you why. I didn't undress; I sat there waiting and listening. For what would you have said, sir? I couldn't have told you; for surely a poor gentleman might be comfortable with his wife and his son. It was as if I expected to hear the marquis moaning after me again. I listened, but I heard nothing. It was a very still night; I never knew a night so still. At last the very stillness itself seemed to frighten me, and I came out of my room and went very softly downstairs. In the anteroom, outside of the marquis's chamber, I found Mr Urbain walking up and down. He asked me what I wanted, and I said I came back to relieve my lady. He said *he* would relieve my lady, and ordered me back to bed; but as I stood there, unwilling to turn away, the door of the room opened and my lady came out. I noticed she was very pale; she was very strange. She looked a moment at the count and at me, and then she held out her arms to the count. He went to her, and she fell upon him and hid her face. I went quickly past her into the room, and to the marquis's bed. He was lying there, very white, with his eyes shut, like a corpse. I took hold of his hand and spoke to him, and he felt to me like a dead man. Then I turned round; my lady and Mr Urbain were there. "My poor Bread," said my lady, "M. le Marquis is gone." Mr Urbain knelt down by the bed and said softly, "*Mon père, mon père.*"* I thought it wonderful strange, and asked my lady what in the world had happened, and why she hadn't called me. She said nothing had happened; that she had only been sitting there with the marquis, very quiet. She had closed her eyes, thinking she might sleep, and she had slept she didn't know how long. When she woke up he was dead. "It's death, my son, it's death," she said to the count. Mr Urbain said they must have the doctor immediately, from Poitiers, and that he would ride off and fetch him. He kissed his father's face, and then he kissed his mother and went away. My lady and I stood there at the bedside. As I looked at the poor marquis it came into my head that he was not dead, that he was in a kind of swoon. And then my lady repeated, "My poor Bread, it's death, it's death"; and I said, "Yes, my lady, it's certainly death." I said just the opposite to what I believed; it was my notion. Then my lady said we must wait for the doctor, and we sat there and waited. It was a long time; the poor marquis neither stirred nor changed. "I have seen death before," said my lady, "and it's terribly like this." "Yes, please, my lady," said I; and I kept thinking. The night wore away without the count's coming back, and my lady began to be frightened. She was afraid he had had an accident in the dark, or met with some wild people. At last she got so restless that she went below to watch in the court for her son's return. I sat there alone and the marquis never stirred.'

Here Mrs Bread paused again, and the most artistic of romancers could not have been more effective. Newman made a movement as if he were turning over the page of a novel. 'So he *was* dead!' he exclaimed.

'Three days afterwards he was in his grave,' said Mrs Bread sententiously. 'In a little while I went away to the front of the house and looked out into the court, and there, before long, I saw Mr Urbain ride in alone. I waited a bit, to hear him come upstairs with his mother, but they stayed below, and I went back to the marquis's room. I went to the bed and held up the light to him, but I don't know why I didn't let the candlestick fall. The marquis's eyes were open – open wide! they were staring at me. I knelt down beside him and took his hands, and begged him to tell me, in the name of wonder, whether he was alive or dead. Still he looked at me a long time, and then he made me a sign to put my ear close to him: "I am dead," he said, "I am dead. The marquise has killed me." I was all in a tremble. I didn't understand him. I didn't know what had become of him. He seemed both a man and a corpse if you can fancy, sir. "But you'll get well, now, sir," I said. And then he whispered again, ever so weak: "I wouldn't get well, for a kingdom. I wouldn't be that woman's husband again." And then he said more; he said she had murdered him. I asked him what she had done to him, but he only replied: "Murder,

murder. And she'll kill my daughter," he said; "my poor unhappy child." And he begged me to prevent that, and then he said that he was dying, that he was dead. I was afraid to move or to leave him; I was almost dead myself. All of a sudden he asked me to get a pencil and write for him; and then I had to tell him that I couldn't manage a pencil. He asked me to hold him up in bed while he wrote himself, and I said he could never, never do such a thing. But he seemed to have a kind of terror that gave him strength. I found a pencil in the room and a piece of paper and a book, and I put the paper on the book and the pencil into his hand, and moved the candle near him. You will think all this very strange, sir; and very strange it was. The strangest part of it was that I believed he was dying, and that I was eager to help him to write. I sat on the bed and put my arm round him, and held him up. I felt very strong; I believe I could have lifted him and carried him. It was a wonder how he wrote, but he did write, in a big scratching hand; he almost covered one side of the paper. It seemed a long time; I suppose it was three or four minutes. He was groaning, terribly, all the while. Then he said it was ended, and I let him down upon his pillows, and he gave me the paper and told me to fold it, and hide it, and to give it to those who would act upon it. "Whom do you mean?" I said. "Who are those who will act upon it?" But he only groaned, for an answer; he couldn't speak, for weakness. In a few minutes he told me to go and look at the bottle on the chimney-piece. I knew the bottle he meant; the white stuff that was good for his stomach. I went and looked at it, but it was empty. When I came back his eyes were open and he was staring at me; but soon he closed them and he said no more. I hid the paper in my dress; I didn't look at what was written upon it, though I can read very well, sir, if I haven't any handwriting. I sat down near the bed, but it was nearly half an hour before my lady and the count came in. The marquis looked as he did when they left him, and I never said a word about his having been otherwise. Mr Urbain said that the doctor had been called to a person in childbirth, but that he promised to set out for Fleurières immediately. In another half hour he arrived, and as soon as he had examined the marquis he said that we had had a false alarm. The poor gentleman was very low, but he was still living. I watched my lady and her son when he said this, to see if they looked at each other, and I am obliged to admit that they didn't. The doctor said there was no reason he should die; he had been going on so well. And then he wanted to know how he had suddenly fallen off; he had left him so very hearty. My lady told her little story again – what she had told Mr Urbain and me – and the doctor looked at her and said nothing. He stayed all the next day at the château, and hardly left the marquis. I was always there. Mademoiselle and Mr Valentin came and looked at their father, but he never stirred. It was a strange, deathly stupor. My lady was always about; her face was as white as her husband's, and she looked very proud, as I had seen her look when her orders or her wishes had been disobeyed. It was as if the poor marquis had defied her; and the way she took it made me afraid of her. The apothecary* from Poitiers kept the marquis along through the day, and we waited for the other doctor from Paris, who, as I told you, had been staying at Fleurières. They had telegraphed for him early in the morning, and in the evening he arrived. He talked a bit outside with the doctor from Poitiers, and then they came in to see the marquis together. I was with him, and so was Mr Urbain. My lady had been to receive the doctor from Paris, and she didn't come back with him into the room. He sat down by the marquis – I can see him there now, with his hand on the marquis's wrist, and Mr Urbain watching him with a little looking-glass* in his hand. "I'm sure he's better," said the little doctor from Poitiers; "I'm sure he'll come back." A few moments after he had said this the marquis opened his eyes, as if he were waking up, and looked at us, from one to the other. I saw him look at me very softly, as you'd say. At the same moment my lady came in on tiptoe; she came up to the bed and put in her head between me and the count. The marquis saw her and gave a long, most wonderful moan. He said something we couldn't understand, and he seemed to have a kind of spasm. He shook all over and then closed his eyes, and the doctor jumped up and took hold of my lady. He held her for a moment a bit roughly. The marquis was stone dead! This time there were those there that knew.'

Newman felt as if he had been reading by starlight the report of highly important evidence in a great murder case. 'And the paper – the paper!' he said, excitedly. 'What was written upon it?'

'I can't tell you, sir,' answered Mrs Bread. 'I couldn't read it; it was in French.'

'But could no one else read it?'

'I never asked a human creature.'

'No one has ever seen it?'

'If you see it you'll be the first.'

Newman seized the old woman's hand in both his own and pressed it vigorously. 'I thank you ever so much for that,' he cried. 'I want to be the first; I want it to be my property and no one else's! You're the wisest old woman in Europe. And what did you do with the paper?' This information had made him feel extraordinarily strong. 'Give it to me quick!'

Mrs Bread got up with a certain majesty. 'It is not so easy as that, sir. If you want the paper, you must wait.'

'But waiting is horrible, you know,' urged Newman.

'I am sure *I* have waited; I have waited these many years,' said Mrs Bread.

'That is very true. You have waited for me. I won't forget it. And yet, how comes it you didn't do as M. de Bellegarde said, show the paper to someone?'

'To whom should I show it?' answered Mrs Bread mournfully. 'It was not easy to know, and many's the night I have lain awake thinking of it. Six months afterwards, when they married Mademoiselle to her vicious old husband, I was very near bringing it out. I thought it was my duty to do something with it, and yet I was mightily afraid. I didn't know what was written on the paper, or how bad it might be, and there was no one I could trust enough to ask. And it seemed to me a cruel kindness to that sweet young creature, letting her know that her father had written her mother down so shamefully; for that's what he did I suppose. I thought she would rather be unhappy with her husband than be unhappy that way. It was for her and for my dear Mr Valentin I kept quiet. Quiet I call it, but for me it was a weary quietness. It worried me terribly, and it changed me altogether. But for others I held my tongue, and no one, to this hour, knows what passed between the poor marquis and me.'

'But evidently there were suspicions,' said Newman. 'Where did Mr Valentin get his ideas?'

'It was the little doctor from Poitiers. He was very ill-satisfied, and he made a great talk. He was a sharp Frenchman, and coming to the house, as he did, day after day, I suppose he saw more than he seemed to see. And indeed the way the poor marquis went off as soon as his eyes fell on my lady was a most

shocking sight for anyone. The medical gentleman from Paris
was much more accommodating, and he hushed up the other.
But for all he could do Mr Valentin and Mademoiselle heard
something; they knew their father's death was somehow against
nature. Of course they couldn't accuse their mother, and, as I
tell you, I was as dumb as that stone. Mr Valentin used to look
at me sometimes, and his eyes seemed to shine, as if he were
thinking of asking me something. I was dreadfully afraid he
would speak, and I always looked away and went about my
business. If I were to tell him, I was sure he would hate me
afterwards, and that I could never have borne. Once I went up
to him and took a great liberty; I kissed him, as I had kissed him
when he was a child. "You oughtn't to look so sad, sir," I said;
"believe your poor old Bread. Such a gallant, handsome young
man can have nothing to be sad about." And I think he
understood me; he understood that I was begging off, and he
made up his mind in his own way. He went about with his
unasked question in his mind, as I did with my untold tale; we
were both afraid of bringing dishonour on a great house. And it
was the same with Mademoiselle. She didn't know what had
happened; she wouldn't know. My lady and Mr Urbain asked
me no questions because they had no reason. I was as still as a
mouse. When I was younger my lady thought me a hussy, and
now she thought me a fool. How should I have any ideas?'

'But you say the little doctor from Poitiers made a talk,' said
Newman. 'Did no one take it up?'

'I heard nothing of it, sir. They are always talking scandal in
these foreign countries – you may have noticed – and I suppose
they shook their heads over Madame de Bellegarde. But after
all, what could they say? The marquis had been ill, and the
marquis had died; he had as good a right to die as anyone. The
doctor couldn't say he had not come honestly by his cramps.
The next year the little doctor left the place and bought a
practice in Bordeaux, and if there has been any gossip it died
out. And I don't think there could have been much gossip about
my lady that anyone would listen to. My lady is so very
respectable.'

Newman, at this last affirmation, broke into an immense,
resounding laugh. Mrs Bread had begun to move away from the
spot where they were sitting, and he helped her through the
aperture in the wall and along the homeward path. 'Yes,' he

said, 'my lady's respectability is delicious; it will be a great crash!' They reached the empty space in front of the church, where they stopped a moment, looking at each other with something of an air of closer fellowship – like two sociable conspirators. 'But what was it,' said Newman, 'what was it she did to her husband? She didn't stab him or poison him.'

'I don't know, sir; no one saw it.'

'Unless it was Mr Urbain. You say he was walking up and down, outside the room. Perhaps he looked through the keyhole. But no; I think that with his mother he would take it on trust.'

'You may be sure I have often thought of it,' said Mrs Bread. 'I am sure she didn't touch him with her hands. I saw nothing on him, anywhere. I believe it was in this way. He had a fit of his great pain, and he asked her for his medicine. Instead of giving it to him she went and poured it away, before his eyes. Then he saw what she meant, and, weak and helpless as he was, he was frightened, he was terrified. "You want to kill me," he said. "Yes, M. le Marquis, I want to kill you," says my lady, and sits down and fixes her eyes upon him. You know my lady's eyes, I think, sir; it was with them she killed him; it was with the terrible strong will she put into them. It was like a frost on flowers.'

'Well, you are a very intelligent woman; you have shown great discretion,' said Newman. 'I shall value your services as housekeeper extremely.'

They had begun to descend the hill, and Mrs Bread said nothing until they reached the foot. Newman strolled lightly beside her; his head was thrown back as he was gazing at all the stars: he seemed to himself to be riding his vengeance along the Milky Way. 'So you are serious, sir, about that?' said Mrs Bread, softly.

'About your living with me? Why of course I take care of you to the end of your days. You can't live with those people any longer. And you oughtn't to, you know, after this. You give me the paper, and you move away.'

'It seems very flighty in me to be taking a new place at this time of life,' observed Mrs Bread lugubriously. 'But if you are going to turn the house upside down, I would rather be out of it.'

'Oh,' said Newman, in the cheerful tone of a man who feels rich in alternatives, 'I don't think I shall bring in the constables, if that's what you mean. Whatever Madame de Bellegarde did, I am afraid the law can't take hold of it. But I am glad of that; it leaves it altogether to me!'

'You are a mighty bold gentleman, sir,' murmured Mrs Bread, looking at him round the edge of her great bonnet.

He walked with her back to the château; the curfew had tolled for the laborious villagers of Fleurières, and the street was unlighted and empty. She promised him that he should have the marquis's manuscript in half an hour. Mrs Bread choosing not to go in by the great gate, they passed round by a winding lane to a door in the wall of the park, of which she had the key, and which would enable her to enter the château from behind. Newman arranged with her that he should await outside the wall her return with the coveted document.

She went in, and his half hour in the dusky lane seemed very long. But he had plenty to think about. At last the door in the wall opened and Mrs Bread stood there, with one hand on the latch and the other holding out a scrap of white paper, folded small. In a moment he was master of it, and it had passed into his waistcoat-pocket. 'Come and see me in Paris,' he said; 'we are to settle your future, you know; and I will translate poor M. de Bellegarde's French to you.' Never had he felt so grateful as at this moment for M. Nioche's instructions.

Mrs Bread's dull eyes had followed the disappearance of the paper, and she gave a heavy sigh. 'Well, you have done what you would with me, sir, and I suppose you will do it again. You *must* take care of me now. You are a terribly positive gentleman.'

'Just now,' said Newman, 'I'm a terribly impatient gentleman!' And he bade her good-night and walked rapidly back to the inn. He ordered his vehicle to be prepared for his return to Poitiers, and then he shut the door of the common salle and strode towards the solitary lamp on the chimney-piece. He pulled out the paper and quickly unfolded it. It was covered with pencil-marks, which at first, in the feeble light, seemed indistinct. But Newman's fierce curiosity forced a meaning from the tremulous signs. The English of them was as follows:

My wife has tried to kill me, and she has done it; I am dying, dying horribly. It is to marry my dear daughter to M. de Cintré. With all my soul I protest – I forbid it. I am not insane – ask the doctors, ask Mrs B——. It was alone with me here, tonight; she attacked me and put me to death. It is murder, if murder ever was. Ask the doctors.

HENRI-URBAIN DE BELLEGARDE

CHAPTER 23

Newman returned to Paris the second day after his interview with Mrs Bread. The morrow he had spent at Poitiers, reading over and over again the little document which he had lodged in his pocket-book, and thinking what he would do in the circumstances and how he would do it. He would not have said that Poitiers was an amusing place; yet the day seemed very short. Domiciled once more in the Boulevard Haussmann, he walked over to the Rue de l'Université and inquired of Madame de Bellegarde's portress whether the marquise had come back. The portress told him that she had arrived, with M. le Marquis, on the preceding day, and further informed him that if he desired to enter, Madame de Bellegarde and her son were both at home. As she said these words the little white-faced old woman who peered out of the dusky gate-house of the Hôtel de Bellegarde gave a small wicked smile – a smile which seemed to Newman to mean, 'Go in if you dare!' She was evidently versed in the current domestic history; she was placed where she could feel the pulse of the house. Newman stood a moment, twisting his moustache and looking at her; then he abruptly turned away. But this was not because he was afraid to go in – though he doubted whether, if he did so, he should be able to make his way, unchallenged, into the presence of Madame de Cintré's relatives. Confidence – excessive confidence, perhaps – quite as much as timidity prompted his retreat. He was nursing his thunderbolt; he loved it; he was unwilling to part with it. He seemed to be holding it aloft in the rumbling, vaguely-flashing air, directly over the heads of his victims, and he fancied he could see their pale upturned faces. Few specimens of the human countenance had ever given him such pleasure as these, lighted in the lurid fashion I have hinted at, and he was disposed to sip the cup of contemplative revenge in a leisurely fashion. It must be added, too, that he was at a loss to see exactly how he could arrange to witness the operation of his thunder. To send in his card to Madame de Bellegarde would be a waste of ceremony; she would certainly decline to receive him. On the other hand he could not force his way into her presence. It annoyed him keenly to think that he might be reduced to the blind satisfaction of writing her a letter; but he consoled himself in a measure with the reflection that a letter might lead to an interview. He went home, and feeling rather tired – nursing a vengeance was, it must be confessed, a rather fatiguing process; it took a good deal out of one – flung himself into one of his brocaded fauteuils,* stretched his legs, thrust his hands into his pockets, and, while he watched the reflected sunset fading from the ornate house-tops on the opposite side of the Boulevard, began mentally to compose a cool epistle to Madame de Bellegarde. While he was so occupied his servant threw open the door and announced ceremoniously, 'Madame Brett!'

Newman roused himself, expectantly, and in a few moments perceived upon his threshold the worthy woman with whom he had conversed to such good purpose on the starlit hill-top of Fleurières. Mrs Bread had made for this visit the same toilet as for her former expedition. Newman was struck with her distinguished appearance. His lamp was not lit, and as her large grave face gazed at him through the light dusk from under the shadow of her ample bonnet, he felt the incongruity of such a person presenting herself as a servant. He greeted her with high geniality, and bade her come in and sit down and make herself comfortable. There was something which might have touched the springs both of mirth and of melancholy in the ancient maidenliness with which Mrs Bread endeavoured to comply with these directions. She was not playing at being fluttered, which would have been simply ridiculous; she was doing her best to carry herself as a person so humble that, for her, even embarrassment would have been pretentious; but evidently she had never dreamed of its being in her horoscope to pay a visit, at nightfall, to a friendly single gentleman who lived in theatrical-looking rooms on one of the new boulevards.

'I truly hope I am not forgetting my place, sir,' she murmured.

'Forgetting your place?' cried Newman. 'Why, you are remembering it. This is your place, you know. You are already in my service; your wages, as housekeeper, began a fortnight ago. I can tell you my house wants keeping! Why don't you take off your bonnet and stay?'

'Take off my bonnet?' said Mrs Bread, with timid literalness. 'Oh, sir, I haven't my cap. And with your leave, sir, I couldn't keep house in my best gown.'

'Never mind your gown,' said Newman cheerfully. 'You shall have a better gown than that.'

Mrs Bread stared solemnly and then stretched her hands over her lustreless satin skirt, as if the perilous side of her situation was defining itself. 'Oh, sir, I am fond of my own clothes,' she murmured.

'I hope you have left those wicked people, at any rate,' said Newman.

'Well, sir, here I am!' said Mrs Bread. 'That's all I can tell you. Here I sit, poor Catherine Bread. It's a strange place for me to be. I don't know myself; I never supposed I was so bold. But indeed, sir, I have gone as far as my own strength will bear me.'

'Oh, come, Mrs Bread,' said Newman, almost caressingly, 'don't make yourself uncomfortable. Now's the time to feel lively, you know.'

She began to speak again with a trembling voice. 'I think it would be more respectable if I could – if I could – ' and her voice trembled to a pause.

'If you could give up this sort of thing altogether?' said Newman kindly, trying to anticipate her meaning, which he supposed might be a wish to retire from service.

'If I could give up everything, sir! All I should ask is a decent Protestant burial.'

'Burial!' cried Newman, with a burst of laughter. 'Why, to bury you now would be a sad piece of extravagance. It's only rascals who have to be buried to get respectable. Honest folks like you and me can live our time out – and live together. Come! did you bring your baggage?'

'My box is locked and corded; but I haven't yet spoken to my lady.'

'Speak to her, then, and have done with it. I should like to have your chance!' cried Newman.

'I would gladly give it you, sir. I have passed some weary hours in my lady's dressing-room; but this will be one of the longest. She will tax me with ingratitude.'

'Well,' said Newman, 'so long as you can tax her with murder – '

'Oh, sir, I can't; not I,' sighed Mrs Bread.

'You don't mean to say anything about it? So much the better. Leave that to me.'

'If she calls me a thankless old woman,' said Mrs Bread, 'I shall have nothing to say. But it is better so,' she softly added. 'She shall be my lady to the last. That will be more respectable.'

'And then you will come to me and I shall be your gentleman,' said Newman; 'that will be more respectable still!'

Mrs Bread rose, with lowered eyes, and stood a moment; then, looking up, she rested her eyes upon Newman's face. The disordered proprieties were somehow settling to rest. She looked at Newman so long and so fixedly, with such a dull intense devotedness, that he himself might have had a pretext for embarrassment. At last she said gently: 'You are not looking well, sir.'

'That's natural enough,' said Newman. 'I have nothing to feel well about. To be very indifferent and very fierce, very dull and very jovial, very sick and very lively, all at once – why, it rather mixes one up.'

Mrs Bread gave a noiseless sigh. 'I can tell you something that will make you feel duller still, if you want to feel all one way. About Madame de Cintré.'

'What can you tell me?' Newman demanded. 'Not that you have seen her?'

She shook her head. 'No, indeed, sir, nor ever shall. That's the dulness of it. Nor my lady. Nor M. de Bellegarde.'

'You mean that she is kept so close.'

'Close, close,' said Mrs Bread, very softly.

These words, for an instant, seemed to check the beating of Newman's heart. He leaned back in his chair, staring up at the old woman. 'They have tried to see her, and she wouldn't – she couldn't?'

'She refused – forever! I had it from my lady's own maid,' said Mrs Bread, 'who had it from my lady. To speak of it to such a person my lady must have felt the shock. Madame de Cintré won't see them now, and now is her only chance. A while hence she will have no chance.'

'You mean the other women – the mothers, the daughters, the sisters; what is it they call them? – won't let her?'

'It is what they call the rule of the house – or of the order, I believe,' said Mrs Bread. 'There is no rule so strict as that of the Carmelites. The bad women in the reformatories are fine ladies to them. They wear old brown cloaks – so the *femme de chambre** told me – that you wouldn't use for a horse blanket. And the poor countess was so fond of soft-feeling dresses; she would never have anything stiff! They sleep on the ground,' Mrs Bread went on; 'they are no better, no better' – and she hesitated for a comparison – 'they are no better than tinkers' wives. They give up everything, down to the very name their poor old nurses called them by. They give up father and mother, brother and sister – to say nothing of other persons,' Mrs Bread delicately added. 'They wear a shroud under their brown cloaks and a rope round their waists, and they get up on winter nights and go off into cold places to pray to the Virgin Mary. The Virgin Mary is a hard mistress!'

Mrs Bread, dwelling on these terrible facts, sat dry-eyed and pale, with her hands clasped in her satin lap. Newman gave a melancholy groan and fell forward, leaning his head in his hands. There was a long silence, broken only by the ticking of the great gilded clock on the chimney-piece.

'Where is this place – where is the convent?' Newman asked at last, looking up.

'There are two houses,' said Mrs Bread. 'I found out; I thought you would like to know – though it's poor comfort, I think. One is the Avenue de Messine;* they have learned that Madame de Cintré is there. The other is in the Rue d'Enfer.* That's a terrible name; I suppose you know what it means.'

Newman got up and walked away to the end of his long room. When he came back Mrs Bread had got up, and stood by the fire with folded hands. 'Tell me this,' he said. 'Can I get near her – even if I don't see her? Can I look through a grating, or some such thing, at the place where she is?'

It is said that all women love a lover, and Mrs Bread's sense of the pre-established harmony which kept servants in their 'place', even as planets in their orbits (not that Mrs Bread had ever consciously likened herself to a planet), barely availed to temper the maternal melancholy with which she leaned her head on one side and gazed at her new employer. She probably felt for the moment as if, forty years before, she had held him also in her arms. 'That wouldn't help you, sir. It would only make her seem farther away.'

'I want to go there, at all events,' said Newman. 'Avenue de Messine, you say? And what is it they call themselves?'

'Carmelites,' said Mrs Bread.

'I shall remember that.'

Mrs Bread hesitated a moment, and then: 'It's my duty to tell you this, sir,' she went on. 'The convent has a chapel, and some people are admitted on Sunday to the mass. You don't see the poor creatures that are shut up there, but I am told you can hear them sing. It's a wonder they have any heart for singing! Some Sunday I shall make bold to go. It seems to me I should know *her* voice in fifty.'

Newman looked at his visitor very gratefully; then he held out his hand and shook hers. 'Thank you,' he said. 'If anyone can get in, I will.' A moment later Mrs Bread proposed, deferentially, to retire, but he checked her and put a lighted candle into her hand. 'There are half-a-dozen rooms there I don't use,' he said, pointing through an open door. 'Go and look at them and take your choice. You can live in the one you like best.' From this bewildering opportunity Mrs Bread at first recoiled; but finally, yielding to Newman's gentle, reassuring push, she wandered off into the dusk with her tremulous taper. She remained absent a quarter of an hour, during which Newman paced up and down, stopped occasionally to look out of the window at the lights on the Boulevard, and then resumed his walk. Mrs Bread's relish for her investigations apparently increased as she proceeded; but at last she reappeared and deposited her candlestick on the chimney-piece.

'Well, have you picked one out?' asked Newman.

'A room, sir? They are all too fine for a dingy old body like me. There isn't one that hasn't a bit of gilding.'

'It's only tinsel, Mrs Bread,' said Newman. 'If you stay there awhile it will all peel off of itself.' And he gave a dismal smile.

'Oh, sir, there are things enough peeling off already!' rejoined Mrs Bread, with a head-shake. 'Since I was there I thought I would look about me. I don't believe you know, sir. The corners are most dreadful. You do want a housekeeper, that you do; you want a tidy Englishwoman that isn't above taking hold of a broom.'

Newman assured her that he suspected, if he had not measured, his domestic abuses, and that to reform them was a mission worthy of her powers. She held her candlestick aloft again and looked round the salon with compassionate glances; then she intimated that she accepted the mission, and that its sacred character would sustain her in her rupture with Madame de Bellegarde. With this she curtsied herself away.

She came back the next day with her worldly goods, and Newman going into his drawing-room, found her upon her aged knees before a divan, sewing up some detached fringe. He questioned her as to her leave-taking with her late mistress, and she said it had proved easier than she feared. 'I was perfectly civil, sir, but the Lord helped me to remember that a good woman has no call to tremble before a bad one.'

'I should think so!' cried Newman. 'And does she know you have come to me?'

'She asked me where I was going, and I mentioned your name,' said Mrs Bread.

'What did she say to that?'

'She looked at me very hard, and she turned very red. Then she bade me leave her. I was all ready to go, and I had got the coachman, who is an Englishman, to bring down my poor box, and to fetch me a cab. But when I went down myself to the gate I found it closed. My lady had sent orders to the porter not to let me pass, and by the same orders the porter's wife – she is a dreadful sly old body – had gone out in a cab to fetch home M. de Bellegarde from his club.

Newman slapped his knee. 'She *is* scared! she *is* scared!' he cried exultantly.

'I was frightened too, sir,' said Mrs Bread, 'but I was also mightily vexed. I took it very high with the porter, and asked him by what right he used violence to an honourable English-woman who had lived in the house for thirty years before he was heard of. Oh, sir, I was very grand, and I brought the man down. He drew his bolts, and let me out, and I promised the cabman something handsome if he would drive fast. But he was terribly slow; it seemed as if we should never reach your blessed door. I am all of a tremble still; it took me five minutes, just now, to thread my needle.'

Newman told her, with a gleeful laugh, that if she chose she might have a little maid on purpose to thread her needles; and he went away murmuring to himself again that the old woman *was* scared – she *was* scared!

He had not shown Mrs Tristram the little paper that he carried in his pocket-book, but since his return to Paris he had seen her several times, and she had told him that he seemed to her to be in a strange way – an even stranger way than his sad situation made natural. Had his disappointment gone to his head? He looked like a man who was going to be ill, and yet she had never seen him more restless and active. One day he would sit hanging his head and looking as if he were firmly resolved never to smile again; another he would indulge in laughter that was almost unseemly and made jokes that were bad even for him. If he was trying to carry off his sorrow, he at such times really went too far. She begged him of all things not to be 'strange'. Feeling in a measure responsible as she did for the affair which had turned out so ill for him, she could endure anything but his strangeness. He might be melancholy if he would, or he might be stoical, he might be cross and cantankerous with her and ask her why she had ever dared to meddle with his destiny: to this she would submit; for this she would make allowances. Only, for Heaven's sake, let him not be incoherent. That would be extremely unpleasant. It was like people talking in their sleep; they always frightened her. And Mrs Tristram intimated that, taking very high ground as regards the moral obligation which events had laid upon her, she proposed not to rest quiet until she should have confronted him with the least inadequate substitute for Madame de Cintré that the two hemispheres contained.

'Oh,' said Newman, 'we are even now, and we had better not open a new account! You may bury me some day, but you shall never marry me. It's too rough. I hope, at any rate,' he added, 'that there is nothing incoherent in this – that I want to go next Sunday to the Carmelite chapel in the Avenue de Messine. You know one of the Catholic ministers – an abbé, is that it? – I have seen him here, you know; that motherly old gentleman with the big waistband. Please ask him if I need a special leave to go in, and if I do, beg him to obtain it for me.'

Mrs Tristram gave expression to the liveliest joy. 'I am so glad you have asked me to do something!' she cried. 'You shall get into the chapel if the abbé is disfrocked for his share in it.' And two days afterwards she told him that it was all arranged; the abbé was enchanted to serve him, and if he would present himself civilly at the convent-gate there would be no difficulty.

CHAPTER 24

Sunday was as yet two days off; but meanwhile, to beguile his impatience, Newman took his way to the Avenue de Messine and got what comfort he could in staring at the blank outer wall of Madame de Cintré's present residence. The street in question, as some travellers will remember, adjoins the Parc Monceau, which is one of the prettiest corners of Paris. The quarter has an air of modern opulence and convenience which seems at variance with the ascetic institution, and the impression made upon Newman's gloomily-irritated gaze by the fresh-looking, windowless expanse behind which the woman he loved was perhaps even then pledging herself to pass the rest of her days was less exasperating than he had feared. The place suggested a convent with the modern improvements – an asylum in which privacy, though unbroken, might be not quite identical with privation, and meditation, though monotonous, might be of a cheerful cast. And yet he knew the case was otherwise; only at present it was not a reality to him. It was too strange and too mocking to be real; it was like a page torn out of a romance, with no context in his own experience.

On Sunday morning, at the hour which Mrs Tristram had indicated, he rang at the gate in the blank wall. It instantly opened and admitted him into a clean, cold-looking court, from beyond which a dull, plain edifice looked down upon him. A robust lay sister with a cheerful complexion emerged from a porter's lodge, and, on his stating his errand, pointed to the open door of the chapel, an edifice which occupied the right side of the court and was preceded by a high flight of steps. Newman ascended the steps and immediately entered the open door. Service had not yet begun; the place was dimly lighted, and it was some moments before he could distinguish its features. Then he saw it was divided by a large close iron screen into two unequal portions. The altar was on the hither side of the screen,

and between it and the entrance were disposed several benches
and chairs. Three or four of these were occupied by vague,
motionless figures – figures that he presently perceived to be
women, deeply absorbed in their devotion. The place seemed to
Newman very cold; the smell of the incense itself was cold.
Besides this there was a twinkle of tapers and here and there a
glow of coloured glass. Newman seated himself; the praying
women kept still, with their backs turned. He saw they were
visitors like himself, and he would have liked to see their faces;
for he believed that they were the mourning mothers and sisters
of other women who had had the same pitiless courage as
Madame de Cintré. But they were better off than he, for they at
least shared the faith to which the others had sacrificed themselves. Three or four persons came in; two of them were elderly
gentlemen. Everyone was very quiet. Newman fastened his eyes
upon the screen behind the altar. That was the convent, the real
convent, the place where she was. But he could see nothing; no
light came through the crevices. He got up and approached the
partition very gently, trying to look through. But behind it there
was darkness, with nothing stirring. He went back to his place,
and after that a priest and two altar-boys came in and began to
say mass.

Newman watched their genuflections and gyrations with a
grim, still enmity; they seemed aids and abettors of Madame de
Cintré's desertion; they were mouthing and droning out their
triumph. The priest's long, dismal intonings acted upon his
nerves and deepened his wrath; there was something defiant in
his unintelligible drawl; it seemed meant for Newman himself.
Suddenly there arose from the depths of the chapel, from behind
the inexorable grating, a sound which drew his attention from
the altar – the sound of a strange, lugubrious chant uttered by
women's voices. It began softly, but it presently grew louder,
and as it increased it became more of a wail and a dirge. It was
the chant of the Carmelite nuns, their only human utterance. It
was their dirge over their buried affections and over the vanity
of earthly desires. At first Newman was bewildered – almost
stunned – by the strangeness of the sound; then, as he compre-
hended its meaning, he listened intently and his heart began to
throb. He listened for Madame de Cintré's voice, and in the very
heart of the tuneless harmony he imagined he made it out. (We
are obliged to believe that he was wrong, inasmuch as she had

obviously not yet had time to become a member of the invisible
sisterhood.) The chant kept on, mechanical and monotonous,
with dismal repetitions and despairing cadences. It was hideous,
it was horrible; as it continued, Newman felt that he needed all
his self-control. He was growing more agitated; he felt tears in
his eyes. At last, as in its full force the thought came over him
that this confused, impersonal wail was all that he or the world
she had deserted should ever hear of the voice he had found so
sweet, he felt that he could bear it no longer. He rose abruptly
and made his way out. On the threshold he paused, listened
again to the dreary strain, and then hastily descended into the
court. As he did so he saw that the good sister with the high-
coloured cheeks and the fan-like frill to her coiffure, who had
admitted him, was in conference at the gate with two persons
who had just come in. A second glance informed him that these
persons were Madame de Bellegarde and her son, and that they
were about to avail themselves of that method of approach to
Madame de Cintré which Newman had found but a mockery of
consolation. As he crossed the court M. de Bellegarde recognised
him; the marquis was coming to the steps, leading his mother.
The old lady also gave Newman a look, and it resembled that of
her son. Both faces expressed a franker perturbation, something
more akin to the humbleness of dismay than Newman had yet
seen in them. Evidently he startled the Bellegardes, and they had
not their grand behaviour immediately in hand. Newman hurried past them, guided only by the desire to get out of the
convent-walls into the street. The gate opened itself at his
approach; he strode over the threshold and it closed behind him.
A carriage, which appeared to have been standing there, was
just turning away from the sidewalk. Newman looked at it for a
moment, blankly; then he became conscious, through the dusky
mist that swam before his eyes, that a lady seated in it was
bowing to him. The vehicle had turned away before he recognised her; it was an ancient landau with one half the cover
lowered. The lady's bow was very positive and accompanied
with a smile; a little girl was seated beside her. He raised his hat,
and then the lady bade the coachman stop.

The carriage halted again beside the pavement, and she sat
there and beckoned to Newman – beckoned with the demonstrative grace of Madame Urbain de Bellegarde. Newman hesitated
a moment before he obeyed her summons; during this moment

he had time to curse his stupidity for letting the others escape him. He had been wondering how he could get at them; fool that he was for not stopping them then and there! What better place than beneath the very prison-walls to which they had consigned the promise of his joy? He had been too bewildered to stop them, but now he felt ready to wait for them at the gate. Madame Urbain, with a certain attractive petulance, beckoned to him again, and this time he went over to the carriage. She leaned out and gave him her hand, looking at him kindly, and smiling.

'Ah, monsieur,' she said, 'you don't include me in your wrath? I had nothing to do with it.'

'Oh, I don't suppose *you* could have prevented it?' Newman answered in a tone which was not that of studied gallantry.

'What you say is too true for me to resent the small account it makes of my influence. I forgive you, at any rate, because you look as if you had seen a ghost.'

'I have!' said Newman.

'I am glad, then, I didn't go in with Madame de Bellegarde and my husband. You must have seen them, eh? Was the meeting affectionate? Did you hear the chanting? They say it's like the lamentations of the damned. I wouldn't go in: one is certain to hear that soon enough. Poor Claire – in a white shroud and a big brown cloak! That's the *toilette** of the Carmelites, you know. Well, she was always fond of long, loose things. But I must not speak of her to you; only I must say that I am very sorry for you, that if I could have helped you I would, and that I think everyone has been very shabby. I was afraid of it, you know; I felt it in the air for a fortnight before it came. When I saw you at my mother-in-law's ball, taking it all so easily, I felt as if you were dancing on your grave. But what could I do? I wish you all the good I can think of. You will say that isn't much! Yes; they have been very shabby; I am not a bit afraid to say it; I assure you everyone thinks so. We are not all like that. I am sorry I am not going to see you again; you know I think you very good company. I would prove it by asking you to get into the carriage and drive with me for a quarter of an hour, while I wait for my mother-in-law. Only if we were seen – considering what has passed, and everyone knows you have been turned away – it might be thought I was going a little too far, even for me. But I shall see you sometimes – somewhere, eh? You know' – this was said in English – 'we have a plan for a little amusement.'

Newman stood there with his hand on the carriage-door, listening to this consolatory murmur with an unlighted eye. He hardly knew what Madame de Bellegarde was saying; he was only conscious that she was chattering ineffectively. But suddenly it occurred to him that, with her pretty professions, there was a way of making her effective; she might help him to get at the old woman and the marquis. 'They are coming back soon – your companions?' he said. 'You are waiting for them?'

'They will hear the mass out; there is nothing to keep them longer. Claire has refused to see them.'

'I want to speak to them,' said Newman; 'and you can help me, you can do me a favour. Delay your return for five minutes and give me a chance at them. I will wait for them here.'

Madame de Bellegarde clasped her hands with a tender grimace. 'My poor friend, what do you want to do to them? To beg them to come back to you? It will be wasted words. They will never come back!'

'I want to speak to them, all the same. Pray do what I ask you. Stay away and leave them to me for five minutes; you needn't be afraid; I shall not be violent; I am very quiet.'

'Yes, you look very quiet! If they had *le coeur tendre** you would move them. But they haven't! However, I will do better for you than what you propose. The understanding is not that I shall come back for them. I am going into the Parc Monceau with my little girl to give her a walk, and my mother-in-law, who comes so rarely into this quarter, is to profit by the same opportunity to take the air. We are to wait for her in the park, where my husband is to bring her to us. Follow me now; just within the gates I shall get out of my carriage. Sit down on a chair in some quiet corner and I will bring them near you. There's devotion for you! *Le reste vous regarde.'**

This proposal seemed to Newman extremely felicitous; it revived his drooping spirit, and he reflected that Madame Urbain was not such a goose as she seemed. He promised immediately to overtake her, and the carriage drove away.

The Parc Monceau is a very pretty piece of landscape-gardening, but Newman, passing into it, bestowed little attention upon its elegant vegetation, which was full of the freshness of spring. He found Madame de Bellegarde promptly, seated in one of the quiet corners of which she had spoken, while before her, in the alley, her little girl, attended by the footman and the lap-dog, walked up and down as if she were taking a lesson in deportment. Newman sat down beside the mamma, and she talked a great deal, apparently with the design of convincing him that – if he would only see it – poor dear Claire did not belong to the most fascinating type of woman. She was too tall and thin, too stiff and cold; her mouth was too wide and her nose too narrow. She had no dimples anywhere. And then she was eccentric, eccentric in cold blood; she was an Anglaise,* after all. Newman was very impatient; he was counting the minutes until his victims should reappear. He sat silent, leaning upon his cane, looking absently and insensibly at the little marquise. At length Madame de Bellegarde said she would walk toward the gate of the park and meet her companions; but before she went she dropped her eyes, and, after playing a moment with the lace of her sleeve, looked up again at Newman.

'Do you remember,' she asked, 'the promise you made me three weeks ago?' And then, as Newman, vainly consulting his memory, was obliged to confess that the promise had escaped it, she declared that he had made her, at the time, a very queer answer – an answer at which, viewing it in the light of the sequel, she had fair ground for taking offence. 'You promised to take me to Bullier's after your marriage. After your marriage – you made a great point of that. Three days after that your marriage was broken off. Do you know, when I heard the news, the first thing I said to myself? "Oh heaven, now he won't go with me to Bullier's!" And I really began to wonder if you had not been expecting the rupture.'

'Oh, my dear lady,' murmured Newman, looking down the path to see if the others were not coming.

'I shall be good-natured,' said Madame de Bellegarde. 'One must not ask too much of a gentleman who is in love with a cloistered nun. Besides, I can't go to Bullier's while we are in mourning. But I haven't given it up for that. The *partie** is arranged; I have my cavalier. Lord Deepmere, if you please! He has gone back to his dear Dublin; but a few months hence I am to name any evening and he will come over from Ireland on purpose. That's what I call gallantry!'

Shortly after this Madame de Bellegarde walked away with her little girl. Newman sat in his place; the time seemed terribly long. He felt how fiercely his quarter of an hour in the convent chapel had raked over the glowing coals of his resentment. Madame de Bellegarde kept him waiting, but she proved as good as her word. At last she reappeared at the end of the path, with her little girl and her footman; beside her slowly walked her husband, with his mother on his arm. They were a long time advancing, during which Newman sat unmoved. Tingling as he was with passion, it was extremely characteristic of him that he was able to moderate his expression of it, as he would have turned down a flaring gas-burner. His native coolness, shrewdness, and deliberateness, his life-long submissiveness to the sentiment that words were acts and acts were steps in life, and that in this matter of taking steps curveting and prancing were exclusively reserved for quadrupeds and foreigners – all this admonished him that rightful wrath had no connection with being a fool and indulging in spectacular violence. So as he rose, when old Madame de Bellegarde and her son were close to him, he only felt very tall and light. He had been sitting beside some shrubbery, in such a way as not to be noticeable at a distance; but M. de Bellegarde had evidently already perceived him. His mother and he were holding their course, but Newman stepped in front of them, and they were obliged to pause. He lifted his hat slightly, and looked at them for a moment; they were pale with amazement and disgust.

'Excuse me for stopping you,' he said in a low tone, 'but I must profit by the occasion. I have ten words to say to you. Will you listen to them?'

The marquis glared at him and then turned to his mother. 'Can Mr Newman possibly have anything to say that is worth our listening to?'

'I assure you I have something,' said Newman; 'besides, it is my duty to say it. It's a notification – a warning.'

'Your duty?' said old Madame de Bellegarde, her thin lips curving like scorched paper. 'That is your affair, not ours.'

Madame Urbain meanwhile had seized her little girl by the hand, with a gesture of surprise and impatience which struck Newman, intent as he was upon his own words, with its dramatic effectiveness. 'If Mr Newman is going to make a scene in public,' she exclaimed, 'I will take my poor child out of the *mêlée*.* She is too young to see such naughtiness!' and she instantly resumed her walk.

'You had much better listen to me,' Newman went on. 'Whether you do or not, things will be disagreeable for you; but at any rate you will be prepared.'

'We have already heard something of your threats,' said the marquis, 'and you know what we think of them.'

'You think a good deal more than you admit. A moment,' Newman added in reply to an exclamation of the old lady. 'I remember perfectly that we are in a public place, and you see I am very quiet. I am not going to tell your secret to the passers-by; I shall keep it, to begin with, for certain picked listeners. Anyone who observes us will think that we are having a friendly chat, and that I am complimenting you, madam, on your venerable virtues.'

The marquis gave three short sharp raps on the ground with his stick. 'I demand of you to step out of our path!' he hissed.

Newman instantly complied, and M. de Bellegarde stepped forward with his mother. Then Newman said: 'Half an hour hence Madame de Bellegarde will regret that she didn't learn exactly what I mean.'

The marquise had taken a few steps, but at these words she paused, looking at Newman with eyes like two scintillating globules of ice. 'You are like a peddler with something to sell,' she said, with a little cold laugh which only partially concealed the tremor in her voice.

'Oh no, not to sell,' Newman rejoined; 'I give it to you for nothing.' And he approached nearer to her, looking her straight in the eyes. 'You killed your husband,' he said, almost in a whisper. 'That is, you tried once and failed, and then, without trying, you succeeded.'

Madame de Bellegarde closed her eyes and gave a little cough, which, as a piece of dissimulation, struck Newman as really heroic. 'Dear mother,' said the marquis, 'does this stuff amuse you so much?'

'The rest is more amusing,' said Newman. 'You had better not lose it.'

Madame de Bellegarde opened her eyes; the scintillations had gone out of them; they were fixed and dead. But she smiled superbly with her narrow little lips, and repeated Newman's word. 'Amusing? Have I killed someone else?'

'I don't count your daughter,' said Newman, 'though I might! Your husband knew what you were doing. I have a proof of it,

whose existence you have never suspected.' And he turned to
the marquis, who was terribly white – whiter than Newman had
ever seen anyone out of a picture. 'A paper written by the hand,
and signed with the name of Henri-Urbain de Bellegarde.
Written after you, madam, had left him for dead, and while you,
sir, had gone – not very fast – for the doctor.'

The marquis looked at his mother; she turned away, looking
vaguely round her. 'I must sit down,' she said in a low tone,
going toward the bench on which Newman had been sitting.

'Couldn't you have spoken to me alone?' said the marquis to
Newman, with a strange look.

'Well, yes, if I could have been sure of speaking to your
mother alone, too,' Newman answered. 'But I have had to take
you as I could get you.'

Madame de Bellegarde, with a movement very eloquent of
what he would have called her 'grit', her steel-cold pluck and
her instinctive appeal to her own personal resources, drew her
hand out of her son's arm and went and seated herself upon the
bench. There she remained, with her hands folded in her lap,
looking straight at Newman. The expression of her face was
such that he fancied at first that she was smiling; but he went
and stood in front of her, and saw that her elegant features were
distorted by agitation. He saw, however, equally, that she was
resisting her agitation with all the rigour of her inflexible will,
and there was nothing like either fear or submission in her stony
stare. She had been startled, but she was not terrified. Newman
had an exasperating feeling that she would get the better of him
still; he would not have believed it possible that he could so
utterly fail to be touched by the sight of a woman (criminal or
other) in so tight a place. Madame de Bellegarde gave a glance
at her son which seemed tantamount to an injunction to be
silent and leave her to her own devices. The marquis stood
beside her, with his hands behind him, looking at Newman.

'What paper is this you speak of?' asked the old lady, with an
imitation of tranquillity which would have been applauded in a
veteran actress.

'Exactly what I have told you,' said Newman. 'A paper
written by your husband after you had left him for dead, and
during the couple of hours before you returned. You see he had
the time; you shouldn't have stayed away so long. It declares
distinctly his wife's murderous intent.'

'I should like to see it,' Madame de Bellegarde observed.

'I thought you might,' said Newman, 'and I have taken a copy.' And he drew from his waistcoat-pocket a small folded sheet.

'Give it to my son,' said Madame de Bellegarde. Newman handed it to the marquis, whose mother, glancing at him, said simply, 'Look at it.' M. de Bellegarde's eyes had a pale eagerness which it was useless for him to try to dissimulate; he took the paper in his light-gloved fingers and opened it. There was a silence, during which he read it. He had more than time to read it, but still he said nothing; he stood staring at it. 'Where is the original?' asked Madame de Bellegarde, in a voice which was really a consummate negation of impatience.

'In a very safe place. Of course I can't show you that,' said Newman. 'You might want to take hold of it,' he added with conscious quaintness. 'But that's a very correct copy – except, of course, the handwriting. I am keeping the original to show someone else.'

M. de Bellegarde at last looked up, and his eyes were still very eager. 'To whom do you mean to show it?'

'Well, I'm thinking of beginning with the duchess,' said Newman; 'that stout lady I saw at your ball. She asked me to come and see her, you know. I thought at the moment I shouldn't have much to say to her; but my little document will give us something to talk about.'

'You had better keep it, my son,' said Madame de Bellegarde.

'By all means,' said Newman; 'keep it and show it to your mother when you get home.'

'And after showing it to the duchess?' asked the marquis, folding the paper and putting it away.

'Well, I'll take up the dukes,' said Newman. 'Then the counts and the barons – all the people you had the cruelty to introduce me to in a character of which you meant immediately to deprive me. I have made out a list.'

For a moment neither Madame de Bellegarde nor her son said a word; the old lady sat with her eyes upon the ground; M. de Bellegarde's blanched pupils were fixed upon her face. Then, looking at Newman, 'Is that all you have to say?' she asked.

'No, I want to say a few words more. I want to say that I hope you quite understand what I'm about. This is my revenge, you know. You have treated me before the world – convened for the express purpose – as if I were not good enough for you. I mean to show the world that however bad I may be, you are not quite the people to say it.'

Madame de Bellegarde was silent again, and then she broke her silence. Her self-possession continued to be extraordinary. 'I needn't ask you who has been your accomplice. Mrs Bread told me that you had purchased her services.'

'Don't accuse Mrs Bread of venality,' said Newman. 'She has kept your secret all these years. She has given you a long respite. It was beneath her eyes your husband wrote that paper; he put it into her hands with a solemn injunction that she was to make it public. She was too good-hearted to make use of it.'

The old lady appeared for an instant to hesitate, and then, 'She was my husband's mistress,' she said softly. This was the only concession to self-defence that she condescended to make.

'I doubt that,' said Newman.

Madame de Bellegarde got up from her bench. 'It was not to your opinions I undertook to listen, and if you have nothing left but them to tell me I think this remarkable interview may terminate.' And turning to the marquis she took his arm again. 'My son,' she said, 'say something!'

M. de Bellegarde looked down at his mother, passing his hand over his forehead, and then, tenderly, caressingly, 'What shall I say?' he asked.

'There is only one thing to say,' said the marquise. 'That it was really not worthwhile to have interrupted our walk.'

But the marquis thought he could improve this. 'Your paper's a forgery,' he said to Newman.

Newman shook his head a little, with a tranquil smile. 'M. de Bellegarde,' he said, 'your mother does better. She has done better all along, from the first of my knowing you. You're a mighty plucky woman, madam,' he continued. 'It's a great pity you have made me your enemy. I should have been one of your greatest admirers.'

'*Mon pauvre ami*,'* said Madame de Bellegarde to her son in French, and as if she had not heard these words, 'you must take me immediately to my carriage.'

Newman stepped back and let them leave him; he watched them a moment and saw Madame Urbain, with her little girl, come out of a by-path to meet them. The old lady stooped and kissed her grandchild. 'Damn it, she *is* plucky!' said Newman, and he walked home with a slight sense of being balked. She was so inexpressively defiant! But on reflection he decided that what he had witnessed was no real sense of security, still less a real innocence. It was only a very superior style of brazen assurance. 'Wait till she reads the paper!' he said to himself; and he concluded that he should hear from her soon.

He heard sooner than he expected. The next morning, before midday, when he was about to give orders for his breakfast to be served, M. de Bellegarde's card was brought to him. 'She has read the paper and she has passed a bad night,' said Newman. He instantly admitted his visitor, who came in with the air of the ambassador of a great power meeting the delegate of a barbarous tribe whom an absurd accident had enabled for the moment to be abominably annoying. The ambassador, at all events, had passed a bad night, and his faultlessly careful toilet only threw into relief the frigid rancour in his eyes and the mottled tones of his refined complexion. He stood before Newman a moment, breathing quickly and softly, and shaking his forefinger curtly as his host pointed to a chair.

'What I have come to say is soon said,' he declared, 'and can only be said without ceremony.'

'I am good for as much or for as little as you desire,' said Newman.

The marquis looked round the room a moment, and then: 'On what terms will you part with your scrap of paper?'

'On none!' And while Newman, with his head on one side and his hands behind him sounded the marquis's turbid gaze with his own, he added: 'Certainly, that is not worth sitting down about.'

M. de Bellegarde meditated a moment, as if he had not heard Newman's refusal. 'My mother and I, last evening,' he said, 'talked over your story. You will be surprised to learn that we think your little document is – a' – and he held back his word a moment – 'is genuine.'

'You forget that with you I am used to surprises!' exclaimed Newman, with a laugh.

'The very smallest amount of respect that we owe to my father's memory,' the marquis continued, 'makes us desire that he should not be held up to the world as the author of so – so infernal an attack upon the reputation of a wife whose only fault was that she had been submissive to accumulated injury.'

'Oh, I see,' said Newman. 'It's for your father's sake.' And he laughed the laugh in which he indulged when he was most amused – a noiseless laugh, with his lips closed.

But M. de Bellegarde's gravity held good. 'There are a few of my father's particular friends for whom the knowledge of so – so unfortunate an – inspiration – would be a real grief. Even say we firmly established by medical evidence the presumption of a mind disordered by fever, *il en resterait quelque chose*.* At the best it would look ill in him. Very ill!'

'Don't try medical evidence,' said Newman. 'Don't touch the doctors and they won't touch you. I don't mind your knowing that I have not written to them.'

Newman fancied that he saw signs in M. de Bellegarde's discoloured mask that this information was extremely pertinent. But it may have been merely fancy; for the marquis remained majestically argumentative. 'For instance, Madame d'Outreville,' he said, 'of whom you spoke yesterday. I can imagine nothing that would shock her more.'

'Oh, I am quite prepared to shock Madame d'Outreville, you know. That's on the cards. I expect to shock a great many people.'

M. de Bellegarde examined for a moment the stitching on the back of one of his gloves. Then, without looking up, 'We don't offer you money,' he said. 'That we suppose to be useless.'

Newman, turning away, took a few turns about the room, and then came back. 'What *do* you offer me? By what I can make out, the generosity is all to be on my side.'

The marquis dropped his arms at his side and held his head a little higher. 'What we offer you is a chance – a chance that a gentleman should appreciate. A chance to abstain from inflicting a terrible blot upon the memory of a man who certainly had his faults, but who, personally, had done you no wrong.'

'There are two things to say to that,' said Newman. 'The first is, as regards appreciating your "chance", that you don't consider me a gentleman. That's your great point, you know. It's a poor rule that won't work both ways. The second is that – well, in a word, you are talking great nonsense!'

Newman, who in the midst of his bitterness had, as I have said, kept well before his eyes a certain ideal of saying nothing rude, was immediately somewhat regretfully conscious of the sharpness of these words. But he speedily observed that the marquis took them more quietly than might have been expected. M. de Bellegarde, like the stately ambassador that he was, continued the policy of ignoring what was disagreeable in his adversary's replies. He gazed at the gilded arabesques on the opposite wall, and then presently transferred his glance to Newman, as if he too were a large grotesque in a rather vulgar system of chamber-decoration. 'I suppose you know that as regards yourself, it won't do at all.'

'How do you mean it won't do?'

'Why, of course you damn yourself. But I suppose that's in your programme. You propose to throw mud at us; you believe, you hope, that some of it may stick. We know, of course, it can't,' explained the marquis in a tone of conscious lucidity; 'but you take the chance, and are willing at any rate to show that you yourself have dirty hands.'

'That's a good comparison; at least half of it is,' said Newman. 'I take the chance of something sticking. But as regards my hands, they are clean. I have taken the matter up with my finger-tips.'

M. de Bellegarde looked a moment into his hat. 'All our friends are quite with us,' he said. 'They would have done exactly as we have done.'

'I shall believe that when I hear them say it. Meanwhile I shall think better of human nature.'

The marquis looked into his hat again. 'Madame de Cintré was extremely fond of her father. If she knew of the existence of the few written words of which you propose to make this scandalous use, she would demand of you proudly for his sake to give it up to her, and she would destroy it without reading it.'

'Very possibly,' Newman rejoined. 'But she will not know. I was in that convent yesterday, and I know what *she* is doing. Lord deliver us! You can guess whether it made me feel forgiving!'

M. de Bellegarde appeared to have nothing more to suggest; but he continued to stand there, rigid and elegant, as a man who believed that his mere personal presence had an argumentative value. Newman watched him, and, without yielding an inch on the main issue, felt an incongruously good-natured impulse to help him to retreat in good order.

'Your visit's a failure, you see,' he said. 'You offer too little.'

'Propose something yourself,' said the marquis.

'Give me back Madame de Cintré in the same state in which you took her from me.'

M. de Bellegarde threw back his head and his pale face flushed. 'Never!' he said.

'You can't!'

'We wouldn't if we could! In the sentiment which led us to deprecate her marriage nothing is changed.'

'"Deprecate" is good!' cried Newman. 'It was hardly worthwhile to come here only to tell me that you are not ashamed of yourselves. I could have guessed that!'

The marquis slowly walked toward the door, and Newman, following, opened it for him. 'What you propose to do will be very disagreeable,' M. de Bellegarde said. 'That is very evident. But it will be nothing more.'

'As I understand it,' Newman answered, 'that will be quite enough!'

M. de Bellegarde stood a moment looking on the ground, as if he were ransacking his ingenuity to see what else he could do to save his father's reputation. Then, with a little cold sigh, he seemed to signify that he regretfully surrendered the late marquis to the penalty of his turpitude. He gave a hardly perceptible shrug, took his neat umbrella from the servant in the vestibule, and, with his gentlemanly walk, passed out. Newman stood listening till he heard the door close; then he slowly exclaimed: 'Well, I ought to begin to be satisfied now!'

CHAPTER 25

Newman called upon the comical duchess and found her at home. An old gentleman with a high nose and a gold-headed cane was just taking leave of her; he made Newman a protracted obeisance as he retired, and our hero supposed that he was one of the mysterious grandees with whom he had shaken hands at Madame de Bellegarde's ball. The duchess, in her arm-chair, from which she did not move, with a great flower-pot on one side of her, a pile of pink-covered novels* on the other, and a large piece of tapestry depending from her lap, presented an expansive and imposing front; but her aspect was in the highest degree gracious, and there was nothing in her manner to check the effusion of his confidence. She talked to him about flowers and books, getting launched with marvellous promptitude; about the theatres, about the peculiar institutions of his native country, about the humidity of Paris, about the pretty complexions of the American ladies, about his impressions of France and his opinion of its female inhabitants. All this was a brilliant monologue on the part of the duchess, who, like many of her countrywomen, was a person of an affirmative rather than an interrogative cast of mind, who made *mots* and put them herself into circulation, and who was apt to offer you a present of a convenient little opinion, neatly enveloped in the gilt paper of a happy Gallicism. Newman had come to her with a grievance, but he found himself in an atmosphere in which apparently no cognisance was taken of grievances; an atmosphere into which the chill of discomfort had never penetrated, and which seemed exclusively made up of mild, sweet, stale intellectual perfumes. The feeling with which he had watched Madame d'Outreville at the treacherous festival of the Bellegardes came back to him; she struck him as a wonderful old lady in a comedy, particularly well up in her part. He observed before long that she asked him no questions about their common friends; she made no allusion to the circumstances under which he had been presented to her. She neither feigned ignorance of a change in these circumstances nor pretended to condole with him upon it; but she smiled and discoursed and compared the tender-tinted wools of her tapestry, as if the Bellegardes and their wickedness were not of this world. 'She is fighting shy!' said Newman to himself; and, having made the observation, he was prompted to observe, further, how the duchess would carry off her indifference. She did so in a masterly manner. There was not a gleam of disguised consciousness in those small, clear, demonstrative eyes which constituted her nearest claim to personal loveliness; there was not a symptom of apprehension that Newman would trench upon the ground she proposed to avoid. 'Upon my word, she does it very well,' he tacitly commented. 'They all hold together bravely, and, whether anyone else can trust them or not, they can certainly trust each other.'

Newman, at this juncture, fell to admiring the duchess for her fine manners. He felt, most accurately, that she was not a grain less urbane than she would have been if his marriage were still in prospect; but he felt also that she was not a particle more urbane. He had come, so reasoned the duchess – Heaven knew why he had come, after what had happened; and for the half hour, therefore, she would be *charmante*.* But she would never see him again. Finding no ready-made opportunity to tell his story, Newman pondered these things more dispassionately than might have been expected; he stretched his legs, as usual, and even chuckled a little, appreciatively and noiselessly. And then as the duchess went on relating a *mot* with which her mother had snubbed the great Napoleon, it occurred to Newman that her evasion of a chapter of French history more interesting to himself might possibly be the result of an extreme consideration for his feelings. Perhaps it was delicacy on the duchess's part – not policy. He was on the point of saying something himself, to make the chance which he had determined to give her still better, when the servant announced another visitor. The duchess, on hearing the name – it was that of an Italian prince – gave a little imperceptible pout, and said to Newman, rapidly: 'I beg you to remain; I desire this visit to be short.' Newman said to himself, at this, that Madame d'Outreville intended, after all, that they should discuss the Bellegardes together.

The prince was a short stout man, with a head disproportionately large. He had a dusky complexion and a bushy eyebrow, beneath which his eye wore a fixed and somewhat defiant expression; he seemed to be challenging you to insinuate that he was top-heavy. The duchess, judging from her charge to Newman, regarded him as a bore; but this was not apparent from the unchecked flow of her conversation. She made a fresh series of *mots*,* characterised with great felicity the Italian intellect and the taste of the figs at Sorrento, predicted the ultimate future of the Italian kingdom (disgust with the brutal Sardinian rule and complete reversion, throughout the peninsula, to the sacred sway of the Holy Father), and, finally, gave a history of the love affairs of the Princess X——. This narrative provoked some rectifications on the part of the prince, who, as he said, pretended to know something about that matter; and having satisfied himself that Newman was in no laughing mood, either with regard to the size of his head or anything else, he entered into the controversy with an animation for which the duchess, when she set him down as a bore, could not have been

prepared. The sentimental vicissitudes of the Princess X— led
to a discussion of the heart-history* of Florentine nobility in
general; the duchess had spent five weeks in Florence and had
gathered much information on the subject. This was merged, in
turn, in an examination of the Italian heart *per se*. The duchess
took a brilliantly heterodox view – thought it the least suscep-
tible organ of its kind that she had ever encountered, related
examples of its want of susceptibility, and at last declared that
for her the Italians were a people of ice. The prince became
flame to refute her, and his visit really proved charming.
Newman was naturally out of the conversation; he sat with his
head a little on one side watching the interlocutors. The duchess,
as she talked, frequently looked at him with a smile, as if to
intimate, in the charming manner of her nation, that it lay only
with him to say something very much to the point. But he said
nothing at all, and at last his thoughts began to wander. A
singular feeling came over him – a sudden sense of the folly of
his errand. What under the sun had he to say to the duchess,
after all? Wherein would it profit him to tell her that the
Bellegardes were traitors and that the old lady, into the bargain,
was a murderess? He seemed morally to have turned a sort of
somersault, and to find things looking differently in consequence. He felt a sudden stiffening of his will and quickening of
his reserve. What in the world had he been thinking of when he
fancied the duchess could help him, and that it would conduce
to his comfort to make her think ill of the Bellegardes? What
did her opinion of the Bellegardes matter to him! It was only a
shade more important than the opinion the Bellegardes entertained of her. The duchess help him – that cold, stout, soft,
artificial woman help him? – she who in the last twenty minutes
had built up between them a wall of polite conversation in
which she evidently flattered herself that he would never find a
gate. Had it come to that – that he was asking favours of
conceited people, and appealing for sympathy where he had no
sympathy to give? He rested his arms on his knees, and sat for
some minutes staring into his hat. As he did so his ears tingled –
he had come very near being an ass. Whether or no the duchess
would hear his story, he wouldn't tell it. Was he to sit there
another half hour for the sake of exposing the Bellegardes? The
Bellegardes be hanged! He got up abruptly, and advanced to
shake hands with his hostess.

'You can't stay longer?' she asked very graciously.

'I am afraid not,' he said.

She hesitated a moment, and then, 'I had an idea you had something particular to say to me,' she declared.

Newman looked at her; he felt a little dizzy; for the moment he seemed to be turning his somersault again. The little Italian prince came to his help: 'Ah, madam, who has not that?' he softly sighed.

'Don't teach Mr Newman to say *fadaises*,'* said the duchess. 'It is his merit that he doesn't know how.'

'Yes, I don't know how to say *fadaises*,' said Newman, 'and I don't want to say anything unpleasant.'

'I am sure you are very considerate,' said the duchess with a smile; and she gave him a little nod for good-bye, with which he took his departure.

Once in the street, he stood for some time on the pavement, wondering whether, after all, he was not an ass not to have discharged his pistol. And then he decided that to talk to anyone whomsoever about the Bellegardes would be extremely disagreeable to him. The least disagreeable thing, under the circumstances, was to banish them from his mind, and never think of them again. Indecision had not hitherto been one of Newman's weaknesses, and in this case it was not of long duration. For three days after this he did not, or at least he tried not to, think of the Bellegardes. He dined with Mrs Tristram, and on her mentioning their name, he begged her almost severely to desist. This gave Tom Tristram a much-coveted opportunity to offer his condolences.

He leaned forward, laying his hand on Newman's arm, compressing his lips, and shaking his head. 'The fact is, my dear fellow, you see, that you ought never to have gone into it. It was not your doing, I know – it was all my wife. If you want to come down on her, I'll stand off: I give you leave to hit her as hard as you like. You know she has never had a word of reproach from me in her life, and I think she is in need of something of the kind. Why didn't you listen to *me*? You know I didn't believe in the thing. I thought it at the best an amiable delusion. I don't profess to be a Don Juan or a gay Lothario* – that class of man, you know; but I do pretend to know something about the harder sex. I have never disliked a woman in my life that she has not turned out badly. I was not at all deceived in Lizzie, for instance; I always had my doubts about her. Whatever you may think of my present situation, I must at least admit that I got into it with my eyes open. Now suppose you had got into something like this box with Madame de Cintré. You may depend upon it she would have turned out a stiff one. And upon my word I don't see where you could have found your comfort. Not from the marquis, my dear Newman; he wasn't a man you could go and talk things over with in a sociable, common-sense way. Did he ever seem to want to have you on the premises – did he ever try to see you alone? Did he ever ask you to come and smoke a cigar with him of an evening, or step in, when you had been calling on the ladies, and take something? I don't think you would have got much encouragement out of *him*. And as for the old lady, she struck one as an uncommonly strong dose. They have a great expression here, you know; they call it "sympathetic". Every-thing is sympathetic – or ought to be. Now Madame de Bellegarde is about as sympathetic as that mustard-pot. They're a d——d cold-blooded lot, anyway; I felt it awfully at that ball of theirs. I felt as if I were walking up and down in the Armoury, in the Tower of London! My dear boy, don't think me a vulgar brute for hinting at it, but you may depend upon it, all they wanted was your money. I know something about that; I can tell when people want one's money! Why they stopped wanting yours I don't know; I suppose because they could get someone else's without working so hard for it. It isn't worth finding out. It may be that it was not Madame de Cintré that backed out first; very likely the old woman put her up to it. I suspect she and her mother are really as thick as thieves, eh? You are well out of it, my boy; make up your mind to that. If I express myself strongly it is all because I love you so much; and from that point of view I may say I should as soon have thought of making up to that piece of pale high-mightiness as I should have thought of making up to the Obelisk in the Place de la Concorde.'*

Newman sat gazing at Tristram during this harangue with a lack-lustre eye; never yet had he seemed to himself to have outgrown so completely the phase of equal comradeship with Tom Tristram. Mrs Tristram's glance at her husband had more of a spark; she turned to Newman with a slightly lurid smile. 'You must at least do justice,' she said, 'to the felicity with which Mr Tristram repairs the indiscretions of a too zealous wife.'

But even without the aid of Tom Tristram's conversational felicities, Newman would have begun to think of the Bellegardes again. He could cease to think of them only when he ceased to think of his loss and privation, and the days had as yet but scantily lightened the weight of this incommodity. In vain Mrs Tristram begged him to cheer up; she assured him that the sight of his countenance made her miserable.

'How can I help it?' he demanded with a trembling voice. 'I feel like a widower – and a widower who has not even the consolation of going to stand beside the grave of his wife – who has not the right to wear so much mourning as a weed* on his hat. I feel,' he added in a moment, 'as if my wife had been murdered and her assassins were still at large.'

Mrs Tristram made no immediate rejoinder, but at last she said, with a smile which, in so far as it was a forced one, was less successfully simulated than such smiles, on her lips, usually were: 'Are you very sure that you would have been happy?'

Newman stared a moment, and then shook his head. 'That's weak,' he said; 'that won't do.'

'Well,' said Mrs Tristram with a more triumphant bravery, 'I don't believe you would have been happy.'

Newman gave a little laugh. 'Say I should have been miserable, then; it's a misery I should have preferred to any happiness.'

Mrs Tristram began to muse. 'I should have been curious to see; it would have been very strange.'

'Was it from curiosity that you urged me to try and marry her?'

'A little,' said Mrs Tristram, growing still more audacious. Newman gave her the one angry look he had been destined ever to give her, turned away and took up his hat. She watched him a moment, and then she said, 'That sounds very cruel, but it is less so than it sounds. Curiosity has a share in almost everything I do. I wanted very much to see, first, whether such a marriage could actually take place; second, what would happen if it should take place.'

'So you didn't believe,' said Newman, resentfully.

'Yes, I believed – I believed that it would take place, and that you would be happy. Otherwise I should have been, among my speculations, a very heartless creature. *But*,' she continued, laying her hand upon Newman's arm and hazarding a grave smile, 'it was the highest flight ever taken by a tolerably bold imagination!'

Shortly after this she recommended him to leave Paris and travel for three months. Change of scene would do him good, and he would forget his misfortune sooner in absence from the objects which had witnessed it. 'I really feel,' Newman rejoined, 'as if to leave *you*, at least, would do me good – and cost me very little effort. You are growing cynical; you shock me and pain me.'

'Very good,' said Mrs Tristram, good-naturedly or cynically, as may be thought most probable. 'I shall certainly see you again.'

Newman was very willing to get away from Paris; the brilliant streets he had walked through in his happier hours, and which then seemed to wear a higher brilliancy in honour of his happiness, appeared now to be in the secret of his defeat and to look down upon it in shining mockery. He would go somewhere; he cared little where; and he made his preparations. Then, one morning, at haphazard, he drove to the train that would transport him to Boulogne* and despatch him thence to the shores of Britain. As he rolled along in the train he asked himself what had become of his revenge, and he was able to say that it was provisionally pigeon-holed in a very safe place; it would keep till called for.

He arrived in London in the midst of what is called 'the season', and it seemed to him at first that he might here put himself in the way of being diverted from his heavy-heartedness. He knew no one in all England, but the spectacle of the mighty metropolis roused him somewhat from his apathy. Anything that was enormous usually found favour with Newman, and the multitudinous energies and industries of England stirred within him a dull vivacity of contemplation. It is on record that the weather, at that moment, was of the finest English quality; he took long walks and explored London in every direction; he sat by the hour in Kensington Gardens and beside the adjoining Drive, watching the people and the horses and the carriages; the rosy English beauties, the wonderful English dandies, and the splendid flunkies.* He went to the opera and found it better than in Paris; he went to the theatre and found a surprising charm in listening to dialogue the finest points of which came within the range of his comprehension. He made several excursions into the country, recommended by the waiter at his hotel, with whom, on this and similar points, he had established confidential relations. He watched the deer in Windsor Forest and admired the Thames from Richmond Hill; he ate whitebait and brown-bread and butter at Greenwich, and strolled in the grassy shadow of the cathedral of Canterbury. He also visited the Tower of London and Madame Tussaud's exhibition. One day he thought he would go to Sheffield, and then, thinking again, he gave it up. Why should he go to Sheffield? He had a feeling that the link which bound him to a possible interest in the manufacture of cutlery was broken. He had no desire for an 'inside view' of any successful enterprise whatever, and he would not have given the smallest sum for the privilege of talking over the details of the most 'splendid' business with the shrewdest of overseers.

One afternoon he had walked into Hyde Park, and was slowly threading his way through the human maze which edges the Drive. The stream of carriages was no less dense, and Newman, as usual, marvelled at the strange dingy figures which he saw taking the air in some of the stateliest vehicles. They reminded him of what he had read of eastern and southern countries, in which grotesque idols and fetiches were sometimes taken out of their temples and carried abroad in golden chariots to be displayed to the multitude. He saw a great many pretty cheeks beneath high-plumed hats as he squeezed his way through serried waves of crumpled muslin; and sitting on little chairs at the base of the great serious English trees, he observed a number of quiet-eyed maidens, who seemed only to remind him afresh that the magic of beauty had gone out of the world with Madame de Cintré: to say nothing of other damsels, whose eyes were not quiet, and who struck him still more as a satire on possible consolation. He had been walking for some time, when, directly in front of him, borne back by the summer breeze, he heard a few words uttered in that bright Parisian idiom from which his ears had begun to alienate themselves. The voice in which the words were spoken made them seem even more like a thing with which he had once been familiar, and as he bent his eyes it lent an identity to the commonplace elegance of the back hair and shoulders of a young lady walking in the same direction

as himself. Mademoiselle Nioche, apparently, had come to seek
a more rapid advancement in London, and another glance led
Newman to suppose that she had found it. A gentleman was
strolling beside her, lending a most attentive ear to her conversation and too entranced to open his lips. Newman did not hear
his voice, but perceived that he presented the dorsal expression
of a well-dressed Englishman. Mademoiselle Nioche was attract-
ing attention: the ladies who passed her turned round to survey
the Parisian perfection of her toilet. A great cataract of flounces
rolled down from the young lady's waist to Newman's feet; he
had to step aside to avoid treading upon them. He stepped aside,
indeed, with a decision of movement which the occasion scarcely
demanded; for even this imperfect glimpse of Miss Noémie had
excited his displeasure. She seemed an odious blot upon the face
of nature; he wanted to put her out of his sight. He thought of
Valentin de Bellegarde, still green in the earth of his burial – his
young life clipped by this flourishing impudence. The perfume
of the young lady's finery sickened him; he turned his head and
tried to deflect his course; but the pressure of the crowd kept
him near her a few minutes longer, so that he heard what she
was saying.

'Ah, I'm sure he will miss me,' she murmured. 'It was very
cruel in me to leave him; I am afraid you will think me a very
heartless creature. He might perfectly well have come with us. I
don't think he is very well,' she added; 'it seemed to me today
that he was not very gay.'

Newman wondered whom she was talking about, but just
then an opening among his neighbours enabled him to turn
away, and he said to himself that she was probably paying a
tribute to British propriety and playing at tender solicitude
about her papa. Was that miserable old man still treading the
path of vice in her train? Was he still giving her the benefit of
his experience of affairs, and had he crossed the sea to serve as
her interpreter? Newman walked some distance farther, and
then began to retrace his steps, taking care not to traverse again
the orbit of Mademoiselle Nioche. At last he looked for a chair
under the trees, but he had some difficulty in finding an empty
one. He was about to give up the search when he saw a
gentleman rise from the seat he had been occupying, leaving
Newman to take it without looking at his neighbours. He sat
there for some time without heeding them; his attention was lost

in the irritation and bitterness produced by his recent glimpse of Miss Noémie's iniquitous vitality. But at the end of a quarter of an hour, dropping his eyes, he perceived a small pug-dog squatted upon the path near his feet – a diminutive but very perfect specimen of its interesting species. The pug was sniffing at the fashionable world, as it passed him, with his little black muzzle, and was kept from extending his investigation by a large blue ribbon attached to his collar with an enormous rosette, and held in the hand of a person seated next to Newman. To this person Newman transferred his attention, and immediately perceived that he was the object of all that of his neighbour, who was staring up at him from a pair of little fixed white eyes. These eyes Newman instantly recognised; he had been sitting for the last quarter of an hour beside M. Nioche. He had vaguely felt that someone was staring at him. M. Nioche continued to stare; he appeared afraid to move, even to the extent of evading Newman's glance.

'Dear me!' said Newman; 'are you here, too?' And he looked at his neighbour's helplessness more grimly than he knew. M. Nioche had a new hat and a pair of kid gloves; his clothes, too, seemed to belong to a more recent antiquity than of yore. Over his arm was suspended a lady's mantilla – a light and brilliant tissue, fringed with white lace – which had apparently been committed to his keeping; and the little dog's blue ribbon was wound tightly round his hand. There was no expression of recognition in his face – or of anything indeed save a sort of feeble fascinated dread. Newman looked at the pug and the lace mantilla, and then he met the old man's eyes again. 'You know me, I see,' he pursued. 'You might have spoken to me before.' M. Nioche still said nothing, but it seemed to Newman that his eyes began faintly to water. 'I didn't expect,' our hero went on, 'to meet you so far from – from the Café de la Patrie.' The old man remained silent, but decidedly Newman had touched the source of tears. His neighbour sat staring, and Newman added: 'What's the matter, M. Nioche? You used to talk – to talk very prettily. Don't you remember you even gave lessons in conversation?'

At this M. Nioche decided to change his attitude. He stooped and picked up the pug, lifted it to his face and wiped his eyes on its little soft back. 'I am afraid to speak to you,' he presently said, looking over the puppy's shoulder. 'I hoped you wouldn't notice me. I should have moved away, but I was afraid that if I moved you would notice me. So I sat very still.'

'I suspect you have a bad conscience, sir,' said Newman.

The old man put down the little dog and held it carefully in his lap. Then he shook his head, with his eyes still fixed upon his interlocutor. 'No, Mr Newman, I have a good conscience,' he murmured.

'Then why should you want to slink away from me?'

'Because – because you don't understand my position.'

'Oh, I think you once explained it to me,' said Newman. 'But it seems improved.'

'Improved!' exclaimed M. Nioche, under his breath. 'Do you call this improvement?' And he glanced at the treasures in his arms.

'Why, you are on your travels,' Newman rejoined. 'A visit to London in the season is certainly a sign of prosperity.'

M. Nioche, in answer to this cruel piece of irony, lifted the puppy up to his face again, peering at Newman with his small blank eye-holes. There was something almost imbecile in the movement, and Newman hardly knew whether he was taking refuge in a convenient affectation of unreason, or whether he had in fact paid for his dishonour by the loss of his wits. In the latter case, just now, he felt little more tenderly to the foolish old man than in the former. Responsible or not, he was equally an accomplice of his detestably mischievous daughter. Newman was going to leave him abruptly, when a ray of entreaty appeared to disengage itself from the old man's misty gaze. 'Are you going away?' he asked.

'Do you want me to stay?' said Newman.

'I should have left you – from consideration. But my dignity suffers at your leaving me – that way.'

'Have you got anything particular to say to me?'

M. Nioche looked round him to see that no one was listening, and then he said, very softly but distinctly, 'I have *not* forgiven her!'

Newman gave a short laugh, but the old man seemed for the moment not to perceive it; he was gazing away, absently, at some metaphysical image of his implacability. 'It doesn't much matter whether you forgive her or not,' said Newman. 'There are other people who won't, I assure you.'

'What has she done?' M. Nioche softly questioned, turning round again. 'I don't know what she does, you know.'

'She has done a devilish mischief; it doesn't matter what,' said Newman. 'She's a nuisance; she ought to be stopped.'

M. Nioche stealthily put out his hand and laid it very gently upon Newman's arm. 'Stopped, yes,' he whispered. 'That's it. Stopped short. She is running away – she must be stopped.' Then he paused a moment and looked round him. 'I mean to stop her,' he went on. 'I am only waiting for my chance.'

'I see,' said Newman, laughing briefly again. 'She is running away and you are running after her. You have run a long distance!'

But M. Nioche stared insistently: 'I shall stop her!' he softly repeated.

He had hardly spoken when the crowd in front of them separated, as if by the impulse to make way for an important personage. Presently, through the opening, advanced Mademoiselle Nioche, attended by the gentleman whom Newman had lately observed. His face being now presented to our hero, the latter recognised the irregular features, the hardly more regular complexion, and the amiable expression of Lord Deepmere. Noémie, on finding herself suddenly confronted with Newman, who, like M. Nioche, had risen from his seat, faltered for a barely perceptible instant. She gave him a little nod, as if she had seen him yesterday, and then, with a good-natured smile, '*Tiens*,* how we keep meeting!' she said. She looked consummately pretty, and the front of her dress was a wonderful work of art. She went up to her father, stretching out her hands for the little dog, which he submissively placed in them, and she began to kiss it and murmur over it: 'To think of leaving him all alone – what a wicked, abominable creature he must believe me! He has been very unwell,' she added, turning and affecting to explain to Newman, with a spark of infernal impudence, fine as a needle-point, in her eye. 'I don't think the English climate agrees with him.'

'It seems to agree wonderfully well with his mistress,' said Newman.

'Do you mean me? I have never been better, thank you,' Miss Noémie declared. 'But with *milord*,' and she gave a brilliant glance at her late companion, 'how can one help being well?'

She seated herself in the chair from which her father had risen, and began to arrange the little dog's rosette.

Lord Deepmere carried off such embarrassment as might be incidental to this unexpected encounter with the inferior grace of a male and a Briton. He blushed a good deal, and greeted the object of his late momentary aspiration to rivalry in the favour of a person other than the mistress of the invalid pug with an awkward nod and a rapid ejaculation – an ejaculation to which Newman, who often found it hard to understand the speech of English people, was able to attach no meaning. Then the young man stood there, with his hand on his hip, and with a conscious grin, staring askance at Miss Noémie. Suddenly an idea seemed to strike him, and he said, turning to Newman, 'Oh, you know her?'

'Yes,' said Newman, 'I know her. I don't believe you do.'

'Oh dear, yes, I do!' said Lord Deepmere, with another grin. 'I knew her in Paris – by my poor cousin Bellegarde, you know. He knew her, poor fellow, didn't he? It was she, you know, who was at the bottom of his affair. Awfully sad, wasn't it?' continued the young man, talking off his embarrassment as his simple nature permitted. 'They got up some story about its being for the Pope; about the other man having said something against the Pope's morals. They always do that, you know. They put it on the Pope because Bellegarde was once in the Zouaves. But it was about *her* morals – *she* was the Pope!' Lord Deepmere pursued, directing an eye illumined by this pleasantry toward Mademoiselle Nioche, who was bending gracefully over her lap-dog, apparently absorbed in conversation with it. 'I daresay you think it rather odd that I should – ah – keep up the acquaintance,' the young man resumed; 'but she couldn't help it, you know, and Bellegarde was only my twentieth cousin. I daresay you think it's rather cheeky, my showing with her in Hyde Park; but you see she isn't known yet, and she's in such very good form – ' And Lord Deepmere's conclusion was lost in the attesting glance which he again directed toward the young lady.

Newman turned away; he was having more of her than he relished. M. Nioche had stepped aside on his daughter's approach, and he stood there, within a very small compass, looking down hard at the ground. It had never yet, as between him and Newman, been so apposite to place on record the fact that he had not forgiven his daughter. As Newman was moving away he looked up and drew near to him, and Newman, seeing the old man had something particular to say, bent his head for an instant.

'You will see it some day in the papers,' murmured M. Nioche.

Our hero departed to hide his smile, and to this day, though the newspapers form his principal reading, his eyes have not been arrested by any paragraph forming a sequel to this announcement.

CHAPTER 26

In that uninitiated observation of the great spectacle of English life upon which I have touched, it might be supposed that Newman passed a great many dull days. But the dulness of his days pleased him; his melancholy, which was settling into a secondary stage, like a healing wound, had in it a certain acrid, palatable sweetness. He had company in his thoughts, and for the present he wanted no other. He had no desire to make acquaintances, and he left untouched a couple of notes of introduction which had been sent him by Tom Tristram. He thought a great deal of Madame de Cintré – sometimes with a dogged tranquillity which might have seemed, for a quarter of an hour at a time, a near neighbour to forgetfulness. He lived over again the happiest hours he had known – that silver chain of numbered days in which his afternoon visits, tending sensibly to the ideal result, had subtilised his good humour to a sort of spiritual intoxication. He came back to reality, after such reveries, with a somewhat muffled shock; he had begun to feel the need of accepting the unchangeable. At other times the reality became an infamy again and the unchangeable an imposture, and he gave himself up to his angry restlessness till he was weary. But on the whole he fell into a rather reflective mood. Without in the least intending it or knowing it, he attempted to read the moral of his strange misadventure. He asked himself, in his quieter hours, whether perhaps, after all, he *was* more commercial than was pleasant. We know that it was in obedience to a strong reaction against questions exclusively commercial that he had come out to pick up aesthetic entertainment in Europe; it may therefore be understood that he was able to conceive that a man might be too commercial. He was very willing to grant it, but the concession, as to his own case, was not made with any very oppressive sense of shame. If he had been too commercial, he was ready to forget it, for in being so he had done no man any wrong that might not be as easily forgotten. He reflected with sober placidity that at least there were no monuments of his 'meanness' scattered about the world. If there was any reason in the nature of things why his connection with business should have cast a shadow upon a connection – even a connection broken – with a woman justly proud, he was willing to sponge it out of his life forever. The thing seemed a possibility; he could not feel it, doubtless, as keenly as some people, and it hardly seemed worthwhile to flap his wings very hard to rise to the idea; but he could feel it enough to make any sacrifice that still remained to be made. As to what such sacrifice was now to be made to, here Newman stopped short before a blank wall over which there sometimes played a shadowy imagery. He had a fancy of carrying out his life as he would have directed it if Madame de Cintré had been left to him – of making it a religion to do nothing that she would have disliked. In this, certainly there was no sacrifice; but there was a pale, oblique ray of inspiration. It would be lonely entertainment – a good deal like a man talking to himself in the mirror for want of better company. Yet the idea yielded Newman several half hours' dumb exaltation as he sat, with his hands in his pockets and his legs stretched, over the relics of an expensively poor dinner, in the undying English twilight. If, however, his commercial imagination was dead, he felt no contempt for the surviving actualities begotten by it. He was glad he had been prosperous and had been a great man of business rather than a small one; he was extremely glad he was rich. He felt no impulse to sell all he had and give to the poor, or to retire into meditative economy and asceticism. He was glad he was rich and tolerably young; if it was possible to think too much about buying and selling, it was a gain to have a good slice of life left in which not to think about them. Come, what should he think about now? Again and again Newman could only think of one thing; his thoughts always came back to it, and as they did so, with an emotional rush which seemed physically to express itself in a sudden upward choking, he leaned forward – the waiter having left the room – and, resting his arms on the table, buried his troubled face.

He remained in England till midsummer, and spent a month in the country, wandering about among cathedrals, castles and ruins. Several times, taking a walk from his inn into meadows and parks, he stopped by a well-worn stile, looked across through the early evening at a grey church tower, with its dusky nimbus of thick-circling swallows, and remembered that this might have been part of the entertainment of his honeymoon. He had never been so much alone or indulged so little in accidental dialogue. The period of recreation appointed by Mrs Tristram had at last expired, and he asked himself what he should do now. Mrs Tristram had written to him, proposing to him that he should join her in the Pyrenees; but he was not in the humour to return to France. The simplest thing was to repair to Liverpool and embark on the first American steamer. Newman made his way to the great seaport and secured his berth; and the night before sailing he sat in his room at the hotel, staring down, vacantly and wearily, at an open portmanteau. A number of papers were lying upon it, which he had been meaning to look over; some of them might conveniently be destroyed. But at last he shuffled them roughly together, and pushed them into a corner of the valise; they were business papers, and he was in no humour for sifting them. Then he drew forth his pocket-book and took out a paper of smaller size than those he had dismissed. He did not unfold it; he simply sat looking at the back of it. If he had momentarily entertained the idea of destroying it, the idea quickly expired. What the paper suggested was the feeling that lay in his innermost heart and that no reviving cheerfulness could long quench – the feeling that after all and above all he was a good fellow wronged. With it came a hearty hope that the Bellegardes were enjoying their suspense as to what he would do yet. The more it was prolonged the more they would enjoy it! He had hung fire once, yes; perhaps, in his present queer state of mind, he might hang fire again. But he restored the little paper to his pocket-book very tenderly, and felt better for thinking of the suspense of the Bellegardes. He felt better every time he thought of it after that, as he sailed the summer seas. He landed in New York and

journeyed across the continent to San Francisco, and nothing
that he observed by the way contributed to mitigate his sense of
being a good fellow wronged.

He saw a great many other good fellows – his old friends –
but he told none of them of the trick that had been played him.
He said simply that the lady he was to have married had changed
her mind, and when he was asked if he had changed his own, he
said, 'Suppose we change the subject.' He told his friends that he
had brought home no 'new ideas' from Europe, and his conduct
probably struck them as an eloquent proof of failing invention.
He took no interest in chatting about his affairs and manifested
no desire to look over his accounts. He asked half-a-dozen
questions which, like those of an eminent physician inquiring for
particular symptoms, showed that he still knew what he was
talking about; but he made no comments and gave no directions.
He not only puzzled the gentlemen on the Stock Exchange, but
he was himself surprised at the extent of his indifference. As it
seemed only to increase, he made an effort to combat it; he tried
to interest himself and to take up his old occupations. But they
appeared unreal to him; do what he would he somehow could
not believe in them. Sometimes he began to fear that there was
something the matter with his head; that his brain, perhaps, had
softened, and that the end of his strong activities had come. This
idea came back to him with an exasperating force. A hopeless,
helpless loafer, useful to no one and detestable to himself – this
was what the treachery of the Bellegardes had made of him. In
his restless idleness he came back from San Francisco to New
York, and sat for three days in the lobby of his hotel, looking
out through a huge wall of plate-glass at the unceasing stream
of pretty girls in Parisian-looking dresses, undulating past with
little parcels nursed against their neat figures. At the end of three
days he returned to San Francisco, and having arrived there he
wished he had stayed away. He had nothing to do, his occupation was gone, and it seemed to him that he should never find it
again. He had nothing to do *here*, he sometimes said to himself;
but there was something beyond the ocean that he was still to
do; something that he had left undone experimentally and specu-
latively, to see if it could content itself to remain undone. But it
was not content: it kept pulling at his heart-strings and thumping
at his reason; it murmured in his ears and hovered perpetually
before his eyes. It interposed between all new resolutions and

their fulfilment; it seemed like a stubborn ghost, dumbly entreating to be laid. Till that was done he should never be able to do anything else.

One day, toward the end of the winter, after a long interval, he received a letter from Mrs Tristram, who apparently was animated by a charitable desire to amuse and distract her correspondent. She gave him much Paris gossip, talked of General Packard and Miss Kitty Upjohn, enumerated the new plays at the theatre, and enclosed a note from her husband, who had gone down to spend a month at Nice. Then came her signature, and after this her postscript. The latter consisted of these few lines: 'I heard three days since from my friend, the Abbé Aubert, that Madame de Cintré last week took the veil at the Carmelites. It was on her twenty-seventh birthday, and she took the name of her patroness, St Veronica.* Sister Veronica has a lifetime before her!'

This letter came to Newman in the morning; in the evening he started for Paris. His wound began to ache with its first fierceness, and during his long bleak journey the thought of Madame de Cintré's 'lifetime', passed within prison walls on whose outer side he might stand, kept him perpetual company. Now he would fix himself in Paris forever; he would extort a sort of happiness from the knowledge that if she was not there, at least the stony sepulchre that held her was. He descended, unannounced, upon Mrs Bread, whom he found keeping lonely watch in his great empty saloons on the Boulevard Haussmann. They were as neat as a Dutch village; Mrs Bread's only occupation had been removing individual dust-particles. She made no complaint, however, of her loneliness, for in her philosophy a servant was but a mysteriously projected machine, and it would be as fantastic for a housekeeper to comment upon a gentleman's absences as for a clock to remark upon not being wound up. No particular clock, Mrs Bread supposed, kept all the time, and no particular servant could enjoy all the sunshine diffused by the career of an exacting master. She ventured, nevertheless, to express a modest hope that Newman meant to remain awhile in Paris. Newman laid his hand on hers and shook it gently. 'I mean to remain forever,' he said.

He went after this to see Mrs Tristram, to whom he had telegraphed, and who expected him. She looked at him a moment and shook her head. 'This won't do,' she said; 'you have come back too soon.' He sat down and asked about her husband and her children, tried even to inquire about Miss Dora Finch. In the midst of this – 'Do you know where she is?' he asked, abruptly.

Mrs Tristram hesitated a moment; of course he couldn't mean Miss Dora Finch. Then she answered, properly: 'She has gone to the other house – in the Rue d'Enfer.' After Newman had sat awhile longer, looking very sombre, she went on: 'You are not so good a man as I thought. You are more – you are more – '

'More what?' Newman asked.

'More unforgiving.'

'Good God!' cried Newman; 'do you expect me to forgive?'

'No, not that. I have not forgiven, so of course you can't. But you might forget! You have a worse temper about it than I should have expected. You look wicked – you look dangerous.'

'I may be dangerous,' he said; 'but I am not wicked. No, I am not wicked.' And he got up to go. Mrs Tristram asked him to come back to dinner; but he answered that he did not feel like pledging himself to be present at an entertainment, even as a solitary guest. Later in the evening, if he should be able, he would come.

He walked away through the city, beside the Seine and over it, and took the direction of the Rue d'Enfer. The day had the softness of early spring; but the weather was grey and humid. Newman found himself in a part of Paris which he little knew – a region of convents and prisons, of streets bordered by long dead walls and traversed by few wayfarers. At the intersection of two of these streets stood the house of the Carmelites – a dull, plain edifice, with a high-shouldered blank wall all round it. From without Newman could see its upper windows, its steep roof and its chimneys. But these things revealed no symptoms of human life; the place looked dumb, deaf, inanimate. The pale, dead, discoloured wall stretched beneath it far down the empty side street – a vista without a human figure. Newman stood there a long time; there were no passers; he was free to gaze his fill. This seemed the goal of his journey; it was what he had come for. It was a strange satisfaction, and yet it was a satisfaction; the barren stillness of the place seemed to be his own release from ineffectual longing. It told him that the woman within was lost beyond recall, and that the days and years of the future would pile themselves above her like the huge immovable slab of a tomb. These days and years, in this place, would always be just so grey and silent. Suddenly, from the thought of their seeing him stand there, again the charm utterly departed. He would never stand there again; it was gratuitous dreariness. He turned away with a heavy heart, but with a heart lighter than the one he had brought.

Everything was over, and he too at last could rest. He walked down through narrow, winding streets to the edge of the Seine again, and there he saw, close above him, the soft, vast towers of Notre Dame. He crossed one of the bridges and stood a moment in the empty place before the great cathedral; then he went in beneath the grossly-imaged portals. He wandered some distance up the nave and sat down in the splendid dimness. He sat a long time; he heard far-away bells chiming off, at long intervals, to the rest of the world. He was very tired; this was the best place he could be in. He said no prayers; he had no prayers to say. He had nothing to be thankful for, and he had nothing to ask; nothing to ask, because now he must take care of himself. But a great cathedral offers a very various hospitality, and Newman sat in his place, because while he was there he was out of the world. The most unpleasant thing that had ever happened to him had reached its formal conclusion, as it were; he could close the book and put it away. He leaned his head for a long time on the chair in front of him; when he took it up he felt that he was himself again. Somewhere in his mind, a tight knot seemed to have loosened. He thought of the Bellegardes; he had almost forgotten them. He remembered them as people he had meant to do something to. He gave a groan as he remembered what he had meant to do; he was annoyed at having meant to do it; the bottom, suddenly, had fallen out of his revenge. Whether it was Christian charity or unregenerate good-nature – what it was, in the background of his soul – I don't pretend to say; but Newman's last thought was that of course he would let the Bellegardes go.

If he had spoken it aloud he would have said that he didn't want to hurt them. He was ashamed of having wanted to hurt them. They had hurt him, but such things were really not his game. At last he got up and came out of the darkening church; not with the elastic step of a man who has won a victory or taken a resolve, but strolling soberly, like a good-natured man who is still a little ashamed.

Going home, he said to Mrs Bread that he must trouble her
to put back his things into the portmanteau she had had
unpacked the evening before. His gentle stewardess looked at
him through eyes a trifle bedimmed. 'Dear me, sir,' she
exclaimed, 'I thought you said that you were going to stay
forever.'

'I meant that I was going to stay away forever,' said Newman
kindly. And since his departure from Paris on the following day
he has certainly not returned. The gilded apartments I have so
often spoken of stand ready to receive him; but they serve only
as a spacious residence for Mrs Bread, who wanders eternally
from room to room, adjusting the tassels of the curtains, and
keeps her wages, which are regularly brought her by a banker's
clerk, in a great pink Sèvres vase on the drawing-room
mantelshelf.

Late in the evening Newman went to Mrs Tristram's and
found Tom Tristram by the domestic fireside. 'I'm glad to see
you back in Paris,' this gentleman declared. 'You know it's
really the only place for a white man to live.' Mr Tristram made
his friend welcome, according to his own rosy light, and offered
him a convenient *résumé* of the Franco-American gossip of the
last six months. Then at last he got up and said he would go for
half an hour to the club. 'I suppose a man who has been for six
months in California wants a little intellectual conversation. I'll
let my wife have a go at you.'

Newman shook hands heartily with his host, but did not ask
him to remain; and then he relapsed into his place on the sofa,
opposite to Mrs Tristram. She presently asked him what he had
done after leaving her. 'Nothing particular,' said Newman.

'You struck me,' she rejoined, 'as a man with a plot in his
head. You looked as if you were bent on some sinister errand,
and after you had left me I wondered whether I ought to have
let you go.'

'I only went over to the other side of the river – to the
Carmelites,' said Newman.

Mrs Tristram looked at him a moment and smiled. 'What did
you do there? Try to scale the wall?'

'I did nothing. I looked at the place for a few minutes and
then came away.'

Mrs Tristram gave him a sympathetic glance. 'You didn't
happen to meet M. de Bellegarde,' she asked, 'staring hopelessly

at the convent-wall as well? I am told he takes his sister's conduct very hard.'

'No, I didn't meet him, I am happy to say,' Newman answered, after a pause.

'They are in the country,' Mrs Tristram went on; 'at – what is the name of the place? – Fleurières. They returned there at the time you left Paris and have been spending the year in extreme seclusion. The little marquise must enjoy it; I expect to hear that she has eloped with her daughter's music-master!'

Newman was looking at the light wood-fire; but he listened to this with extreme interest. At last he spoke: 'I mean never to mention the name of those people again, and I don't want to hear anything more about them.' And then he took out his pocket-book and drew forth a scrap of paper. He looked at it an instant, then got up and stood by the fire. 'I am going to burn them up,' he said. 'I am glad to have you as a witness. There they go!' And he tossed the paper into the flame.

Mrs Tristram sat with her embroidery-needle suspended. 'What is that paper?' she asked.

Newman, leaning against the fireplace, stretched his arms and drew a longer breath than usual. Then after a moment, 'I can tell you now,' he said. 'It was a paper containing a secret of the Bellegardes – something which would damn them if it were known.'

Mrs Tristram dropped her embroidery with a reproachful moan. 'Ah, why didn't you show it to me?'

'I thought of showing it to you – I thought of showing it to everyone. I thought of paying my debt to the Bellegardes that way. So I told them, and I frightened them. They have been staying in the country, as you tell me, to keep out of the explosion. But I have given it up.'

Mrs Tristram began to take slow stitches again. 'Have you quite given it up?'

'Oh yes.'

'Is it very bad, this secret?'

'Yes, very bad.'

'For myself,' said Mrs Tristram, 'I am sorry you have given it up. I should have liked immensely to see your paper. They have wronged me too, you know, as your sponsor and guarantee, and it would have served for my revenge as well. How did you come into possession of your secret?'

'It's a long story. But honestly, at any rate.'

'And they knew you were master of it?'

'Oh, I told them.'

'Dear me, how interesting!' cried Mrs Tristram. 'And you humbled them at your feet?'

Newman was silent a moment. 'No, not at all. They pretended not to care – not to be afraid. But I know they did care – they were afraid.'

'Are you very sure?'

Newman stared a moment. 'Yes, I'm sure.'

Mrs Tristram resumed her slow stitches. 'They defied you, eh?'

'Yes,' said Newman, 'it was about that.'

'You tried by the threat of exposure to make them retract?' Mrs Tristram pursued.

'Yes, but they wouldn't. I gave them their choice, and they chose to take their chance of bluffing off the charge and convicting me of fraud. But they *were* frightened,' Newman added, 'and I have had all the vengeance I want.'

'It is most provoking,' said Mrs Tristram, 'to hear you talk of the "charge" when the charge is burnt up. Is it quite consumed?' she asked, glancing at the fire.

Newman assured her that there was nothing left of it.

'Well then,' she said, 'I suppose there is no harm in saying that you probably did not make them so very uncomfortable. My impression would be that since, as you say, they defied you, it was because they believed that, after all, you would never really come to the point. Their confidence, after counsel taken of each other, was not in their innocence, nor in their talent for bluffing things off; it was in your remarkable good-nature! You see they were right.'

Newman instinctively turned to see if the little paper was in fact consumed; but there was nothing left of it.

NOTES

---

Chapter 1

p. 19 Salon Carré, in the Museum of the Louvre: the chief location assigned to the Italian school, including Leonardo da Vinci's *Mona Lisa*.

p. 19 Murillo's beautiful moon-borne Madonna: Bartolomé Esteban Murillo (1617–82) painted *The Immaculate Conception* (*c*. 1655). See Revelation 13:1. Newman commissions Mlle. Nioche to copy six paintings, of these three are marriage paintings 'symptomatic of Newman's desire to marry someone of the quality of the Museum pieces'. Adeline Tintner, *The Museum World of Henry James* (Ann Arbor, Michigan: UMI Research Press, 1986) p. 58.

p. 19 Bädeker: Karl Baedeker's *Handbook for Paris* first appeared in 1865. Asterisks were used as marks of commendation.

p. 20 physical capital: see Mark Selzer's essay 'Physical Capital: *The American* and the Realist Body', part of which is in the James and His Critics section.

p. 20 muscular Christian: term applied from 1857 to the ideal of religious character in the works of Charles Kingsley (1819–75).

p. 20 Café Anglais: famous Parisian restaurant listed as High Class – located on the Boulevard des Italiens.

p. 20 homeopathy: a system of medicine developed by Hahnemann in 1796 based on the notion of curing by use of drugs which mimic the symptoms of the disease being treated. Became fashionable in the mid-19th century.

p. 22 *splendide*: splendid.

p. 22 *pas insulté*: you aren't insulted, are you?

p. 22 '*Donnez!*': Give it to me!

p. 22 '*Pas beaucoup?*': A great deal?

p. 23 Sèvres *biscuit*: Sèvres is a porcelain factory near Versailles (fl. 1756); *biscuit* means unglazed, therefore unready.

p. 23 '*Bien sûr!*': Of course!

p. 23 He invented: he came upon.

p. 24 portemonnaie: purse.

p. 24 Mdlle. Noémie Nioche: Noémie is the first name of the American heroine, Mrs Clarkson in Alexandre Dumas *fils*'s play *L'Étrangère* (1875), a play which annoyed James no end. See James and His Critics, pp. 371–2.

p. 25 *très-supérieure*: very superior, high-class.

p. 26 'He says thou art very clever': thou art – the English translation of *tu es*.

p. 26 '*Pas de raisons!*': Don't argue!

p. 26 *esprit*: spirit, intelligence, feeling.

p. 26 '*Hélas, oui!*': Alas, yes!

p. 27 an *homme du monde*: a man of the world.

p. 27 *commerçant*: trader or merchant.

p. 28 *Dame*: why yes.

Chapter 2
p. 28 Paul Veronese has depicted the marriage feast of Cana: in the Louvre (1562) painted by Paolo Cagliari Veronese (1528–88). See John 2:1–11.

p. 31 Palais Royal: the Palais Royal is historically one of the more interesting buildings in Paris. There are two parts: the Palace and the Gardens, flanked by galleries. It was erected by Cardinal Richelieu in 1629–34 from designs by J. Lemercier. Later it became a complex of 'tripots' gaming houses, cafés and restaurants.

p. 31 Avenue d'Iéna: the area known as the *Colonie Américaine*.

p. 31 '*C'est le bel âge . . .*': that's still a good age, that's still young.

p. 33 Grand Hotel: one of the hotels of the highest class, 12 Boulevard des Capucines, next to the Opéra.

p. 34 brevet: a certificate awarded to officers on the battlefield for distinguished service.

p. 35 haircloth shirt: the shirt worn by ascetics.

p. 36 golden stream: Zeus changes himself into a shower of gold so that he can gain access to Danae locked in a tower by Acrisus, King of Argos. She becomes the mother of Perseus.

p. 36 his philosophy had hitherto dreamt of: cf. Shakespeare's *Hamlet* I.v.

p. 36 original: natural.

p. 36 The Occidental: a club modelled on the British club.

p. 37 'Well, if I'm not the rose . . .': cream of the crop.

p. 38 Irish funerals: the adjective Irish was used frequently in slang, Irish weddings for example referred to cess-pools; this might be a pun on the phrase meaning shabby or dirty.

p. 39 *caprice de prince*: whims of the prince.

p. 39 Bois de Boulogne: or simply le Bois, is a splendid park of 2115 acres bounded by fortifications of Paris, on the east of the River Seine.

p. 39 Trouville: a fashionable resort on the coast of Normandy.

p. 39 French Newport: Newport is a resort city on Rhode Island, USA.

Chapter 3
p. 40 Baron Haussmann: Baron Georges-Eugène Haussmann (1809–91), adminstrator and developer. Responsible for the transformation of Paris into a modern city.

p. 41 ten-button gloves: long evening gloves. From 1868 the fashionable ladies of Europe wore gloves with several buttons.

p. 44 *cocottes*: loose women.

p. 47 Cut the knot or untie it: the Gordian knot.

p. 48 *'Voilà ce qui s'appelle parler!'*: Now you are talking!

p. 50 Rolla and Fortunio: Rolla is the titular hero of a poem (1833) by Alfred de Musset and Fortunio the titular hero of a prose tale (1837) by Théophile Gautier.

p. 50 a fair Circassian, with a dagger in her belt: see Byron's *Don Juan* (canto IV, stanzas 113–14).

p. 51 Sardanapalus: the name applied to any wealthy, extravagant, egotistic tyrant. It is the Greek name of an Assyrian King in the 7th century BC. Byron wrote a poetic drama about the King (1821).

p. 51 Rue de l'Université: most of the action of the novel takes place here and in the Rue de Lille and the Rue de Bellechasse. See Leon Edel, *Henry James: The Conquest of London, 1870–1881* (London: Rupert Hart-Davis, 1962). p. 249.

p. 52 *monde*: circle or set.

p. 52 *noblesse*: nobility, nobleness.

p. 52 a Legitimist is, or an Ultramontane: i.e. extremists. The Legitimists wanted the restoration of the Bourbon Monarchy in France which had been overthrown in 1830. The Ultramontanes ('over the mountain') were an Ultra Papal party who maintained the infallibility of the Pope.

p. 52 fifty quarterings: the quarterings on a shield denoting family alliances or generations.

p. 54 *sang-froid*: coolness, composure.

p. 55 Faubourg St Germain: opposite the Louvre and the Tuileries, within the 6th Arrondissement (Luxembourg), it is the most aristocratic area.

p. 55 Eastern seraglios: harems.

Chapter 4
p. 57 youth in a blouse: a smock.

p. 57 Boulevard: the Boulevard des Capucines is in front of the Grand Hotel.

p. 58 napoleons: French gold coins from the second empire of Napoleon III.

p. 59 hasn't the sou: penniless.

p. 59 converted into specie!: *espèces*: a coin.

p. 60 *'Voyons!'*: Let's see!

p. 60 *beaux jours*: my day.

p. 61 *demitasse*: half a cup of coffee.

p. 61 con: peruse.

p. 61 *charcutière*: pork butcher.

p. 61 Rue de Clichy: a street in the working-class area of northern Paris.

p. 61 Lamartine: French novelist Alphonse Marie Louis Prat de Lamartine (1790–1869).

p. 62 Théâtre Français: was erected in 1785 by Victor Louis for the 'Variétés-Amusantes'. It is the south-west part of the Palais Royal building.

p. 63 *franche coquette*: flirt.

p. 63 *coup de tête*: act of desperation.

p. 64 *quartier*: neighbourhood.

p. 64 *dame de compagnie*: lady's servant or companion.

p. 66 '*Quelle folie!*': What nonsense!

p. 66 *comme il faut*: decent or proper.

p. 67 St Catherine: *The Mystical Marriage of St Catherine* with the martyrdom of St Sebastian in the background, painted in 1526–7 by Antonio Allegri da Correggio (Parmese) *c.* 1494–1534.

p. 67 Italian portrait of a lady: the famous *Bella Nani*, a portrait of an Italian lady in the Louvre by Veronese painted in 1555.

p. 67 large as the original: copyists had to alter the scale thus preventing forgeries.

p. 68 *en prince*: princely fashion.

p. 68 '*Je le veux bien!*': I confess it freely!

p. 69 Marie de Médicis: daughter of Francis, grand-duke of Tuscany married in 1610 to Henry IV. The painting is the allegorical *The Marriage of Henry IV with Marie de Médicis* by Peter Paul Rubens (1577–1640).

p. 71 *dot*: marriage portion or dowry.

p. 71 *maîtres de cafés*: head waiters.

Chapter 5

p. 72 blue-cloaked Madonna: Virgin Mary as she is commonly depicted.

p. 73 Hôtel de Ville: the Hôtel was begun in 1533 and after its enlargement became the headquarters of municipal government. In its long history it has played an important role in different French revolutions.

p. 73 cicerone: guide for sight-seers.

p. 73 Counts Egmont and Horn: Lamoral graafran van Egmond(t) (1522–68) and Count Horn (d. 1568) were beheaded for their opposition to Philip of Spain. See John Lothrop Motley's *The Rise of the Dutch Republic* (3 vols. London: George Routledge and Sons, 1889): 'Tall magnificent in costume, with dark flowing hair, soft brown eyes, smooth cheek, a slight moustache, and features of almost feminine delicacy; such was the gallant and ill-fated Lamoral Egmont . . .' (vol. 1 p. 91). See also Goethe's play *Egmont* (1788).

p. 73 Champs Élysées: begun at the end of the 17th century, and substantially altered in 1815, the Champs-Élysées is a park with a long avenue running past the Rond-Point to the Arc de Triomphe.

p. 73 Grand Tour: in the 18th century English aristocrats went on a Grand Tour of Europe visiting the main cities as part of their cultural education.

p. 74 *valets de place*: couriers.

p. 75 New England metropolis: Boston.

p. 75 *table d'hôte*: (ordinary) dinner.

p. 75 American Agency: a provisions store.

p. 76 Mrs Jameson's works: Anna Brownell Jameson's books entitled the *Sacred and Legendary Art* (1848–60).

p. 77 Goethe recommended seeing human nature in the most various forms: German writer Johann Wolfgang von Goethe (1749–1832). Refers to *Wilhelm Meister* translated by Thomas Carlyle.

p. 77 Simplon: the famous mountain pass between Switzerland and Italy.

p. 79 Luini: Milanese painter Bernardino Luini (*c.* 1485–1532).

p. 83 'L'appétit vient en mangeant': proverb: appetite comes in the eating.

p. 83 I am in the shafts: hitched up to the carriage.

p. 84 art for art: L'art pour l'art: the aesthetic movement slogan.

Chapter 6
p. 86 Boulevard Haussmann: a long Boulevard named for Baron Haussmann. In parallel with the Avenue de Friedland it leads to the Arc de Triomphe de l'Étoile.

p. 86 Church of St Sulpice: the wealthiest and most important church on the left bank of the Seine.

p. 86 Grand Turk: the Sultan of the Ottoman Empire (1482), used later to refer to someone who is cruel, savage or tyrannical.

p. 87 ma mère: my mother.

p. 87 nabob: a person of fortune and rank.

p. 88 Mysteries of the Fifth Avenue: pun on Ann Radcliffe's The Mysteries of Udolpho (1794).

p. 88 spread eagle: aggressive or assertive of US national interests – from the Great Seal of the United States.

p. 91 was a date – 1627: the year when Rubens completed his painting of St Catherine and the date of the Duke of Buckingham's invasion of France.

p. 95 dans le monde: in the world.

Chapter 7
p. 101 morgue: haughty look.

p. 102 gentilhomme: gentleman.

p. 103 Bonapartes: line descended from Napoleon Bonaparte.

p. 103 roturière: plebeian; commoner.

p. 103 de notre bord: our side of the ship.

p. 103 Castle of St Angelo: the Pope's refuge until 1870 after his forces had been defeated by Victor Emmanuel in 1860.

p. 106 C'est égal: no matter, it is all one.

p. 108 white cap and pink ribbons: the person who sells *libretti* for foreigners in theatres.

p. 109 a blue spot: literally a bruise.

p. 109 *hôtel garni*: furnished accommodation: rooming house.

Chapter 8
p. 111 Orestes and Electra: the son and daughter of Agamemnon and Clytemnestra. After Clytemnestra killed their father, Agamemnon, the children killed her.

p. 111 *grande dame*: great lady.

p. 111 She looks like a statue . . . long trains: Pygmalion, the legendary king of Tyre, fell in love with a statue. He prayed for a wife as beautiful as the statue. Aphrodite brought the statue to life and Pygmalion married her.

p. 112 *'Parbleu!'*: By Jove!

p. 114 *bourgeoisie*: middle class.

p. 114 King Cophetua: an imaginary King of Africa who fell in love with Penelophon (Zenelophon in *Love's Labour's Lost*, IV.i). See Percy's *Reliques* and Shakespeare's *Romeo & Juliet* (II.i) and *Richard II* (V.iii).

p. 114 *petite noblesse*: petty aristocracy below the *haute noblesse* (peerage).

p. 116 *Ouf!*: Oh!

p. 118 *vous m'imposez*: you impress me.

p. 120 *Touchez-là*: shake hands on it; put it there!

Chapter 9
p. 125 *naïf*: naive.

Chapter 10
p. 130 according to the French phrase: *abonder de le même sens*: (trans.) in complete agreement with her.

p. 130 Desdemona: see Shakespeare's *Othello* (I.iii).

p. 132 *beaucoup de cachet*: lots of character, style.

p. 132 Turkey carpet: Turkish carpet.

p. 133 Lady Emmeline Atheling: the maiden name of Mme. Henri-Urbain de Bellegarde.

p. 133 Books of Beauty: an English fashion magazine of the 1830s.

p. 136 *Monsieur mon frère:* my brother.

p. 139 Tuileries: the old French Palace, burned down by the Communards in 1871.

p. 140 '*En voilà, du nouveau!*': That's news!

Chapter 11

p. 143 long hall of the Italian masters: the Grande Galerie.

p. 144 *ennuis:* worries or anxieties.

p. 145 The two men passed into the long gallery ... smaller apartment devoted to the same school, on the left: Salle des Primitifs Italiens.

p. 146 '*Mon Dieu!*': My God!

p. 147 blue devils: depression.

p. 148 through the door behind her, which opens on one of the great white stone staircases of the Louvre: the Escalier Daru that connects the Salon des Italien Primitifs to the Grande Galerie.

p. 149 *Diable, diable, diable!:* The devil!

p. 150 *des malheurs:* bad luck.

p. 150 Virginius: in the *Roman de La Rose*: refers to Virginius, father of Virginia. Virginius killed his daughter to save her from being violated. See *The Romance of the Rose*, translated by Charles Dahlberg (Hanover and London: University of New England Press, 1983), p. 114.

Chapter 12

p. 154 flesh-tints of Rubens and the good-taste of Sansovino: the Venetian architect and sculptor, Jacopo Sansovino (1486–1570).

p. 155 Corps Législatif: the legislation in France from 1795 to 1814.

p. 159 '*C'est un beau choix*': It is a good choice.

p. 159 you owe me a famous taper: *Vous me devez un cierge fameux.* You should be grateful.

p. 160 *talon rouge:* aristocrat, nobleman: aristocrats were known for wearing red heels.

p. 160 *vieille roche*: Old Rock, i.e. the Old Order.

p. 160 '*Ce que c'est que la gloire!*': That's enough of family pride!

p. 160 Empire: the Napoleonic Empire.

p. 165 cap over the mill: from the French: *Jeta son bonnet par-dessus les moulins*: to let one's hair down.

p. 165 Andromeda has found another Perseus: in Greek mythology Andromeda, daughter of Cepheus, is tied to a rock as a sacrifice. She is rescued by Perseus who changes the sea-monster to stone.

Chapter 13

p. 170 Henry of Bourbon, Fifth of his name: Henry Charles-Ferdinand Marie Dieudonné d'Artois, Comte de Chambord, duc de Bordeaux (1820–83). A direct descendant from Louis (1214–70) and the 'legit-imate' heir to the French throne. If he had been crowned in 1870 by the Legitimists, he would have been Henri V.

p. 171 tirewoman: servant.

p. 174 *portière*: door curtain.

p. 178 vice: a photographer's vice used for holding the subject's head while the photograph is being taken.

p. 179 Offenbach: the opera composer, Jacques Offenbach (1819–80).

p. 179 La Pomme de Paris: possibly Offenbach's *Pomme d'Api* (1873).

p. 179 'Gazza Ladra': *La Gazza Ladra* ('The Thieving Magpie') (1817) by Gioacchino Antonio Rossini (1792–1868).

Chapter 14

p. 184 '*Oui, ma mère*': Yes, my mother.

p. 185 '*Arrivez donc, messieurs!*': Come in, gentlemen!

p. 190 Madame Frezzolini's singing: Eminia Frezzolini (1818–84) the Italian soprano. Her voice went into decline after her tour of the USA in 1858–61.

p. 190 *fête champêtre*: an open-air entertainment.

p. 190 fête: a party.

Chapter 15

p. 192 *Figaro*: *Figaro*, founded in 1854, began as a satirical journal.

p. 193 **inflated gloves**: kid gloves inflated and hung up to dry.

p. 194 **Garçon**: waiter.

p. 194 '*Quelle horreur!*': How horrible!

p. 195 *galant*: gallant.

p. 196 *Au revoir*: Good-bye.

p. 198 **Montmartre**: Montmartre, approx 400 feet above the River Seine, is a predominantly working-class area.

p. 199 **musical-glasses**: glass harmonica.

p. 199 **antique intaglio**: a precious stone with a figure or design engraved on its surface.

p. 200 *tableaux vivants*: a motionless representation of a critical moment/action in a play.

p. 201 **little jade**: a disreputable woman, a hussy.

p. 202 *en somme*: all things considered.

p. 202 *mots*: witticisms.

Chapter 16

p. 203 **clock-image in** *papier-mâché*: automaton.

p. 204 '*Malheureux!*': Wretch!

p. 204 '**Green bows . . . illegitimate!**': The wearing of a green bow was doubly offensive as it was the badge of prostitution.

p. 205 **chère belle**: (French) dear beauty.

p. 206 **looked like an old lady painted by Vandyke**: Anthony Van Dyck the Flemish painter (1599–1641) in his early period painted several portraits of burgers and their wives.

p. 207 **Young Madame de Bellegarde . . . full discs**: the colours of the dress are shocking because they go against the French custom which forbade the wearing of certain colours.

p. 207 *disponible*: available.

p. 210 *beaux noms*: great names.

p. 210 'C'est positif': That is definite.

p. 210 légende: legend.

p. 210 bizarre: bizarre, outlandish.

p. 212 a bear-leader: a trainer of bears.

p. 213 "Belle Dame sans Merci": Lady without Mercy (1820); this ballad by John Keats (1795–1821) tells the story of a knight fatally attracted to a woman.

p. 214 café glacé: iced coffee.

p. 216 rez-de-chaussée: ground level, ground floor.

Chapter 17

p. 218 'Don Giovanni': the titular hero in Amadeus Wolfgang Mozart's opera Don Giovanni (1787), based upon the legendary 14th-century rake and libertine of Seville, Don Juan.

p. 218 orchestra-chair: a seat in front of the orchestra pit.

p. 218 high drags: a drag is a private horse-drawn carriage.

p. 218 making a toilet: grooming oneself.

p. 219 Madame Alboni: Italian contralto (1823–94); one of the finest.

p. 219 entr'actes: between the acts, intermissions.

p. 219 baignoire: a ground box in a theatre.

p. 220 au sérieux: seriously.

p. 220 carbuncle: a red precious stone.

p. 221 'Vous parlez d'or': literally you speak gold – you speak wisely.

p. 222 feuilleton in the Figaro: Figaro, founded in 1854, began as a satirical journal.

p. 222 Donna Elvira: a lady of Burgos who is deserted by Don Giovanni.

p. 223 Zerlina: a peasant girl betrothed to Masetto in Don Giovanni.

p. 223 man of stone: in Don Giovanni the statue of the dead Commendatore Giovanni invites to supper; it later comes to life and Giovanni is engulfed in flames after touching it.

p. 223 Poitiers: the location of the Bellegardes' country house, Fleurières.

p. 224 Latin Quarter: Quartier Latin on the left bank of the River Seine, includes the 5th Arrondissement (Panthéon) and the East part of the 6th Arrondissement.

p. 224 *drôle*: droll; funny.

p. 225 *contrat*: the marriage contract.

p. 225 kicking off young men's hats: the cancan.

p. 226 *raffiné*: refined, delicate.

p. 226 Boulevard des Italiens: a fashionable boulevard named from the Théâtre des Italiens in 1783.

p. 227 El Dorado: fabulous city in South America – the 'golden city'.

p. 228 *ouvreuse*: female usher.

p. 228 fire-eater: a person fond of quarrelling.

p. 229 *'C'est ça qui pose une femme!'*: That will establish me as a lady!

p. 229 theological noun in four letters: hell.

p. 231 Strasbourg: in north-eastern France.

p. 233 portmanteau: suitcase.

p. 233 ducks and drakes: trifle with or use recklessly.

p. 234 *'Que voulez-vous?'*: What do you expect?

p. 235 tail-piece: an illustration or decoration at the end of a chapter in a book.

Chapter 18
p. 244 *enceinte*: an enclosure; city walls.
p. 245 Auteuil: former village of the department of Seine, now part of Paris; a residential area on the right bank where famous writers and artists lived.

p. 245 Trocadero: named from one of the forts of Cadiz taken by the French in 1823.

p. 246 Peerage: i.e. *Burke's Peerage.*

Chapter 19

p. 247 **Jura**: a mountain range on the Franco-Swiss border.

p. 247 **curé**: beneficent, clergyman, priest, parson.

p. 248 *commode*: accommodating.

p. 248 **canton**: in Switzerland a geographical, administrative area of state.

p. 248 *procès-verbal*: official report.

p. 249 *cabinet de toilette*: dressing-room.

p. 249 *bonne*: maidservant.

p. 250 **Pontifical Zouaves**: French soldiers serving the Vatican.

p. 250 **Croix Helvétique**: literally Swiss Cross, the inn's name.

p. 250 '*C'est plus qu'un Anglais – c'est un Anglomane!*': He is more than an Englishman – he is an Anglomaniac! French dandies had a taste for all things English. This scene also echoes the death of Rudin in Ivan Turgenev's novel *Rudin*, where the hero is mistaken for a Pole (*Polaise*). See p. 181 of Richard Freeborn's translation (Harmondsworth: Penguin, 1975), and the discussion of Anglomania in Turgenev's *A Nest of Gentlefolk* (1858).

p. 251 *que diable!*: for heaven's sake!

p. 251 **sabots**: wooden slippers worn by the peasantry of France.

p. 252 '**Les Liaisons Dangereuses**': a famous epistolary novel (1782) by the French author Pierre-Ambrose-François Choderlos de Laclos (1741–1803). The novel was a substitute for *Les Amours du Chevalier de Faublas* which had been used in the serialisation of *The American* in the *Atlantic*. Both works contain seduction scenes and detailed description of courtship which would have shocked the American reader.

p. 253 'let us eat and drink, for tomorrow – tomorrow': 'we die' – so concludes the proverb.

p. 254 *cabinet*: study.

p. 254 *va!*: go!

p. 255 **Rothschild**: a famous Jewish banking family.

p. 259 '*Voilà!*': There it is!

p. 261 sacred vessel: the Communion chalice.

Chapter 20
p. 262 *petit bourg*: small town.

p. 263 Henry IV: King of France and Navarre (1553–1610); assassinated by Ravaillac. His second wife was Marie de Medicis.

p. 263 liveried gentry: servants.

Chapter 21
p. 272 Poitiers: the Black Prince defeated the French at Poitiers in 1356.

p. 274 calèche: calash, barouche, an open four-wheeled carriage.

p. 278 Soeur Catherine: an allusion to St Catherine of Alexandria, the 4th-century Christian martyr who claimed she had been mystically married to Christ; the first nun. See Chapter 4 in which a small Italian picture, Correggio's 'A Marriage of St Catherine', is pointed out to Newman.

p. 279 '*Le misérable!*': The rogue! or scoundrel.

p. 282 *salle*: parlour.

p. 282 Armes de France: name of the inn.

p. 282 very Low: Low church.

Chapter 22
p. 291 "*Mon père, mon père.*": My father, my father.

p. 294 apothecary: pharmacist or drug seller.

p. 294 looking-glass: mirror used to ascertain whether someone is dead or alive.

Chapter 23
p. 300 brocaded fauteuils: armchair.

p. 303 *femme de chambre*: waiting-woman, parlour-maid.

p. 303 Avenue de Messine: runs from Place St Augustin to Rue de Monceau.

p. 303 Rue d'Enfer: see Thomas Carlyle, *Sartor Resartus* (1833) and the fictitious Rue Saint-Thomas de l'Enfer – Thomas hell-fire street.

(*Sartor Resartus*, eds Kerry McSweeney and Peter Sabor [Oxford University Press, 1987] p. 128)

Chapter 24
p. 310 *toilette*: habit.

p. 311 *le coeur tendre*: tenderhearted.

p. 311 *Le reste vous regarde*: From now on you can look after yourself.

p. 312 **Anglaise**: Englishwoman.

p. 312 *partie*: the date.

p. 313 *mêlée*: scuffle or fray.

p. 317 '*Mon pauvre ami*': My poor friend.

p. 319 *il en resterait quelque chose*: there remained something odd or unusual.

Chapter 25
p. 321 **pink-covered novels**: this is an anachronism as George Sand's pink-covered novels (because of their binding) were published in 1871. On Sand's influence on James see Patricia Thomson, *George Sand and the Victorians* (London: Macmillan, 1977) especially p. 234 on *The American*.

p. 323 *charmante*: charming.

p. 323 *mots*: witticisms.

p. 324 **heart-history**: *histoire de coeur, histoire intérieure*.

p. 325 *fadaises*: trifles, nonsenses.

p. 325 **Lothario**: a seducer. See the play, *The Fair Penitent*, by Nicholas Rowe (1674–1718).

p. 326 **Obelisk in the Place de la Concorde**: the Place de la Concorde is one of the largest squares in the world. The Egyptian Obelisk in the centre once stood in front of the great temple at Luxor (Thebes) erected by Ramses II.

p. 327 **much mourning as a weed**: the black band worn by men in mourning.

p. 328 **Boulogne**: a French port.

p. 328 **flunkies:** liveried servants.

p. 333 *Tiens*: Well, well.

Chapter 26
p. 339 **St Veronica:** legendary woman who gave Christ her kerchief to wipe his brow. The image of Christ was imprinted on the kerchief.

JAMES AND HIS CRITICS

Early Reception

Henry James's second significant novel, *The American*, was first turned down for serialisation by the editor of the American journal, *The Galaxy*. William Dean Howells (1837–1920), a more sympathetic editor, accepted the novel for a twelve-month run in his journal *The Atlantic Monthly* in 1877. James earned $1,350 from the serialisation. The novel was published by James R. Osgood of Boston shortly after it had been serialised. An imprint of this Bostonian publication was used for the first British publication by Macmillan. There were also, as was common before an effective international copyright law was brought in 1891, several pirate editions and unauthorised translations published in Europe. From its earliest days, readers and critics alike felt a deep disappointment with the novel. George Grove (1820–1900), the editor of *Macmillan's Magazine*, informed Frederick Macmillan that he could not finish the novel. Those who did complete the novel found the ending unsatisfactory, including William Dean Howells. James responded, defending his conclusion:

> I quite understand that as an editor you should go in for 'cheerful endings'; but I am sorry that as a private reader you are not struck with the evitability of the American denouement . . . It was cruelly hard for poor N. to lose, certainly; but there are tall stone walls which fatally divide us. I have written my story from Newman's side of the wall, and I understand so well how Mme. de Cintré couldn't really scramble over from her side! If I had represented her as doing so I should have made a prettier ending, certainly; but I should have felt as if I were throwing a rather vulgar sop to readers who don't really know the world and who don't measure the merit of a novel by its correspondence to the same.
>
> . . . I suspect it is the tragedies in life that say more to my imagination.

(Letter to William Dean Howells, 30 March 1877, quoted in Charles R. Anderson, *Person, Place, and Thing in Henry James's Novels* [Durham, North Carolina: Duke University Press, 1977] pp. 41–2)

Early critics thought there must be a reason why the narrative went off the tracks at the end. George Saintsbury (1845–1933) reviewing for the *Academy* blamed Balzac for spoiling the novel.

We have but one thing against Mr James, and we wish we could say as much for most of the novelists whose work comes before us. He has read Balzac, if it be possible, just a little too much; has read him until he has fallen into the one sin of his great master, the tendency to bestow refined dissection and analysis on characters which are not of sufficient intrinsic interest to deserve such treatment. No doubt this is a fault which savours of virtue; but still it is a fault, and a fault which renders it extremely difficult to fix one's attention on *The American* until the excellence of Mr James's manipulation fairly forces one for very shame to interest oneself in his story.

There are several minor characters who are decidedly better than the principals. Such are the old Marquise, who bears, however, a rather perilous likeness to Lady Kew;* her younger son, a capital fellow and partisan of the ill-treated Yankee; a match-making and platonically flirtatious American matron, and others. Also we have a ghastly family secret, a fatal duel, and a retirement to a convent; so that Mr James has been by no means stingy of what some people regard as the solids of his feast. The portrait of his countryman must of course be taken as accurate, and is evidently sympathetic. But if not only the *naif* consciousness and avowal of being good as anybody else, but also the inability to understand how the anybody else may possibly differ from him on this point, be taken from life, the defect of repulsion strikes us as a serious one. There is, moreover, something exceedingly jarring to our possibly effete nerves in the idea of a man who seriously entertains the idea of revenging himself for a personal slight by making use of a family secret which he has surreptitiously got hold of. It is true he does not do it, but he threatens to do so, and tries to make profit of scoundrels as they are. And the lady, though her temperament and French ideas of duty explain her conduct not insufficiently, is far too shadowy and colourless. The book is an odd one, for, though we cannot call it a good book, there is no doubt whatever that it is worth a score of books which we are wont truly enough in a sense to call good.

(George Saintsbury, review, *Academy* July 1877, xii, 33) * Lady Kew appears in William Makepeace Thackeray's *The Newcomes*.

The novel was well received in the United States, the title and the character Christopher Newman promised a lot, but there was still disappointment with the 'miserable ending'. The reviewer for the *Scribner's Monthly* sounded at first triumphant.

Those who have faith in the growth of literature according to seed and soil, have long cherished the hope – deferred from season to season – that the 'great'-ness which characterizes so many American things would soon develop itself in fiction. A great American novel has seemed to many a confident and hopeful patriot to be heralded with the incoming of each new writer. Mr James early showed qualities which justified the turning of expectant gaze in his direction. The 'Passionate Pilgrim', 'A Modern Madonna' and 'the Last of the Valeri', showed some qualities which might well grow to greatness. It is true that in 'Madame De Mauves' and in *Roderick Hudson*, expectation received a warning; but Mr James had given such unmistakable evidence of originality and delicacy, and of skillful *technique*, that when the first chapters of *The American* made their appearance we were justified in looking for a novel thoroughly American in character and sufficiently good to satisfy our national literary longing. It was evident that the movement of the story was to be on foreign soil, – where its author is so much at home, – and that but one of its important characters was to be of our people, but this one character was so thoroughly of the best typical American sort as to afford a safe basis for the highest hopes that might be built upon it. Big, rich, frank, simplehearted, straightforward, and triumphantly successful, he satisfied us entirely by his genuine and hearty manliness, and he seemed to carry in his very blood a genius for success in any direction toward which his modest strength might be turned [. . .]

But it was Ivan Turgenev, however, not Balzac, who ruined the novel:

It is the best compliment we can pay to Mr James's writing to say that he gave us such a living interest in his hero, that we are made angry by his own failure to comprehend the character he had created. Can it be that we owe such a fiasco in some degree to the fact that the author has been unconsciously twisted out of his own individuality by the strong influence of Tourguéneff's example? Tourguéneff', however, would justify so miserable an ending; he is remorseless, but does not shock nor disappoint.

(From an unsigned review, *Scribner's Monthly*, July 1877, xiv, 406–7)

Early Twentieth-Century Reception

Joseph Warren Beach (1880–1957) in *The Method of Henry James* (1918) examined the important theme in *The American*, that of the contrast between the Old World and the New World, and later looked at the techniques used in the novel including comic devices. He also looked at the 'point of view' in the novel comparing it unfavourably with maturer works.

'The American' is the first large essay of James in treatment of the theme that was to occupy so much of his attention all along, – the contrast of the American and European cultures. And it remains to this day an effective piece of work. The self-made American without antecedents and traditions brought in contrast with a group of persons for whom these are almost the whole of life; the man of strong and unlimited self-reliance in contrast to men and women hedged and thwarted in every direction by the restraints of family and caste – the simple, straightforward, easy-going westerner in his dealings with these formal, sophisticated, inordinately polite and treacherous people; it makes a story and a spectacle of endless richness and variety. The idea is clearly conceived, and there is no detail of the story that it does not inform and make relevant. The sub-plot of Valentin de Bellegarde and Noémie Nioche is obviously introduced for the purpose of illustrating certain aspects of the social contrast which do not come out in Newman's love affair. (pp. 199–200)

The social contrast comes out most strikingly, however, and certainly to our greatest amusement, in the series of scenes in which the blunt and humorous westerner is opposed to the frigid courtliness of elder Bellegardes, above all on those occasions when, having accepted him as a suitor for the hand of Claire, they yet endeavor, largely without success, to make him understand the enormous condescension in their friendly treatment of a 'commercial' person. (p. 200)

I will not dwell on the superficial points of technique in which it resembles 'Roderick Hudson'. The dialogue is often very good; but not at all in the way the dialogue is good in 'The Awkward Age'. It is refreshing to have the hero 'bet his life on' something, or to have him urge an amused Parisian to 'give' somebody 'one in the eye'. There are passages of talk, however, which have somewhat lost their savor. We cannot help feeling at times Valentin and even his sister are permitted to show themselves younger and less practiced hands than the author intended. And we are conscious of a certain perfunctory character in most of Newman's exemplary love-making. (pp. 201–2)

But the early manner is exhibited in ways more important than these. It resides essentially in what we may call the greater objectivity of the work. The chief concern of the author seems to be for scenic effectiveness of what is said and done. In the later work the scene is used chiefly to objectify the idea. Here the idea is the opportunity for scene. The characters express themselves more violently here, in a word and gesture. The emotional emphasis reaches its culmination in the chapter [20] in which Claire announces her intention of becoming a nun. (p. 202)

Nowhere else in James, I think, is there such a lavish use of irony as that indulged in by Newman and the grim Marquise. Their remarks are as good as lines in a smart play. And that is the point. These scenes in which new world and old world are pitted against one another are introduced for their theatrical effectiveness, like certain brilliant scenes in Thackeray or in Dumas *père*. Such is the scene in which the Marquis is obliged to introduce to all his *monde* the 'commercial' person who is going to marry his sister. Such is the scene in the Park Monceau in which Newman announces to the Marquis and the old Marquise his possession of the incriminating paper. It makes a fine show, the bravery with which his adversaries, deep-stricken as they are, bear-up in the face of the world, – their display of that 'very superior style of brazen assurance, of what M. Nioche called *l'usage du monde*, and Mrs Tristram called the grand manner'. (pp. 202–3)

The point of view is throughout chiefly that of Newman. But not the same use is made of this as would have been made in a later book. We see what Newman sees, but he does not interpret it to us. The author interprets it, and he is sometimes obliged – in order to get Newman into the picture – to give us a glimpse or two beyond what Newman sees. (pp. 203–4)

A story in which the main actor is so uninitiated can bear no very close resemblance to the story of Isabel Archer or Fleda Vetch or Lambert Strether. There is here no revelation of anything through Newman's consciousness – nothing that depends on his understanding. There is in fact no spiritual dilemma. That is why the book is not among the greatest of its author's. There is a gallant fight for a woman. There is an amusing and finally tragic social contrast in which the American hero is one of the terms. And that is the main point in which this is recognizable as a novel of Henry James. (pp. 204–5)

(Joseph Warren Beach, *The Method of Henry James* [Philadelphia, Albert Saifer, 1954. Originally Yale University Press, 1918])

Constance Rourke (1885–1941) in *Native American Humor: A Study of the National Character* (1931) placed *The American* in its cultural context: the American comic tradition (fables, long tales, jokes) with its development of the American 'innocent abroad'. Her study was an important foundation for later studies such as Richard Poirer, *The Comic Sense of Henry James: A Study of the Early Novels* (New York: Oxford University Press, 1967) and Ronald Wallace, *Henry James and the Comic Form* (Ann Arbor: University of Michigan Press, 1975):

The Civil War has been considered a prime destructive agent in the life of the nation, warping or even destroying a native culture. But the literature of the '50's had never been truly complete. Uncalculating digressions might have followed even though there had been no catastrophe. In spite of the disruption of the War a determined experiment continued through the '60's, '70's, and '80's. The international scene became a great American scene, even in a sense *the* great American scene.

Few ideas had disturbed the American mind more acutely than those which had to do with the European relationship. In the '60's

the early commentaries of European travelers still rankled: Tuck-
erman gathered them into a compendious volume, with rejoinders.
But the old fable had undergone a change. In its last notable
version, *Our American Cousin*, the nationalistic hero had exhibited his character and enjoyed his adventures in England, and
possessed an English heritage. He was in fact one of those 'dispossessed princes and wandering heirs' of whom Henry James was to
write. In spite of the burlesque the gesture of disseverance had
grown less positive in Mark Twain's long skits. The American
went abroad, often to stay; sentiment overspread his return to 'our
old home', and that preoccupation with art which had been satirised in *Innocents Abroad* became one of his larger preoccupations.

This was mixed with a consideration which had long since been
borne in upon the American mind by British criticisms. Culture
was an obvious proof of leisure, of long establishment, of half a
hundred desirable assurances that had been lacking in American
life; it even seemed to resolve the vexing problem of manners.
Culture was sought abroad as a tangible emblem. The resultant
'pillage of the past' was to mount to monstrous proportions, and
to include the play of many unworthy instincts – ostentation,
boredom, a morbid inversion of personal desires; often, no doubt,
it represented a natural response to the fine accumulations of time.
Yet surely on the wide scale it was something more than these.
Fumbling and fantastic, the restless habit seemed an effort to find
an established tradition, with the solidity, assurance, and justifi-
cation which traditions may bring. The American wish for establishment had often seemed a fundamental wish, with all the
upheaval.

Many Americans continued to make extravagant denials of
Innocents Abroad, but the exodus was unbroken, and found an
interpreter in Henry James. His talk of 'dispossessed princes and
wandering heirs' was not without personal connotation. As a
young man, considering Europe, he had wondered how he was to
come into his 'own'. 'The nostalgic poison had been distilled for
him,' he declared, speaking of himself. James became indeed as
Van Wyck Brooks has said, 'an immortal symbol'. Strangely
enough in this connection, he was something more: an American
artist who worked within native sequence. (pp. 186–7)

Even the title was a fulfillment. Who ever heard of a significant
English novel called *The Englishman* or an excellent French novel

JAMES AND HIS CRITICS

called *Le Français*? The simple and aggressive stance belonged to
an imagination perennially engaged by the problem of the national
type. The name Newman had significance, faintly partaking of
that comic symbolism by which a hero in one of the Yankee fables
was called Jedidah Homebred. (p. 194)

The tone, as one knows Newman, was jocose, with an admixture
of serious conviction. It was the comic belligerent tone that had
spread through the assertive nationalism of the Yankee fables; and
James seemed to enjoy the mixed quality. He glossed over nothing,
writing with gusto of Newman's early preoccupation with money,
which had also been dominant in Yankee swapping and bargain-
ing. He admitted that his hero considered 'what he had been
placed in the world for was ... simply to gouge a fortune, the
bigger the better, out of its hard material. This idea completely
filled his horizon and contented his imagination. Upon the uses of
money, upon what one might do with a life into which one had
succeeded in injecting the golden stream, he had up to the eve of
his fortieth year very scantly reflected.' (p. 197)
(Constance Rourke, *Native American Humor: A Study of the
National Character* [New York: Doubleday, 1953. Originally
Harcourt, Brace & Co., 1931])

Daniel Lerner in an important essay, 'The Influence of Turgenev
on Henry James' (1941), explored the similarities between *The
American* and Ivan Turgenev's (1818–83) novel *A Nest of
Gentlefolk* (1858):

James's next novel, *The American* (1877), is based largely on
Turgenev's *Nest of Gentlefolk* (1858). The home of the Bellegardes, in *The American*, is evidently also a 'nest of gentlefolk'. In
each novel the hero does not 'belong' – Lavretski's family background, half-peasant and half-landlord, is incongruous; Newman
is American middle-class. Perversely, each falls in love with the
rarest bird in the nest. In each novel one of the lovers has been
married; 'the theme,' James writes of *A Nest of Gentlefolk*, 'is an
unhappy marriage and unhappy love.' In Turgenev's novel Lavretski has been unhappily married and the problem derives from
Lisa's religion, which will not permit her to love a married man.
In James's novel, however, it is the heroine who has been
unhappily married. There the past marriage becomes only a small

factor in the 'conflict', which consists mainly in the opposition of
the aristocratic Bellegarde family to their daughter's projected
marriage to the bourgeois-democratic American Newman (imagine their horror of the man who declares that he wants for his
wife 'the best article in the market'). Another reason for shifting
the past marriage to the heroine was James's desire to locate the
dramatic conflict even more centrally in her consciousness. For in
both novels, it should be noted, the determining 'crisis' takes place
within the heroine. It is in, James's phrase, 'the dusky, antique
consciousness of sin in this tender, virginal soul' (re Lisa) that
carries the day. In each novel, the conflict is resolved by the
heroine's decision to enter a convent. James was fascinated by the
final scene of *A Nest of Gentlefolk*, in which the hero gains
admission to the heroine's convent: 'She knows of his presence,
but does not even look at him; trembling of her downcast lids
betrays her sense of it. "What must they both have thought, have
felt," asks the author . . . With an unanswered question his story
characteristically closes' (229). In *The American* James reproduced
both the scene and unanswered question at the end. But nothing
could be more relevant of the lesson James learned from Turgenev,
and of his own development, than the comparison of these two
scenes – and then the comparison of each with the greatly revised
'ambiguous ending' which James wrote for the New York edition.
Before leaving these two novels, we should note James's final
comment on *A Nest of Gentlefolk*: 'In this tale, as always with
our author, the drama is quite uncommented; the poet never plays
chorus; situations speak for themselves' (231). The author had
made his Exit, and the 'dramatic method' was in progress.
(pp. 43–4).
(Daniel Lerner, 'The Influence of Turgenev on Henry James', *The
Slavonic Year-Book* vol. 20, December 1941, pp. 28–54)

The 1950s to 1990s

Oscar Cargill's *The Novels of Henry James* (1961) provided
readers with more information on the French influences, most
notably, Émile Augier (1820–89) and Alexandre Dumas *fils*
(1824–95):

James began work on *The American* shortly after reaching Paris
at the end of 1875. Going constantly to the theater and devouring

printed plays while he was developing his novel from Turgenev's
A Nest of Gentlefolk, Henry James must have been struck by the
parallel afforded to the situation in Turgenev's novel in a device
being exploited with great effectiveness by Émile Augier upon the
French stage – the 'intrusion-plot'. As many as twenty-two of
Augier's twenty-five plays, according to Professor Girdler B. Fitch,
utilize this device as their principal plot mechanism:

To state this theme in its simplest form, suspending qualifications
for the moment, the basic action of a typical Augier play is this:
*Into a group there comes an intruder whose presence is resisted
by one or more persons and accepted by one or more, with
resulting conflict, until someone's eyes are opened to the true
situation, to the danger, or to a possible solution.* Different
outcomes are possible, but the most frequent is the elimination of
the intruder.
[Cargill's italics and taken from Professor Girdler B. Fitch, 'Émile
Augier and the Intrusion-Plot', *PMLA*, *LXIII* (March 1948)
pp. 274–80] (Cargill pp. 42–4)

But while James was working at *The American* there was put on
at the Théâtre Français a play by Alexandre Dumas *fils*, on 14
February 1876, entitled *L'Étrangère*, which boldly infused inter-
nationalism into the intrusion-plot. James was not only drawn to
this play by the extended advance notice of it in *Figaro*, which
filled most of the issue, but because of his special interest in the
work of Dumas *fils*, which had provided him, as Viola Dunbar
has convincingly shown, with the main features of the plot of
Roderick Hudson. James reacted violently and at length to this
play:

... *L'Étrangère* strikes me as a rather desperate piece of flounder-
ing in the dramatic sea ... The 'Foreigner' who gives its title to
the piece and who is played by that very interesting actress Mme
Sarah Bernhardt, is a daughter of our own democracy, Mrs
Clarkson by name. She explains in the second act, by a mortal
harangue – the longest, by the watch, I have ever listened to – that
she is the daughter of a mulatto slave girl by a Carolinian planter.
As she expresses it herself, 'My mother was pretty: he remarked
her; I was born of remark.' Mrs Clarkson, however, has next to
nothing to do with the play, and she is the least successful figure
the author has ever drawn. Why she should be an American, why

she should have Negro blood, why she should be the implacable demon she is represented, why she should deliver the melodramatic and interminable *tirade* I have mentioned, why she should come in why she should go out, why, in short, she should exist – all this is the perfection of mystery. She is like the heroine of an old-fashioned drama of the Boulevard du Crime who has strayed unwittingly into a literary work, in which she is out of time with all her companions. She is, on Dumas' part, an incredible error of taste. It must be confessed, however, that her entrance into the play has masterly effectiveness. [Letter to *New York Tribune* published on 25 March 1876] (Cargill, pp. 43–4)

Cargill points out that *The American* is very much an inversion of *L'Étrangère*. His points can be summarised as

1) Clarkson wants to go back to the West to make money in gold mining.
   Newman has made his money in Californian mining and has no desire to return.
2) Clarkson brags about money.
   Newman is indifferent to society and wishes only the hand of Claire.
3) Clarkson doesn't hesitate to use his gun in the West, as a substitute duellist kills the villain of the play, the Duc Maximin de Septmonts.
   Newman is a pacifist and looks upon duelling as being barbaric.
4) Clarkson is a philistine when it comes to art.
   Newman wants to learn more about art and culture.
5) Mistress Clarkson is animated by revenge.
   Newman rejects the revenge motive.

(Oscar Cargill, *The Novels of Henry James* [New York: Macmillan, 1961])

In the 1950s there was a spate of articles and theses on the revisions of *The American* and its ambivalent ending. William T. Stafford favours, as many critics do, the earlier version:

Although I consider it somewhat perilous to disagree with Henry James's judgments about his own work, I cannot agree that the revised ending of *The American* is superior to the early version or that the revision as Floyd C. Watkins contended in this journal, is 'evidence of maturity and superior craftsmanship at the time of the revision'. In fact, here is one instance, in my opinion, wherein James's strategy led him woefully astray. 'The free play of . . . unchallenged instinct', the phrase James later used to characterize his method at the time he wrote *The American*, a method he viewed at the time of writing the Preface with 'a certain sad envy', might well, in this particular, have been the better method to have followed.

(William T. Stafford, 'The Ending of James's *The American*: A Defense of the Early Version', *Nineteenth Century Fiction* 18 [1963], pp. 86–9)

The concern with James's revision of the novels culminated in the publication of a book given over entirely to that subject, Philip Horne, *Henry James and Revision: The New York Edition* (Oxford: Clarendon Press 1990). The chapter on *The American*, pp. 148–83.

The process which we have seen undergone by the 1883 text of *The American* emerges then as neither a rewriting nor a non-committal half-measure. We could liken its development to that undergone by a Jamesian 'germ', first into the Notebooks and then into story form, as an eliciting of inner logic. There is an incremental relation and re-relation of expressive elements progressively prompting and shifting and metamorphising as each makes and settles into its place in the whole, altering that whole, but as part of a single evolution, each new link connecting with something in the old matter to form a continuity of intention. We may want to ask in a few instances whether the fact of imaginative connection makes the revisions as infallible as James's confidence makes him, in the Prefaces, want to suggest, for it may be impossible to guard entirely against the trap which catches Balzac's Frenhofer, in which the necessary renewal of the illusion can become delusive and self-incited. What, moreover, are we to make of the losses which inevitably accompany the gains in any process of change? What I hope the examples here demonstrate, though, is the creative truth of James's principle as his practice mostly shows it. His conception of the novel as a coherent record of experience receives extraordinary tribute as we examine the pages documenting his vast labour – in our sense in him of the energy he ascribes to Balzac, 'the never-extinct operation of his sensibility'. (*Henry James Literary Criticism* ii, 1336)

These cases also show the intensity of James's imaginative dependence on and liberation by the very substance of his expressive art, the words with which he grasps the matter of fictional experience. The revisions of the NYE [New York Edition], taken together with his 1905 lecture on *The Question of Our Speech*, express his passionate belief in the value of the development of a power of nuance and exact expression as the shaping condition of a truer consciousness. In this belief the details of writing and speech are enlivened.

(It all comes back to that, to my and your 'fun' – if we but allow the term its full extension; to the production of which no humblest question involved, even to that of the shade of a cadence or the position of a comma, is not richly pertinent.) (*Henry James Literary Criticism*, eds. Leon Edel and Mark Wilson, 2 vols [New York and Cambridge, 1984], ii, 1358)

James allows the term its full extension. (pp. 182–3)

The related topic of the 'ambivalent' ending was treated by Mutlu Blasing in the article 'Double Focus in *The American*', *Nineteenth Century Fiction* 28 (1973), pp. 74–84.

We may conclude, then, that the presence of a double focus in *The American* results in two distinct movements, each with its characteristic plot, humor, and technique of character presentation, for after the Bellegardes' rejection of Newman the novel does not proceed on the same premises. The frame of reference clearly changes from the narrator to Newman, and this shift allows Newman's self-image to dominate the second movement of the novel without, as we have seen, implying James's endorsement. Newman's character does not change; his idealized self-image survives the test intact. And it is here that we can detect James's ambivalence: while the narrator snubs, patronizes, and satirizes Newman, James lets Newman triumph on *his own terms*. Like James, then, we can be attracted to Newman without ever losing sight of his obvious short-comings.

This double focus in the novel reflects not only James's ambivalence toward a type like Newman but the nature of the technical problem that confronted James in *The American*. According to his

1907 Preface to *The American*, James's intention was to present in Newman an American type – a 'generous nature engaged with forces, with difficulties and dangers, that it but half understands'. At the same time, however, James intended to make Newman the 'lighted figure' – to make '*his* vision, *his* conception, *his* interpretation' the center of the novel. James writes: at the window of his wide, quite sufficiently wide, consciousness we are seated, from that admirable position we 'assist'. Yet it seems that James's objectives here are contradictory. If Newman is to be the legendary type complete with 'social innocence', he can hardly be the central intelligence in a novel set within a social context, in which perception itself depends upon a degree of social knowledge. Once again, then, if Newman's vision was to be central, James had to take him out of society into melodrama. (pp. 82–3)

Henry James's Preface to *The American* has been considered as an important contribution in the development of the American Romance, having something of the status of Nathaniel Hawthorne's declaration in his preface to *The House of the Seven Gables* (1851). Hawthorne's definition however is more conservative and controlled than James's. There have been several articles on James and the Romance. George Knox's article is representative of the 1960s' approach to the subject:

Since its publication, the novel's critics have placed too literal an emphasis on the purely social factors instead of reaching into its psychic depths for the fable. Indeed, one does not have to reach deeply. The fable is from one angle the story of the American innocent ('passionate pilgrim'). The equations he worked out in *The American* reappear with fine variations in novel after novel: they are like the image clusters of a poem. James's Romances have been widely discussed in the terminology of poetry criticism, dramatic alignments being thought of as analogous to the symbolic patterns in poems. Therefore, we will discover that Newman's tale projects a cultural fable of success and failure, superimposed on various fairy-tale motifs, allusions to marriage-immurement themes in renaissance paintings, and the employment of eighteenth-century Gothic conventions. In developing his conventions, and stock plot, he ties the narrative together by interconnecting two climacteric incidents: the Carriage Crisis in Chapter 2 and the Church Crisis in Chapter 26. All minor incidents clustering around these moments reflect and support them. The fairy-tale elements converge in Newman's failure to release and then to possess the princess, or sleeping beauty, and constitute the reversal that results from the hero's cultural inferiority, in spite of all his insistence to Valentin that he is a 'civilized' man. At least he knows what he wants – 'Goodness, beauty, intelligence, a fine education, personal elegance – everything, in a word, that makes a splendid woman.' Claire has these things, plus noble birth, and thus is Newman's 'dream realized'.

But though the Bellegardes succeed in thwarting him at the moment when success seemed sure, the Yankee is not to be cheated. He triumphs morally through renunciation. This told American readers what they wanted to know – that it is they (and their 'hero') and not the European aristocrats who are really superior. Therefore, the 'mythology' or fable falls between a nineteenth-century realist mode of innocents-abroad critical fiction (cf. De Forest, Mark Twain, and William Dean Howells) and the idealizations of Romance. The structure is a cyclic analogizing of states of ignorance-innocence and wisdom-wickedness. In addition we find shadows of the nineteenth-century 'proletarian' (Alger-esque) striver, as in *Roderick Hudson* (1875), *The Rise of Silas Lapham* (1885), *The Princess Casamassima* (1886), *The Damnation of Theron Ware* (1896). Each of these in its way exemplifies the Romance mode. Twain's *Connecticut Yankee in King Arthur's Court* (1898) pushed the Romance genre to the outer limits of parody, becoming also one of the major (and darker) anti-utopian fictions in American literature. (pp. 311–12)

(George Knox, 'Romance and Fable in James's *The American*', *Anglia* 83 [1965]: pp. 308–23)

Charles R. Anderson covered many themes found in the novel. Here Anderson looks at the name-game in *The American*:

James himself gives sufficient warrant for playing this game. At the beginning, in introducing himself to Noémie, Newman calls attention to the fact that he was named for a famous Christopher, leaving the reader to bear it in mind as he reads on through to the end of this tale of a Columbus-in-reverse – the new man from America coming over to rediscover the Old World. The pattern, obvious enough in the hero's name, can be extended to many of the characters. *Valentin*, the younger Bellegarde who favors

Newman's suit, has for his name-saint the patron of young lovers. *Claire* ('Light') is the ideal of all that is pure and lovely, but after her unhappy marriage to the Comte de *Cintré* she had been left, in her widowed state, bound ('girdled') by her family's will. The older brother, *Urbain*, is the embodiment of a formal civility so extreme as to suggest that it is merely a superficial ornamentation or veneer. Finally, the family name *Bellegarde* sums up all the 'walls' that separate Newman from his heart's desire. It may be freely translated as Finecastle (or great house, as in *The Princess Casamassima*). More literally *garde* signifies the castle 'keep' or innermost fortress, where the very existence of the family can be protected against intruders. Some readers may find these comic names too broadly farcical. But they are only showy when the critic pulls them out for examination; allowed to slip back into place in the novel, they are unobtrusive. The name-game, added to the other evidence, makes it clear James was conscious of the native tradition of humor when writing *The American*. But that tradition accounts for only part of its comedy.

(Charles R. Anderson, *Person, Place, and Thing in Henry James's Novels* [Durham, North Carolina: Duke University Press, 1977] pp. 54–5)

Peter Brooks examined the melodramatic imagination at work in James's novels and the influence of Balzac.

The American can stand for the use of melodrama in the early fiction. As we noted in the first chapter, Newman's experience in that novel brings into play a number of melodrama's specific devices, even its claptrap. James is not content to have American innocence baffled and betrayed by the manipulations of decadent French aristocrats in their fortress-like hôtel in the Faubourg Saint-Germain. He must further intensify the clash by creating a hidden crime in the Bellegarde heritage, the murder of the old marquis by his wife, who had denied him his medicine and transfixed him with her fully Balzacian glance: 'You know my lady's eyes, I think, sir; it was with them she killed him; it was with the terrible strong will she put into them'. The deed is recounted by old Mrs Bread, the English governess, as the dusk gathers on a bleak hillside by the ruined castle of Fleurières; and Newman is provided with documentary evidence in the form of the deathbed accusation scribbled by the old marquis. Underlying

the social drama played out in Newman's courtship of Claire de
Cintré is this bloodcurdling deed, rendered with all possible shades
of horror, supported by sure signs to the determination of guilt.
After his encounter with Mrs Bread, Newman appears to be in a
position to act as the providential hero of melodrama: he possesses
the signs necessary to expose the villain and perhaps to free the
innocent heroine from her claustration in the convent in the rue
d'Enfer, to purge the positioned air of the social order.

That Newman does not so rout the villains is a first sign of the
typical Jamesian transmutation of melodrama, his primary interest
in the melodrama of consciousness. The clash of good innocence
and sophisticated villainy in this novel at the last works to an
intensification of the terms of Newman's choice between revenge
and renunciation, a choice that is the final test of his inner being,
that must call upon his deepest moral inwardness for a difficult
victory of generosity and natural nobility. Newman's renunciation
of revenge should not be construed as James's renunciation of
melodrama. It marks on the contrary a deep understanding of the
fundamental concerns of melodrama and its possible uses. If
melodrama as a form exists to permit the isolation and dramati-
zation of integral ethical forces, to impose their evidence and a
recognition of the force of the right, the mode and terms of
Newman's choice stand squarely within the tradition. What differs
is that the melodrama of external action – the suspenseful menace,
pursuit, and combat – all are past by the time he resolves the
ethical conflict. External melodrama has been used to lead into
the melodrama of ethical choice.
(Peter Brooks, *The Melodramatic Imagination* [New York:
Columbia University Press, 1985], pp. 156–7)

Elizabeth Allen and Carolyn Porter have treated the novel from
a feminist perspective:

I am suggesting that Newman's function as the great Western
Barbarian is modified by his function as an active, predatory
individual with American qualities who is engaged in a hostile
struggle with alien people with alien ideas. The comparison of
European and American ideas is engendered through this struggle,
yet not centred in an interpretation of Newman by an observing
consciousness. That Newman is not a catalyst for another subject
experience does not detract from his symbolic reverberation for

the reader, but it does mean that we are not focused on any sense of his existence as sign in relation to his world. He is finally only an 'American' to the Bellegardes as they are 'European' to him. Claire, representing the potential best in both, is portrayed as inexplicable and motiveless, and her powerlessness in relation to both Newman and the Bellegardes consistently levels the power balance between the two cultures to sets of different yet predatory impulses, with Claire as prey.

There seem to be two modes of subject experience, that of appropriation and that of interpretation. The first is a male preserve; women can aid, but not appropriate for themselves. Living, however, through their ability to be interpreted, women can construct their subjecthood not only through conscious awareness of themselves as a sign be read, but in the offer of a reading, an explanation. Newman is not so concerned with the interpretative side of life, indeed both Mrs Tristram and Claire appear to offer to take care of it for him; he is more concerned with acquisition and ownership as a means of establishing his existence in the world.

(Elizabeth Allen, *A Woman's Place in the Novels of Henry James* [London: Macmillan, 1984], pp. 48–9)

Carolyn Porter in her essay 'Gender and Value in *The American*' argues that:

Noémie's entire performance in this scene signals her high ambition to join the ranks of those courtesans whose talent for copying the habits and fashions of the upper-classes provoked complaints such as the following from a contemporary Parisian journalist: 'Everything brings together the *demi-monde* and the *monde entier*: everything allows us to confuse things which should not even be aware of one another's existence . . . The nobleman's wife from the Faubourg St Germain passes, on the staircase at Worth's, the elegant female from the Quartier Breda.'

If Noémie is a copy of the upper-class women whose ranks she aspires to join, Claire de Cintré is the original par excellence. The scene in which Newman appears before Madame de Bellegarde to offer his suit for Claire echoes the opening scene, although now the commercial offer is made in the sanctified space not of the Louvre, but of the Faubourg. Newman appeared to Noémie as a potential client, a man who might provide financial support for his rise into society in exchange for her sexual services. Now he appears to Madame de Bellegarde as a potential financial resource, one whose fortune might be large enough to buy her daughter's hand in marriage. Her response, 'How rich?' echoes his opening 'Combien?' Like Newman at the Louvre, what Madame de Bellegarde has to sell is theoretically of inordinate value. Claire de Cintré is an original, so that the only question here is whether Newman has sufficient millions to buy the social equivalent of the 'Mona Lisa'.

(In *New Essays on the The American*, edited by Martha Banta [Cambridge: Cambridge University Press, 1987], pp. 109–10)

Richard A. Hocks in a survey of recent studies had this to say about works on *The American*:

For years it was of great importance by virtue of being James's first attempt at the international novel. But it was also critically salient because of James's celebrated censure in his late preface of its 'fatal flaw' of succumbing to 'the romantic'. Well, to begin with, postmodern criticism of James already celebrates the romantic, or at least dismisses the notion of James as 'mere' realist – or else dismisses the notion of realism itself as realistic. In any event, the 1987 volume *New Essays on The American* by several fine contemporary literary theoreticians suggests the quiet sea change this always popular book – popular because in part very lively and easy to read – has undergone. Since the last decade, it would be anything but out of place to affirm that James in his famous preface had already 'deconstructed' his own earlier novel, *The American*, but that it is now appropriate to deconstruct his critique itself in the New York preface.

(Richard A. Hocks, 'Recanonizing the Multiple Canons of Henry James' in *American Realism and the Canon*, edited by Tom Quirk and Gary Scharnhorst [Newark: University of Delaware Press, London and Toronto: Associated University Press, 1994], p. 163)

Representative of the new criticism is Mark Selzer. Here he outlines his investigation:

In these pages I investigate this configuration of relations – relations of bodies, economies, and forms of representation – in the novel. My primary focus is Henry James's *The American*, a novel that enacts, in an almost diagrammatic fashion, a set of relations, relays, and displacements between the bodily and the economic. My treatment of the novel centers on the ways in which social and economic practices are physically embodied, and with the ways in which imperatives of embodiment and personification constitute the novel's account of the 'commercial person'. At one extreme, the imperative of embodiment appears as a problem, at once literary and economic, of putting persons, meanings, and values 'on paper', and I am concerned with the novel's uneasy investments in what writers and economists in the later nineteenth century described as the American 'paper-system'. Most generally, I attempt to define what I would call the logistics or *social logistics* of James's novel, the practical and exigent deployment and disposition of persons, things and representations. My concern is with how both James's contradictory and radically unstable styles of representation – 'romance' and 'realism' – engage such a logistics, and moreover, with how these contradictions and instabilities become functional within the novel, at once registering and securing the complicated nexus of bodies and commerce that make up James's account of 'physical capital'.

(Mark Selzer, 'Physical Capital: *The American* and the Realist Body' in *New Essays on the American* edited by Martha Banta [Cambridge: Cambridge University Press, 1987], pp. 132–3)

Haralson, with a number of recent critics, has concentrated on Newman's masculinity and read it in terms of Kingsley's muscular Christianity' and other nineteenth-century constructs. He concludes by looking at the legacy of Newman:

James's engagement with the figure of the resolute, manly man did not, of course, end with *The American*. Interestingly, the ghost of Charles Kingsley and his muscular protagonist continued to hover over his later incarnations of the Christopher Newman type. In the hard-driving cotton magnate Caspar Goodwood of *The Portrait of a Lady* (1881), James presented the type with mixed sympathy and satire as a former college athlete – 'a gymnast and an oarsman [rather] than . . . a votary of culture – and a would-be military hero who regretted living in 'such a confoundedly peaceful nation'. In Basil Ransom of *The Bostonians* (1886) – originally conceived as a Westerner like Newman – James offered a Southern version of the Kingsleyan kind, replete with rough 'muscular force' and a zealous intention to keep up the 'masculine tone' of society. Like Kingsley a devotee of Thomas Carlyle, Ransom conducted himself (James wrote) as if 'inhabited by some transmitted spirit of a robust but narrow [English] ancestor' with a 'primitive conception of manhood'. Finally, in *The Tragic Muse* (1890) James restored the Kingsleyan type to its native soil in Nick Dormer – a true son of 'the energetic race' with 'his inches, his limbs', and his amiable 'combination of the muscular and the musing'. As if to complete the arc that had started with Newman's renunciation of Wall Street, James arranges for Dormer to reject a parliamentary career and a political marriage – in short, the sphere of manly action – in order to become, like his creator, a painter of portraits. James reverted to the Newman brand of manhood several times, then, but never with the web of uneasy affiliations that had beset him in the telling of the story of Christopher Newman himself. As the author's sense of his own gender/vocational definition became sharper, so too did his command of narrative and his critique of hypermasculinity. Newman, Goodwood, Ransom, Dormer – each marks a stage in James's movement away from the traditional imperatives of male performance and toward a radically different model of strength and health: the 'strong, sane joys of the artistic life'.

(Eric Haralson, 'James's *The American*: A [New]man Is Being Beaten' in *American Literature* vol. 64, No. 3, September 1992 pp. 489–90)

SUGGESTIONS FOR FURTHER READING

The American

Editions of The American
Osgood, 1877
Macmillan, 1879
Macmillan, 1883
See also the Norton Critical Edition for text variants: *The American*, ed. James W. Tuttleton (New York: W. W. Norton, 1981).

The New York Edition of the Novels and Tales of Henry James (New York: Scribner, 1907–9), 24 vols (2 added in 1918).
The Novels and Stories of Henry James, ed. P. Lubbock (London: Macmillan, 1921–3), 5 vols.
The Complete Tales of Henry James, ed. L. Edel (London: Rupert Hart-Davis, 1962–4), 12 vols.
The Letters of Henry James, ed. P. Lubbock (London: Macmillan, 1920), 2 vols.
Henry James's Letters, ed. L. Edel (Cambridge, Mass.: Belknap Press, 1974–84), 4 vols.
The Complete Notebooks of Henry James, eds L. Edel and L. A. Powers (New York: Oxford University Press, 1987).
The Notebooks of Henry James, eds F. O. Mattiessen and Kenneth Murdock (New York: Oxford University Press, 1961).
The Complete Plays of Henry James, ed. L. Edel (London: Rupert Hart-Davis, 1949).

Literary Criticism

Literary Criticism: Vol 1: *Essays on Literature, American Writers, English Writers*; *Literary Criticism*: Vol 2: *French Writers, Other European Writers, the Prefaces to the New York Edition*, ed. L. Edel with assistance from Mark Wilson (New York: Literary Classics of the United States Inc., 1984).

Useful Essays and Letters

James, Henry, *The Art of the Novel, Critical Prefaces*, with an introduction by R. P. Blackmur (New York: Scribner, 1934).

The Painter's Eye: Notes and Essays on the Pictorial Art by Henry James, ed. J. L. Sweeney (London: Rupert Hart-Davis, 1956).

James, Henry, *Henry James's Letters*, ed. L. Edel (Vols I–III) (London: Macmillan, 1975, 1978, 1980, 1982): Vol IV, Cambridge, Mass. and London: Belknap Press, 1984).

James, Henry, *The Complete Notebooks*, eds L. Edel and L. A. Powers (New York: Oxford University Press, 1987).

Biography

Edel, L., Henry James: *The Untried Years, 1843–1870* (London: Rupert Hart-Davis, 1953).

Edel, L., Henry James: *The Conquest of London, 1870–1881*, Vol. 2 of *The Life of Henry James* (London: Rupert Hart-Davis, 1962).

Edel, L., Henry James: *Henry James: The Middle Years, 1882–1895*, Vol. 3 of *The Life of Henry James* (London: Rupert Hart-Davis, 1963).

Edel, L., Henry James: *The Treacherous Years, 1895–1901*, Vol. 4 of *The Life of Henry James* (London: Rupert Hart-Davis, 1969).

Hyde, Montgomery H., *Henry James at Home* (London: Methuen, 1969).

Edel, L., Henry James: *The Master, 1901–1916*, Vol. 5 of *The Life of Henry James* (London: Rupert Hart-Davis, 1972).

Edel, L., *The Life of Henry James* (Harmondsworth: Penguin, 1977), 2 vols.

Edel, L., *Henry James: A Life* (New York and London: Harper & Row, 1985).

Kaplan, Fred, Henry James: *The Imagination of Genius – A Biography* (London: Hodder, 1992).

Graham, Kenneth, *Henry James: A Literary Life* (London: Macmillan, 1995).

Bibliography and Reference

Blanck, J., 'Henry James', in *Bibliography of American Literature* 5 vols (New Haven, Conn.: Yale University Press, 1955–69), Vol. V, pp. 117–81.

Budd, J., *A Bibliography of Criticism 1975–1981* (Westpoint, Conn.: Greenwood, 1983).

Edel, L., and D. H. Laurence, *A Bibliography of Henry James* 3rd edn, revised by James Rambeau (Oxford: Clarendon Press, 1982).

Brabury, Nichola, *An Annotated Critical Bibliography of Henry James* (New York: St Martin's Press, 1987).

Edel, L. and Adeline R. Tintner, *The Library of Henry James* (Ann Arbor, Mich.: UMI Research Press, 1987).

Gale, Robert L., *A Henry James Encyclopedia* (Westport, Conn.: Greenwood Press, 1989).

Fogel, Daniel Mark (ed.), *Companion to Henry James* (Westport, Conn.; London: Greenwood Press, 1993).

Revision

Horne, Philip, *Henry James and Revision: The New York Edition* (Oxford: Clarendon Press, 1990).

Visual Arts

Winner, Viola Hopkins, *Henry James and the Visual Arts* (Charlottesville: University Press of Virginia, 1970).

Tintner, Adeline R., *The Museum World of Henry James* (Ann Arbor, Mich.: UMI Research Press, 1986).

Freedman, Jonathan, *Professions of Taste: Henry James, British Aestheticism, and Commodity Culture* (Stanford, Calif.: Stanford University Press, 1990).

Griffin, Susan M., *The Historical Eye: The Texture of the Visual in Late James* (Boston: Northeastern University Press, 1991).

Romance and Realism

Goetz, William R., *Henry James and the Darkest Abyss of Romance* (Baton Rouge: Louisiana Press, 1974).

Long, Robert Emmet, *The Great Succession: Henry James and the Legacy of Hawthorne* (Pittsburgh: University of Pittsburgh Press, 1979).

Fogel, Daniel Mark, *Henry James and the Structure of the Romantic Imagination* (Baton Rouge: Louisiana State University Press, 1981).

Habegger, Alfred, *Gender, Fantasy, and Realism in American Literature* (New York: Columbia University Press, 1982).

Stowe, William, *Balzac, James and the Realistic Novel* (Princeton, N.J.: Princeton University Press, 1983).

Evan, Carton, *The Rhetoric of American Romance* (Baltimore, London: Johns Hopkins University Press, 1985).

Auerbach, Jonathan, *The Romance of Failure: First-Person Fictions of Poe, Hawthorne, and James* (New York: Oxford University Press, 1989).

Borus, Daniel H., *Writing Realism: Howells, James, and Norris in the Mass Market* (Chapel Hill: University of North Carolina Press, 1989).

Greenwald, Elissa, *Realism and Romance: Nathaniel Hawthorne, Henry James, and American Fiction* (Ann Arbor, Mich.: UMI Research Press, 1989).

Gender

Sicker, Philip, *Love and the Quest for Identity in the Fiction of Henry James* (Princeton, N.J.: Princeton University Press, 1980).

Allen, Elizabeth, *A Woman's Place in the Novels of Henry James* (London: Macmillan, 1984).

Fowler, Virginia C., *Henry James's The American Girl: The Embroidery on the Canvas* (Madison: University of Wisconsin Press, 1984).

Habegger, Alfred, *Henry James and the 'Woman Business'* (Cambridge: Cambridge University Press, 1990).

Walton, Priscilla L., *Disruption of the Feminine in Henry James* (Toronto: University of Toronto Press, 1992).

Collections of Essays

Dupee, F. W. (ed.), *The Question of Henry James: A Collection of Critical Essays* (London: Allen Wingate, 1945).

Edel, L. (ed.), *Henry James: A Collection of Critical Essays* (Englewood Cliffs, NJ.: Prentice-Hall, 1963).

Tanner, Tony (ed.), *Henry James: Modern Judgments* (London: Macmillan, 1968).

Goode, J. (ed.), *The Air of Reality: New Essays on Henry James* (London: Methuen, 1972).

Bell, Ian F. A. (ed.), *Henry James: Fiction as History* (London and Totowa, N.J.: Vision and Barnes and Noble, 1984, 1985).

Bloom, Harold (ed.), *Henry James* [Modern Critical Views series] (Chelsea House, 1991).

Rawlings, Peter (ed.), *Critical Essays on Henry James* (Scolar Press, 1993).

Criticism

Anderson, C. R., *Person, Place, and Thing in Henry James's Novels* (Durham, N.C.: Duke University Press, 1977).

Anesko, Michael, *'Friction with the Market': Henry James and the Profession of Authorship* (New York: Oxford University Press, 1986).

Auchard, John, *Silence in Henry James: The Heritage of Symbolism and Decadence* (University Park: Pennsylvania State University Press, 1986).

Beach, Joseph Warren, *The Method of Henry James* (New Haven, Conn.: Yale University Press, 1918; 2nd edn, 1954, Albert Saifer).

Bell, Millicent, *Meaning in Henry James* (Cambridge: Harvard University Press, 1991).

Berland, A., *Culture and Conduct in the Novels of Henry James* (Cambridge: Cambridge University Press, 1981).

Bewley, Marius, *The Complex Fate* (London: Chatto & Windus, 1952).

Bradbury, Malcolm, *Dangerous Pilgrimages: Trans-Atlantic Mythologies and the Novel* (London: Secker & Warburg, 1995).

Cameron, Sharon, *Thinking in Henry James* (Chicago: University of Chicago Press, 1989).

Cannon, Kelly, *Henry James and Masculinity: The Man at the Margins* (London: Macmillan Press, 1994).

Cargill, Oscar, *The Novels of Henry James* (New York: Macmillan, 1961).

Cross, Mary, *Henry James* (London: Macmillan Press, 1993).

Delbaere-Garant, Jeanne, *Henry James: The Vision of France* (Paris: Société des Éditions Belles Lettres, 1970).

Dupe, F. W., *Henry James* (New York: Sloane, 1951).

Dupee, F. W., *Henry James: His Life and Writings* (New York: Anchoer, 1956).

Gale, R. L., *The Caught Image: Figurative Language in the Fiction of Henry James* (Chapel Hill, N. C.: University of North Carolina Press, 1964).

Gard, R., *Henry James: The Critical Heritage* (London: Routledge & Kegan Paul, 1968).

Holland, L. B., *The Experience of Vision: Essays on the Craft of Henry James* (Princeton: Princeton University Press, 1964).

Jacobson, Marcia, *Henry James and the Mass Market* (University: University of Alabama Press, 1983).

Jolly, Roslyn, *Henry James: History, Narrative, Fiction* (Oxford: Oxford University Press, 1994).

Kappeler, Susanne, *Writing and Reading in Henry James* (London: Macmillan, 1980).

Kaston, Carren, *Imagination and Desire in the Novels of Henry James* (New Brunswick, N.J.: Rutgers University Press, 1984).

Kelley, C. P., *The Early Development of Henry James* (Urbana, Ill.: University of Illinois Press, 1930).

Leavis, F. R., *The Great Tradition* (London: Chatto & Windus, 1948).

Leavis, F. R., *The Common Pursuit* (London: Chatto & Windus, 1952).

Lee, B., *The Novels of Henry James: A Study of Culture and Consciousness* (London: Edward Arnold, 1978).

Lubbock, Percy, *The Craft of Fiction* (London: Jonathan Cape, 1921).

Margolis, Anne T., *Henry James and the Problem of Audience* (Ann Arbor, Mich.: UMI Research Press, 1985).

McCarthy, H. T., *Henry James: The Creative Process* (New York: Yoseloft, 1958).

Mizruchi, Susan L., *The Power of Historical Knowledge: Narrating the Past in Hawthorne, James and Dreiser* (Princeton, N.J.: Princeton University Press, 1988).

Mull, D. L., *Henry James's 'Sublime Economy': Money as Symbolic Center in the Fiction* (Middletown, Conn.: Wesleyan University Press, 1973).

Perosa, Sergio, *Henry James and the Experimental Novel* (Charlottesville, Va.: University Press of Virginia, 1978).

Poirer, Richard, *The Comic Sense of Henry James* (London: Chatto & Windus, 1960).

Putt, S. G., *A Reader's Guide to Henry James* (London: Thames and Hudson, 1996).

Rourke, Constance, *Native American Humor: A Study of the National Character* (New York: Harcourt Brace Jovanovich, 1931).

Rowe, John Carlos, *The Theoretical Dimension of Henry James* (Ithaca, N.Y.: Cornell University Press, 1976).

Segal, O., *The Lucid Reflector: The Observer in Henry James's Fiction* (New Haven, Conn.: Yale University Press, 1969).

Selzer, Mark, *Henry James and the Art of Power* (Ithaca, N.Y.: Cornell University Press, 1984).

Smith, Virginia Llewellyn, *Henry James and the Real Thing: A Modern Reader's Guide* (London: Macmillan, 1994).

Tintner, Adeline R., *The Book World of Henry James: Appropriating the Classics* (Ann Arbor, Mich.: UMI Research Press, 1987).

Wegelin, C., *The Image of Europe in Henry James* (Dallas: Southern Methodist University Press, 1958).

Woolf, Judith, *Henry James: The Major Novels* (Cambridge: Cambridge University Press, 1991).

On The American

Articles in alphabetical order by author

Antush, John V., 'The "Much Finer Complexity" of History in *The American*', *Journal of American Studies* 6 (1972): 85–95.

Banta, Martha, 'Rebirth and Revenge: The Endings of *Huckleberry Finn* and *The American*', *Modern Fiction Studies* 15 (Summer 1969): 191–207.

Blasing, Mutlu, 'Double Focus in *The American*', *Nineteenth Century Fiction* 28 (1973): 74–84.

Brooks, Cleanth, 'The American Innocence', *Shenandoah* 16 (1964): 21–37.

Brooks, Peter, 'The Turn of *The American*', in Banta, Martha (ed.), *New Essays on The American* (Cambridge: Cambridge University Press, 1987).

Butterfield, R. W., '*The American*' in Goode, John (ed.), *The Air of Reality: New Essays on Henry James* (London: Methuen, 1972).

Cargill, Oscar, 'The First International Novel', *PMLA* 73 (1958): 418–25.

Clair, John A., '*The American*: A Reinterpretation', *PMLA* 74 (1959): 613–18.

Fussell, Edwin, 'Time and Topography in *The American*', *The Henry James Review* (1989) Fall 10 (3): 167–78.

Gargano, James W., 'Foreshadowing in *The American*', *Modern Language Notes* 74 (1959): 600–1.

Goldsmith, Arnold L., 'Henry James's Reconciliation of Free Will and Fatalism', *Nineteenth Century Fiction* 13 (1958): 109–126.

Haralson, Eric, 'James's *The American*: A (New)man Is Being Beaten', *American Literature* (1992) 64 (3): 475–95.

Hays, H. R., 'The Limitations of Christopher Newman', in *Henry James: The American*, ed. Gerald Willen (New York: Thomas Y. Crowell, 1972).

Higdon, David Leon, 'Henry James and Lillian Hellman: An Unnoted Source', *The Henry James Review* (1985) Winter 6 (2): 134–5.

Hobbs, Michael, 'Reading Newman Reading: Textuality and Possession in The American', *The Henry James Review* (1992) Winter 13 (1): 78–81.

Hoffman, Frederick J., 'Freedom and Conscious Form: Henry James's and the American Self', *Virginia Quarterly Review* 37 (1961): 115–25.

Horowitz, Floyd R., 'The Christian Time Sequence in Henry James's *The American*', *CLA Journal* 9 (1966): 234–45.

Jobe, Steven H., 'The Discrimination of Stoicisms in *The American*', *Studies in American Fiction* (1988) Autumn 16(2): 181–93.

Johnson, William A., 'The Moment of *The American* in L'Écriture Judéo-Chrétienne', *The Henry James Review* (1984) Spring 5 (3): 216–20.

Keyishan, Harry, 'Cross-currents of Revenge in James's *The American*', *Modern Language Studies* (1987) Spring 17(2): 3–13.

Knox, George, 'Romance and Fable in James's *The American*', *Anglia* 83 (1965): 308–23.

Leeming, David Adams, 'Henry James's Self-made Man', pp. 71–82 in Ricard, Serge (introd.) *From Rags to Riches: Le Mythe du self-made man* (Aix-en-Province: Univ. de Provence, 1984).

Lerner, Daniel, 'The Influence of Turgenev on Henry James', *The Slavonic Year-Book* 20 (1941): 28–54.

Morrow, Nancy, 'Playing the Game of Life: The Dilemma of Christopher Newman and Isabel Archer', *Studies in American Fiction* (1988) Spring 16(1): 65–82.

Park, Hershel, 'An Error in the Text of Henry James's *The American*', *American Literature* 38 (1965): 316–18.

Probert, K. G., 'Christopher Newman and the Artistic View of Life', *Studies in American Fiction* (1983) Autumn 11(2): 203–15.

Reising, Russell J., 'Condensing the James Novel: *The American* in Hugh Selwyn Mauberley', *Journal of Modern Literature* (1988) Summer 15(1): 17–34.

Reynolds, Larry, 'Henry James's New Christopher Newman', *Studies in the Novel* 5 (Winter 1973): 457–68.

Rowe, John Carlos, 'The Politics of Innocence in Henry James's *The American*', pp. 66–97 in Banta, Martha (ed.), *New Essays on The American* (Cambridge: Cambridge University Press, 1987).

Rowe, John Carlos, 'The Politics of the Uncanny: Newman's Fate in *The American*', *The Henry James Review* (1987) Winter 8 (2): 79–90.

Scharnhorst, Gary, 'Henry James and the Reverend William Rounsville Alger', *The Henry James Review* (1986) Fall 8 (1): 71–5.

Schloss, Dietmar, 'The Standard of "One's Own Good-Humoured Prosperity": Henry James's Critique of American Innocence in *The American*', *Archiv fur das Studium der Neuren Sprachen und Literaturen* (1988) 225 (2): 285–99.

Shackelford, Lynne P., 'Forsaking the Bridal Veil: Henry James's Illusion to Correggio's "The Marriage of St Catherine" in *The American*', *The Henry James Review* (1992) Winter 13 (1): 78–81.

Shackelford, Lynne P., 'James's *The American*', *Explicator* (1990) Summer 48(4): 254–7.

Sharma, Jatindra Kumar, 'Response to Alien Culture in Henry James and Raja Rao: Comparative Observations on *The American* and *The Serpent and Rope*', *Panjab University Research Bulletin* (1984) 15(1): 11–25.

Schulz, Max F., 'The Bellegardes' Feud with Christopher Newman: A Study of Henry James's Revision of *The American*', *American Literature* 27 (1955): 42–55.

Sherfick, Kathleen A., 'Claire de Cintré in Henry James's *The American* and St Clare of Assisi', *The Henry James Review* (1991) Spring 12 (2): 117–19.

Secor, Robert, 'Christopher Newman: How Innocent is James's American?', *Studies in American Fiction* 1 (1973): 141–53.

Selzer, Mark, 'Physical Capital: *The American* and the Realist Body' pp. 131–67 in Banta, Martha (ed.), *New Essays on The American* (Cambridge: Cambridge University Press, 1987).

Stafford, William T., 'The Ending of James's *The American*: A Defense of the Early Version', *Nineteenth Century Fiction* 18 (1963): 86–9.

Steele, Elizabeth, 'Chaucer and Henry James: Surprising Bedfellows', *The Henry James Review* (1992) Spring 13 (2): 126–42.

Stowe, William W., 'Interpretation in Fiction: *Le Père Goriot* and *The American*', *Texas Studies in Literature and Language* (1981) Summer 23 (2): 248–67.

Taylor, Michael, 'Reluctant Romancers: Self-Consciousness and Derogation in Prose Romance', *English Studies in Canada* (1991) 17 (1): 89–106.

Tick, Stanley, 'Henry James's *The American Voyons*', *Studies in the Novel* (North Texas State University) 2 (1970): 276–91.

Traschen, Isodore, 'An American in Paris', *American Literature* 26 (1954): 57–77.

Tuttleton, James W., 'Henry James: The Superstitious Valuation of

Europe' from *The Novel of Manners in America* (New York: W. W. Norton, 1974) pp. 48–85.

Tuttleton, James W., 'James's *The American*: The Novel and the Play', *The Henry James Review* (1989) Spring 10 (2): 112–16.

Van Der Beets, Richard, 'A Note on Henry James's Western Barbarism', *Western Humanities Review* 17 (1963): 175–8.

Vanderbilt, Kermit, 'James, Fitzgerald, and the American Self-Image', *Massachusetts Review* 6 (1965): 289–304.

Ware, Cheryl L., 'Americans Abroad: Anti-Intellectualism in Mark Twain and Henry James', *McNeese Review* (1980–1) 27: 50–62.

Watkins, Floyd, C., 'Christopher Newman's Final Instinct', *Nineteenth Century Fiction* 12 (1957): 85–8.

Zeitlow, Edward R., 'A Flaw in *The American*', *CLA Journal* 9 (1966): 246–54.

French Culture

Richardson, *La Vie Parisienne (1852–1870)* (London: Hamish Hamilton, 1971).

Pinkey, David, *Napoleon III and the Rebuilding of Paris* (Princeton, N.J.: Princeton University Press, 1994).

Steele, Valerie, *Paris Fashion: A Cultural History* (New York; London: Oxford University Press, 1988). This book has an excellent bibliography.

Perot, Philippe, *Fashioning the Bourgeoisie* (trans. Richard Bienvenu) (Princeton, N.J.: Princeton University Press, 1994).

TEXT SUMMARY

Chapter 1

May 1868 a gentleman (Christopher Newman) is reclining on a couch in the Salon Carré in the Louvre, Paris. He is described as being a fine specimen of an American. While viewing the paintings his attention turns to a copyist (Mademoiselle Noémie Nioche). He approaches her and asks how much is her copy. *Combien?* They talk. Newman meets her father, M. Nioche, and agrees to take French lessons.

Chapter 2

He returns to his divan and is surprised by an old friend, Mr Tom Tristram. They talk briefly about their past and their immediate circumstances. They discuss Newman's intentions. They go to the Palais Royal for a drink. Newman tells his 'rags to riches' story. He tells Tristram how his options are still open for returning to his business. Tom invites Newman to meet his wife, Lizzie Tristram.

Chapter 3

The following day Newman dines with the Tristrams at their apartment. Mrs Tristram is described and her sophistication is contrasted with her 'light weight' husband interested in gambling and loose women. Newman takes a great fancy to her. He visits the Tristrams many times. Mrs Tristram on one occasion observes to Newman it is time he took a wife. The three of them discuss the ideal wife for Newman. At the end of their discussion, the name of Madame Claire de Cintré is mentioned. Some days later he briefly meets Claire in the Tristram's drawing-room. On the advice of Mrs Tristram, Newman goes to Claire's Paris residence. There he sees le Comte and le Marquis. Claire is not at home.

Chapter 4

M. Nioche visits Newman at his apartment. The copy is finished and examined. They discuss his daughter and her various 'talents'. Newman wants her to paint half-a-dozen copies and also decides upon having lessons with M. Nioche. For the following three weeks, M. Nioche comes to give Newman French lessons and Newman learns a great deal about the old man and his daughter and Parisian society. He talks to Noémie and concurs with her father's statement that 'she was a frank coquette'.

Chapter 5

Newman, after his fruitless visit to Madame de Cintré's, decides to embark upon a 'Grand Tour' of Europe. He lounges through Belgium, Holland and the Rhineland. In Holland he encounters Benjamin Babcock, a young Unitarian minister. They travel together but part company because Babcock believes Newman is not being as serious as he should. In Baden-Baden he receives a letter from Mrs Tristram to which he replies.

Chapter 6

Upon his return to Paris he meets Mrs Tristram. She tells him that Claire has returned from the country. She also informs Newman about the Bellegarde family history and their pride. Later he visits the Hôtel de Bellegarde and manages to see Claire. They talk about their respective countries. The Bellegarde family is further discussed. Her younger brother, Valentin, offers to show the house to Newman, but Newman would rather talk to his sister. He meets her sister-in-law. Newman is invited by Claire to visit again.

Chapter 7

A week after his visit Valentin visits Newman. They talk about the Bellegardes. Valentin narrates his life and career. Valentin envies Newman for being free. Newman takes a liking to Valentin and dines out with him. On one such evening Valentin proposes new entertainment. They will visit Madame Dandelard, an Italian lady married to a French brute. Newman is upset by her 'drama'. He thinks Claire should intervene to save her.

Chapter 8

Newman asks Valentin to tell him all about Claire and her past. She married at eighteen to M. de Cintré, a sixty-year-old. After his death a lawsuit was brought against her by her late husband's relatives. The older brother is described and so too is the mother. Valentin warns Newman about the obstacles to be overcome.

Chapter 9

The next day Newman finds Claire alone. He proposes to her, taking into account the cultural differences and his low antecedents. Claire listens to the long marriage proposal and doesn't reject him. She tells him that he must solemnly promise for six months not to court her, but he can visit the house. Valentin offers to introduce Newman to his older brother the Marquis.

Chapter 10

Newman turns down an invitation by Princess Borealska and visits his old friends the Tristrams. Mrs Tristram advises Newman to try his fortune with Claire. Newman is taken by Valentin to meet the old Marquise de Bellegarde and her eldest son the Marquis. He tells the family about his background and past hardships. The Bellegardes will go to a ball later. Newman sees Claire and thinks she is 'tremendously handsome'. The younger Bellegardes go to the ball leaving Newman with Madame de Bellegarde. He tells her about his 'project' to marry Claire.

Chapter 11

M. Nioche informs Newman that his daughter is still working on the copies. Newman goes to the Louvre where he meets Valentin. The latter is there to 'point out the "principal beauties"' to his English cousin. The two walk together and meet up with Mademoiselle Nioche. Valentin is smitten by her prettiness. They discuss her future success.

Chapter 12

Three days after his first introduction to the Bellegarde family Newman is invited to dinner. He sees Claire with her niece on her lap. Claire is telling her the fairy story of Florabella. In the smoking-room he is told by Valentin that the family has accepted Newman as a candidate for the hand of their sister in marriage. He meets the elderly Rochefidèle couple. Valentin tells Newman that Mademoiselle Noémie has left her father and 'launched' herself into society.

Chapter 13

Newman keeps his promise to Claire but visits her many times. He discusses the Bellegardes with Mrs Tristram. He thinks there might be some awful family secret involving the old Marquise and her eldest son. One afternoon he meets Mrs Bread the English servant. They talk about his marriage proposal. Lord Deepmere the thirty-three-year-old cousin arrives at the Bellegarde house.

Chapter 14

Claire consents to Newman's proposal. Madame de Bellegarde congratulates Newman. However, Claire is not entirely convinced by her mother and the Marquis. Plans go ahead for the wedding.

Chapter 15

Newman learns from Valentin more shocking details of Mademoiselle Noémie's career. Newman visits the Nioche lodgings and is told the old man is at the Café de la Patrie. He sees that Valentin was right, the old man hadn't taken the 'high moral ground'. Noémie has been transformed into a beautiful lady. He meets Valentin and talks about Noémie and Claire. He receives an invitation from Madame de Bellegarde to her ball on the 27th of the month.

Chapter 16

The next ten days are the happiest that Newman has ever known. Wedding preparations are discussed. At the ball Newman meets French aristocrats and other dignitaries. Lord Deepmere has a private interview with the old Marquise and then dances with Claire. Newman is suspicious about the Lord's intentions. Claire placates him.

Chapter 17

Newman attends the opera. On one occasion with Dora Finch his American friend, on another by himself. At the opera, *Don Giovanni*, he meets up with various members of the Bellegarde family. He talks privately to the young Marquise and she tells him about her unhappy life with Henri-Urbain. He sees Noémie with a young man. Valentin sees this and is enraged. The outcome is a duel with his rival M. Stanislas Kapp – which Newman seeks to prevent. Noémie claps her hands and says '*C'est ça qui pose une femme!*'

Chapter 18

Newman goes to the Bellegarde house. Claire tells him that something unfortunate has happened and that she cannot marry him now. She leaves for the family home Fleurières near Poitiers. Her mother and brother have used their 'authority' over her. Newman is amazed by this news and wonders what the Bellegardes did to reverse his fortunes. He seeks the advice of Lizzie Tristram who tells him to follow Claire. He receives a telegram from Count Valentin informing him that he has been fatally wounded.

Chapter 19

Newman travels to Switzerland and is told that the doctor has 'condemned' Valentin. Valentin's friend, M. Ledoux, describes the duel. At the point of death Valentin confides in Newman that there is a 'family secret' – something about his father. He advises Newman to ask Mrs Bread who knows the secret.

Chapter 20
Valentin dies tranquilly. Newman goes to Poitiers to see Claire. Fleurières is described. Claire's appearance has changed – she is 'pale, heavy-browed, almost haggard, with a sort of monastic rigidity in her dress'. He pleads with Claire to reconsider her decision to 'give him up'. Claire announces to Newman that she is going into a convent.

Chapter 21
Newman arranges a rendezvous with Mrs Bread. Newman confronts the Bellegardes. He says that he knows they have done something dastardly. Their reaction is cool. The Marquis sends a letter letting Newman know that they think he has been impertinent.

Chapter 22
Mrs Bread tells the story of the Bellegarde 'dark secret'. The old Marquis who was ill had been against the arranged marriage between Claire and M. de Cintré. However the Marquise and son were for the match and as the note left by the dying Marquis testifies, they wouldn't let anyone get in their way. The Marquis died because his wife and son refused to give him his medicine.

Chapter 23
Newman is encouraged by his discovery to seek another confrontation with the Bellegardes. He wants desperately to see Claire. Mrs Bread and Mrs Tristram assist him. The latter promises to obtain permission from the abbé.

Chapter 24
Newman goes to the Carmelite chapel. The Bellegardes have chosen the same means to visit Claire. She has refused to see them. Newman threatens the Bellegardes with exposure by telling the Duchesse d'Outreville.

Chapter 25
He visits the Duchesse d'Outreville intent on exposing the Bellegardes, but realises that there is a 'polite wall' between him and the Duchesse. Frustrated, he leaves her and decides to 'banish' the Bellegardes completely from his mind. Believing a change of scene would do him good, Newman goes to England. He meets Noémie in London with her father and new partner, Lord Deepmere. M. Nioche tells Newman that there will be an announcement later in the newspapers.

Chapter 26
After spending the appointed time in England Newman decides to leave for America. He surprises those at the Stock Exchange by being indifferent to business matters. In the winter he receives a letter from Mrs Tristram informing him about the latest Parisian gossip including the news that Madame de Cintré has taken the veil at the Carmelites on her twenty-seventh birthday. He returns to Paris to 'remain there forever'. Newman throws the incriminating note written by the old Marquis into a fire. The Bellegardes have spent a year in seclusion at Fleurières.

ACKNOWLEDGEMENTS

The editor and publishers wish to thank the following for permission to use copyright material:

Columbia University Press for material from Peter Brooks, *The Melodramatic Imagination: Balzac, Henry James, and the Mode of Excess* (1985), pp. 156-7;

Harcourt Brace and Company for material from Constance Rourke, *Native American Humor: A Study of the National Character*, pp. 186-7, 194, 197. Copyright © 1931 by Harcourt Brace and Company and renewed 1958 by Alice D. Fore;

Max Niemeyer Verlag GmbH & Co. for material from George Knox, 'Romance and Fable in James's *The American*', *Anglia* 83 (1965), pp. 311-12;

School of Slavonic and East European Studies for material from Daniel Lerner, 'The Influence of Turgenev on Henry James', *The Slavonic Year-Book* 20 (December 1941), pp. 43-4;

The University of California Press for material from Mutlu Blasing, 'Double Focus in *The American*', *Nineteenth Century Fiction* 28:1 (1973), pp. 82-3. Copyright © 1973 by the Regents of the University of California.

Every effort has been made to trace the copyright holders but if any have been inadvertently overlooked the publishers will be pleased to make the necessary arrangement at the first opportunity.

CLASSIC FICTION
IN EVERYMAN

**The Impressions of
Theophrastus Such**
GEORGE ELIOT
*An amusing collection of character
sketches, and the only paperback
edition available*
£5.99

Frankenstein
MARY SHELLEY
*A masterpiece of Gothic terror in
its original 1818 version*
£3.99

East Lynne
MRS HENRY WOOD
*A classic tale of melodrama,
murder and mystery*
£7.99

**Holiday Romance and
Other Writings for Children**
CHARLES DICKENS
*Dickens's works for children,
including 'The Life of Our Lord'
and 'A Child's History of England',
with original illustrations*
£5.99

The Ebb-Tide
R. L. STEVENSON
*A compelling study of ordinary
people in extreme circumstances*
£4.99

The Three Impostors
ARTHUR MACHEN
*The only edition available
of this cult thriller*
£4.99

Mister Johnson
JOYCE CARY
*The only edition available of this
amusing but disturbing twentieth-
century tale*
£5.99

The Jungle Book
RUDYARD KIPLING
*The classic adventures of Mowgli
and his friends*
£3.99

Glenarvon
LADY CAROLINE LAMB
*The only edition available of the
novel which throws light on the
greatest scandal of the early nineteenth century – the infatuation of
Caroline Lamb with Lord Byron*
£6.99

**Twenty Thousand Leagues
Under the Sea**
JULES VERNE
*Scientific fact combines with
fantasy in this prophetic tale
of underwater adventure*
£4.99

All books are available from your local bookshop or direct from:
Littlehampton Book Services Cash Sales, 14 Eldon Way, Lineside Estate,
Littlehampton, West Sussex BN17 7HE (*prices are subject to change*)

To order any of the books, please enclose a cheque (in sterling) made payable to
Littlehampton Book Services, or phone your order through with credit card details (Access,
Visa or Mastercard) on 01903 721596 (24 hour answering service) stating card number
and expiry date. (*Please add £1.25 for package and postage to the total of your order.*)

In the USA, for further information and a complete catalogue call 1-800-526-2778

AMERICAN LITERATURE
IN EVERYMAN

The Marble Faun
NATHANIEL HAWTHORNE

The product of Hawthorne's two years in Italy, the thrilling story of young Americans in Europe
£5.99

The Portrait of a Lady
HENRY JAMES

A masterpiece of psychological and social examination, which established James as a major novelist
£5.99

Billy Budd and Other Stories
HERMAN MELVILLE

The compelling parable of innocence destroyed by a fallen world
£4.99

The Red Badge of Courage
STEPHEN CRANE

A vivid portrayal of a young soldier's experience of the American Civil War
£3.99

Leaves of Grass and Selected Prose
WALT WHITMAN

The best of Whitman in one volume
£6.99

The Age of Innocence
EDITH WHARTON

A tale of the conflict between love and tradition by one of America's finest women novelists
£4.99

Nineteenth-Century American Short Stories
edited by Christopher Bigsby

A selection of the works of Henry James, Edith Wharton, Mark Twain and many other great American writers
£6.99

Selected Poems
HENRY LONGFELLOW

A selection spanning the whole of Longfellow's literary career
£7.99

The Last of the Mohicans
JAMES FENIMORE COOPER

The tale that shaped American frontier myth
£5.99

The Great Gatsby
F. SCOTT FITZGERALD

Much loved story of passion and betrayal, glamour and the powerful allure of the American dream
£4.99

All books are available from your local bookshop or direct from:
Littlehampton Book Services Cash Sales, 14 Eldon Way, Lineside Estate,
Littlehampton, West Sussex BN17 7HE *(prices are subject to change)*

To order any of the books, please enclose a cheque (in sterling) made payable to
Littlehampton Book Services, or phone your order through with credit card details (Access,
Visa or Mastercard) on 01903 721596 (24 hour answering service) stating card number
and expiry date. *(Please add £1.25 for package and postage to the total of your order.)*

In the USA, for further information and a complete catalogue call 1-800-526-2778